Business ethics and
business behaviour

Business ethics and business behaviour

Edited by

Ken Smith

and

Phil Johnson

INTERNATIONAL THOMSON BUSINESS PRESS
I⬤P An International Thomson Publishing Company

London • Bonn • Boston • Johannesburg • Madrid • Melbourne • Mexico City • New York • Paris
Singapore • Tokyo • Toronto • Albany, NY • Belmont, CA • Cincinnati, OH • Detroit, MI

Business ethics and business behaviour

Copyright ©1996 K. Smith and P. Johnson

First published by International Thomson Business Press

 I⊤P A division of International Thomson Publishing Inc.
The ITP logo is a trademark under licence

British Library Cataloguing-in-Publication Data
A catalogue record for this book is available from the British Library

First edition 1996

Typeset in the UK by Gray Publishing, Tunbridge Wells, Kent
Printed in the UK by Clays Ltd, St Ives plc, Bungay, Suffolk

ISBN 0-415-11383-0

International Thomson Business Press   International Thomson Business Press
Berkshire House   20 Park Plaza
168–173 High Holborn   14th Floor
London WC1V 7AA   Boston MA 02116
UK   USA

http://www.thomson.com/itbp.html

Contents

Preface

Ken Smith and Phil Johnson

When one raises the issue of business ethics in general conversation it is not uncommon for the response to be one of hilarity at the naivety of the misnomer – that business and ethics do not mix. Such a reaction says much about the way in which the business community is perceived by the general public and how they understand what it is to behave ethically. To make matters worse, there is often a similar response from managers. However managers' initial cynicism often becomes tempered by observations that there are ethical standards to which they refer, but that they are personal and rarely explicitly articulated or sanctioned by their organizations.

Another reaction to the topic of business ethics takes the form of an argument: while there may be *some* ethics, moral standards, or principles underlying the way in which business people conduct themselves, they are not the same as those that are used in life outside the business context. As Jackall contends

> bureaucratic work causes people to bracket, while at work, the moralities they hold outside the workplace or that they might adhere to privately and to follow instead the prevailing morality of their particular organizational situation. (1988, p.6)

In a different manner this notion that there is a dichotomy between work-life and home-life, is illustrated by the idea that business could be likened to a game of poker – a game played by a different set of rules to the rest of social life (Carr, 1968; Ladd, 1970). It followed that in the world of business one was not expected to be quite as honest and fair as in other areas of life. If one was, then it was a bad mistake – a sign of weakness or naivety. Such an individual is a sucker and could expect to be exploited by those more attuned to the mores of the marketplace. If one wanted to survive and prosper in business, one had to 'sharpen up' and learn those rules of engagement.

The view that business is analogous to a game whose rules diverge from the morality of other aspects of life, and therefore must entail ethical schizophrenia for players, has prompted much debate (e.g. Sullivan, 1984; Keeley, 1981). Some critics argue that business is, or should be, conducted with honesty and integrity. Moreover, the managers of business organizations have a set of social obligations and responsibilities that go beyond those stakeholder interests which are articulated by a desire to profit-maximize. For example, Goodpaster and Matthews (1982) maintain that fairness, honesty, and trust are essential in any business activity while Freeman and Gilbert (1988) argue that in order to be ethical companies have to ensure that employee tasks are compatible with employee interests. Other critics have argued that the competitive ethos which underpins the game analogy is misleading since any business must also entail cooperation between organizations (Solomon, 1992). These various arguments display both the controversy that surrounds the role of business organizations in contemporary society and the uncertainty about what should be the responsibilities, obligations and duties of business towards that society.

It is plainly absurd to suggest that are no values and beliefs, principles and standards which find expression within the working of the modern business organization. Indeed the demand (e.g. Friedman, 1962; Hayek, 1969) that the only responsibility of business is to make maximum profits for the shareholder is just as laden with ethical commitments as the pluralistic argument that business must be socially responsible to a wider constituency of stakeholders (e.g. Epstein, 1989; Nash, 1990). The point is that the underlying ethical commitments are merely different.

What is perhaps most surprising is that the (varying) ethical principles which underpin so many aspects of business behaviour have been rarely made explicit, or discussed and reflected upon. For instance, the public statements of corporate executives either in the form of corporate mission statements or annual reports, etc., provide important indications of the ethics which the authors think that their organization embodies. Yet such statements do tend to be just that – statements. Often they are divorced from the perceived realities of everyday organizational life and with little influence on the organizational behaviour of members as they confront, and try to cope with, the various dilemmas which arise out of the tensions between personal concerns and organizational imperatives that are formally and informally sanctioned. So while it is wrong to suggest that there is an ethical vacuum within business, it is perhaps more accurate to suggest that there is, or until fairly recently there has been, a relative silence since the ethical dimension to business behaviour has been sublimated – a veritable 'moral muteness' (Bird and Walters, 1987, 1989).

The developing importance of business ethics

The silence is now being broken as business ethics becomes an issue for contemporary debate. The reasons for this are numerous. One possible reason might lie in the negative reaction to the exclusive dictates of neoclassical economics which located managerial responsibility in the pursuit of what were assumed to be shareholder interests. For Stark (1993) this has resulted in the devaluation of traditional business interests in favour of ostensibly more important, or equally important, interests that derive from other organizational stakeholders. How far neoclassical prescriptions penetrated the psyche of business communities might be open to debate, nevertheless Rossouw (1994) argues that moral dissension and debate is a feature of today. Dissension and debate now pose severe difficulties for the process of moral decision making as they increase the possibility of personal moral dilemmas and public moral disputes. As Primeaux comments ...

> we can no longer presume a common, universal, prevailing consensus for personal and corporate ethics. Neither academic philosophy, religious morality, or legal proscriptions command the kind of definitive, universal authority that we once thought they had. That is, we can no longer assume that everyone with whom we work ascribes to some single, all-encompassing ethical code. (1992, p. 780)

The suggestion is that such uncertainty regarding ethical conditions has served to impel a re-examination of the moral basis of business behaviour. However, this has also been prompted by a growing awareness of the impact of business organizations on the natural and social environment (Vogel, 1991). The continuing concentration of capital into larger units, together with its globalization, have resulted in the increasing power and influence of the industrial corporation. Their policies and actions can threaten or enhance the natural environment, the political stability and the prosperity of host societies (Prost, 1991). Given such a potential it is hardly surprising that the ethical basis of their behaviours has become a focus of concern (DeGeorge, 1987; Donaldson, 1989).

Meanwhile the consensus that people could, through the medium of science and technology, assert and benefit from more control over the vagaries of their natural environments has been challenged (e.g. Hickman, 1990). Spectacular environmental tragedies such as Chernobyl, Bhophal and the *Exxon Valdez* have added impetus to these growing concerns. Similarly the view that economic development and growth would bring material well-being and financial security is questioned. Many critics argue that an emphasis on economic growth is open to question, and that there is a need for society as a whole to consider what its priorities are (Handy, 1989, 1994). While some commentators seem to extol the application of science and technology to the pursuit of economic growth, others have questioned the impact of developments such as microelectronic technology on both the quality of working life and employment levels (Hines and Searle, 1979; Jenkins and Sherman, 1979, 1981).

In Britain, in contrast to the demand-management policies of successive postwar governments, recent Conservative governments have vigorously implemented the monetarist economic principles of the 'new right'. Not only has this resulted in the abandoning of 'full' employment as a policy objective, but it has also created a new legitimacy for both entrepreneurism and aggressive individualism. So the last 17 years have witnessed an increased emphasis on the role of the market economy as the primary vehicle for economic growth and international competitiveness. Yet the processes of rationalizing British industry to create 'leaner', flexible and more competitive organizations, have not resolved the continuing problem of high levels of unemployment and the increasing incidence of crime.

The new organizational forms that seem to be developing out of what has been called the 'flexibility offensive' (Atkinson and Gregory, 1986, p. 15) appear to be characterized by functionally flexible cores of skilled, permanently employed workers surrounded by numerically flexible peripheries of less skilled temporary employees (Atkinson, 1984; Nichols, 1986; Prowse, 1990). The existence, extent and pace of this trend has been subject to much debate (e.g. MacInnes, 1988; Storey, 1989; Pollert, 1991), however, a possible future scenario is invoked by Clegg (1990, p. 234) when he describes a series of exclusive and privileged enclaves surrounded by a marginalized and underprivileged majority. The resultant differentiation may be at best constructed on possibly spurious operationalizations of merit, or at worst characterized by insidious sexism and racism. Whatever its basis it

> creates social polarisation and tensions as the labour markets are divided into elites in the core and a growing peripheral mass of unemployed, underemployed and casual workers. (Leadbeater and Lloyd, 1987)

The uncertainties and concerns created by these developments have probably given further impetus to moral dissension and debate. If these debates are primarily concerned with uncertainty regarding the socially approved objectives of business, a variety of business 'scandals' also further highlight uncertainty about the institutionally approved means of achieving those objectives. Clearly, North America has put its business system under critical examination through the trial and imprisonment of such figures as Michael Milken, Ivan Boesky and Dennis Levine (Stewart, 1991; Levine and Hoffer, 1991; Kornbluth, 1992) and Britain has not been exempt. In recent years cases such as Barlow Clowes, Blue Arrow, BCCI, Guinness, Robert Maxwell, and the British Airways–Virgin Atlantic controversy, all have prompted questions concerning not only the ability of current legislation to adequately regulate business activity, but also about the motives and behaviour of leading companies and the people who manage them (see Truell and Gurwin, 1992; Beaty and Gwynne, 1993, Gregory, 1994) – concerns fuelled by apparent avarice of some senior managers (Cannon, 1993). Perhaps something of the confusion surrounding the ethical resolution of such issues is illustrated by the recent controversy, and subsequent withdrawal, of a Department of Trade and Industry publication entitled *Marketing Your Business*. This 40-page publication recommended going through competitors rubbish bins, lying about who you represent and making friends with secretaries from rival firms who had access to a photocopier (Cusick 1994a, b).

Thus, in recent years the issues and concerns addressed by business ethics have become both more complex and diverse. They reflect the increased rate of innovation and change occurring in both business and society, as well as the uncertainties and anxieties that accompany the processes of change. So, along with the now almost commonplace concern for the natural environment, there is an interest in the ethical issues which arise from the implications of corporate takeovers (e.g. Hanley, 1992; Meade and Davidson, 1993); the increasing use of computerized information systems within the workplace (e.g. Cohen and Cornwall, 1989); the use of expert systems in organizational decision-making (e.g. Khalil, 1993); the use of computers to monitor employee performance (e.g. Hawk, 1994) and the rise of the surveillance society (Lyon, 1994); the ethics of 'business intelligence' (e.g. Hallaq and Steinhorst, 1994); the increasing prevalence of part-time employment (e.g. Bartkowiak, 1993); the implications of a global economy (e.g. Buller et al., 1991) and its impact on the 'Third World' (e.g. Amba-Roa, 1993) and 'fair trade' (e.g. Dobson, 1993).

Business, has been one of the most (perhaps the single most) important agents of change within British society for the last 250 years. Debates about the ethical basis of business are not simply about the 'misuse' of science and technology, nor are they about business practitioners becoming corrupted by the pursuit of profit and hence requiring additional legislation to bring them back into line. Such apparently 'simple' solutions whilst being anything but simple in their design and execution, are not in themselves adequate for the task at hand. Merely to try and impose more effective external controls over the activities and behaviour of the business community may be well intentioned, but could be ineffectual and misguided. Alternatively, perhaps the regulation of business could be sought within the workings of business organizations through reflection on, and critique of, existing business practices. It is here that business ethics has a key role to play; not as one more set of external constraints or rules to abide by, but as a mechanism of self-appraisal and re-evaluation of the moral dimensions of business behaviour.

One of the problems that confront attempts to define the nature and scope of business ethics is its evident range and diversity. Several writers have tried to identify the various 'levels' of analysis into which the subject can be subdivided. For instance, McHugh (1988) observes that the subject is concerned with the moral aspects of capitalism and democracy at one end of the continuum, and with the issue of individual morality at the other. Meanwhile Hoffman and Moore (1990) provide a more structured approach by identifying four levels of analysis relevant to business ethics:

1. The system level, concerned with the nature of capitalism and the free market system.
2. The analysis of the nature and role of the business organization within the economic system.
3. The examination of particular ethical issues as they arise within the course of economic activity, e.g. employee rights, product safety, hiring and firing.
4. The examination and ethical assessment of the values which are encapsulated within the structure and nature of business activity, e.g. freedom of opportunity, economic growth and materialism.

Alternatively, De George (1987) identifies three levels of analysis:

1. The macrolevel, i.e. the economic system of free enterprise.
2. The study of business operating within the free-market system.
3. The morality of individuals operating within the context of the business system.

For his part, Epstein (1989) sees business ethics as encompassing four distinct levels of analysis:

1. The macro or systemic – involving the nature and performance of 'total political economies'.
2. Intermediate, involving the conduct of 'collective business actors', e.g. industry or trade associations, or professions.
3. Organizational – consideration of the policies and actions of specific firms.
4. Individual – the behaviour of identifiable human actors.

In contrast, MacDonald and Zepp (1989) focus attention primarily on the internal processes of the organization by identifying the individual, group or peer influence, and organizational strategies. If one attempts to amalgamate the views of the writers who have commented on the levels analysis one is confronted with a model which resembles the following figure.

The
systemic

Intermediary   The organization
bodies

Specific
Groups   issues   The individual

By partitioning the subject into such subdivisions, there is a danger that such a 'piecemeal' approach, while understandable as a means of facilitating analysis, may lend itself to the oversimplification and fragmentation of the subject matter. To an extent this is already evident in the way in which much of the literature distinguishes between 'business ethics' and 'corporate social responsibility', the former being concerned with the behaviour of the individual, the latter with the organization. So although these frameworks do help to map various possible aspects of the territory of business ethics, there is also the need to take account of their 'interconnections' (De George, 1987). It is one thing to identify the different levels for analysis, so as to construct more manageable areas for investigation, but it is essential to remain aware of their interrelationships. For example, the individual does not operate as a social isolate. Her or his behaviour is affected by the immediate organizational environment as well as the broader social and economic context. The production and reproduction of capitalism as a mode of economic and social relations is partly founded on its ability to influence the ways in which individuals both perceive, make sense of, and behave in their everyday working lives. Likewise, the process by which an organization's senior management construct corporate strategy is a function of both cultural factors and organizational political processes (Johnson, 1990, 1992; Peattie, 1993; Whittington, 1993).

Therefore the identification of various levels of analysis, provided by the above models, is one of heuristic value rather than a fundamental division. If there is a need to 'take apart' in order to analyse and investigate, there is also the need to 're-assemble' in order to comprehend the systemic complexity of the phenomena under investigation. Goodpaster (1985) echoes De George in this respect when, by identifying three interacting levels of analysis (the ethics of the person, of the organization and of the system), he suggests that there might be relationships among the three levels of moral accountability which contribute to the understanding of each issue or problem ...

> ... Phenomena on one level might be expected to illuminate or even explain phenomena on other levels. (Goodpaster, 1985, p. 167)

Such an observation serves to illustrate the interdisciplinary nature of business ethics as an area of study. Taking the figure as an example, it is possible to hypothesize that there will be interconnections between all six levels or foci of analysis. The particular way in which issues are identified and articulated within the context of any given business organization will be influenced by a variety of situational factors which will both influence the way in which an individual perceives and identifies the nature of the problem, and feels able to deal with it. In effect, the way in which ethical dilemmas are expressed and perhaps resolved within a given organizational context is not simply a reflection of the individual's moral values. How the individual gives expression to his or her concern will be influenced by such factors as the structural aspects of the organization, and the particular values and beliefs which find overt and covert expression within the cultural milieux of the organization. The way in which such issues will be expressed, if at all, will be contingent on the strength and nature of both internal and external support, or hostility.

This complex state of affairs is usefully expressed by writers such as Trevino (1986), Bommer *et al.* (1987) and Stead *et al.* (1990) who set out a variety of models concerned with the factors influencing ethical and unethical decision making within business organizations. What is apparent from such models is that they draw on an interdisciplinary approach in order to create a more comprehensive model of individual decision making and behaviour within an organizational context. Drawing particularly on the disciplines of psychology, sociology and organizational behaviour they offer a useful framework for attempting to understand the variety of factors which influence business behaviour.

From the preceding discussion it should be evident that the study of business ethics is not straightforward. This situation is compounded by the problem that recourse to existing ethical theories to resolve issues of uncertainty within the business context is inadequate. Raphael (1981) expressed himself quite succinctly when he observed that anyone hoping to find an answer to their personal dilemma within the pages of a textbook on moral philosophy is going to be disappointed. At best one can hope to find aids towards solving one's problem. One is still left with the task of choosing which ethical 'guide' or 'map' to make use of, and then defending that choice against advocates of competing, or at best merely different, orientations. This ambiguity is exacerbated by the probability that individuals, who have to cope with the stress of modern business organizations, have limited opportunity for prolonged philosophical reflection. Decisions are often made under conditions of stress and urgency. Nevertheless, the study of business ethics does have important and constructive contributions to make to business behaviour. Firstly, as we have tried to indicate, it can provide a framework, or ethical 'map', which individuals (whether managers, salaried professional or shopfloor workers) can use in order to help them determine what they believe to be 'correct' or acceptable behaviour within the workplace. Secondly, it can both encourage and facilitate a process of self-reflection regarding both past behaviour, current issues, and future action. In this respect it contributes to both the development of the individual, and the business organization. Thirdly, where the potential value of business ethics is recognized and an attempt is made to 'institutionalize' ethics, it can provide a mechanism for organizational change and development.

However, these potential contributions take place in complex organizational contexts that can either facilitate or obstruct their implementation. It is all very well for the individual to want to do the 'right thing', but if peer group, subordinate or superordinate pressure is telling him or her otherwise, then individual choice may well lose out to situational pressures. Whether such pressures to behave in a manner that is socially construed as unethical are always deliberate and conscious may be open to doubt. Often it is the inadvertent pressure exerted by the organization's control and evaluation system which may incline the individual to behave in a way which he or she feels unhappy about.

For Nash (1990) there are three major systemic factors which appear to exert a powerful influence on the nature and prevalence of unethical behaviour within the business organization: the importance attached to the bottom line; the prevalence of short-termism and expediency; and organizational self-interest – which itself raises ethical concerns regarding the 'moral status' of the corporation (Ladd, 1970; Goodpaster and Matthews, 1982; Buchholz, 1989; Ewin, 1991).

A concern with the bottom line demonstrates the importance that business organizations place on results, especially financial ones, and the criteria which are all-too-often used to measure both corporate and individual performance. Particularly important here are the information and control systems designed to facilitate and coordinate organizational performance. An obvious example of this is the importance placed on keeping within budget, and the consequent pressure on individual managers to trim costs even if it results in a loss of product quality. Likewise, time controls may exert pressure on a manager to ensure that an order goes out on time to a customer, even if this means that maintenance duties are neglected and the health and safety of employees and the wider community become compromised.

Short-termism indicates the on-going pressure on business personnel to meet day-to-day demands placed on them by the exigences of the business situation. It embodies the need to firefight and meet a series of on-going demands placed on individuals and organizations faced with an increasingly competitive business environment, and operating under conditions of uncertainty and change. Such observations are important in that they again emphasize that business ethics is not an exercise in 'armchair ethics'. It is of little use to business organizations, the community or society in general, if business ethics does not have practical implications for the way in which individuals behave within the business environment, and business activity is conducted. It is worth emphasizing the earlier observation that business ethics involves *considerably* more than the application of ethical beliefs to business practice – it implies organizational change.

Organizational self-interest represents the personal dilemmas facing the manager or employee when deciding how to respond to such pressures. Does one 'fit-in' and meet the organizational targets, and thereby play safe? Or should one do what one feels to be correct, even if such an action will put oneself in conflict with senior management's directives and/or peer group pressure? It is very easy to advocate that irrespective of the consequences, one should always do the 'right thing', and that in the long run this will result in a beneficial outcome for both oneself and/or the 'organization'. The situation, however, is often very different. To make a stand, on principle or belief, is very often to court disfavour and censure. Whistleblowers within business organizations often act out of their personal apprehension of moral principle – and usually they are punished for doing so (Vinten, 1994). It would be good to be able to believe that the business community would give support to such an individual who has 'turned in' his or her employer out of a sense of moral rectitude. Unfortunately this does not always prove to be the case. Business organizations place considerable value on employee commitment and loyalty, and on occasion can override socially established concerns for business integrity, honesty and fair-play. Determining where the responsibility for such behaviour lies is often difficult. It is not always as simple as identifying the guilty party and punishing them. Ernest Saunders was found guilty of illegal behaviour resulting in the Guinness affair, but to locate the blame on a single individual may serve the purpose of providing the public with a sacrificial victim, without removing the institutional pressures which provoked the behaviour in the first instance.

This is why business ethics is important, not because it can provide incontrovertible ethical guidelines for decision making, but because it can provide frameworks for understanding individual and collective behaviour within an organizational context. As such it is inherently inter-disciplinary in nature. The challenge it presents is to work towards a synthesis of approaches in order to further understanding of the phenomenon known as business ethics.

The complexity involved in such a task is both considerable, and on-going. Given the evolutionary and changing nature of business practice in a rapidly changing socioeconomic and political environment, it will be a brave, and naively optimistic person who ever claims to have reached a definitive 'end-point' regarding business ethics as an area of both thought and practice. The relationship between business ethics and business behaviour is inherently dialectical. As business activity changes as the result of scientific and technological developments, or economic business cycles, or changing attitudes and expectations, then so too will business ethics evolve and develop as a means of seeking to understand, evaluate and influence the nature of such changes.

By their very nature one can expect there to be an inherent tension to exist between business behaviour and business ethics. This tension, we would argue, needs to be acknowledged and recognized, but not necessarily in the form of the old joke that there is no such thing as 'business ethics', and that ethics and business are inherently incompatible with each other. The attempt to laugh-away the subject is a cop-out, an easy way of avoiding the issues which business ethics can raise. Rather, we would contend that business ethics is not only an essential area of study and investigation for anyone who has a stake in business activities, it is also an extremely difficult one. This is why there is the temptation to 'laugh it away'. It is a source of embarrassment. It draws attention to the relationship between the systemic nature of the economy and business organizations on the one hand, and the individual on the other. It is a way of restating that business and financial institutions, however complex they may appear to be, do not have a life of their own. Individuals need not, and should not, believe that their working and social lives are somehow determined by, and dependent on, the 'hidden hand' of the market economy, as if the market system has somehow taken on a life of its own and seems to be beyond human understanding and control.

This is a key contribution that business ethics, as an area of study and discourse, has to make to the activity of business. It serves to focus attention on the things that really matter: the relationship between business and the society within which it lies; the production of goods and services for customer and client; the quality of working life experienced by employees, regardless of rank and status; and the importance of the individual as a social agent.

Our concern in this book is not to identify a coherent definition of business ethicality. Rather the overall aim is to explore the different ethical dimensions to business behaviour in a variety of organizational contexts. There are several reasons for this, which when taken together, justify the chosen approach.

The rationale of this book

Firstly, the chapters are written not by ethicists or moral philosophers, but by members of the Sheffield Business School and the School of Financial Studies and Law at Sheffield Hallam University. While it can be taken for granted that the contributors do have ethics, it would be arguably wrong to describe them as being ethicists, in the sense of having a broad knowledge of ethical theory and moral philosophy. What the authors do share in common is the belief that business ethics is a broad multidisciplinary field of knowledge and practice, and that this reflects both the importance and relevance of the subject for both business practitioners and academics alike.

Secondly, there is the common concern that the subject should be more than a matter for abstract academic debate. If business ethics, as a field of knowledge and practice is to be relevant in the world of business, then it must be seen to have a practical role to play in both the analysis and conduct of business. In this respect, while theorizing can act as an aid to both personal self-reflection and critical analysis it is the variety of ways in which this is expressed in terms of both personal behaviour and organizational practice which serves to both sustain and legitimate the subject as an area worthy of serious consideration.

Thirdly, there is the need to both acknowledge and take account of the complexity of the subject in its various social, political and economic contexts. The extent and duration of change within British society have exacerbated doubt regarding the existing mechanisms of social regulation. The age-old question of 'how should I live my life?', takes on an added urgency and relevance in such times. Thus, the appeal for comprehensive guidelines is perhaps both readily understandable and laudable, but inherently problematic.

Adopting such a rationale presents business ethics as being a social product of knowledge and practice. In sociological terms, one could argue that the above account is essentially functionalist. Contemporary society has a need for some mechanism by which to reduce feelings of both individual and collective uncertainty and doubt concerning the nature and conduct of business practice which cannot be fulfilled by reliance on existing legal custom and practice. Business ethics, as a set of both evaluative criteria and institutionalized organizational practices, provides a means by which doubt can be assuaged. Social equanimity is restored. Life can continue.

The problem with the above functionalist view is that it is theoretically and ideologically suspect. It fails to deal adequately with the complexity inherent in business ethics. If it is possible to contextualize business ethics as being a social product of uncertainty, then it is also necessary to acknowledge that such uncertainty is also inherent in business ethics itself. It is not a homogeneous area of knowledge and agreement – an island of theoretical and practical stability amid the complexity and chaos of contemporary social life. Rather, business ethics is a multidisciplinary area of theoretical discourse and practice which exhibits a similar degree of uncertainty as the social milieux within which it is located. Paradoxically, business ethics could be said to be both an expression of, and a reaction to, the uncertainty and heterogeneity manifested in contemporary society.

A central objective of this book is to indicate the problematical nature of business ethics. It is not a 'managerial problem' which can be easily defined, analysed and resolved through the development of a set of nostrums. To present it as being a coherent, homogeneous body of knowledge, would be a disservice. This book therefore is concerned to provide the reader with a range of subject matter which, when viewed as a collectivity, provides a means of contextualizing the complexity and heterogeneous nature of business ethics while also emphasizing the importance of the particular issues which are dealt with by contributors.

As a means of achieving this, the editors deliberately did not attempt to be overly prescriptive in their approach to the contributors. It was felt that encouraging the writers to address particular aspects of business behaviour and express their particular perspectives is itself an important indicator of the both the richness, complexity, diversity and topicality of business ethics. The reader is encouraged to both consider, and challenge the views expressed in the chapters that follow. Discussion, debate, and argument and counterargument should be essential ingredients of any text dealing with business ethics. The exercises and occasional case study found at the end of a chapter are designed to further stimulate this reflexive process. To question and disagree with the views contained within the text is essential, but it is equally important to ask oneself, why do I disagree?

In *Chapter 1*, Ken Smith and Phil Johnson provide an introduction to the 'field' of business ethics. They review and evaluate two key approaches to the subject – the prescriptive and the descriptive. The authors conclude that each approach has severe philosophical and practical problems which are inevitably expressed in any attempt at comprehending the ethical dimensions of business behaviour.

The book structure

The rest of the book is divided into parts and a concluding chapter.

Part One provides a contextual framework which elaborates the different levels of analysis through which the subject of business ethics can be approached. While the initial emphasis may appear to focus on a systemic level of analysis, it becomes apparent that this level is itself dependent on the social production of knowledge and practice undertaken by individuals situated within organizational contexts. This part is also important for making the reader aware of the issues of power and organizational politics which play an important role in influencing the nature and processes of organizational activity – a process which affects both the ethicality of individual behaviour, and how such behaviour is interpreted and evaluated by the individuals affected by it.

In *Chapter 2*, Kevan Scholes and Tony Wood focus attention on the difficulties encountered in seeking to apply business ethics within the complex and dynamic arena of corporate strategy. The interrelationships existing between the systemic, organizational, and individual levels of analysis are readily apparent in considering the process by which the analysis, creation, implementation, and evaluation of an organization's corporate strategy is undertaken. Reflecting both the need to take account of socioeconomic and political factors affecting the organization's environment and the internal, cultural and political processes affecting the formulation of strategy, they indicate the importance of incorporating an ethical dimension to the process of strategy formulation.

In *Chapter 3*, Alex Dunlop provides a critical appraisal of contemporary approaches toward corporate governance. Contending that the current concerns reflect a desire for self-regulation rather than government intervention he locates the phenomenon within the parameters of the market economic system, which thereby both constrains and influences the form and content of the controversy regarding how it should be enacted. Observing that the recommendations of the Cadbury Report appear to be overly concerned with the responsibilities and duties of the board of directors, he draws attention to the need to take more account of the problematic nature of organizational shareholders and their varied aspirations, and for this to be accorded more importance when considering the forms and processes of corporate accountability and control.

In *Chapter 4*, David Hawley and Don White, in setting out a model for scanning the ethical environment, illustrate both the complexity involved in adopting an ethical perspective and its importance for analysing and evaluating organizational and individual behaviour. The complex situation confronting the individual ethical decision-maker operating within an organizational context is ably illustrated by reference to the situation of the systems analyst employed as a salaried professional. Concerned to apply his or her professional skills and knowledge within the political–cultural milieux of the organization, the case of the systems analyst illustrates the dilemma of many organizational employees concerned to apply their knowledge and skills responsibly within a context of conflicting interests and concerns.

In *Chapter 5*, Colin Gilligan illustrates the pivotal role which marketing plays in providing a crucial interface between the business organization and the market. He highlights the ethical conflicts that managers are often faced with in increasingly competitive markets and how this conflict is manifested in both the development of a competitive stance, and in the management of the marketing mix. In this respect, any discussion of the ethics of marketing could perhaps also be seen as incorporating, in microcosm, the concerns regarding the ethics of business in general.

In *Chapter 6*, Sue Whittle challenges the assumption of a close relationship existing between the concern for organizational competitiveness and efficiency, and the acceptance and legitimation of an increasingly capital intensive and technologically determined workplace. She contends that ethics can provide a means of both investigating and challenging the widespread acceptance of a technologically determinist approach towards justifying the re-organization of the workplace and the design of jobs. By facilitating a process of critical self-analysis and re-appraisal of existing techniques and rationales adopted by management it is suggested that the explicit adoption of an ethical perspective to organizational analysis can contribute to alternative processes of both organizational redesign and consequently the experience of work.

In *Chapter 7*, Peter Cooke and John Shipton focus on the ethical dimensions inherent in both the concept and practice of human resource management (HRM). In an increasingly competitive and dynamic work environment HRM practices have become more important for both facilitating organizational change and increasing both individual and organizational efficiency. As a consequence of this, HRM practices have themselves become subject to critical analysis and appraisal regarding both their role and substance. HRM may be expected to play an important part in the process of institutionalizing ethics within the workplace, all the more reason therefore to adopt an ethical perspective towards investigating the practice of HRM.

Part Two focuses on a variety of issues which were selected on the basis of their importance in contemporary business organizations. Thus, the chapters in Part Two examine the problematic nature of establishing control over ethicality and the ethical debates and dilemmas surrounding discrimination, leadership, managing change and the globalization of business. In examining these issues, the contributors illustrate something of both the complexity and importance of business ethics for both business organizations, perceived as a social entity, and for the groups and individuals who comprise their membership.

In *Chapter 8*, Phil Johnson, Catherine Cassell and Ken Smith investigate the processes through which members determine what and how things get done in business organizations. Using corporate codes of ethics as an example, they examine how the impact of attempts at influencing the ethical dimensions of organizational behaviour are mediated by formal and informal organizational contexts. They conclude that while a corporate code may specify ethicality, alone it cannot create ethical behaviour without the collateral development of contextual 'fit'.

In *Chapter 9*, Catherine Cassell discusses the meaning of 'discrimination', its nature and incidence in the UK, and the extent to which it is an important ethical issue. By applying a contextualist approach to business ethics she evaluates the main approaches to reducing discrimination and finds them wanting.

In *Chapter 10*, John Gill argues that conventional approaches to leadership are essentially different ways of controlling and coercing subordinates which pose ethical dilemmas. Such notions of leadership socially validate beliefs about the necessity for hierarchy and engender alienation. In contrast Gill argues for the development of organizations based on the intrinsic motivation of self-controlling members. 'Leadership' in this context is unlikely to be based on overcontrol through command and authority but rather on supportive behaviour that promises more ethical and less exploitative relationships.

In *Chapter 11*, John McAuley analyses the ethical issues which arise with the management of change in business organizations. He extends this initial analysis to explore the ethical presuppositions and rhetoric of three key approaches: transformational leadership, force-field analysis and organizational development. To avoid 'ethical muddles', McAuley argues that it is critical to establish consensus among internal and external stakeholders.

In *Chapter 12*, Robin Lowe reviews the ethical issues that arise in international business. He argues that as firms globalize their operations, they become exposed to new tensions which create a variety of new ethical challenges. This increasingly common scenario requires managerial 'proaction', at both strategic and operational levels, which is sensitive to the needs and interests of those who have a stake in the activities of a multinational enterprise.

In *Chapter 13*, through a critical review of the debates about modernism and postmodernism, Ken Smith and Phil Johnson attempt to contextualize business ethics as a social phenomenon. In this they argue that the 'field' of business ethics may be understood as both an expression of, and reaction to, the anomic (i.e. normless) conditions inherent in contemporary society.

References   Amba-Roa, S.C. (1993) Multinational corporate social responsibility, ethics, interaction and Third World governments: an agenda for the 1990s. *Journal of Business Ethics*, **12**, 553–72.

Atkinson, J. (1984) Manpower strategies for flexible organisations. *Personnel Management*, **26**(8), 28–31.

Atkinson, J. and Gregory, D. (1986) A flexible future: Britain's dual labour force. *Marxism Today*, April, 12–17.

Bartkowiak, J.J. (1993) Trends towards part-time employment: ethical issues. *Journal of Business Ethics*, **12**, 811–15.

Beaty, J. and Gwynne, S.C. (1993) *The Outlaw Bank: A Wild Ride into the Secret World of BCCI*. Random House, London.

Bird, F. and Walters, J.A. (1987) The nature of managerial standards. *Journal of Business Ethics*, **6**, 1–13.

Bird, F. and Walters, J.A (1989) The moral muteness of managers. *California Management Review*, Fall, 73–88.

Bommer, M., Gratto, C., Gravaander, J. and Tuttle, M. (1987) A model of ethical and unethical decision making. *Journal of Business Ethics*, **6**, 265–80.

Buchholtz, R.A. (1989) *Fundamental Concepts and Problems in Business Ethics*. Prentice-Hall, Englewood Cliffs, NJ.

Buller, P.F., Kohls, J.J. and Anderson, K.S. (1991) The challenge of global ethics. *Journal of Business Ethics*, **12**, 767–75.

Cannon, H. (1993) Standard Life attacks bosses pay bonanzas. *The Independent*, 10 May.

Carr, A. (1968) Is business bluffing ethical? *Harvard Business Review*, **46**, 143–55.

Clegg, S.R. (1990) *Modern Organizations: Organizations in the Postmodern World*. Sage, London.

Cohen, E. and Cornwall, L. (1989) A question of ethics: developing informations system ethics. *Journal of Business Ethics*, **8**, 431–7.

Cusick, J. (1994a) Secrets of success by Dirty Tricks Inc. *The Independent*, 4 November.

Cusick, J. (1994b) DTI's dirty tricks manual in use for two years. *The Independent*, 5 November.

Derry, G. and Green, R.M. (1989) Ethical theory in business ethics. *Journal of Business Ethics*, **8**, 521–33.

De George, R.T. (1986) Replies and reflections on theology and business ethics. *Journal of Business Ethics*, **5**, 521–524.

De George, R.T. (1987) The status of business ethics: past and future. *Journal of Business Ethics*, **6**, 201–11.

De George, R.T. (1990) *Business Ethics*, 3rd edn. Prentice-Hall, Englewood Cliffs, NJ.

Dobson, J. (1993) TNCs and the corruption of GATT. *Journal of Business Ethics*, **12**, 573–8.

Donaldson, J. (1989) *Key Issues in Business Ethics*. Academic Press, London.

Donaldson, T. and Werhane, P.H. (eds) (1988) *Ethical Issues in Business: A Philosophical Approach*, 3rd edn. Prentice-Hall, Englewood Cliffs, NJ.

Epstein, E.M. (1989) Business ethics, corporate good citizenship and the corporate social policy process: a view from the United States. *Journal of Business Ethics*, **8**, 583–95.

Ewin, R.E. (1991) The moral status of the corporation. *Journal of Business Ethics*, **10**, 749–56.

Freeman, R.E. and Gilbert, D.R. (1988) *Corporate Strategy and the Search for Ethics*. Prentice-Hall, New York.

Friedman, M. (1962) *Capitalism and Freedom*. University of Chicago Press, Chicago, IL.

Goodpaster, K.E. (1985) Toward an integrated approach to business ethics thought. *Thought*, **60**(2), 161–80.

Goodpaster, K.E. and Matthews, (1982) Can a corporation have a conscience? *Harvard Business Review*, 132–40.

Gregory, M. (1994) *Dirty Tricks: British Airways Secret War Against Virgin Atlantic*. Little Brown, London.

Hallaq, J.H. and Steinhorst, K. (1994) Business intelligence methods – how ethical? *Journal of Business Ethics*, **13**, 787–94.

Handy, C. (1989) *The Age of Unreason*. Business Books, London.

Handy, C. (1994) *The Empty Raincoat: Making Sense of the Future*. Hutchinson, London.

Hanley, K. (1992) Hostile takeover and methods of defence: a stakeholder analysis. *Journal of Business Ethics*, **11**, 859–913.

Hawk, S.R. (1994) The effects of computerised performance monitoring. *Journal of Business Ethics*, **13**, 949–57.

Hayek, F.A. (1969) The corporation in a democratic society: in whose interest ought it and will it be run?, in *Business Strategy* (ed. H.I. Ansoff). Penguin, Harmondsworth.

Hickman, L.A. (ed.) (1990) *Technology as a Human Affair*. McGraw-Hill, London.

Hines, C. and Searle, G. (1979) *Automatic Unemployment*. Earth Resources, London.

Hoffman, W.M. and Moore, J.M. (1990) *Business Ethics: Readings and Cases in Corporate Morality*, 2nd edn. McGraw-Hill, New York.

Hosmer, L.T. (1987) The institutionalisation of unethical behaviour. *Journal of Business Ethics*, **6**, 439–47.

Jackall, R. (1988) *Moral Mazes: The World of Corporate Managers*. Oxford University Press, Oxford.

Jenkins, C. and Sherman, B. (1979) *The Collapse of Work*. Eyre-Methuen, London.

Jenkins, C. and Sherman, B. (1981) *The Leisure Shock*. Eyre-Methuen, London.

Johnson, G. (1990) Managing strategic change: the role of symbolic action. *British Journal of Management*, **1**, 183–200.

Johnson, G. (1992) Managing strategic change: strategy, culture and action. *Long Range Planning*, **25**(1), 28–36.

Keeley, M. (1981) Organizations as non-persons. *Journal of Value Inquiry*, **15**, 149–55.

Khalil, O.E.M. (1993) Artificial decision-making and artificial ethics: a management concern. *Journal of Business Ethics*, **12**, 312–13.

Kornbluth, J. (1992) *Highly Confidential: The Crime and Punishment of Michael Milken*. William Morrow, New York.

Ladd, J. (1970) Morality and the ideal of rationality in formal organizations. *The Monist*, **54**(4), 488–516.

Leadbeater, C. and Lloyd, J. (1987) *In Search of Work*. Penguin, Harmondsworth.

Levine, D.B., with Hoffer, W. (1991) *Insider Out: An Insider's Account of Wall Street*. Putnam, New York.

Lyon, D. (1994) *The Electronic Eye: The Rise of Surveillance Society*. Polity Press, Cambridge.

MacDonald, G.M. and Zepp, R.A. (1989) Business ethics: practical proposals. *Journal of Management Development*, **8**(1), 55–66.

MacInnes, J. (1988) The question of flexibility. *Personnel Review*, 17(3), 12–15.

Meade, N.L. and Davidson, D. (1993) The use of shark repellents to prevent corporate takeovers: an ethical perspective. *Journal of Business Ethics*, **12**, 83–92.

McHugh, F.P. (1988) *Keyguide to Information Sources in Business Ethics*. Nichols Publishing, New York.

Nash, L.L. (1990) *Good Intentions Aside: A Manager's Guide to Resolving Ethical Problems*. Harvard Business School Press, Boston, MA.

Nichols, T. (1986) *The British Worker Question*. Routledge & Kegan Paul, London.

Peattie, K. (1993) Strategic planning: its role in organizational politics. *Long Range Planning*, **26**(3), 10–17.

Pollert, A. (1991) *Farewell to Flexibility*. Basil Blackwell, Oxford.

Primeaux, P. (1992) Experiential ethics: a blueprint for personal and corporate ethics. *Journal of Business Ethics*, **11**, 779–88.

Prost, J.E. (1991) Managing as if the Earth mattered. *Business Horizons*, 3(4), 32–8.

Prowse, P. (1990) Assessing the flexible firm. *Personnel Review*, 19(6), 13–17.

Raphael, D.D. (1981) *Moral Philosophy*. Oxford University Press, Oxford.

Rossouw, G.J. (1994) Rational interaction for moral sensitivity: a postmodern approach to moral decision-making in business. *Journal of Business Ethics*, **13**, 11–20.

Solomon, R.C. (1992) *Ethics and Excellence: Cooperation and Integrity in Business*. Oxford University Press, Oxford.

Stark, A. (1993) What's the matter with business ethics? *Harvard Business Review*, May–June, 38–48.

Stead, W.E., Worrell, D.L. and Stead, J.G. (1990) An integrative model for understanding and managing ethical behavior in business organizations. *Journal of Business Organisations*, **9**, 233–42.

Stewart, J.B. (1991) *Den of Thieves*. Simon & Schuster, New York.

Storey, J. (ed.) (1989) *New Perspectives on Human Resource Management.* Routledge, London.

Sullivan, R.J. (1984) Is business bluffing ethical? *Business and Professional Ethics Journal*, 3(2), 1–17.

Trevino, L.K. (1986) Ethical decision making in organisations: a person–situation interactionist model. *Academy of Management Review*, 11(3), 601–17.

Truell, P. and Gurwin, L. (1992) *BCCI: The Inside Story of the World's Most Corrupt Financial Empire.* Bloomsbury, London.

Velasquez, M.G. (1988) *Business Ethics: Concepts and Cases*, 2nd edn. Prentice-Hall, Englewood Cliffs, NJ.

Vogel, D. (1991) New perspectives on old problems. *California Management Review*, 35(4), 101–17.

Vinten, P. (ed.) (1994) *Whistle Blowing: Subversion or Corporate Citizenship.* Paul Chapman, London.

Waters, J.A. and Bird, F. (1987) The moral dimension of organisational culture. *Journal of Business Ethics*, 6, 15–22.

Whittington, R. (1993) *What is Strategy – And Does It Matter?* Routledge, London.

Business ethics and business behaviour: towards an understanding

1

Ken Smith and Phil Johnson

Introduction

Although philosophical debates about ethics can be traced back to antiquity (Small, 1993), it is only relatively recently that there appears to have been a marked surge in interest in the area of business ethics (Mahoney, 1990). But in trying to conceptualize business ethics as a discipline we are immediately confronted by its problematic nature. This is because any definition of business ethics articulates particular assumptions about the subject. It is the nature of these underlying assumptions which may be problematic.

For instance, one orientation is to identify business ethics with the application of normative ethical theory to business (e.g. Ozar, 1979; Davis, 1982; Goodpaster and Matthews, 1982; Velasquez, 1988). Typically Velasquez argues that ...

> ... business ethics is applied ethics. It is the application of our understanding of what is good and right to the assortment of institutions, technologies, transactions, activities, and pursuits which we call 'Business'. (1988, p.1)

This implies that through the systematic application of the canons of moral philosophy it becomes possible to objectively arbitrate what is good and right for the various activities associated with 'business' (Donaldson, 1989a). However, if

> ... business ethics is any systematic attempt to integrate models of moral problem solving with practical moral dilemmas in business ... there may be no one correct solution to a given problem. Rather, there may be competing models of explanation that provide reasonable solutions. (Cooke, 1986, p. 261)

This situation raises two issues. Firstly, that of 'praxis' – business ethics is an applied, practical, area of investigation. It is not simply the study of ethical thought divorced from the social contexts of business activities. Its test-bed must be business environments with all their complexity, confusion and uncertainty. Secondly, there is no one set of universally agreed canons. Instead any business practitioner is confronted by an array of competing views, derived from different moral philosophies, each articulating different prescriptions about what is good or bad for the conduct of business behaviour. He or she is faced with the dilemma of choosing which ethical theory to draw upon for guidance – a decision which will influence how events are interpreted. Raphael puts the issue quite succinctly when he observes that

> ... in philosophy, far more than in science, one is left in the end with a number of possible theories, none of them proved, none of them definitely disproved. The individual must then decide for himself which, if any, to accept. – So do not expect moral philosophy to solve the practical problems of life or to be a crutch on which you can lean. A study of philosophy makes it more necessary, not less, to stand on your own feet, to be self-critical, and to be obliged to choose for yourself. (1981, p. 10)

Rather than providing a definitive guide, the business practitioner is faced with a variety of potential guides, or axioms, and the problem of deciding which one to make use of. Alternatively, he or she could try to combine the differing approaches and thereby discern the optimum solution to the problem. But this raises the problem of whether different moral philosophies are commensurable and can be combined in this manner (see MacDonald and Beck-Dudley, 1994). If moral recourse to ethical theory cannot resolve personal ethical dilemmas, it is even more important where overt ethical disputes between parties with rival moral views exist. The plurality of normative ethical theories means that there is no neutral position from which to adjudicate the claims of those rival parties (Rossouw, 1994). Therefore, as Raphael implies, perhaps the main value of moral philosophy to the business person lies its ability to facilitate critical self-reflection rather than in the provision of clear guidelines that enable the construction of optimal solutions.

Because of the problems noted above, some commentators avoid defining business ethics purely in terms of the application of ethical theory to business affairs. For instance, De George (1986, p. 20) argues that business ethics is an interdisciplinary field in which the methodologies of the various areas of business education are as applicable as those of ethical and philosophical analysis. McHugh (1988) provides a good indication of this variety of academic influence when he indicates that there are a dozen or so disciplines which can be said to have a claim to providing an input to business ethics. These include philosophy, sociology, psychology, history, law, politics and economics.

Thus, McHugh rejects the view that business ethics is the preserve of one academic discipline (philosophy) and the hope that business ethics provides any easy solutions to the problems of contemporary business practice through appeal to incontrovertible moral authority. If it was that easy there could be a rule-book on business ethics supplied to every new entrant to business schools and potential or practising managers could be tested with regard to their ethicality.

McHugh's elucidation of a variety of disciplinary inputs adds weight to De George's contention that business ethics is a 'field' rather than a discipline in its own right. A consideration of these 'disciplinary contributors' serves to lend force to the argument that business ethics entails more than applying the prescriptions of various ethical philosophers. It also suggests that the subject is dynamic rather than static, a behavioural subject that attempts to describe and explain the ethical dimension to organization members' everyday interactions rather than prescribe them through an appeal to incontestable moral certainties.

The dynamic aspect inherent in business ethics can be interpreted in a number of ways. Firstly, there is the argument that to rely on the moral arguments put forward over the years by philosophers, theologians and other social commentators may be helpful, but they are insufficient since the issues facing today's business community are complex and subject to unpredictable change. Secondly, there is the question of where responsibility for such matters lies? It is all very well to maintain that responsibility lies with the individual, but the very complexity of the modern business organizations points to the need to look beyond the single individual, no matter how well-versed he or she is in the virtues of Socratic contemplation.

It can be concluded that the subject matter of business ethics is more than an individual responsibility and the application of moral beliefs to business practice. For one thing, just as contemporary debate in business ethics can draw upon existing ethical thought, so contemporary business practice can contribute, and probably has contributed, to the evolution of ethical thought since such thought is itself a social product (see MacIntyre, 1989) that cannot be divorced from the context of its articulation. Moreover, as we have emphasized, there will be different answers to ethical issues depending on the assumptions, or 'mode of engagement', of whoever is proposing the answers. With this particular issue in mind, many commentators (e.g. Buchholz, 1989; Stace, 1988; Sumner, 1988) have differentiated what may called **'prescriptive'**, **'cognitive'** or **'absolutist'** moral statements from what are termed **'descriptive'**, **'non-cognitive'** or **'relativist'** moral statements. This dichotomy is of crucial importance to the study of ethics in general, and to the definition and study of business ethics in particular. To put it crudely, how a person is oriented with regard to this dichotomy determines the extent to which he or she believes it is possible to prespecify what is good or bad, right or wrong, for people in general and, in particular, for the behaviour of members of business organizations. Now we shall review each approach in turn and thereby elaborate some of the themes identified so far in this chapter.

Prescriptive business ethics

From this perspective business ethics entails the prescriptive application of normative ethical theory to business (e.g. Velasquez, 1988; Donaldson, 1989a, Hoffman and Moore, 1990). Typically, Hoffman and Moore observe that it is

> ... the study of what is good and right for human beings. It asks what goals people ought to pursue and what actions they ought to perform. Business ethics is a branch of applied ethics; it studies the relationship of what is good and right to business. (1990, p. 1).

This approach is based on the notion that ultimately there exist eternal moral principles which are universally applicable and cognitively accessible to everyone in the conduct of business regardless of social or historical context. Although there is some disagreement as to the extent, it is possible to fully elucidate a coherent set of absolute ethical principles, there is a concern to formulate a framework of ethical standards that are taken to approximate those principles. Into this framework are encoded prescriptions about what is right and wrong, or good and bad, for the conduct of business. This entails specifying what should be avoided and done in order to achieve those prescribed standards.

So underpinning a prescriptive approach to business ethics is the assumption that it is possible to discern what is good or bad in the conduct of business affairs and develop guidelines that will promote the good which are often inextricably linked to explicit, or implicit, conceptions of human welfare. An important aspect of this programme is a concern to evaluate current and past business practices in the light of these philosophically grounded criteria. Therefore, adherents share the assumption that it is possible to objectively judge the behaviour of others in the light of their conformity to, or deviance from, some universally applicable framework of moral standards as interpreted and evaluated through the medium of ethical concepts and criteria (e.g. Goodpaster, 1985, p. 163). Importantly, this is to be accomplished without reference to the subjective state of the person(s) whose behaviour is being adjudicated. In other words, whether or not a person thinks that what he or she is doing is morally right or wrong, according to their own understanding and moral precepts, is irrelevant to that adjudication process. However, it is difficult to find unambiguous criteria that enable any subsequent adjudication process. As we have already noted, this is because there is a variety of different ethical theories each of which embraces different assumptions about what is good or bad in the conduct of business affairs.

For instance, it is apparent that prescriptive approaches often draw on two quite different schools of ethical thought that vary in terms of the ethical precepts deployed. One is called a *teleological* or *consequentialist* approach. This claims that judgements as to whether or not human actions are right or wrong can only be accomplished with reference to the nature of the consequences of those actions for human beings. The most important version of this approach is known as *utilitarianism* which stresses the greatest good to the greatest number. An important alternative to utilitarianism is concerned with *rights* and *duties*. It derives from the *deontological* tradition and has a basis in Judeo-Christian philosophical beliefs and the writings of Immanuel Kant. This deontological approach articulates the view that if a human action is to be judged as right, it has to have certain characteristics that are independent of its consequences. Therefore there is no appeal to the beneficial or harmful consequences of actions in determining their ethicality, rather it is in the virtue of being a particular action, according to particular principles, which bestows ethicality.

Although these two key prescriptive approaches contradict one another, and although they cannot be expected to supply complete answers to contemporary problems, that is not to maintain that they should be ignored. To do so would loose their reflexive value. It is not the intention here to embark on a detailed exposition of both schools of thought. Instead we intend to briefly delineate these beliefs. This will provide an indication of their contribution to prescriptive business ethics and demonstrate the problems encountered by the prescriptive approach since given this variability in ethical theory, how does one decide which axioms to follow in defining 'ethicality'?

UTILITARIANISM: THE COSTS AND BENEFITS OF DECISIONS

Utilitarianism is closely associated with the work of Jeremy Bentham and John Stuart Mill. It argues that the actions and policies arising from decisions should be evaluated in terms of the costs and benefits which they will have for society. The 'correct' course of action is that which will result in the greatest net gain, or benefit for society as a whole – the greatest good for the greatest number. Here there is an apparent dilemma since utilitarianism could justify acts which benefit the majority yet entail terrible costs to the minority. This dilemma is compounded by further quandaries.

For instance, costs and benefits are often calculated in monetary terms. Economics textbooks have sometimes argued in terms of a decision creating so many 'utils of satisfaction'. The idea being that one can somehow measure or quantify how many 'utils' can be derived from each potential action or decision, thereby determining which course of action is preferable. The assumption is that one can somehow put a 'price' on any given action or happening and thereby convert costs and benefits into the parlance of economics – an operationalization into a common medium of comparison, money.

Thus, some underlying difficulties with utilitarianism lie in the very complexity of the task it sets itself. An action is ethically correct only if the total amount of utility produced by that action is greater than the total amount of utility that could have been produced by the pursuit of any alternative course. The assumption is that the relevant costs and benefits arising from any given course of action are amenable to some form of common numerical measurement. In this way the costs can be added together and then subtracted from the sum of the benefits. What one is left with is a quantity, or amount of utility, which can be compared with the outcomes of similar calculations appertaining to alternative potential courses of action. Having compared the results the decision maker should then opt for the course of action which produces the most utility.

It is hardly surprising that such an exercise is very difficult to put into practice. Firstly, the decision-maker has to find the *single best decision* compared with all other potential decisions. Utilitarianism has a perfectionist stance – there can be only one best course of action. Secondly, the 'correct' action is not that which produces the most utility for the individual actually taking the action. The course of action is only the correct one if it results in the most utility for everybody who is affected by that action, including the individual initiating the action. The decision maker has to contend with the task of identifying *everybody* who may be affected by the intended action, and then engaging in a much larger round of arithmetical calculations – assuming of course that he or she is able to calculate arithmetical values on the costs and benefits of the individuals involved. Moreover the utilitarian has to take account of 'time'. In making the arithmetical calculations regarding the costs and benefits arising from any potential course of action, the individual is also obliged to take into account both short- and long-term costs and benefits. It is not sufficient merely to make the calculation for the immediate context.

Even if the decision maker was able to make the calculations, he or she is forced into making the assumption that it is possible to correctly determine the arithmetical values for those affected by the decision. It is therefore evident that it assumes a high degree of uniformity in the values held by those potentially affected by the decision. A unitary assumption which is difficult to sustain in today's complex and pluralistic society. Such problems are compounded by naivety – it assumes that decision makers are free to operate in line with all perceived interests. Thereby it ignores the impact, on decision-making processes, of inequalities between interest groups in terms of symbolic, ideological and material power.

To operationalize the original tenets of utilitarianism, is a daunting task. There is a temptation to dismiss utilitarianism as an approach which is impossible to use in practice. But whatever the problems inherent in the approach it should not be dismissed out-of-hand. Despite its utopian nature, utilitarianism could serve several important functions.

Firstly, it focuses upon outcomes and their consequences for others. Secondly, basic to the approach is the intent to maximize beneficial outcomes, and to try and ensure that the benefits accruing from any decision choice outweigh the costs, damage or harm that may also derive from consequent courses of action. Thirdly, by trying to measure the costs and benefits involved it seeks to avoid the more obvious pitfalls arising from personal interest and bias. It makes it very clear that in determining the appropriate course of action, the decision maker must take into account the effects upon all those influenced by that action. He or she should not be swayed by personal advantage, or bias or personal animosity towards others affected by the decision. In this manner it could aid the reconciliation of the various demands that might impact upon decision making that stem from a multiplicity of stakeholders.

Perhaps the greatest damage done to utilitarian thought in today's society has been the extent to which it has been associated with certain approaches to economics. Specifically, they attempt to resolve the problem of measurement in utilitarianism by adopting an approach to cost-benefit analysis that disenfranchises stakeholder interests beyond those of the shareholder. In effect this articulates the dismissal, by both Hayek (1969) and Friedman (1962), of the view (e.g. Berle and Means, 1932, p. 356) that management should be socially responsible through balancing the claims made by a variety of interest groups. For Hayek and Friedman the purpose of business was the profitable use of capital entrusted to management by shareholders because

> ... if anything is certain to destroy our free society ... it would be a widespread acceptance by management of social responsibilities ... other than to make as much money as possible. (Friedman, quoted in Hayek, 1969, p. 239)

Thus management's social responsibility becomes redefined as 'making maximum profits for their shareholders'. But utilitarianism originally embraced a far wider constituency of interests (e.g. 'the common good') than those prescribed by such economists – a point which needs to be borne in mind when seeking to apply utilitarianism to real-life organizational issues. The temptation is to fall back upon economic measures that merely operationalize the shareholder interest because they appear to be objective (see, Tinker, 1985).

In sum, a fundamental problem for utilitarianism is that notions like 'cost' and 'benefit' are not concepts which may be neutrally operationalized, rather they are socially constructed artefacts that people use to make sense of their world(s) and as such vary according to their perceptions, values and interests. The paradox is that utilitarianism could be a valuable aid to decision making within the context of business whilst being difficult to operationalize. The likelihood of consensus over what constitutes costs and benefits must be low given the plurality of interests that constitute society and its institutions.

An alternative tradition within prescriptive business ethics derives from a view that considers that the whole consequentialist basis of utilitarianism is fundamentally misguided. This is because since utilitarianism merely focuses upon outcomes it devalues people as individuals and thereby their rights give way to a calculative expediency. An expression of this position is illustrated by the work of Immanuel Kant.

RIGHTS AND DUTIES

Kant's approach (1964) highlights the motivations underlying actions rather than their consequences. For Kant, an action had 'moral worth' if it was motivated by 'good will', that is from a sense of duty (i.e. deontological), from a belief that it was the right way to behave – reasons that everyone would agree to act on. Therefore Kant ties morality to a view of rationality which is grounded in compliance with consistent, absolute and universal maxims.

Thus his first formulation of the categorical imperative maintained that:

> I ought never to act except in such a way that I can also will my maxim should become a universal law. (1964, p. 70)

In other words Kant argues that it is possible to derive moral laws by the individual asking himself or herself if the maxim that underpinned his or her behaviour could become a universal law. For instance, a person's refusal to pay a debt would only be moral if he or she was consistently prepared for everyone else, in similar circumstances, to also refuse to settle their debts.

Kant's second formulation of the categorical imperative appears to complement his first. He argues that an individual should act with respect for people in the sense that he or she should:

> Act in such a way that you always treat humanity, whether in your own person or in the person of any other, never simply as a means, but always at the same time as an end. (1964, p. 96)

At the risk of oversimplifying Kant, the main message for business is the concern for the individual's intrinsic worth and that the individual should not be treated merely as a means to an end. To treat people instrumentally is to act unethically, rather people must be accorded dignity and treated with respect. Kant's position thereby has an affinity with the issue of 'rights' as it entails the prescription that it is a moral duty to ensure and respect the rights of others. Generally, a right is an individual's entitlement to something. It can be that an individual is entitled to behave, or act in a certain way, or in addition, to have others behave in certain ways towards him or her. In this sense Kant provides an ethical defence against both the tyranny of a minority over the majority and, importantly, a utilitarian pursuit of the common good at the expense of minorities.

At a very formal level, the issue of rights might be highlighted by contracts – the limited rights and related duties which occur when one person enters into a formal agreement with another. Modern business might be said to almost run on contracts, whether it be between a buyer and a seller, or between an employer and employee. The general rules governing contracts are worth consideration as they can be said to incorporate a number of moral constraints or obligations on those involved. Broadly speaking, they require that (see also Velasquez, 1988):

1. Both parties to the contract fully understand the nature of the contract which they are entering into.
2. Neither of the parties must intentionally misrepresent the contents of the contract to the other party.
3. Neither party to the contract should be coerced into accepting the terms of the contract.
4. The contract should not require the parties to take part in an immoral act.

Whether every contract entered into between business organizations, or between employer and employees meets all the requirements of such a contract is open to some debate, and perhaps helps explain why so much time and effort is spent analysing the 'fine print' before signing. Whether expressed as a contact, or embodied in laws, or informally expressed through social conventions, rights can be either positive or negative.

Negative rights can be described in terms of the duties that others have not to interfere in the various activities to which the individual has a right. An example of this might be the right of an individual to privacy, and hence the obligation upon either an employer, or perhaps the state, not to infringe that right through, for example, the computerization of employee information and the transmission of such data to other parties.

Positive rights advocate that individuals, or organizations, have a positive duty to provide the holder of any such right with the means by which such a right can be enacted – such as the right to health care.

Applying the debate over positive and negative rights to the realm of employment is ambiguous and controversial. Do workers have a (positive) right to work? If so, what are the duties and obligations placed on employers for providing such opportunity? How might the (negative) right to work free from harassment, clash with the (positive or negative) right to strike? Should there be a (positive or negative) right for employees to join a trade union? One might argue so on grounds of such an activity being an expression of a negative right – the freedom of association. But if this is so, are employers also obligated to recognize and negotiate with such a body? For example, to what extent does the right of employees to join a trade union and collectively attempt to influence organizational decision-making impinge on management's (positive and negative) right to manage?

The above examples serve to indicate the variety and complexity of the controversies surrounding rights relating to the world of business. The debates are long-running, controversial and demonstrate a lack of consensus. Firstly, there is the question of prioritizing. How does one rank the various rights in order of importance? Secondly, while some rights are legally expressed and sanctioned through contracts and statutes, others are more ephemeral and socially contingent – the result of informal social convention and practices. Thirdly, what happens when two rights appear to come into conflict with each other? For example, when an individual's right to freedom of conscience finds expression in whistleblowing, does this override the obligations placed on the individual by his or her contract of employment? It might be argued that it does, on the grounds that one of the criteria of such a contract is that it should not result in an individual being required to perform, or condone through silence, an immoral act. However, there is not always agreement upon what precisely constitutes an immoral act within the realm of business activity. When is a business practice 'unfair' or a production practice dangerous? Where does the individual's duties and obligations lie – to the customer, or to the employer or to colleagues? For all the importance attached to freedom of expression and conscience, the evidence points to the fact that whistle-blowers are usually punished for their behaviour, either implicitly by being passed-over for promotion, or denied a salary increase, or more directly by being dismissed and made redundant (see James, 1990; Behrman, 1988).

In sum, rights focus primarily on the individual. They are concerned with promoting the well-being of the individual against injury or damage by society. In contrast, utilitarianism in its original form is concerned with society as a whole, and with determining what is of most benefit for that collectivity. In the case of rights, it is the individual who is important, and it is his or her interest which must be protected, even if by doing so harm may be experienced by others. For example, if the right to equal pay for equal work results in redundancies in order to control labour costs, then for those involved it may be perceived as something of a Pyrrhic victory. This example demonstrates that, as with the case of utilitarianism, rights do not provide an unambiguous mechanism for resolving the dilemmas of, and disputes in, business. It relies on the establishment of agreement, firstly about whose rights are to be protected and secondly, about any order of precedence – like utilitarianism it presumes the prior establishment of consensus, something which might neither exist nor be achievable in a pluralistic society.

This brief consideration of prescriptive ethical theories cannot be expected to do adequate justice to the complexity of their relative positions and arguments. Rather the objective has been to illustrate three important issues:

1. Inevitably, people make choices regarding the affairs of business that have an ethical dimension – whether or not they are conscious of it. The approaches reviewed above conceptualize and evaluate these choices in terms of different notions of ethicality and thereby prescribe different possible courses of action.
2. The choice to apply a particular ethical theory entails the projection of value-laden preferences and assumptions by the decision maker.
3. No ethical theory or school of thought is without practical and philosophical problems. How either approach reviewed above is applied entails the conceptualization of notions such as cost and benefit, or rights and duties. The operationalization of those conceptualizations within a particular school of thought can vary, indeed there appears little consensus as to the best way of operationalizing and applying them in practice.

It is unlikely that many people are consistently and exclusively either utilitarians, or wholehearted advocates of either Kantian imperatives. Most commentators who adopt a prescriptive approach will draw on both approaches (and possibly other prescriptive theories) for help in deciding what to do, or what is for the best in any given situation. Indeed such theory can be an aid to problem solving and decision making, but one should not expect to find ready-made solutions to every contemporary business dilemma. Even if there were such solutions, they would vary both between and within schools of thought depending on the interpretative procedures of those trying to use them. Nevertheless the consideration of these approaches can enable people to embark on a process of both self-reflection and learning. Perhaps the greatest benefit arising from the conscious consideration of the debates provoked by these theories is that they do encourage consideration of how, and why, certain decisions were made together with an on-going evaluation of their effects and outcomes. It is in this respect this kind of theory is most evident in the various analyses and critiques of business actions and decisions (see Pastin, 1988; Walton, 1988; Hoffman and More, 1990). By using such theory as a means for reflection on everyday practices, rather than as some philosophical watchdog to regulate business behaviour, it might avoid some of the problems with a prescriptive orientation that are further revealed by a consideration of a descriptive approach to the study of business ethics.

A descriptive approach to the study of business ethics derives from the premise that the ways in which people reason about ethical issues, and thereby subjectively construct ethical principles that are applicable to human behaviour, varies between and within different societies both contemporaneously and historically. While cross-cultural evidence (Donaldson, 1989b; Hofstede, 1991) is used to support this assertion of

Descriptive business ethics: ethical relativism

ethical plurality, what is perhaps more important is how this basic point of departure becomes translated into a distinctive perspective for the study of ethics in general and business ethics in particular. If ethical judgements about human behaviour are an outcome of variable human subjective processes (Payne and Giacalone, 1990; Primeaux, 1992), schemes of ethical principles are intimately connected with the cultures to which people defer and refer to in making sense of their worlds and in constructing their behaviour. As such, the ethical dimension of human behaviour is a product of the social and historical context of that behaviour and therefore is relative to the particular constellation of beliefs, values and recipes of knowledge that characterize a particular culture. In support of this view, Sumner (1988) points to how shared ethical systems are social constructions which are bounded by cultural traditions and are therefore always relative to a tradition from which human actors can never escape. Thus he claims that

> ... the notion of right is in the folkways. It is not outside them, of independent origin, and brought to them to test them. In the folkways whatever is, is right. (1988, p. 20)

From this position of ethical relativism, it follows that it is impossible to extricate oneself from the cultural tradition into which one has been socialized. Therefore it is impossible to neutrally, or objectively, construct a set of universal ethical principles applicable to all people regardless of social and historical contexts. Because human values vary socially and historically, and since they cannot be pragmatically discarded so as to attain a position of cognitive neutrality, it is impossible to prescribe a universal ethical code since all the prescriber is doing is attempting to impose his or her own culturally derived subjectivity on others who happen to belong to alternative cultures. Such is the route to cultural imperialism which can only be avoided by the realization that no one set of ethical assertions can have a greater claim to a privileged status than any other. Even though there may be a degree of social agreement about morality within and between modern societies and even though the people who make moral claims will often allude to their universality, there is no ultimate, universal, or absolute set of ethical principles that can be discerned and applied to evaluate or prescribe the ethical behaviour of others. Thus everything is relative to particular social and historical contexts. For the relativist there are no cognitive grounds, in terms of rationality or objectivity, for determining right and wrong.

Relativism has important implications for the study of business ethics. Since all business organizations create, propagate and sustain particular values, into which members are socialized to varying extents, it follows that all business enterprises are ethical in one way or another – they just differ. From this view, it follows that it is not possible to specify what members should do in order to be ethical in their organizational behaviour in an absolute sense. Thus business ethics becomes reconcept-ualized as a concern with how and why particular ethical discourses become established and how they subsequently affect members' organizational behaviour.

However, supporters of a prescriptive approach would attempt to counter this argument by claiming that such variation is explicable in terms of human ignorance regarding the nature of those absolute moral standards (e.g. Stace, 1988, p. 31). If left at this, they would appear to have an important challenge to relativism, at least in the sense that the evidence of moral diversity does not necessarily support a relativist view. Indeed it may be possible to contend that, even allowing for variations between cultures, it is still possible to discern commonly held ethical beliefs, such as the notion that members of a group bear some form of responsibility for the well-being of other members (Hosmer, 1991, p. 105), which indicate the existence of universally held principles. But this contention ignores the difficulty of disentangling and identifying such universals from the cultural milieux in which they are embedded and expressed – a problem exacerbated for MacIntyre (1981, 1989) because the notion of ethicality is itself also a social construct.

Moreover relativists can counter an absolutist challenge by drawing on a further argument. Even if an absolute moral code does exist, how could we as human actors ever know it? In other words, what is the source of authority, or cognitive grounds, for the absolutist's specification of one moral code as being superior to all others? In particular, relativists would argue that it is impossible to pragmatically stand outside one's own cultural tradition and thus neutrally, or objectively, discern and establish a universally applicable ethical code. The absolutists who must claim that this is possible in order to justify their position, are, in the view of the relativists, merely imposing their subjective beliefs upon others by according to those beliefs a privileged status. This whole issue is worthy of further exploration because it is around this issue of privilege that it is possible to distinguish the rival points of departure of the prescriptive and descriptive approaches to business ethics.

THE ISSUE OF PRIVILEGE

Those who would propose that it is possible to prescribe and adjudicate what is ethically right or wrong, in an objective manner independent of their own cultural tradition, adopt what may be called a cognitively privileged position. This is in the sense that they assign a superior status to their own view of ethicality over those other actors. This provides the prescriber with the role of arbiter of an ethical reality external to the subjectivity, or common sense, of those people whose actions he or she is adjudicating.

The notion of privilege position is illustrated by the allegory of the cave in Plato's *Republic*. This allegory suggests that the subjectivity, or commonsense, of ordinary people is like the shadows cast on the walls of a cave. Within this cave people are chained so that they can only see the shadows cast on the walls by the light of a fire at the entrance. For the cave dweller, the shadows are taken to be reality because they have no conception of any alternative. They can see the shadows but cannot see, and have no knowledge of, the things that cast those shadows. But if one of the imprisoned cave dwellers managed to escape, that person would realize that the shadowy world of those 'ordinary people' still trapped inside the cave was a distorted image of a real world which he or she could now perceive. Metaphorically, the shadows in the cave might be taken to represent the world of commonsense illusion and ignorance – the culture of the cave dweller. The escape to the outside can be taken to represent the development of privileged knowledge – since it is knowledge of the reality that casts the shadows that constitutes an understanding superior to that of those still imprisoned. The journey to the outside metaphorically represents the development of human reason. Those who manage to undertake that journey become, intellectually, the arbitrators of the reality which the cave dwellers are unable to apprehend. It is the accomplishment of such a journey that those who put forward a prescriptive view of business ethics must claim to have achieved. For it is only through making such a claim to privilege that they become empowered to denigrate the subjectivity and everyday experience of 'ordinary' people whose understanding of ethicality is dismissed as peripheral to the study of business ethics. So those who promulgate a prescriptive approach to business ethics are overtly, or inadvertenly, proposing that renditions of what is ethical can only be made by those in specially privileged positions of detachment. A view similar to Mannheim's contention that an objective standpoint can only be achieved by 'intellectuals' in that

> ...only a state of mind that has been sociologically fully clarified operates with situationally congruous ideas and motives. (Mannheim, 1960, p. 175)

So the claim that prescription and adjudication is possible and warranted, must be based on a claim to privilege. It is hardly surprising that the claim that there is some neutral point, from which it is possible for an observer to stand back and perceive the world in an objective fashion that is independent of the values and assumptions that stem from his or her own culture, has been subject to much debate and attack.

For instance, in the philosophy of science, the epistemological assumption that there exists some neutral standpoint from which the observer can observe the world objectively and free from distortion, is called a subject–object dualism. This means that when an observer (the subject) attempts to observe some aspect of the reality (the object) that surrounds him or her, the observations that are registered are independent of the process of the observer observing. Therefore it is claimed that 'truth' is to be found in the observer's passive sensory registration of the facts that constitute external reality through the application of a neutral observational language. Thus the veracity of various competing accounts of reality may be adjudicated through reference to their correspondence with the facts. This might be often articulated as the empiricist maxim that science should be, and can be, a neutral, value-free and disinterested endeavour. Moreover this is a maxim that those who pursue a prescriptive approach to the study of business ethics must support, otherwise their claim to a privileged position *vis-à-vis* the subjectivity of those people they study would be vacuous. It is only their claim to be able to stand outside their own cultural tradition, and thereby neutrally apprehend the facts of the world, that can justify their approach. But it is precisely this maxim, and its notion that a neutral observational language is available, that has been challenged.

Rorty (1979, 1982) argues that the view that different competing accounts might be adjudicated through an appeal to their correspondence with the facts of an external objective reality inevitably relies on the received wisdom that such facts can be 'mirrored' in the 'glassy essence' of the observer (1979, p. 46). In terms of this 'ocular' or 'mirror' metaphor, a correspondence approach is based on the assumption that there is a mirror inside the mind that must be polished so as to allow the mind's eye to gaze on the reflections of reality in the mirror – it is through such 'polishing' that a privileged position is possible. Specifically, it is this notion of privileged knowledge that Rorty and others have attacked. Indeed Rorty dismisses those philosophers who argue that such a privileged position is possible as 'cultural overseers' (1979, p. 317). The question here is why has the idea that a privileged position is possible provoked so much controversy?

If one assumes that it is possible for an observer to passively register the facts of reality, that assumption ignores the possibility that the observer's perceptual apparatus does not provide mere reflections of what is out there, and is instead proactive and creative in influencing what we apprehend. We are continually bombarded by sensations and stimuli and we project on to those inputs a form and substance that derives from within us, from what may be called our 'cognitive processing mechanisms' (Unwin, 1986, p. 300) and our 'horizons of expectations' (Habermas, 1974, p. 199). Such projection entails selection as we choose what we sense by giving attention to particular stimuli while de-emphasizing, filtering out or ignoring others. The selected sensory stimulations are simultaneously organized and interpreted by being put into a coherent and meaningful whole (Spinelli, 1989, p. 38). The processes by which sensory inputs are organized and interpreted may be highly influenced by the schemas built up from our previous experience, or which have been received as stocks of knowledge through our social interactions in various cultural milieux. We usually do these things rapidly, automatically and unconsciously. Although the result may appear as objective and separate from ourselves, as 'out there', in many respects we are active participants in creating what we apprehend (Berger and Luckmann, 1967).

This brief discussion of the processes of perception must cast doubt on the possibility that human beings have the ability to separate themselves from their own cultural traditions so as to neutrally apprehend a cognitively accessible external reality. To use Plato's allegory of the cave as a point of reference, perhaps we cannot ever cast off our chains and fully leave the cave and thereby see the reality beyond the shadows in the cave. Indeed, as Gadamer (1975) argues, the notion that there exists an ahistorical Archimedian (i.e. neutral) position is a myth – any attempt at assuming the possibility of an 'infinite intellect' or 'transcendental' position devoid of our own historicity, are self-delusions. For Gadamer, interpretations cannot escape the background preconceptions embedded in the language and life of their authors. Thus those who might advocate a prescriptive approach to business ethics, which must be grounded in the assumption that it is possible to attain a neutral or privileged position, fail to acknowledge what is know as the 'hermeneutic circle' – that no observation can be free from the observer's interpretation based upon his or her often unconscious presuppositions and culturally derived values and so on.

It follows that any propositions about morality or ethicality, and indeed any recipes of knowledge, are artefacts that have been socially constructed through human behavioural and perceptual processes – even though these social artefacts might become reified and thereby appear as external to, and with an existence separate from, their human creators. It is in this context that it is possible to understand the observation that research into business ethics is influenced by the disciplinary background and metatheoretical assumptions of the researcher (Goodchild, 1986; De George, 1987; McHugh, 1988; Trundle, 1989; Jensen and Wygant, 1990).

So consider the following three statements:

1. Any ethical judgement about human behaviour is ultimately an expression of human subjective values that vary historically and socially.
2. The possibility of achieving a privileged position whereby an observer can neutrally apprehend the world free from the distortions of the culture into which he or she has been previously socialized is an illusion.
3. People who claim to be able to neutrally apprehend the world might be likened to Rorty's cultural overseers in that they are merely imposing their socially constructed beliefs upon other people.

If one agrees with these three statements then the only appropriate approach to studying business ethics is a relativist approach that eschews prescription and is based on attempts at description. At one level this approach manages to avoid the problems previously associated with a prescriptive approach to business ethics. At another level it creates a distinctive agenda for organizational research which might be conceptualized around the issues identified below:

❑ **Issue 1** – to describe members' ethical discourses in different social and organizational contexts.
❑ **Issue 2** – to identify the social processes that have lead to the establishment of particular ethical discourses.
❑ **Issue 3** – to analyse how different levels of credibility are assigned to differing definitions of what is ethical in particular social and organizational contexts.
❑ **Issue 4** – to identify the impact of such discursive practices in everyday organizational contexts.
❑ **Issue 5** – to identify the nature of the ethical dilemmas and disputes that confront members with reference to the ethical mores to which they defer and describe how those dilemmas are resolved in everyday organizational interaction.
❑ **Issue 6** – to explain how and why ethical discourses might change.

So, important to a descriptive/relativist approach to business ethics would be a concern to understand the nature of the beliefs that organizational members might hold, to elucidate how such social constructs influence their organizational behaviour and to analyse how and why they develop and change. As we have already noted, this orientation has, as a central concern, the phenomenon of organizational culture. Although they do not consider that ethics and culture are necessarily identical, some writers (e.g. Schein, 1985) do suggest that business ethics is as Pastin (1988) puts it, 'the core' of organizational culture. In this way the 'ethical climate' that prevails influences the individual's interpretation of organizational experience and his or her own behaviour (Victor and Cullen, 1987, 1988; Cullen *et al.*, 1989). In a similar vein, McCoy (1985), with reference to the work of Deal and Kennedy (1982) and Peters and Waterman (1982), argues that the link between corporate culture and the moral agency of the corporation (i.e. where should the responsibility for organizational policy and action be located?) is an important area for research.

In a similar manner some writers have approached the relationship between organizational culture and business ethics by exploring how particular organizational cultures might inhibit or prevent the discussion of ethical issues (e.g. Bird and Waters, 1987, 1989; Waters and Bird, 1987; Jackall, 1988; Kram *et al.*, 1989). Other writers have explored the relationship between business ethics and organizational culture by creating models that identify the sociopsychological and cultural factors which influence the nature of ethical and unethical decision making (Trevino, 1986; Bommer *et al.*, 1987; Stead *et al.*, 1990; Jones, 1991).

In this context, McCoy perceives that collective and individual moral agency are 'mutually interdependent' (1985, p. 68), a view which receives some support from Pastin (1988, p. 24), who, while differentiating between the ethics of individuals and those of organizations, argues that as with the ground rules of individuals, organizational ground rules determine which actions are possible for the organization and what actions mean. However, what is not clarified by these writers is the nature of the relationship(s) between individual and collective/organizational value systems.

An evident link between organizational culture and business ethics is provided by consideration of the role of senior managers in socialization processes in the sense of providing ethical role models for subordinates. So while Schein (1985) points to the importance of the founder and senior management as creators and maintainers of organizational culture, other writers have either argued that senior managers should provide ethical role models (e.g. Newstrom and Ruch, 1975; Lincoln, *et al.*, 1982; Laczniak, 1983), or maintain that senior managers are a moral factor in the organization who create guides for others to follow (Hosmer, 1987) in a fashion that is more influential than written policies (Andrews, 1989).

Pastin (1988) and Nash (1990) attempt to encourage the development of an ethical awareness on the part of managers, especially senior management. They seem to envisage the creation of an ethical organization as a 'top-down' exercise that has parallels with the ways in which other writers have identified as viable methods for managing organizational culture (e.g. Deal and Kennedy, 1982; Peters and Waterman, 1982; Sathe, 1985; Sethia and Von Glinow, 1985).

For the relativist, a 'top-down' approach to managing ethicality is interesting as a set of social processes that may lead to the establishment of particular ethical discourses which variably impact on members' organizational behaviour. What is important here is the attitude of the relativist to this genre. For the relativist, a 'top-down' approach to ethical–cultural management could be perceived as problematical because, given our prior discussion of privilege, the basis of management authority must also be considered to be precarious. This raises one of the paradoxes of ethical relativism. At first sight its strictures against cultural imperialism seem to imply cultural tolerance – no culture is any better than any other, they are just different. Therefore all culturally sanctioned practices are on an equal ethical footing since there are no empirical or rational grounds for judging whether one set of beliefs and practices are superior to any other. But an outcome of this anti-absolutist liberalism is the denial of critique – a quietism and indifference that disempowers and which is not without political significance since by default it is supportive of the *status quo*. Moreover, as Donaldson (1989b, pp. 16–17) argues, the irony is that since ethical relativism claims an absence of any objective grounds for ethicality it cannot sanction cultures that impose ethical intolerance or endorse those that articulate ethical tolerance. The danger is that relativism may deny itself, not just in the manner alluded to by Donaldson but also in the sense that

> ... the assertion of relativity itself claims absolute validity and hence its very form presupposes a principle which its manifest content rejects. (Mannheim, 1952, p. 130)

Conclusions

In many respects a descriptive/relativistic approach to the study of business ethics provides a fundamental challenge to those who would implicitly, or explicitly, adopt a prescriptive approach. It points to the socially constructed nature of all ethical discourse and thereby argues that there are no good reasons for preferring one representation over another. As such it undermines the prescriptive impulse that characterizes many commentaries upon business ethics – but in doing so it is disempowering for it also seems to destroy the basis of critique. Tacit support for the *status quo* may well be the result. A possible escape route from this quandary for the relativist may be in the form of encouraging members' reflection on, and debate, about the basis of ethicality in their organizations. Through such disruption of taken-for-granted assumptions members themselves might begin to challenge the status quo and engender critique and organizational change that could conceivably be based upon consensus. So perhaps relativists can have their cake and eat it. Indeed it is in this context that the relevance of prescriptive theory to relativism is evident. Prescriptive theory, such as utilitarianism, may be useful in helping to categorize and understand organizational members' preferences, prejudices, disputes and dilemmas and how they influence their business behaviour. Moreover they provide useful schemes for helping people reflect upon their own views about ethical behaviour provided they are used with great caution in respect to their claims to a cognitively privileged status.

Exercise

Choose a decision which you have recently had to make at work, or in any other aspect of your life, which inevitably affected other people. Revisit that decision and re-evaluate the your potential options by:

❑ Applying a utilitarian cost-benefit analysis.
❑ Applying Kant's categorical imperative.

Critically discuss the strengths and weaknesses of each approach and identify their implications for the decision that you would make.

Further reading

Useful overviews of the issues discussed in this chapter may be found in both Rachels (1993) and Snare (1992). MacDonald and Beck-Dudley (1994) provide an interesting discussion of the extent of commensurability between different moral philosophies. Accessible introductions to the philosophical debates surrounding relativism are presented in Phillips (1987) and Gellner (1985). For a more general discussion of the implications of human subjectivity see Spinelli (1989). The organizational role of variable subjective processes in constituting ethicality is directly discussed by Primeaux (1992) and by Payne and Giacalone (1990).

References

Andrews, K. (1989) Ethics in practice. *Harvard Business Review*, September–October, 99–104.

Berger, P. and Luckmann, T. (1967) *The Social Construction of Reality*. Penguin, Harmondsworth.

Berle, A.A. and Means, G.C. (1932) *The Modern Corporation and Private Property*. Macmillan, London.

Behrman, S.N. (1988) *Essays on Ethics in Business and the Professions*. Prentice-Hall, London.

Bird, F. and Walters, J.A. (1987) The nature of managerial standards. *Journal of Business Ethics*, **6**, 1–13.

Bird, F. and Walters, J.A. (1989) The moral muteness of managers. *California Management Review*, Fall, 73–88.

Bommer, M., Gratto, C., Gravaander, J. and Tuttle, M. (1987) A model of ethical and unethical decision making. *Journal of Business Ethics*, **6**, 265–80.

Buchholtz, R.A. (1989) *Fundamental Concepts and Problems in Business Ethics*. Prentice-Hall, Englewood Cliffs, NJ.

Cooke, R.A. (1986) Business ethics at the crossroads. *Journal of Business Ethics*, **5**, 259–63.

Cullen, J.B., Victor, B. and Stevens, C. (1989) An ethical weather report: assessing the organisation's ethical climate. *Organisation Dynamics*, **8**(2), 50–62.

Davis, M. (1982) Conflict of interest 2. *Business and Professional Ethics Journal*, **1**(4), 17–29.

Deal, T. and Kennedy, A. (1982) *Corporate Cultures: The Rites and Rituals of Corporate Life*. Penguin, Harmondsworth.

De George, R.T. (1986) Replies and reflections on theology and business ethics. *Journal of Business Ethics*, **5**, 521–4.

De George, R.T. (1987) The status of business ethics: past and future. *Journal of Business Ethics*, **6**, 201–11.

Donaldson, T. (1989a) *Key Issues in Business Ethics*. Academic Press, London.

Donaldson, T. (1989b) *The Ethics of International Business*. Oxford University Press, Oxford.

Friedman, M. (1962) *Capitalism and Freedom*. University of Chicago Press, Chicago, IL.

Gadamer, H. (1975) *Truth and Method*. Sheed & Ward, London.

Gellner, E. (1985) *Relativism and the Social Sciences*. Cambridge University Press, Cambridge.

Goodchild, L.F. (1986) Towards a foundational normative method in business ethics. *Journal of Business Ethics*, **5**, 485–99.

Goodpaster, K.E. (1985) Toward an integrated approach to business ethics thought. *Thought*, **60**(2), 161–80.

Goodpaster, K.E. and Matthews (1982) Can a corporation have a conscience? *Harvard Business Review*, 132–40.

Habermas, J. (1974) *Theory and Practice*. Heinemann, London.

Hayek, F.A. (1969) The corporation in a democratic society: in whose interest ought it and will it be run? in *Business Strategy* (ed. H.I. Ansoff). Harmondsworth, Penguin.

Hoffman, W.M. and Moore, J.M. (1990) *Business Ethics: Readings and Cases in Corporate Morality*, 2nd edn. McGraw-Hill, New York.

Hofstede, G. (1991) *Culture and Organization: Software of the Mind*. McGraw-Hill, London.

Hosmer, L.T. (1987) The institutionalisation of unethical behaviour. *Journal of Business Ethics*, **6**, 439–47.

Hosmer, L.T. (1991) *The Ethics of Management*, 2nd edn. Richard D. Irwin, Homewood, IL.

Jackall, R. (1988) *Moral Mazes: The World of Corporate Managers*. Oxford University Press, Oxford.

James, G.G. (1990) Whistle blowing: its moral justification, in *Business Ethics: Readings and Cases in Corporate Morality* (eds W.M. Hoffman and J.M. Moore). McGraw-Hill, New York.

Jensen, L.C. and Wygant, S.A. (1990) The developmental self-valuing theory: a practical approach for business ethics. *Journal of Business Ethics*, **9**, 215–25.

Jones, T.M. (1991) Ethical decision making by individuals in organisations: an issue-contingent model. *Academy of Management Review*, **16**(2), 366–95.

Kant, I. (1964) *Groundwork of the Metaphysics of Morals*. Harper & Row, London.

Kram, K.E., Yeager, P.C. and Reed, G.E. (1989) Decisions and dilemmas: the ethical dimension in the corporate context, in *Research in Corporate Social Performance and Policy* (ed. J.E. Post). JAI Press, Greenwood, CT.

Laczniak, G. (1983) Business ethics: a manager's primer. *Business*, January–February, 23–9.

Lincoln, D.L., Pressley, M.M. and Little, T. (1982) Ethical beliefs and personal values of top level executives. *Journal of Business Research*, **10**, 475–87.

MacDonald, J.E. and Beck-Dudley, C.L. (1994) Are deontology and teleology mutually exclusive? *Journal of Business Ethics*, **13**(8), 615–23.

MacIntyre, A. (1981) *After Virtue*. Duckworth, London.

MacIntyre, A. (1989) *A Short History of Ethics*. Macmillan Press, London.

Mahoney, J. (1990) An international look at business ethics. *Journal of Business Ethics*, **9**, 545–50.

Mannheim, K. (1952) *Essays on the Sociology of Knowledge*. Routledge & Kegan Paul, London.

Mannheim, K. (1960) *Ideology and Utopia*. Routledge & Kegan Paul, London.

Mattick, Jr, P. (1986) *Social Knowledge*. Hutchinson, London.

McCoy, C. (1985) *Management of Values*. Harper & Row, New York.

McHugh, F.P. (1988) *Keyguide to Information Sources in Business Ethics*. Nichols, New York.

Nash, L.L. (1990) *Good Intentions Aside: A Manager's Guide to Resolving Ethical Problems*. Harvard Business School Press, Boston, MA.

Newstrom, J. and Ruch, W.A. (1975) The ethics of management and the management of ethics. *MSU Business Topics*, winter, pp. 29–37.

Ozar, D.T. (1979) The moral responsibility of corporations, in *Ethical Issues in Business* (eds T. Donaldson and P. Werhane). Prentice-Hall, Englewood Cliffs, NJ.

Payne, S.L. and Giacalone, R.A. (1990) Social psychological approaches to the perception of ethical dilemmas. *Human Relations*, **43**(7), 649–65.

Pastin, M. (1988) *The Hard Problems of Management: Gaining the Ethics Edge*. Jossey-Bass, San Francisco, CA.

Phillips, D.C. (1987) *Philosophy, Science and Social Inquiry*. Pergamon Press, Oxford.

Peters, T. and Waterman, Jr, R. (1982) *In Search of Excellence*. Harper & Row, London.

Primeaux, P. (1992) Experiential ethics: a blueprint for personal and corporate ethics. *Journal of Business Ethics*, **11**, 779–88.

Rachels, J. (1993) *The Elements of Moral Philosphy*, 2nd edn. McGraw-Hill, New York.

Raphael, D.D. (1981) *Moral Philosophy*. Oxford University Press, Oxford.

Rorty, R. (1979) *Philosophy and the Mirror of Nature*. Princeton University Press, Princeton, NJ.

Rorty, R. (1982) *Consequences of Pragmatism (Essays: 1972–1980)*. University of Minnesota Press, Minneapolis, MN.

Rossouw, G.J. (1994) Rational interaction for moral sensitivity: a postmodern approach to moral decision-making in business. *Journal of Business Ethics*, **13**, 11–20.

Sathe, V. (1985) How to decipher and change corporate culture, in *Gaining Control of the Corporate Culture* (eds R.H. Kilmann, M.J. Saxton and R. Serpa). Jossey-Bass, San Francisco, CA.

Schein, E.H. (1985) *Organizational Culture and Leadership*. Jossey-Bass, San Francisco, CA.

Sethia, N.K. and Von Glinow, M.A. (1985) Arriving at four cultures by managing the reward system, in *Gaining Control of the Corporate Culture* (eds R.H. Kilmann *et al.*). Jossey-Bass, San Francisco, CA.

Small, M.W. (1993) Ethics in business and administration: an international and historical perspective. *Journal of Business Ethics*, **12**, 293–300.

Snare, F. (1992) *The Nature of Moral Thinking*. Routledge, London.

Spinelli, E. (1989) *The Interpreted World*. Sage, London.

Stace, W.T. (1988) Ethical relativity and ethical absolutism, in *Ethical Issues in Business: A Philosophical Approach*, 3rd edn (eds T. Donaldson and P.H. Werhane). Prentice-Hall, Englewood Cliffs, NJ.

Stead, W.E., Worrell, D.L. and Stead, J.G. (1990) An integrative model for understanding and managing ethical behavior in business organizations. *Journal of Business Organisations*, **9**, 233–42.

Sumner, W.G. (1988) A defence of cultural relativism, in *Ethical Issues in Business: A Philosophical Approach*, 3rd edn (eds T. Donaldson and P.H. Werhane). Prentice-Hall, Englewood Cliffs, NJ.

Tinker, A.M. (1985) *Paper Prophets: A Social Critique of Accounting*. Holt, Reinhart & Winston, London.

Trevino, L.K. (1986) Ethical decision making in organisations: a person-situation interactionist model. *Academy of Management Review*, **11**(3), 601–17.

Trundle, R. (1989) Is there any ethics in business ethics? *Journal of Business Ethics*, **8**, *161–269*.

Unwin, N. (1986) Beyond truth. *Mind*, XV, 300–17.

Velasquez, M.G. (1988) *Business Ethics: Concepts and Cases*, 2nd edn. Prentice-Hall, Englewood-Cliffs, NJ.

Victor, B. and Cullen, J.B. (1987) A theory and measure of ethical climate in organizations, in *Research in Corporate Social Performance and Policy* (ed. W.C. Frederick). JAI Press, Greenwich, CT, Vol. 9, pp. 51–71.

Victor, B. and Cullen, J.B. (1988) The organisational bases of ethical work climates. *Administrative Science Quarterly*, **33**, 101–25.

Walton, C.C. (1988) *The Moral Manager*. Ballinger, Cambridge, MA.

Waters, J.A. and Bird, F. (1987) The moral dimension of organisational culture. *Journal of Business Ethics*, **6**, 15–22.

Part One

Business ethics: its
organizational and
managerial contexts

Corporate strategy – the importance of an ethical perspective

2

Kevan Scholes and Tony Wood

All organizations have strategies in some shape or form – whether these are developed in a rational and open way – for example, through formal planning approaches or whether through more incremental and evolutionary changes – often less visible but nonetheless generally strategic. Corporate strategy is essentially concerned with how the *scope* of an organization's activities change and develop over time. Strategic change therefore is about the *long-term direction* of the organization and is likely to have major implications to how the resources of the organization are deployed and therefore affect the detailed operational activities of most parts of the organization.

There are many factors which will influence and change the strategic direction of an organization. Traditionally discussions of strategic development tended to emphasize the importance of understanding the organization's *business environment* and the *resources or capability* of the organization. This was often summarized in a SWOT analysis (Johnson and Scholes, 1993, pp. 148–52) outlining the major strengths, weaknesses, opportunities and threats. The danger of this approach was that it gave the impression that strategy formulation was a neat and tidy rational process and it did not properly acknowledge that strategy is actually developed and implemented in a *cultural and political* context (Johnson, 1990, 1992; Peattie, 1993) where a number of individuals and groups (stakeholders) (Mitroff, 1983) have quite different – often conflicting – views of the organization's *purposes* and hence different *expectations* of strategic priorities.

This chapter will explore this last area from an ethical perspective – trying to explain how these various expectations can be reconciled whilst allowing the organization to develop and function successfully. These ethical issues exist at three levels (Hoffman and Moore, 1990; De George, 1987; Epstein, 1989; Goodpaster 1993):

❏ At the *macro* level there are issues about the role of business (and public sector organizations) in the national and international organization

Introduction

of society. This will differ depending on the sociopolitical system, the type of enterprise (private or public sector) and between national and international operation. The following section will explore these issues in detail.

❑ At the *corporate* level the issues concern *corporate social responsibility* (CSR) which is concerned with the ethical issues facing individual corporate entities (private or public sector) when formulating and implementing strategies. The third section deals with *philosophy* and *content* of a CSR approach and the fourth section deals with the process by which a successful CSR programme can be devised, implemented and monitored.

❑ At the *individual* level the ethical issues concern the behaviour and actions of individuals within organizations. This is clearly an issue which affects both the formulation and implementation of strategy – since these are important management tasks in most organizations (Carr, 1968).

The role of business in society

ISSUES IN A MARKET ECONOMY

Business and the state

In a market economy business organizations are allowed a significant degree of discretion. They are ostensibly free to choose what goods and services they produce, the markets they aim to serve and the processes by which they produce. The state will play a greater or lesser part in these processes depending on the social and political complexion of society at large.

The legislative framework of any country will include a raft of laws, statutes and precedents which will affect how organizations are able to go about their business. In the European Union much of this legislation is being harmonized but throughout the world there is likely to be found laws relating to employment practices, restrictive practices, consumer protection, financial reporting and conduct and many other areas of business life. How all embracing the legal framework is depends on the social values in the country and the political processes in place.

It can be argued that ethics or corporate social responsibility (CSR) begins where the law ends (Friedman, 1970). Organizations are expected to observe the law but of course there will always be the issue of interpretation of that law. Legal departments found in many organizations are evidence that understanding and interpreting the law consume resources and time. Organizations also can and do quite legitimately become involved in the formation and framing of law either directly or through their industry associations. Lobbying of governments is a sophisticated activity in many parts of the world, the object being to restrain moves to tighten legislation perceived to be against business interests or to attempt to gain relaxation of laws which are perceived to be inhibiting.

In Britain the historical perception of business is that Conservative administrations will enact a legislative framework which is more favourable to business than would a Labour administration. Hence it is argued that 'big business' will usually support the election of a Conservative government.

Business discretion

Whatever the legislative framework many organizations can and will choose to use their discretion to go beyond the legal baseline and this can be conceived as exercising ethical judgement (Carroll, 1979, p. 497). The reasons why business organizations may choose to do this are many and complex. It can be that there is a particular culture which was imprinted on the organization in earlier times. For example some organizations had Quaker origins and these values have been carried forward into the present time resulting in organizations almost unconsciously accepting an ethical role in all their dealings. Alternatively it may be that adverse publicity in some area may have prompted a firm to embark on a process to restore a battered image. One view is that business not only reflects the values of society but also plays a part in creating those values. To that extent some organizations may well feel that they need to demonstrate some positive values to society.

ISSUES IN A COMMAND ECONOMY

Business and state

In large parts of the world, until recently, the relationship between the state and business was highly integrated. Central planning was the instrument by which many countries ran their business. Enterprises were state owned and highly prescribed in terms of their activities. The state decided what was to be made and how. It also decided how the output was to be distributed and to whom. It prescribed how much labour would be used and how much they were to be paid.

Business discretion

Overall managers in these enterprises had very little discretion and were frequently subject to political pressure to sustain the state ideology.

In these circumstances responsibility for most activities of a strategic nature were not in the hands of the management and ethical judgements were probably only articulated in meeting the demands put on the enterprise by the state and reflecting the values of the government.

The objectives of the state in terms such as production or hard-currency earnings were dominant and one outcome of such policies is reflected in the high levels of environmental pollution and the dangerous state of plant and machinery frequently found in many of the former communist countries.

ISSUES IN THE PUBLIC SECTOR

Since public sector organizations are essentially there to serve the public it might be assumed that these organizations do not face the dilemmas of the profit-seeking private sector between commercial pursuit of profit and notions of ethical behaviour.

Recent experience both in Britain and elsewhere indicates that public sector strategies are changing dramatically and in some instances throwing into sharp focus ethical and social responsibility issues. Many public utilities have been privatized and this has fundamentally changed their operating paradigm and strategies to pursuit of profit rather than purely service delivery. Of the organizations remaining in public ownership attempts are being made to create a business ethic within them. Examples of this are the trust status of hospitals and the internal market created, the creation of agencies from civil service activities and the opting out of schools to grant-maintained status.

It could be argued that these moves have been made to bring a more economic or commercial perspective to strategy in the public sector. The stated aim of the present government is to achieve higher efficiency and better-quality services. Whether this conflicts with the wider social responsibilities of the public sector is a matter of great debate (Hutton, 1995, Chapter 4). The government argues that it is not a matter of economic versus social imperatives but that social goals are achieved through a tighter economic framework. Opponents argue that the government is simply attempting to cut public expenditure for budgetary and dogmatic reasons and are imperilling the ability of many public service organizations to carry out their basic task.

THE ROLE OF CHARTERS

One continuing criticism of some public sector organizations is that they are inflexible, remote, bureaucratic and unresponsive to the public they are designed to serve. Machine bureaucracy is perhaps endemic in large mature organizations in relatively stable environments (Mintzberg and Quinn, 1991). In addition, many public sector organizations were and are professionally driven, for example education and health where the 'customer' is given what is good for them by the professionals. Notions of social responsibility here can revolve around what is best from a professional point of view rather than what the customer may require.

To cope with this and also the fear that in many of the privatized utilities a monopoly situation still exists leading to charges of exploitation of the customer, the British government has introduced a series of charters (examples are those related to railway travel and the Inland Revenue) which specify individuals' rights when they deal with public sector organizations. Other organizations have followed suit – for example the banks have a collective charter for customers and British Telecom specify minimum service levels in theirs. These are designed to orientate organizations to be more responsive and responsible to users of the service. What the longer term success will be remains to be seen but at present charters have aroused significant scepticism from many quarters.

ISSUES IN AN INTERNATIONAL WORLD

Organizations with activities crossing international boundaries can be faced with a particular dilemma with regard to their ethical stance (see Chapter 12 on ethics in international business).

Firstly it is quite possible that the organization can be larger in terms of the resources at its disposal than a small overseas country in which it locates part of its activity. To that extent the organization is extremely powerful and could exercise its power for its own interest where this conflicts with the interest of the host country.

This may result in the organization imposing its own style and culture either consciously or unconsciously. Few of the larger multinationals have escaped the charge of cultural imperialism. The issue here could be whether organizations are pursuing local or global strategies.

Organizations that aim for an integrated production policy on a global basis may make the manufacturing strategy dominant with local variations at a minimum. Hence, adaptations to local custom and practice may be secondary. McDonald's aim to present an identical service wherever a McDonald's is found in the world. The strategy will be perceived by some as cultural imperialism but McDonald's would probably argue that people have the discretion to buy a Big Mac or not and franchisees in many countries are willing to accept the franchise as it adds to rather than replaces existing eating places. However, if an organization is serving a local market as part of its world-wide strategy it is likely that some recognition will be made for local custom and practice. The degree to which an organization brings its 'back home' values into another society should be one aspect of its global strategy. This area like many other ethical issues is fraught with dilemmas. One example could be an organization setting up in a country where wage rates were very low. If the company pays the prevailing low wages it could stand accused of exploitation. On the other hand if it paid somewhat better wages to get better quality employees it could stand accused of being irresponsible by disturbing local wage patterns. A recurring dilemma was posed for many years for many companies in relation to South Africa. International companies who did not pull out of South Africa believed they were being responsible to their black employees and improving their lot. However, they were often accused of being *irresponsible* for giving tacit support to apartheid.

Thinking through corporate social responsibility (CSR)

AN ORGANIZATIONAL PHILOSOPHY FOR CSR

In market economies where organizations and managers do have a considerable degree of autonomy, the way organizations incorporate notions of CSR into their policies and strategies becomes in itself a matter of discretion and one where an organization's needs to develop a clear philosophy or stance (see Chapter 8 on control):

❑ It is possible to conceive of organizations who are **leaders** in the field – setting the pace. They are the ones who go way beyond what the law requires and set an agenda of best practice.
❑ There are many organizations who are **followers**. They observe the pace-setters and make a decision as to how and where they might reasonably act.
❑ A third category could be described as the **minimalists**. They do what the law requires and no more unless there is some pressing reason.

Another view (Frederick *et al.*, 1992) of the varying stances of CSR suggests that three broad approaches are often found:

❑ *Social obligation*. Companies who do what is only absolutely necessary or required by law are acting according to **social obligation**.
❑ *Social responsibility*. Those who recognize a wider circle of relationships and are willing to make charitable donations as well as interact with stakeholder groups who have an interest in what the company does, are acting according to the principle of **social responsibility**.
❑ *Social responsiveness*. Other companies are far more open to social influence and communication with external groups. They give attention to broad **ethical** principles of right and wrong behaviour. Frederick *et al.* say these companies are acting according to the principle of **social responsiveness**.

The stance any organization takes in terms of CSR is likely to arise from both custom and practice and/or, more recently, a carefully worked out position. However, any position taken is likely to be subject to change as social expectations change. The progressive companies are likely to be in the forefront of developments in their position and the more conservative organizations will be likely only to change their position along with changes in legislation. But as society becomes more complex and turbulent it is likely that many organizations will feel it necessary to review their stance on social responsibility.

ARGUMENTS IN FAVOUR OF CSR

Organizations which take a progressive stance may argue that there are several good reasons for them to do so (Frederick *et al.*, 1992):

❏ *Balances power with responsibility.* Modern corporations have considerable power and along with this should go responsibility. If not the company will ultimately attract hostility from many quarters.
❏ *Discourages government legislation.* This is attractive to many groups, not least executives themselves. Self-regulation is perceived to be preferable since legislation can prove draconian, costly and restrictive. In addition if legislation is called for by other interest groups goodwill is likely to have already been lost. Whatever the outcome the more enlightened companies rarely wait for legislation – they are well ahead of it.
❏ *Promotes long-run profit.* A well-rehearsed argument. The belief is that a positive policy builds trust and respect and consequently the company enjoys a good reputation.
❏ *Good company image.* This is clearly related to the previous point. Surveys appear to suggest that business has not enjoyed a good public image. Events such as insider dealing and other financial scandals only serve to confirm some of the fears held. The effect could be reluctance to deal with low image companies or sectors and public support for repressive legislation.

Overall the proponents of social responsibility sum up the case in terms of good business. There is no real alternative and a positive policy actually promotes enlightened self-interest. To that extent, corporate strategy and a strategy for CSR are intertwined. Even in emergent and bottom-up strategy making scenarios where formal strategy making processes are not dominant, a defined and accepted policy on CSR will be a factor in conditioning the decision making of all those involved in the process.

ARGUMENTS AGAINST CSR

Very few firms would say they oppose social responsibility but they would take up the minimalist position of doing no more than the law prescribes. The reasons against going beyond the legal minimum might be:

❏ *Lower economic efficiency and profits.* Incurring unnecessary costs could jeopardize the whole operation to the detriment of all stakeholders.

❑ *Firms penalize themselves against competition.* In being responsible a company might put itself at a competitive disadvantage if others do not follow suit. A case in point here is the issue of training in the UK. Some companies might feel severe foreign competition from firms in countries (particularly developing countries) where the legal minimum is much lower. The belief of the British government in opting out of the Social Chapter of the Maastricht Treaty was that the obligations to employees that it would impose would prejudice the competitive position of British industry.

❑ *Compromises and confuses objectives.* A former chairman of British Steel Corporation was reputed to have once asked the government if British Steel existed to make steel or to act as an arm for the Department of Employment. At this time the economic objective of making steel profitably was in sharp conflict with the responsibility (perceived to have been thrust on British Steel by the government) to maintain jobs. Confusion about objectives may be dysfunctional to the executives of the organization. Taken together the critics of corporate social responsibility would argue that pursuing active social responsibility policies adds burdens on both business and society without producing the intended effect of social improvement.

A STAKEHOLDER APPROACH TO CSR

To whom are organizations responsible?

Possibly the most difficult question for corporate executives is to whom the organization believes it has a responsibility. At one level it is clear that in the private sector the responsibility is to the shareholders; the owners, whilst in the public sector the responsibility is to the politicians as elected representatives of the people.

At a broader level the **stakeholder** concept is useful to give a wider view of relationships the organization has. With these relationships come responsibilities.

What is a stakeholder?

> Those who depend on the organization for the realization of some of their goals and in turn the organization depends on them for the realization of *its* goals. (Mitroff, 1983)

Any organization relates to a wide range of stakeholders and each one will have an interest or expectation of the organization. This interest, when examined, will indicate the perceived relationship between the organization and each stakeholder or stakeholder group.

Some stakeholders will have a vital interest for the achievement of their own objectives in the decisions the organization makes and the way it performs and behaves. For others the interest may be more marginal. In considering relationships with stakeholders from a strategic perspective writers such as Mitroff and Edward Freeman (Freeman, 1984) refer not only to interest but power. It is asserted that the stakeholders who need most carefully monitoring and managing are those with both a high **interest** in the focal organization and high **power** as well. Other stakeholders will have low interest and low power and from a strategic point of view demand less time and effort from management. However, the power and interest of any stakeholder is not static and a change in conditions can significantly alter the status of stakeholders.

In dealing with stakeholders from the management strategy point of view, it is usually difficult to fully take into account all the perceived expectations of the wide number of stakeholders. The result is that the focus of strategy is likely to be directed on the **key** stakeholders, i.e. those with high interest *and* high power as they provide most direct threats or opportunities.

When examining stakeholders from the point of view of social responsibility it may be questioned whether responding to stakeholders on the basis of power and interest is adequate. It could be argued that organizations should not determine their responsibilities on the basis of power and interest as this in itself would be socially irresponsible. Weaker stakeholders may not be taken into account where a strategic move is deemed necessary but it may be argued that longer term responsibilities to the wider constituency demand action. The dilemma is whether an organization in formulating its strategy accepts responsibility to each stakeholder or to stakeholders collectively. Coupled with this is the question of whether or not it is feasible or appropriate to consider the organization as being a 'moral agent'. It is a subject of debate as to where responsibility resides within an organization: at an individual level or collective (organizational) level (Buchholz, 1989, Chapter 8).

The relationship between strategy and social responsibility can be very close. Key strategic moves by organizations such as acquisitions, rationalization, relocation, product diversification and so on, inevitably result in an increase in satisfaction for some stakeholders but dissatisfaction for others. Modern organizations facing an increasingly turbulent environment often need to make significant strategic moves for defensive or offensive reasons. It is at this stage that firms may find themselves facing serious dilemmas. Closing a plant will pose a threat to employees but may help the organization to remain viable. The firm is faced from a social responsibility point of view with conflicting obligations to one stakeholder (*some* employees) and the wider constituency of stakeholders. The dilemma is not purely between strategic imperatives and social responsibility but it is also a dilemma of responsibility to different stakeholders.

THE CSR AGENDA

It appears from a survey carried out by David Clutterbuck and Deborah Snow (Clutterbuck and Snow, 1991) that the issues which attract most attention are those shown in Table 2.1.

In terms of stakeholder expectations the first two on the list above would clearly be the concern of customers while the next three would affect employees. The community is the stakeholder concerned with pollution prevention and education and schools liaison while suppliers are the stakeholder group concerned with purchasing ethics. The potential list of issues can be quite extensive addressing a very wide range of stakeholder interests.

A series of questions are posed in Table 2.2 which direct the attention of organizations to the elements they may wish to embrace in the formulation of their corporate and social responsibility strategies (Johnson and Scholes, 1993, p. 195).

What came out of the survey for Clutterbuck and Snow were some issues of concern. One was that despite a large number of companies having produced guidelines on some or all of the issues above, a significant number of them had no programme to put them into effect – 'the picture which emerges is one of good intentions often unfulfilled'. In their conclusion they say companies in Britain are generally increasing in awareness and activity in social responsibility but they seem to limit their involvement to a relatively narrow range of issues. They also indicated that most organizations fail to seek out best practice elsewhere and this, they suggest, indicates that social responsibility considerations are not pursued as keenly as commercial activities despite the fact that social responsibility ultimately underpins commercial endeavour.

In the late 1980s and early 1990s attention has been given to the issue of **corporate governance** (see Chapter 3). This arose mainly due to a rise in corporate failures, the publicity surrounding scandals such as the Maxwell and Polly Peck affairs, and the large pay rises and financial benefits awarded to senior management recently against a background of recession.

Table 2.1

1. Fair trading, fair marketing and service
2. Product safety
3. Equal opportunities
4. Health and safety
5. Employment security
6. Pollution prevention
7. Education and schools liaison
8. Purchasing ethics

Table 2.2

Should organizations be responsible for ...

Employee welfare
... providing medical care, assistance with mortgages, extended sickness, leave, assistance for dependants, etc.?

Working conditions
... enhancing working surroundings, social and sporting clubs, above minimum safety standards, etc.?

Job design
... designing jobs to the increased satisfaction of workers rather than economic efficiency?

Internal aspects

Green issues
... reducing pollution below legal standards if competitors are not doing so?
... energy conservation?

Products
... danger arising from the careless use of product by consumers?

Markets and marketing
... deciding not to sell in some markets?
... advertising standards?

Suppliers
... fair terms of trade?
... blacklisting suppliers?

Employment
... positive discrimination in favour of minorities?
... maintaining jobs?

Community activity
... sponsoring local events and supporting local good works?

External aspects

Reproduced with permission from Johnson and Scholes (1993).

Proposals for wide-ranging reform in Britain were unveiled in May 1992 after a year-long study of corporate fraud by a committee under the chairmanship of Sir Adrian Cadbury. The report had the backing of the Bank of England and the Stock Exchange. It sought to improve corporate practice through self-regulation by the Stock Exchange, non-executive directors and significant city shareholders, but it held out the prospect of legislation should self-policing fail.

From a legal point of view the corporate governance of a profit-seeking company is clear. The shareholders own the company and they elect a board of directors who in turn appoint managers to run the company on behalf of the shareholders. Recent events appeared to indicate that in a few instances this was not happening.

The majority of **stakeholders** are outside the legal interpretation of corporate governance but in reality the power and interest of some of the groups means they cannot be ignored. Consequently corporate governance is not a simple 'right to manage' concept. Rather key stakeholders concede corporate governance to the management group providing the company is being run with respect to their interests. This means that CSR and corporate governance are very closely related.

SOCIAL RESPONSIBILITY AND ISSUES OF THE DAY

Despite the narrowness of approach alleged by Clutterbuck and Snow many organizations find they are drawn into taking positions on some of the wider issues of the world. The position a company proposes to take may not only be to give a guiding context for business decisions but it may be felt by some organizations that they may need to contribute to public debate. Taking stands on specific issues might also be highly symbolic in transmitting to those inside and outside the organization its nature, style and character.

There is a feeling that the 'power' of business in the community is significant enough for business leaders being encouraged to take a more active/visible role in public debate (Epstein, 1976, 1977). Epstein observed that one difference between British and US business was that Americans were more socially active. Is it possible that there now is an increased role for the business leader/manager/ corporation to be seen as adopting a more socially active role, even if this is controversial for some?

Oliver Wendell Holmes, the American philosopher said 'The opportunity and challenge is there to go beyond the merely profitable and to take part in the action and the passion of our time.' Many companies have declared their positions on some of the issues of our time. These have ranged from the Co-operative Bank's 1992 statement which gave their position on blood sports, the fur trade and armaments to positions which many companies have taken up on issues of pollution, equal opportunities and education. Some companies have taken very strong positions on smoking in the workplace and many companies clearly indicate their position on bribery which can create problems in doing business in some parts of the world. The problem of the inner cities and urban regeneration has been an important feature for some companies and many are actively considering how they can incorporate a responsibility to the Third World. However, there is often some ambiguity which means positions are not easily taken despite good will. A good example was the issue of trading with South Africa referred to earlier.

DEVISING A PROCESS FOR MANAGING CSR

Making CSR work in practice

The formulation of most strategies tends to be incremental and evolutionary. For most organizations the movement towards a strategy of social responsibility proves to be the same. In addition early efforts may be fragmented and piecemeal – almost being made up as issues arise. Dominant values and precedents will prove to be important at this stage along with considerations of economic implications (see Chapter 9 covering issues of discrimination).

For many of the larger companies this becomes intolerable because reacting to stimuli as they arise is likely to lead to contradiction and inconsistency and also some degree of puzzlement on behalf of affected stakeholders. Consequently many large organizations have developed and published position statements on a corporate view of social responsibility. These are sometimes issued as codes of conduct or codes of practice (see Chapter 8 for a discussion on codes).

Some of these may be quite general – attempting to encapsulate the company's philosophy or they may be directed at particular stakeholder groups. The banking code of practice along with the charters produced by some of the privatized industries, such as British Telecom, and some government agencies such as the Inland Revenue, are primarily aimed at one stakeholder group – the customer. The process is still incremental, however, despite the published positions since organizations will find that as developments occur in society and new expectations arise they will be frequently revising and updating their stance.

Most social responsibility policies emanate from senior management/ the board. It is difficult to imagine any policy which could be so far reaching in terms of the conduct, style and nature of the company having any credibility either inside or outside the company unless it had the active support of the people at the top.

IMPLEMENTING CSR

If companies are to avoid the situation of 'good intentions unfulfilled' then positions on social responsibility need to be turned into action programmes. Successful implementation requires several elements.

First and foremost it needs the commitment of senior management and other high profile champions. It needs a place in the formal or informal structures implying staffing and other resources. Resources may also be necessary for research, development and dissemination of the policy. There may also be a need for a training programme and possibly some type of change management initiative (see Chapter 7 on human resource management issues).

The method of implementation is likely to be dependent on the existing style and culture of the organization as well as how well developed is the sense of social responsibility within the organization. In addition, implementation may be affected by how management *wish* to see it working.

Some organizations may conceive such an initiative as a cultural change. They may wish it to be enshrined in the core values of the organization so that it is a factor in almost every decision taken by all managers. On the other hand a bureaucratic organization which is governed by rules and procedures may draft new rules and set up systems to ensure that these rules are adhered to. Both approaches are valid but the rule-driven approach, facing the wide ranging and complex issue of social responsibility, runs the risk of running out of rules as new situations arise.

One other aspect which can be of great value in any policy change is symbolic action at the top. Symbols play a very significant part in the management of any organization and often indicate the closeness or otherwise between what is espoused and what is the reality. Tom Farmer, chairman of Kwik-Fit used to give his telephone number and invite dissatisfied customers to ring him personally. Not too many chairmen are known to do that.

Symbolic action on the part of top management may also help reduce the cynicism which often surrounds any change in organizations. If the senior management are seen to act out the policy then others inside and outside the organization are more likely to take it more seriously.

One fundamental question about implementation is how to judge when it is complete. With a complex and developing issue like social responsibility it is probably true to say it is never complete but as it develops new aspects of policy will have to be implemented. Perhaps implementation may be judged to have happened when everyone has the new rulebook or it may be when one perceives fairly consistent behaviour throughout the organization. Clearly monitoring is only possible if there is some clear and general understanding of what outcomes are expected and these, as already indicated, are likely to be very different between organizations and within a specific organization at different stages of its development.

EVALUATING OUTCOMES

Evaluating CSR is problematic and likely to remain so. In some areas it is possible to look for a measurable return. For example, attempting to act more responsibly towards customers should have the effect of gaining new customers and not losing existing ones. If this were not happening then it should be closely scrutinized to see if policy or implementation are failing. Similarly it might be anticipated that good employee policies should reduce turnover, attract better quality staff, and encourage higher commitment. Some measurable return is possible here. Responsible behaviour to suppliers is hoped to bring better and closer relationships.

Improvements in quality, delivery performance and cooperation are measurable on a variety of parameters. Community programmes are perhaps less easy to evaluate but many large organizations attempt to assess the impact of their community programmes on their corporate image. This sort of assessment has led some organizations to focus their community activities on areas where they have an accepted competence. An example of this was a financial literacy package for schools sponsored by one of the large banks.

Conclusions

The purpose of this chapter has been to demonstrate that the corporate strategies of organizations are *necessarily* developed within an ethical context. The detailed nature of this context will vary depending on the *circumstances* of the organization – the sociopolitical systems; whether the enterprise is private or public sector and whether it is a national or international operator.

The core area of concern for most enterprises are the issues of *corporate social responsibility* (CSR). Organizations need to take a 'stance' on CSR which makes sense in relation to the overall corporate (or competitive) strategy of the organization. This will vary from doing the absolute minimum (*social obligation*) to that of *social responsiveness*. It is dangerous to disconnect this CSR stance from the overall strategy of the organization. For example, a stance of social responsiveness may add costs to such a degree that the firm becomes uncompetitive *vis-à-vis* competition and goes out of business. The reverse problem can also occur where doing the minimum results in a poor corporate image resulting in loss of contracts or the ability to employ good calibre staff – or both!

A well-constructed CSR policy could and should be a source of competitive advantage or part of the value-for-money provided by a public sector organization. Stakeholders will feel able confidently to deal with the organization. This competitive advantage may be recognized as an asset which is not reproducible by competitors in the short run .

Whatever position a business takes on the issue of social responsibility it will become an integral element of corporate strategy. Strategically it helps a company to decide what kind of company it wishes to be. So there is likely to be a strong relationship between the corporate attitude to social responsibility and the character of the company.

Secondly the idea of corporate social responsibility helps to determine *how* the firm will try to reach its goals and how it will do business with its stakeholders. Many organizations now issue statements as to their stance on CSR. This is felt to be necessary to set the tone for executive decision making at both a strategic and operational level. It also gives consistency which would not be present if no statement were there. It is felt that the absence of a declared position can result in social responsibility being a series of reflex and uncoordinated actions despite good intentions. However, it must be remembered that many statements are good intentions unfulfilled according to Clutterbuck and Snow (1990). Stated positions which are *not* acted on are likely to be counterproductive. Thus it is important that aspirations are turned into practice.

In the opening paragraph of this chapter it was stated that 'All organizations have strategies in some shape or form – whether these are developed in a rational and open way – for example, through formal planning approaches or whether through more incremental and evolutionary changes – often less visible but nonetheless generally strategic'. Both notions of and approaches to understanding corporate strategy have been changing. The writings of Whittington (1993), Stacey (1993) and Mintzberg (1994) are examples of the impact of postmodernist concepts and 'chaos' on the traditional nostrums and paradigms of strategy formulation.

As understandings of the strategy process has been changing, it follows that the understanding of business ethics in relation to corporate strategy is also changing and evolving. Managers face a complex world.

> Certainty is stolen away from every side. Classical confidence in analysis, order and control is undermined by Processual scepticism about human cognition, rationality and flexibility. The incrementalist learning of the Processualists is challenged in turn by the impatient markets of the Evolutionists. But even Evolutionary markets can be bucked if, as Systemic analysts of social systems allege, the state is persuaded to intervene. (Whittington, 1993, p. 134)

So the question remains as to how one makes sense of corporate social responsibility in a period of postmodernity (see Chapter 13). This chapter has attempted to sketch out *some* of the parameters of the debate but it has not been concerned to adopt or recommend any prescriptive approach. In this respect the chapter is indicative of the broad framework and approach adopted by the book.

Exercise

In groups or individually consider your own organization or one known to you.

❑ Who are the key stakeholders, or stakeholder groups, in and around the organization?
❑ Are we aware of their expectations of us, the management?
❑ Do they appear to be satisfied with us or not – do we care?
❑ Is our policy balanced or is it focused on a narrow stakeholder set? Did we intend it that way?
❑ Do we want to be leaders, followers or minimalists?
❑ How do we turn our aspirations into action?
　How do we achieve ownership?
　Do we have a structure for debate of issues and delivery of policy?
　Do we have top management commitment?

❑ Do we know where we stand on some or all of the issues of the day?
❑ Do we know what *we* expect from our policy?

Further reading

For a comprehensive coverage of the corporate strategy process the reader can refer to Johnson and Scholes (1993). Whittington (1993) provides a succinct and critical discussion of the way in which thinking about corporate strategy has changed, and the implications arising from adopting a particular theoretical approach to the subject.

In considering the relationship between corporate strategy and business ethics, the reader can consult either Freeman and Gilbert, (1988) or Frederick *et al.* (1992).

References

Buchholz, R.A. (1989) *Fundamental Concepts and Problems in Business Ethics.* Prentice-Hall, London.

Carr, A.Z. (1968) Is business bluffing ethical. *Harvard Business Review*, **46**(1), 143–53.

Carroll, A. (1979) A three dimensional model of corporate performance. *Academy of Management Review*, **4**(4), 497–505.

Clutterbuck, D. and Snow, D. (1991) *Working With The Community – A Guide to Corporate Social Responsibility.* Wiedenfeld & Nicholson, London.

De George, R.T. (1987) The status of business ethics past and future. *Journal of Business Ethics*, **8**, 201–11.

Epstein, E.M. (1976) The social role of business enterprise in Britain: an American perspective: part 1. *Journal of Management Studies*, **13**, 213–33.

Epstein, E.M. (1977) The social role of business enterprise in Britain: an American perspective: part 2. *Journal of Management Studies*, **14**, 281–316.

Epstein, E.M. (1989) Business ethics – corporate good citizenship and the corporate social policy process. A view from the United States. *Journal of Business Ethics*, **8**, 583–95.

Freeman, R.E. (1984) *Strategic Management: A Stakeholder Approach.* Pitman, Marshfield.

Freeman, R.E. and Gilbert, D.R. (1988) *Corporate Strategy and the Search for Ethics.* Prentice-Hall, Englewood Cliffs, NJ.

Frederick, W.C., Post, J.E. and Davis, K. (1992) *Business and Society – Management; Public Policy; Ethics*, 7th edn. McGraw-Hill, New York.

Friedman, M. (1970) The social responsibility of business is to increase its profits. *New York Times Magazine*, 13 September, 32–126.

Goodpaster, K. (1993) Business ethics and stakeholder analysis, in *Applied Ethics – A Reader* (eds E.R. Winkler and J. R. Coombs). Blackwell, Oxford.

Hoffman, M. and Moore, J.M. (1990) *Business Ethics: Readings and Cases in Corporate Morality*, 2nd edn. McGraw-Hill, New York.

Hutton, W. (1995) *The State We're In.* Jonathan Cape, London.

Johnson, G. (1990) Managing strategic change; the role of symbolic action. *British Journal of Management*, **1**, 183–200.

Johnson, G. (1992) Managing strategic change – strategy, culture and action. *Long Range Planning*, **25**(1), 28–36.

Johnson, G and Scholes, K. (1993) *Exploring Corporate Strategy*, 3rd edn. Prentice-Hall, London.

Mintzberg, H. (1994) *The Rise and Fall of Strategic Planning*. Prentice-Hall, London.

Mintzberg, H. and Quinn, J.B. (1991) *The Strategy Process, Concepts, Contexts, Cases*. Prentice-Hall, London.

Mitroff, I.I. (1983) *Stakeholders of the Organizational Mind*. Jossey-Bass, San Francisco, CA.

Peattie, K. (1993) Strategic planning: its role in organisational politics. *Long Range Planning*, 26(3), 10–17.

Stacey, R.H. (1993) *Strategic Management and Organizational Dynamics*. Chapman & Hall, London.

Whittington, R. (1993) *What is Strategy and Does it Matter?* Routledge, London.

Corporate accountability: more form than substance?

3

Alex Dunlop

Alex Dunlop

Discussion of the need for reform of existing structures of corporate governance and accountability has been taking place in the UK and in most other countries with developed economies and capital market systems for at least the last few years. The reasons for this are not difficult to trace – the many large-scale business failures and executive remuneration excesses in the UK, the capital market abuses in the USA and corporate and political fraud in Japan have been the main motive forces behind the demands for change.

Introduction: the current state of corporate governance and accountability

Not only did a large number of investors lose substantial amounts of money in many of these cases, but the whole concept of the corporate entity as a vehicle for mobilizing large scale investment and for managing complex commercial enterprises has come under scrutiny.

As far as the UK is concerned, the emphasis of reform has been in attempting to tighten up the ways in which boards of directors carry out their duties and discharge their responsibilities. The Committee on the Financial Aspects of Corporate Governance (the Cadbury Committee) was established in 1991 by the accountancy bodies and the Stock Exchange. It reported in December 1992 and proposed the establishment of a code of best practice, the adherence to which would be a Stock Exchange listing requirement.

The main thrust of the Committee's recommendations centred on the principles of increasing board objectivity and improving control systems, by:

1. The inclusion on boards of directors of independent non-executive directors of sufficient number and calibre for their views to carry significant weight in board decisions. They are to bring independent judgement to bear on issues of strategy, performance, resources and on standards of conduct. They should be appointed for specified terms, with no automatic reappointment. Their selection should be a formal board process.
2. The board should establish an audit committee of at least three non-executive directors with written terms of reference to deal with its authority and duties. The external auditor would normally attend audit

committee meetings, as would the finance director. The committee should have a discussion with the external auditors at least once a year, without executive board members present, to ensure that there are no unresolved issues of concern. It should review the half-year and annual financial statements before submission to the board and should review the external auditor's letter to the board on perceived internal control deficiencies.

Where an internal audit function exists, the audit committee should ensure that it is adequately resourced and has appropriate standing within the company. The head of internal audit should also normally attend its meetings.

The chairman of the audit committee should be available to answer questions about its work at the annual general meeting.

3. The directors should explain their responsibility for preparing the financial statements. There should be, in addition, a statement by the auditors about their specific reporting responsibilities.
4. The directors should report on the effectiveness of the company's system of internal control.
5. The directors should report that the business is a going concern, with supporting assumptions or qualifications as necessary.

The system will remain, however, one of self-regulation, with the only real sanction the threat of delisting, which, many commentators feel is just that. The possibility, and what some people see as the only effective solution, that of legislative intervention in the process, has been avoided. The US model of a Securities and Exchange Commission to police the behaviour of listed companies has been ruled out as too draconian.

The dimension which has been conspicuously omitted by the Cadbury Committee is the one which is said to be the underlying principle of all corporate regulatory legislation in this country, i.e. that of accountability to the owners of the companies: the shareholders. Companies seem to have become synonymous with their boards of directors, with shareholders having become a marginalized, disadvantaged group. Rather than enabling the organization to become more accountable to its real owners, not to mention the other groups who might have an interest in its financial and operating performance, the recommendations address only one side of the corporate paradigm.

It is not surprising, however, that a strong ethical underpinning can be detected in the Cadbury code, as the American Treadway Commission had sponsored a groundbreaking report on internal control in corporations (published in 1991), which has proved to be influential in this area. The report identifies several important characteristics which it considers should be present before a system of internal control can be considered to be effective, namely:

1. Integrity, ethical values and competence: integrity must be accompanied by ethical values and must start with the chief executive and senior management and permeate the organization.
2. Control environment: this includes the attention and direction provided by the board of directors.
3. Objectives: objectives and strategies must be clearly communicated and reasonably attainable, or control breakdowns are more likely to occur.

But what could be the alternatives to the corporatist Cadbury approach? We read a great deal about governance systems in other countries, such as Germany and in Japan, including their systems of large-scale bank involvement and cross-shareholdings. These are often held up as being desirable models for corporate governance, compared with the so-called unfettered, law of the marketplace systems said to operate in the UK and to some extent in the USA. Overly simplistic parallels are frequently drawn between the one type of system which is said to encourage corporate entities to adopt a longer-term, more notionally responsible approach, and the other deal driven, short-term approaches to commercial activities.

Is this, in fact, a realistic interpretation of the true situation in these countries, or is the truth somewhat different; or are there changes taking place there? Changes which to some extent are being precipitated by the increasingly global nature of much large-scale business and by the ever improving systems of international communication?

And who are the shareholders anyway? It is well known that listed company shareholdings are dominated by institutional investors. Surely they are capable of taking steps to protect their own interests. And what about the position played in corporate investment by large-scale lenders, receiving a prescribed rate of interest each year from corporate profits, in advance of shareholders' dividends? Are they, as some commentators state, a force for the improvement of corporate efficiency and long-term stability, or are they unlikely to play much of a meaningful part in the decision-making process?

This chapter sets out to investigate these and other related questions and attempts to address some aspects which have become perceived wisdom. At the same time the substance of the impact of existing systems of corporate accountability will be explored with a view to undertaking an objective assessment of their effectiveness.

THEORIES OF THE CORPORATE SYSTEM

The creation of the concept of the joint stock, limited liability company, is claimed by Tricker (1990), to be one of the most significant human systems ever, only surpassed by the invention of the wheel. It has enabled

Tracing the development of corporate accountability

huge amounts of capital to be attracted in very efficient ways and has facilitated the growth of world trade and business activities.

The boundaries of the corporate system were clearly defined and easy to comprehend: it would have a separate legal persona from that of its founders and/or owners (i.e. its shareholders) and would therefore be able to enter into contracts and other binding arrangements with third parties, independently of its shareholders. The consequence of this situation would be that, if the company were to fail financially, its creditors would have no direct claim on the assets of the owners, only to the extent of their capital originally, and subsequently, contributed to the company.

Secondly, following from the initial establishment of these boundaries, ownership constituted power over the company: power to nominate and elect the directors who were to manage the organization on behalf of the shareholders; power to require and enforce accountability of these directors for the stewardship of company assets and power to appoint independent auditors, as their agents, to review and report on the truth and fairness of the financial statements prepared and presented by the directors.

The overriding principle, however, is one of stewardship, with the directors having delegated authority from the company (i.e. the share-holders in general meeting) and required to evidence accountability to it. This approach is based very heavily on jurisprudence, and what has become known as classical management theory, in that it believes in the just and honest person, acting in the best interests of the others.

There are, on the other hand, those who present opposing theories, and point to the extent to which the corporation relies on the principle of groups of people with sometimes conflicting interests, acting on behalf of others: in other words, it is a very good example of the operation of agency theory.

Agency theory regards the company as a framework of contracts between principals (the shareholders) and agents (the directors). In contrast to the stewardship model, agency theory assumes that agents will act with rational self-interest, which gives rise to a requirement for a system of independent verification of the actions of the agents. This is the basis for the establishment of the statutory audit process, which, in itself gives rise to additional agency costs, to be borne by the company.

Armstrong (1991), however, cautions against the adoption of a static, functionalist (and tacitly prescriptive) view of agency theory and argues that it is a more dynamic framework and should be viewed from a processual and social action standpoint.

On the other hand, Coase (1937) advances the case for the firm from an economic standpoint, in that in a specialized exchange economy, in which it is generally assumed that the distribution of resources is 'organized' by the price mechanism, the entrepreneur, operating within the firm, has the opportunity to counteract some of these forces through improved direction of resources and thus benefit from cost savings.

An interesting question concerning the rationale for the continuing existence of the usual corporate form is posed by Jensen and Meckling (1976), who paraphrase Alchian (1968): How does it happen that millions of individuals are willing to turn over a significant fraction of their wealth to organizations run by managers who have so little interest in their welfare? What is even more remarkable, why are they willing to make these commitments purely as residual claimants, i.e. on the anticipation that managers will operate the firm so that there will be earnings which accrue to the stockholders?

Writing from a decision-control system perspective, Fama and Jensen (1983) adduce the proposition that the separation of decision and risk-bearing functions is common also to other forms of organization than stock ownership corporations, such as large professional partnerships, financial mutual funds and not-for-profit organizations. Fama and Jensen consider this to be the case due to the common contract structures of the organizations, in that they all contain a separation of the functions of initiation and implementation from those of monitoring and ratification. For example, a board of trustees or managing partners will ratify and monitor important decisions and choose, dismiss and reward important decision agents.

As stated earlier, the corporate system has, in general terms, served its purpose very well, and no doubt, in the majority of cases (as the majority consists of relatively small, privately owned companies) will continue to do so: but the validity of the system as a means of exercising and controlling the operation of large-scale corporate power, where there is an ever-growing degree of separation between ownership and management, is being called into question.

But are we justified in expecting corporations to adopt a moral stance in their decision making at all? According to commentators such as Milton Friedman (1970), they are not moral entities; they are legal beings at best and their social responsibility is to increase their profits. De George (1990) refutes this view on the grounds that their rationally arrived-at decisions and actions affect people and so these actions can be evaluated from a moral standpoint.

In assessing the arguments for and against the extension of the social responsibility of companies beyond the purely wealth increasing, Gray *et al.* (1987) consider the issue from the standpoints of several groups, each espousing a different sociopolitical standpoint, namely the 'pristine capitalists' the 'expedients', proponents of the 'social contract', the 'social ecologists' and the 'socialists'. They conclude that the solution is likely to be a dual one: both informal and formal acknowledgement of responsibility, with the disclosure and measurement procedures appropriately adapted to each approach.

Is it, perhaps, something in the Anglo-Saxon culture which requires the outward appearance of efficiency, flexibility and adaptability and yet involves the need for a complex, regulatory system. It would be useful to look in a little detail at how we got to where we are currently.

EVOLUTION OF THE CORPORATE SYSTEM

For the first part of the nineteenth century, according to Tricker (1990), the principle of personal financial commitment in cases of business failure was strictly adhered to. Business was carried out by means of sole proprietorships, partnerships or unincorporated companies. There was little consideration given to the separation of ownership from management and any possible limitation of personal liability for business debts appeared to contravene the then current perceptions of morality. By the end of the century, however, both were commonplace.

The move towards incorporation was begun by the 1844 Joint Stock Companies Act, which provided for the registration and regulation of all unincorporated firms. This move was prompted by a desire to protect outside investors from overenthusiastic and occasionally fraudulent company promoters. There was, however, no removal of the personal liability of all partners for corporate debts. Over the next 15 years, less than 2000 unincorporated companies were registered, mainly in shipping, insurance and public utilities, but few in the manufacturing sector.

Although a relatively short Act (30 pages), it laid the foundations for company legislation for the next century and a half. It required that directors should manage the affairs of the company, including the appointment of corporate officers, such as the company secretary and that they should arrange for the holding of periodic general meetings of the company, as well as appointing a chairman to preside at them. It stipulated that proper accounting records were to be maintained and balanced and that a balance sheet was to be produced periodically. Auditors were to be appointed by the members, often from among their own number, because professional auditing firms were in their infancy. The names of the auditors were required to be registered with the Companies' Registrar.

Full incorporation, with the liability of shareholding members limited to their initial equity, was not pursued in the first half of the nineteenth century, although interest in it had been kindled before then. Businessmen were suspicious of the propriety, even the morality, of such a development, associating it with the kinds of monopoly privileges which had been granted earlier by the Crown to Chartered Companies, such as the Hudson Bay Company or the East India Company. Such thinking appeared to be contrary to the self-help norms of Victorian Britain.

In 1855, however, an act for limiting the liability of all members of joint stock companies was passed. The precise reason as to why it was felt necessary at that point in time remains something of a mystery: there are those who consider it to have been as a result of parliamentary confusion and drafting errors, in an attempt to create a continental European type of structure in which the liability of non-executive, outside directors was limited, whilst the owner–managers who ran the firm remained personally exposed.

Other commentators (Tricker, 1990) consider that the real driving rationale was, in fact, the familiar economic one, of a need for capital by growing firms, on the one hand, and the existence of investors seeking outlets for accumulating wealth, with a reluctance to stake their personal fortunes, on the other, which created the right climate for the move.

The word 'limited' had to be in the company name and the deed of settlement had to state that the company had such limited liability. Further legislation, consolidated in an act of 1862, specified that seven or more people, by subscribing their names to a Memorandum of Association, could form an incorporated company. The purposes of the company were to be registered, together with the amounts of capital to be subscribed, the location of the registered office, and the fact that liability was to be limited. It is astonishing just how little this process has changed in 130 years, particularly considering the current levels of international trade and commerce and the increasing sophistication of business methods and communications systems – either the Victorian legislators were extraordinarily prescient, or we are now making use of a system which has become dysfunctional!

In fact, Tricker (1990) argues persuasively that this elegant form of nineteenth century corporate governance is unable to cope with the complexities of late twentieth century business life and that the time has come to remodel corporate forms to better reflect the reality of corporate power and responsibility. He posits that the framework of the corporate system ought to incorporate more of the influences of the cultural aspect of human systems management to better reflect observed practice and sources of real power within and surrounding the corporation. The present prevailing forms of corporate structure are substantially influenced by a western bias towards the democratic protection of individual property rights by means of the shareholder primacy approach.

SOME INTERNATIONAL COMPARISONS

With the spread of British influence around the world in Victorian and Edwardian times, it was natural that British systems of corporate governance would follow. Consequently, they became the basis for company legislation in colonies such as India, Hong Kong, Singapore, South Africa, New Zealand, Australia and Canada.

Although developments in the USA were not so directly influenced by British precedents, there were sufficient similarities in national approaches to the recognition of individual freedoms, that the systems adopted contain a high degree of similarity. Individual states passed legislation during the nineteenth century to facilitate the incorporation of companies. Governance was again through the members' meeting, which had the power to nominate and elect the directors and to require regular accountability from them. Federal incorporation was not, and is still not, available.

Developments in continental Europe followed a different path, reflecting again, the differing cultural norms. The regulation of corporate entities in Germany adopted a far more prescriptive and tightly controlled model, which lacked the flexibility of British common law. Shareholders' interests were represented and protected by a supervisory board, quite separate from the management of the company. The supervisory board annually examined and reported on the financial statements prepared by the management directors. Moreover, they could call meetings of the members and, if cause was shown, change the management. It could, therefore, be argued (Tricker, 1990) that top management in German companies is subject to greater, independent scrutiny than their counterparts in this country – a criticism which would have been redressed if the European Community's Fifth Draft Company Law Directive had been adopted, as it originally called for the two-tier, supervisory form of governance, instead of the unitary board with executive and non-executive directors, for all public companies registered in the member states.

In France, the 1807 Napoleonic Code provided the basis for company law, which was consequently prescriptive, providing detailed rules for the conduct of corporate affairs. In 1863 the Société à Responsabilité Limitée was created for companies with capital up to 20 million francs, giving limited liability to both managing (who had previously been excluded) and outside shareholders. The size restriction was subsequently removed.

In Japan, according to Nobes and Parker (1991), the first commercial code was established in 1899, based on the prescriptive Franco-German model and oriented towards creditors and tax collection. Until at least the Second World War, the Japanese economy was dominated by a small number of Zaibatsu, industrial–political consortia, usually involving a bank and originally based on noble families. The importance of banks in the system and the existence of somewhat feudal aspects of business control still survive.

The most common form of business organization in Japan is the Kabushiki Kaisha, which is similar in many respects to the public limited company in the UK. The liability of shareholders is limited to the amount of the subscribed nominal capital, a benefit which requires compliance with the requirements for publicly accessible financial reporting. In addition, the Ministry of Finance administers the Securities and Exchange Law, which applies only to those Kabushiki Kaisha whose shares are publicly traded.

The Securities and Exchange Law was enacted shortly after the Second World War, when General MacArthur was responsible for the Allied administration of Japan. The MacArthur regime naturally adopted the US system of corporate regulation as the model for the revised Japanese system. Consequently, the functions and powers of the Ministry of Finance in relation to financial reporting and corporate control are similar in many respects to those of the US Securities and Exchange Commission, although there is not a directly equivalent body in Japan.

THE US PERSPECTIVE

Life in the New World, through the eyes of leaders, following the War of Independence, as described by Monks and Minow (1991), was based on a suspicion of power. This concern manifested itself in the development of an elaborate written constitution explicitly designed to balance different potential elements of power against each other.

The colonial-era citizens were, however, familiar with the concept of the corporation. Indeed, the early colonies began their existence in the form of joint stock companies. The earliest history of the Massachusetts Bay and Plymouth companies demonstrates the evolution of governmental powers from a commercial charter. Thus, corporations themselves were not suspect – what was essential was that the corporate form be available on a free and open basis.

The Constitution, however, makes no mention of the word 'corporation' and it and its attendant Bill of Rights did not easily cater for the rights of these 'artificial citizens'. As recently as 1990, the Supreme Court was still trying to decide how the protections of the Bill apply to corporations. On the one hand, the American tradition of denying express power to government encouraged the belief that power granted to corporations would further the interests of the individual against the state. On the other, the same year that the USA declared its independence, Adam Smith was writing in the *Wealth of Nations* that directors of publicly held corporations could not be expected to watch the company

> with the same anxious vigilance with which the partners in a private copartnery frequently watch over their own ... Negligence and profusion, therefore, must always prevail, more or less, in the management of such a company.

Louis Brandeis (1933) warned that it was a mistake to 'accept the evils attendant upon the free and unrestricted use of the corporate mechanism as if these evils were the unescapable price of civilised life'. He continued:

> Incorporation for business was commonly denied long after it had been freely granted for religious, educational and charitable purposes. It was denied because of fear. Fear of encroachments upon the liberties and opportunities of the individual. Fear of the subjection of labour to capital. Fear of monopoly. Fear that the absorption of capital by corporations, and their perpetual life, might bring evils similar to those which attended mortmain. There was a sense of some insidious menace inherent in large aggregations of capital, particularly when held by corporations.

To resolve these concerns, an essential part of the system was a kind of corporate democracy, with each 'citizen' entitled to vote according to his investment. If government was permitted to exercise public power through the accountability imposed by the electoral system, it would be logical to permit corporations to exercise private power on the same basis.

It was this involvement of the shareholder/owner in the decision-making process which imbued the corporate system with its validity as being a reasonable representation of the public will. The famous statement of former General Motors president, Charlie Wilson, at his confirmation hearing for Secretary for Defence, was uttered with absolute conviction: 'For years I thought what was good for the country was good for General Motors, and vice versa'. The frequent potential conflicts of interest were becoming more and more apparent as big business grew bigger and began to take on a stance of its own. Commentators began to attribute the US's faltering international competitiveness to a dysfunction in the corporate system, a system which up until then had served the country so well.

According to Monks and Minow (1991), the aspects of the system designed to help the corporation preserve itself have worked, but the aspects of the system designed to make sure that its self-preservation was consistent with the public interest have not. Government, boards of directors and even the marketplace itself, have all been unable to keep the interests of the corporation aligned with those of the community, or to put it another way, to keep it from making everyone else pay the costs of its profits.

This dysfunction was evidenced during the 1980s by the violence in the market for corporate control, with the previously mentioned corporate raiders and leveraged buy-out (LBO) specialists adopting a cavalier approach to 'liberating' shareholder value, by buying out traditional shareholders and restructuring corporations.

The power/accountability interface

PRESSURES ON CORPORATE ACCOUNTABILITY

It can be argued that the massive use of the corporate form in modern times must provide vindication for the robustness and flexibility of the system (Tricker, 1990) – this would be, however, to ignore the countless instances when the very system has proved to be less than satisfactory in the resolution of competing claims on corporate assets or the within the corporate power base. The problems, it appears, become more difficult to manage the bigger the corporation becomes.

British Petroleum plc has in excess of 550,000 registered shareholders, many other public companies have more than 100,000 shareholders, and it would be difficult to find a member of the FT-SE 100 with less than 20,000. As has already been stated, control in the British company rests firmly with the shareholder – but how can 100,000 shareholders arrive at a reasoned, objective, collective decision? There is bound to be a widely differing level of knowledge and understanding of corporate and financial affairs, differing levels of interest in them, differing perspectives, from the potential short-term gain to longer-term investment security and annual income.

At this level, for the company just to be able to communicate effectively with its shareholders is an achievement in itself – for shareholders to communicate with each other in an effective manner is virtually impossible. Hence the development of widely-known and understood corporate reporting codes and signals, such as earnings per share (EPS), price/earnings ratios (P/E), return on capital employed (ROCE) and dividend yields: in other words, utilization of a series of common denominators, on which are based major decisions about a corporation's future.

Should a shareholder wish to become more informed as to the status of a shareholding, it will involve reading and understanding complex reports containing large volumes of high-level financial information; either that or making use of professional analysts and commentators who, in general, may well have access to more relevant information, obtained from first-hand dealings with the company, and which could give some insight into the all-important dimension, usually omitted, relating to the company's future operating prospects.

These problems of communication and understanding, do not, of course, exist at all levels of corporate activity. The vast majority of incorporated entities in this country (and the others which have adopted comparable systems) are smaller, privately-owned companies, where the prime motivation for incorporation was to seek the protection of limited liability, rather than a means of accessing larger-scale capital markets. There are fewer problems of communication and understanding, growth is more likely to be financed from retained earnings, and the transfer of ownership on succession is facilitated.

It is, however, on the activities of the larger corporate entity that attention is most frequently focused. Apart from the already mentioned problems of communication and control, the prescribed legal structure can cause operational difficulties. All major enterprises now trade through a group of subsidiary and associated companies. In some cases these groups are relatively simple, with a small hierarchy of wholly-owned companies under a common parent company. In other cases, groups can be exceedingly complex, with many companies wholly or partly held at many levels in the network, with cross-holdings of shares between group companies, minority interests in such companies and with cross-directorships, intragroup transactions and other inter-dependencies.

It is common for group structures to be designed to facilitate management control, or for international tax planning purposes, to limit financial disclosure, to extend the limitation of liability, or for other regulatory reasons (Tricker, 1990): in such cases, management control structures can fit uneasily into legally prescribed formats, causing operating and control inefficiencies.

To a large extent, these aspects can be considered technicalities which can be managed by the use of appropriate devices – the main problem continues to lie elsewhere. According to Michael Jensen (1989) it is the continuing conflict of interest between boards of directors and share-holders which puts the very long-term future of the public corporation at risk.

Its genius is rooted in its capacity to spread financial risk over the diversified portfolios of thousands of individuals and institutions and to allow investors to customize risk to their own circumstances and predilections. By diversifying risks that would otherwise have been borne by owner-entrepreneurs and by facilitating the creation of a liquid market for exchanging risk, the public corporation has lowered the cost of capital.

This ability to quickly garner large amounts of investment capital, and to spread the portfolio risk over large numbers is likely to continue to be useful, particularly in the cases of companies operating in growth industries, such as computers and electronics, biotechnology, pharmaceuticals and financial services. In these cases, companies are likely to be able to choose from amongst a surplus of potentially profitable projects and unlikely to systematically choose unprofitable ones.

The real problem for the public corporation to resolve is where it is operating in a mature industry, where long-term growth is likely to be low. In such cases, internally generated funds can easily outstrip the opportunities to invest them profitably, or where changes in technology or markets dictate a switching of resources to alternative products or projects.

Industries falling into this category might well include steel, chemicals, brewing, tobacco, wood and paper products. In these and other cash-rich, low-growth or declining sectors, there are often great, sometimes insidious, pressures on management to dissipate cash flow through investment in risky or unsound projects, or just through organizational inertia.

Managers have incentives to retain, rather than distribute cash, partly because cash reserves increase their autonomy *vis-à-vis* the capital markets; this can sometimes serve a competitive purpose, but there is a tendency towards ineffective use and inertia. Cash distributions are also resisted for other less than accountable reasons – retaining cash increases the size of the company, a factor which appears to play an important part in the determination of executive remuneration (which in itself is a source of much shareholder unrest) and social prominence.

A radical approach is put forward by Jensen as a possible solution to this corporate malaise – the replacement of equity by debt (borrowings). Debt is said to be a powerful instrument for change and for instilling greater efficiency into corporations and for creating greater shareholder value. Borrowing commits managers to pay out future cash flows to the providers of capital and removes the element of discretion. To a large extent, what he is recommending is something of a validation of a process which had been having a major impact on corporate USA for a large part of the 1980s – the arrival of the LBO and the LBO association.

The intensive use of debt dramatically shrinks the amount of equity necessary within a company, and it is, therefore, possible to concentrate ownership holdings without the previously attendant requirement to commit large amounts of permanent equity capital. To a large extent, the necessity of the largest funding source taking the form of debt has the effect of transferring the risk diversification process to it, rather than leaving it with the equity.

Arranging these high-yielding (high risk) securities became the province of a few well-known specialist firms, the best known of which was the now deceased Drexel Burnham Lambert which employed the most famous dealer, Michael Milken. The process of portfolio risk diversification, previously applied to equity investments was supposed to apply in a similar manner to these new debt securities, particularly when the diversification process was considered at its secondary level in the holdings of the ultimate investors in the pension and mutual funds themselves.

Issue was taken with Jensen's contentions, most notably by Rappaport (1990), who emphasized the necessity for corporate entities to have long-term planning horizons, in order to retain the confidence of customers, suppliers and employees.

He also recommended the adoption by companies of an institutionalized approach to shareholder value, which would result in at least similar performance improvements to those claimed of LBOs. In any event, these recent developments have had the effect of increasing institutional involvement in corporate affairs and Jensen went so far as to draw comparisons between what was happening with LBO associations in the USA with the Japanese keiretsu business groupings.

THE GERMAN AND JAPANESE PERSPECTIVES

The foregoing analogy was based on the similarities with the substantial bank holdings of debt and equity in large Japanese corporations, and the long-term involvement of the banks and designated executives in corporate strategies and problem solving.

The Japanese Commercial Code requires a Kabushiki to have at least three directors (torishimariyaku), who are elected by the shareholder members. The board of the typical Kabushiki, however, is much larger, with 25–35 being quite normal, and 50 or more not unknown. The composition of a Japanese board is markedly different from a typical western one, in that it is made up almost entirely of inside, executive directors, with no involvement from independent, outside ones.

Moreover, its mode of operation is essentially hierarchical, unlike the US/UK model, which is based on equal responsibility. Indeed, the typical board represents the top three or four echelons of the corporate organizational pyramid.

The chairman is the most senior representative director and meets with his opposite numbers from other firms in the industry, and fosters relations with government, through personal links with politicians. The president is the top operating officer in the corporation. Eventually he would expect to become chairman, a position with considerable honour. The representative directors are the most senior members of the board, which directs the activities of the company, supervising the performance of the managing directors, who might head up divisions, with the directors under them heading up subdivisions. Toyota, for example, has had five representative directors, ten managing directors and 33 directors.

With the corporation seen as a social unit and with a consensus approach to decision making, there is no call for outside directors, who would not be part of the social network; nor would there be a place for them within the board's executive and extremely competitive, hierarchy. The case for independent board membership to provide a system of checks and balances is less apparent given life-time employment and loyalty to the company evidenced by the humiliation of dismissal.

Due to the stability of bank and institutional shareholding and industrial cross-holdings, there has been little merger and acquisition activity, although this is now increasing. Consequently, directors have not had to be concerned about prospective predators, nor have boards been under pressure from outside interests seeking representation. Unlike the notion of shareholder democracy in the western model, with members voting for nominated directors, at the Japanese shareholders' meeting, approval for newly promoted directors is typically shown by a round of applause!

Ironically, however, this much lauded Japanese system, said to encourage stability and the long-term view, is undergoing dramatic change. Japanese corporations have been so commercially successful in their global product markets over the last two decades that they have generated substantial cash resources and have thus been able to reduce their dependence on their traditional sources of bank funding. Also, the emergence of sophisticated international funds markets, particularly the Eurobond, has enabled Japanese companies to even reduce dependence on their domestic market for funding.

In addition, in the last few years, the Japanese stock market has not been performing well, which has caused banks and insurance companies to offload poor performing shares, due to concern about capital–adequacy ratios and returns for policyholders. This has in turn, introduced a greater element of liquidity into the market for equities.

There is also evidence that the pace of product market-led change will have an impact on the structure of Japanese industry – the composition of the top 100 companies is changing quite substantially: in each of the last two decades, 20 firms were displaced and only one firm in three has remained even as long as 30 years. Many of the industries which currently have Japanese domination are maturing and Japanese corporations will be required to downsize, divest and restructure to remain competitive, again introducing substantial elements of change.

They would, thus, appear to be moving towards more of a US/UK approach to corporate funding, which, if these trends continue, will eventually lead to similar problems of investor accountability which currently beset the first two countries.

The German system for funding corporate enterprises has been described as heavily bank-based and has been endowed with similar beneficially stabilizing, long-term attributes to the Japanese system: but do such circumstances actually exist, and, if so, are they also likely to come under major pressures which will cause change to take place? These were some of the questions investigated by Edwards and Fischer (1991) and in respect of which their findings were quite surprising.

Due to the difficulties in obtaining directly comparable financial information in the UK, due mainly to the fact that in Germany all assets are required to be included in financial statements at historical cost, whereas in the UK it is relatively common for land and buildings to be revalued, usually resulting in a corresponding uplift to shareholders' capital, they used sources and uses of funds data for the period 1960–89 to carry out their evaluation.

They found that by far the largest source of corporate funding during the period was retained profits, with the 1980–9 period showing 85% of the total deriving from this category and only 12.6% being provided by long-term bank borrowings, a figure which is less than the UK level of around 20%.

They then went on to look at the nature of bank lending in Germany, compared with the UK. A characteristic of the German system is claimed to be the existence of housebanks, whereby individual companies use one large bank which provides most of their financial requirements and acts as lead bank wherever syndicated credits and other facilities are required. Also the presence of representatives of these banks on supervisory boards is argued to reduce the extent of information asymmetry between borrowers and lenders, so that bank loans are available on more favourable terms than in the UK.

A further consequence of these relationships is said to be that the banks will be more supportive of companies in financial distress than would be the case in the UK, due to the fact that it would be possible to have this risk-taking compensated for in future and not eroded by competition from other banks. German banks are also seen to be better equipped to handle funding requirements, due to the existence of sizeable staffs of technical advisors, well versed in the assessment of industrial prospects and risks.

Almost all of these preconceptions about German banking relationships were found to be misplaced. The banks do not, in fact, have specialist departments which have the technical expertise to assess whether particular projects for which finance is being sought are likely to be successful. Neither is bank representation on supervisory boards a generally significant source of information for the bank concerned: this is largely due to the ethical stance taken within the banks towards the use of information gained in this way.

Nor is the housebank concept prevalent – larger companies, i.e. those with turnovers in excess of DM500 million were found to have in excess of ten active bank connections, and even the smallest companies had between two and five active bank connections. Competition amongst banks for corporate business is, in fact, fierce. It is more likely that banking relationships will be shared among several banks, with the one with the longest-standing connection taking the role of lead banker in syndicated business.

It is also clear that unlike in Japan, German banks do not usually get involved in corporate reorganizations at operational management levels, and do not possess any specialists at turning round unprofitable companies. The main reasons for this appear to be that there is a strong convention that bank and industrial management are separate and distinct and that the direct involvement of a bank in a corporate rescue could raise liability questions for the bank should the rescue fail.

The area wherein the research did indicate there to be some truth in commonly held perceptions was that of bank control of equity voting rights. It has been estimated that German bank direct equity shareholding levels were at the level of 10.3% in 1984 and 11.6% in 1988, and that only in a small minority of cases were the banks able to exercise control as a result of their own shareholdings. Due to the fact, however, that German shares are unregistered bearer shares, which are commonly deposited with the banks by small shareholders for custody and administration purposes, the banks (who are bound to consult with the beneficial owners) are able to exercise the votes of these shares on a proxy basis.

As the larger corporations tend to have the most widely-dispersed shareholdings, and therefore likely to have the largest number of proxy votes, it is in this area that the banks appear to exercise the most control. In 30 cases out of the largest 100 industrial corporations, bank holdings, together with their committed proxy votes, were found to control in excess of 50% of the votes available, whilst in a further 11 cases the combined vote was above 25%, sufficient to block a resolution requiring a 75% majority. Also, the bank vote is concentrated in the hands of the big three banks, namely Deutsche Bank, Dresdner Bank and Commerzbank, a fact which indicates an enormous concentration of power.

Such an enormous power base leads, of course, to large-scale participation as shareholder representatives on supervisory boards. In Aktiengesellschaft (AG) with more than 2000 employees, one half of the supervisory board membership must consist of employee representatives, with the other half being representatives of the shareholders – but the most important requirement is that the chairman of the board is elected by the shareholder representatives and has the right to cast a second vote in cases of board deadlock. Bank representatives hold a significant proportion of positions as supervisory board chairman, in many cases even where they do not have majority voting control, either alone or with proxy votes.

The supervisory board has as its main function, according to the Aktiengesetz (Stock Corporation Act), the control of management: in this capacity it has the power to appoint and dismiss members of the management board (Vorstand) and to fix their remuneration. There is evidence, however, which casts doubts on the extent to which supervisory boards are capable of monitoring the activities of the management board: a 1988 study found that the vast majority of supervisory boards taking part in a study (86%) met for only the legal minimum of twice a year, obviously too seldom to be able to provide any meaningful input to corporate decision making.

In any event, the claim that at the macro-level, the bank voting power is a reasonable representation of the public will, and therefore a force for encouraging management accountability, must itself be called into question: the banks themselves are AGs, and as such have a management board, a supervisory board and a chairman elected by the shareholders – but the banks, in an anacronistic twist of the system, also hold and can exercise proxy votes at their own general meetings, thus giving them, effectively, control of themselves! A recent estimate of the proxy votes held by the big three at their own shareholders' meetings was Deutsche

Bank 47.2%, Dresdner Bank 59.3% and Commerzbank 30.3%. So where is the incentive for the banks to act as shareholders' representatives elsewhere and a force for improved corporate accountability in general?

There are clearly many anomalies and inconsistencies in the German system of accountability and also, it must be borne in mind that the extent of shareholding in Germany is much smaller than in the UK, which again might encourage a less accountable approach from managers and institutions.

In an interesting parallel to the already perceived characteristics of governance systems, Puxty *et al.* (1987), in discussing modes of regulation of accountancy in advanced capitalist societies, make use of Streeck and Schmitter's exploration of models of social order, which uses a combination of the organizing principles of market, state and community.

In this paradigm, the UK is classed as principally associationist, being located between market and state, with important influences from both. Germany, on the other hand is perceived as largely being influenced by the state and therefore being legalist in form. Both these interpretations could as easily be applied to the countries' governance and accountability systems.

The way forward – the consensual approach?

The corporate control scene in the USA has moved on from the era of the hostile takeover and the leveraged buy-out; but at congressional hearings, at annual meetings and in proxy contests, senior executives and powerful shareholders continue to confront each other. The basic issues remain remarkably consistent – what kinds of accountability do directors owe shareholders in terms of strategic consultation and disclosure? What is the precise role of the board of directors as a representative of shareholders? What are the limits of appropriate shareholder involvement?

These issues have had, of necessity, to be addressed over the last few years by many pension funds and other large investors for a variety of very practical reasons: as owners overall of between 40% and 50% of the common stock of the US's large and medium-sized businesses, the trustees had woken up to the fact that they were no longer investors – an investor can, by definition, sell holdings. A small fund might still be able to do so, but the shareholdings of even a medium-sized fund are already so large that they are not easily sold – or more precisely, they can only be sold to another pension fund. According to Drucker, writing in the *Harvard Business Review* in 1991, the funds are thus beginning to learn what George Siemens, founder of Deutsche Bank, said 100 years ago, when he was criticized for spending so much of his and the bank's time on a troubled client company: 'If one can't sell, one must care'.

Perceptions such as these, of frequent share dealing by institutional shareholders and consequently a lack of long-term commitment to investee companies, were also largely refuted by Marsh (1990) in respect of the UK situation, who identified a holding period of investments within institutional portfolios of some five years on average.

Although encouraging greater dialogue between corporate management and institutional investors, Marsh made a strong case for preserving the market mechanism *status quo*, by asserting that even if the UK were to get corporate governance 'right' overnight, actual improvement in business performance would be relatively modest.

The reasoning behind this assertion is that the UK has historically suffered from a relative lack of profitable investment opportunities, reflecting mostly the detrimental impact of supply side factors, such as shortcomings in the quality of management and of workforces and not through any failure due to the nature of the workings of the capital market. Attention should instead be directed to improving government macro-economic policies to create longer-term industrial stability and to increasing infrastructure investment in areas such as education, particularly management education, and training.

In the USA, however, a more proactive climate has been developing and pension funds have caused corporate management to seriously embrace the concept of objective performance measurement, involving financial accountability, even though it is generally accepted that performance and results go beyond the financial 'bottom line'. If there had not been such a concentration of voting power in the hands of pension funds, the activities of the corporate raiders and LBO sponsors would have been seriously curtailed – a raider who has to gain the support of hundreds of thousands of dispersed shareholders soon runs out of time and money!

One reason for their support was that these transactions kept alive the illusion that pension funds could, in fact, sell their shares. The result has been a shake-out of benevolent despotic management, to be replaced by more professional, performance-oriented boards, with a clearer view of long-term strategy: for it is to the long-term that pension fund investors should be looking. Final-salary-based pension schemes (which required the accumulation of market-led gains to keep pace with the inflationary aspects of salary increases) are being rapidly replaced by fixed contribution schemes which make it possible for the funds to plan more effectively on a long-term basis – the most appropriate time scale, i.e. the time until its future beneficiaries will retire, is on average some 15 years, and so, planning on this scale is appropriate.

To enable institutional investments to be systematically monitored on a long-term basis requires a reasonably formal mechanism to be set up. There is no question, for reasons already discussed, of funds taking a more interventionist role in operational management of the investee companies, but it is, nevertheless necessary for them to continuously evaluate the companies on the basis of meeting their agreed performance objectives.

One method which has been suggested, and which is already beginning to find favour, is for annual business performance reviews to be carried out by independent, professional agents, such as consulting firms. Their remits would encompass such aspects of a corporation's activities as mission and strategy development, marketing, innovation, productivity, human resources, community relations and lastly, the manifestation of the success of the foregoing, profitability: in other words, all the areas for which a well-run company might be expected to have developed agreed performance indicators.

Unlike the hostile transactions of the past decade, the new 'political' mechanisms do not depend on the availability of finance. Nor do they depend on high-cost, all-or-nothing techniques aimed at achieving quick control. Indeed, the new approaches to corporate control have arisen as a direct result of the failure of the old ones. In the case of an institution with a sizeable holding in a large public corporation, to become informed about the details of a contentious issue facing the company and to back a particular course of action, will usually be more cost effective than selling, or alternatively, losing value through inactivity with the resultant outcome being detrimental to the investee company.

Some other mechanisms which have been proposed, and, in some cases, are already operating as a result of this more consensual approach, as described by Pound (1992) are:

(a) Shareholder committees: this can act like a 'shadow cabinet', to provide shareholders with an alternative view. At USX, in 1990 Carl Icahn established a shareholders' enhancement committee which carried out independent analysis of the company on behalf of shareholders, and has since become something of a model approach.
(b) Director nominating committees and petitions: convened or organized by the major institutional investors to get together a consensus view of alternative directors who can either be agreed with the existing board, or if necessary, voted in at the general meeting.
(c) Issue campaigns: the canvassing of major shareholders on specific business issues, with a view to their being a mechanism for achieving corporate change.
(d) Friendly monitoring: already mentioned – the use of external consultants to carry out business performance reviews.

In many cases, however, the best results are being obtained through constructive discussion and on-going consultation between investor and corporation, particularly where there is a specifically targeted issue about which the pension fund is unhappy. It is becoming clear that corporations which make an effort can build long-term relationships with their major shareholders and create a new kind of consensus which can ultimately lead to greater stability.

There is every reason to believe that the more consensual management/ institutional shareholder relationship could work effectively in the UK. After all, we have a similar open, market-led stock exchange system as the USA and similar trends in shareholdings, i.e. increasing domination by institutional and other large investors.

It is evident that individual shareholding, as a proportion of overall share capital holdings is continuing to drop: this despite the fact that, in numerical terms, individual shareholders have increased from just three million in 1979 to more than 11 million today.

The important point, in any event, is to track the levels of readily identifiable and easy to contact shareholders, as coordination of shareholder response is primarily a question of communication and the provision of relevant information, to enable a reasoned response to be effected. There is already plenty of evidence to indicate that large shareholders in the UK are beginning to make their views known to company boards on contentious issues such as board/chairman appointments, executive remuneration, and environmental matters, *vide* Burton Group, Brent Walker, Saatchi & Saatchi, etc.

Further, more coordinated activity in this area is evidenced by the work of the Institutional Shareholders' Committee (ISC), which brings together fund managers in pension schemes, life assurance funds and investment and unit trusts. The biggest problem which members of the ISC have identified so far is the insider trading legislation. By acting in a concerted manner by, say, pressing for the replacing of a chief executive of an investee company, institutions involved could be said to be in possession of price-sensitive information, which they would be unable to make use of before it was generally available to the market as a whole. Where does the line get drawn in cases like this? There are bound to be so many marginal instances, that it could effectively become a potential minefield for institutional investors, who not unexpectedly, continue to tread very cautiously.

The crux of the matter comes round again to the fundamental principle of accountability – not just accountability of corporate boards to shareholders, but within the market community, accountability of investor to investor, or more specifically, large investor(s) to other investors, both large and small.

It seems to be generally felt to be undesirable (at least on the part of corporate board representatives), for there to be too rigid a system of shareholder involvement established, such as, for example, the German system of supervisory boards (whose power has been shown to be more apparent than real), but it is clear that there is a real desire to see the establishment of an effective mechanism which would represent shareholder interests to corporate management.

The main drawback of the Cadbury proposals for greater involvement of non-executive directors is the fact that they are not representing any definitive constituency, which is bound to weaken their position and power within the organization.

Following a similar line of argument to that used earlier by Pound (1992), Hanson (1993), also writing in the *Harvard Business Review*, in refutation of the claims that institutional shareholders are not equipped to become more involved in the governance of investee companies stated that, on the contrary, shareholders alone have both the economic interest to monitor corporate performance and the legal power to replace directors who fail to perform adequately. He agreed that some shareholders have a short-term perspective, but those shareholders who control the largest tranches of corporate stock adopt, through the extensive use of the indexing technique, an inherently long-term approach.

One of the largest US pension funds, the Californian State Teachers Retirement Scheme (CALSTRS) (total assets in 1990 of $30 billion) is quoted by Charkham (1994) as stating that it considers itself too large to escape by trying to buy and sell constantly to avoid poor (or simply under-performing) companies and that sometimes even confrontation may be necessary to protect their investment.

Many of the questions faced by the corporate director involve similar types of economic enquiry techniques as those used regularly by investment analysts; but, perhaps most importantly, institutional investors have the resources to consult with the best minds in the country, so even though investors may not know how to make better widgets, they can certainly find someone who does.

A further proposal for the formalization of this consultation process is to encourage boards to establish an investor relations committee, in much the same way as an audit committees and a remuneration committees. The composition of the committee could be the chairman and or the chief executive, a mixture of executive and non-executive directors and the chairmen of the audit and remuneration committees.

Such a committee would provide a conduit for investor communication and would improve relations by:

1. Placing the function of communicating with larger investors on governance issues primarily in the hands of the senior directors elected by all the shareholders.
2. Providing companies with a way to invite their major shareholders in for periodic briefings on what the company is doing and giving these investors an opportunity to air their concerns before they become major points of disagreement.
3. Making a public statement that the company cares enough about its shareholders to create a special committee that will represent their concerns to the entire board.

Admirable as these suggestions are, however, there still exists the possibility of criticism for apparent unfair treatment of smaller shareholders who do not have the resources to instigate or attend such meetings. To counter such objections, the investor relations committee would require to operate to a strict code of conduct, such that formal records of these meetings were kept and available for inspection by any interested shareholder, and that no specific financial information would be divulged without simultaneous notification to the Stock Exchange and the 'wire' services.

There is, obviously, a major role to be played in such an arena by a shareholder representational body, i.e. one which would represent the interests of smaller shareholders. If potential independence problems could be overcome, ProShare (an industry-funded representative body), or a still-to-be-established body could be required to be invited to the previously mentioned meetings of investor relations committees, to represent the smaller shareholders' interests. In any event, the fiduciary relationship of the directors to all shareholders and not just to the major ones, and with the committee being a formal subcommittee of the board, should result in equitable treatment.

One of the common complaints of large shareholders is of the free ride which is being created by them for the smaller ones – this assumes a commonality of interest between the two groups. In recent years just such a situation has become easier to justify, due to the already mentioned widespread use of indexing as an investment technique of the institutional investors, resulting in a longer-term investment time horizon.

There would appear to be much merit in building on these most recent US instances of shareholder communication mechanisms and in creating a UK version, probably involving formal board representation, with opportunities for smaller shareholder participation.

Many other groups of stakeholders are also interested in the performance (not necessarily just financial) of corporate entities, for a variety of reasons. Such groups might be employees, pensioners, customers, suppliers, government departments and agencies and local communities in areas where the corporation operates.

The conventional annual report and financial statements, prepared and published in satisfaction of the Companies Act 1985, were designed to provide relevant financial information for shareholders and were never intended to furnish the wide range of information regularly sought from corporations.

Types of information falling into this category might relate to health and safety issues, employment conditions, waste disposal and pollution control, energy use and environmental matters.

In the course of writing this chapter, the author reviewed the 1993–4 annual reports and financial statements of the ten largest UK companies (by market capitalization) and in most cases information was provided on the corporate mission, as well as some reference being made to environmental matters and community involvement.

The most notable development in corporate accountability, however, was not to be found in the conventional report and accounts, but in the additional material which now seems to be routinely produced by large companies and provides information particularly about their interaction with the environment and with the communities in which they operate. A selection of such reports would be:

- British Telecommunication plc – Environmental Performance Report
- The Shell Transport and Trading Company plc – Shell and the Environment; Shell in Society
- The British Petroleum Company plc – New Horizons
- Glaxo Holdings plc – Glaxo and the Environment; Glaxo in the Community.

Particularly effective among the various types of document available was a straightforward statement from Marks & Spencer plc on company principles and from Shell one on general business principles (although the company has subsequently been the subject of adverse comment). A relevant commentary on these aspects of corporate conduct is provided by Albrecht (1992), who, after describing the system of development and monitoring of the code of ethical conduct within the Ford Motor Company, concludes that corporate ethical behaviour begins and ends with individuals – it is a matter of individual awareness, integrity and commitment.

Publications such as these are helpful to readers interested in corporate accountability beyond just the financial, but the main problem with them is, of course, their objectivity. A few of the companies have attempted to address this issue by commissioning reports on their approach to environmental and health and safety matters from independent consultants. This is a step in the right direction, but the process is still in its infancy and the reports tend to comment on the process of data collection and on the extent of perceived corporate commitment, but do not comment on the apparent effectiveness of the systems and procedures in place.

This process is a further example of the consensual approach to corporate accountability and is a good example of the operation of the Coase theorem (Coase, 1960). The essential points of Coase's proposition were effectively paraphrased by Johnson (1991) as follows:

> Whenever the law adopts an inefficient rule, people will bargain and contract around it. They will eventually arrive at an efficient result – one the law should have adopted in the first place – only they will have wasted effort and resources in negotiating and contracting.

Such a situation pertains in most areas of ethical development – legislation usually follows some way behind. On this basis we should be prepared for substantial legislative involvement in corporate accountability in the foreseeable future.

Benston (1982) is, however, sceptical about the role of the accountant in future systems of social responsibility accounting, due to the subjective nature of much of the data which might be produced – he concludes, in fact, by maintaining that the social responsibility of accountants can be expressed best by their forbearing from social responsibility accounting!

In addition, Gray *et al.* (1993) quote the results of research which has been directed towards assessing whether shareholders rewarded, penalized or were indifferent towards companies with a better than average social performance. Although inconclusive, the results seem to suggest that investors only care about social disclosure and social performance when it will affect financial performance, and to the extent that investors take into consideration the ethical stance of an organization, they do so only in a very limited way.

It rather appears that, based on these findings, the proponents of improvements to corporate accountability, in terms of a greater emphasis being placed on aspects of social responsibility accounting, are likely to have their work cut out.

To end on a more positive note, however, Woodward *et al.* (1993), in discussing organizational legitimacy theory, note that corporate disclosure is reactive to environmental factors and that disclosures legitimize actions. They also note the close links between organizational legitimacy and corporate governance, which, inter alia, establishes the firm's legitimacy as a social entity. As companies continue to adapt to their changing environments we will undoubtedly see more examples of the legitimizing impact of an ever widening range of corporate information disclosures.

Exercises

❑ The UK system of corporate supervision and control is said to be based on the principle of self-regulation. Describe the main features of the UK system and suggest and describe at least one possible alternative.

❑ Commentators such as Milton Friedman maintain that it is wrong to expect corporations to adopt a moral stance in their decision making. Frame a case to support and justify the Friedman stance. How might it be possible to argue from the opposing standpoint?

❑ The western system of corporate governance depends for its successful operation on the tenet of shareholder primacy. What is meant by this description? Suggest reasons as to why it might now be desirable to introduce changes to the system and how this might be accomplished.

❑ Jensen (1989) outlined a radical change to the conventional corporate financial structure, which he considered would improve accountability. Describe and evaluate his proposals.

❑ The claim that the shareholder voting power exercised by German banks is a reasonable representation of public will has been called into question by Edwards and Fischer (1991). Discuss the system of bank representation in Germany and the reasons for Edwards and Fischer's contention.

❏ What is meant by the consensual approach to corporate governance, as is becoming established in the USA? Identify some of the potential problems which any attempt to establish a similar system in the UK might encounter.

Further reading

Monks, R.A.G. and Minow, N. (1995) *Corporate Governance*. Blackwell, Cambridge, MA.

Cannon, T. (1994) *Corporate Responsibility*. Pitman Publishing, London.

Smith, D. (ed.) (1993) *Business and the Environment: Implications of the New Environmentalism*. Paul Chapman, London. 1993.

Watts, R.L. and Zimmerman, J.L. (1983) Agency problems, auditing and the theory of the firm: some evidence. *Journal of Law and Economics*, XXVI, 613–33.

Watts, R.L. and Zimmerman, J.L. (1986) *Positive Accounting Theory*. Prentice-Hall, Englewood Cliffs, NJ.

Welford, R. and Gouldson, A. (1993) *Environmental Management and Business Strategy*. Pitman, London.

References

Albrecht, W.S. (ed.) (1992) *Ethical Issues in the Practice of Accounting*. South-Western, Cincinnati, OH.

Armstrong, P. (1991) Contradiction and social dynamics in the capitalist agency relationship. *Accounting, Organizations and Society*, 16(1), 1–25.

Benston, G.J. (1982) Accounting and corporate accountability. *Accounting, Organizations and Society*, 7(2), 87–105.

Charkham, J.P. (1994) *Keeping Good Company*. Clarendon Press, Oxford.

Coase, R. (1937) The nature of the firm. *Economica*, **4**, November.

Coase, R. (1960) The problem of social cost. *Journal of Law and Economics* 3, October.

Committee on the Financial Aspects of Corporate Governance (1992) Report of the Committee on the Financial Aspects of Corporate Governance (the Cadbury Committee). Gee & Company, London.

De George, R.T. (1990) *Business Ethics*, 3rd edn. Macmillan, New York.

Edwards, J.S.S. and Fischer, K. (1991) An overview of the German financial system. Research paper.

Fama, E.F. and Jensen, M.C. (1983) Separation of ownership and control. *Journal of Law and Economics*, June.

Friedman, M. (1970) The social responsibility of business is to increase its profits. *The New York Times Magazine*, 13 September.

Gray, R., Bebbington, J. and Walters, D. (1993) *Accounting for the Environment*. Paul Chapman, London.

Gray, R., Owen, D. and Maunders, K. (1987) *Corporate Social Reporting: Accounting and Accountability*. Prentice-Hall, London.

Jensen, M.C. and Meckling, W.H. (1976) Theory of the firm: managerial behavior, agency costs and ownership structure. *Journal of Financial Economics*, October.

Jensen, M.C. (1989) Eclipse of the public corporation. *Harvard Business Review*, September/October.

Johnson, N. (1991) Proximity and the expectations gap: Anglo-American perspectives on auditors' liability. Paper presented to Conference of the Association of Law Teachers, Nottingham, April.

Marsh, P. (1990) *Short-termism on Trial*. Institutional Fund Managers' Association, London.

Monks, R.A.G. and Minnow, N. (1991) *Power and Accountability*. HarperCollins.

Nobes, C. and Parker, R. (1991) *Comparative International Accounting*. Prentice-Hall, London.

Pound, J. (1992) Beyond takeovers: politics comes to corporate control. *Harvard Business Review*, March/April, 1992.

Puxty, A.G., Willmott, H.C., Cooper, D.J. and Lowe, T. (1987) Modes of regulation in advanced capitalism: locating accountancy in four countries. *Accounting, Organizations and Society*, **12**(3), 273–91.

Rappaport, A. (1990) The staying power of the public corporation. *Harvard Business Review*, January/February, 1990.

Tricker, R.I. (1990) The corporate concept – redesigning a successful system. *Human Systems Management*, **9**, 65–76.

Woodward, D., Birkin, F. and Edwards, P. (1993) Organisational legitimacy and stakeholder informational perspectives. Paper presented to Northern Accounting Group Conference, Sheffield, September.

4 Modelling the ethical environment: a systems analyst and designer perspective

David Hawley and Don White

Introduction

In this chapter we intend to focus on just one aspect of the organization environment – the ethical environment. There are of course many other aspects. The relationship between the organization, its suppliers, its customers, its workforce, its management, etc. raises many complex issues which may impinge on the successful operation of the organization; issues of power, influence and control to name but three. The environmental models and frameworks of analysis which are presented in this chapter are ones which are often used when considering a variety of complex organizational environmental issues and are suggested as being appropriate in coming to terms with the organization/ethical environment (see Fig. 4.1).

Ethics and morality, as defining what is considered good and bad, right and wrong, are almost inextricably linked with social action being a manifestation of 'good action(s)' arising from the two definitions. In organizational terms there are key factors in the organizational environmental relationship and identifying and understanding those factors is an organizational requirement and not simply a managerial elective.

The way and extent to which the organization comes to terms with the ethical issues in its environment could depend largely upon the way the organization perceives and chooses to interpret societal aspirations and expectations through its environmental scanning system. This is a complicated and difficult process because, *inter alia*, the organization is dealing with uncertain complex phenomena. To say that organizations produce this or that – or organizations behave well or badly is nothing more than a semantic convenience. To claim otherwise is to reify the organization – organizations, *per se*, do not do anything either good or bad. It is individuals and groups within organizations that deal with a variety of situations placed upon it.

Constructing models of the environment, has provided a variety of perspectives of the organization environmental relationship. Many

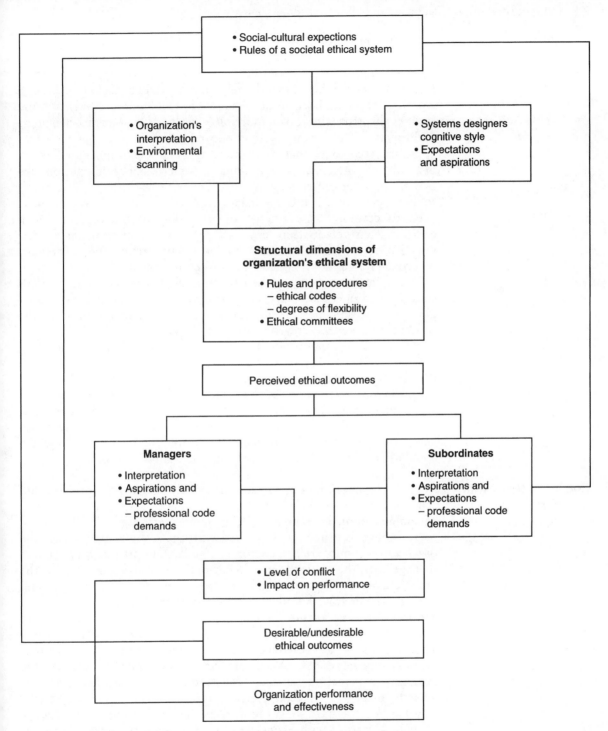

Figure 4.1 Modelling the ethical environment – a framework of analysis.

organizations see the development of a *symbiotic relationship* with their environment as prerequisite to organizational performance and effectiveness. These range from the classicists, who adopted a *closed perspective* by suggesting that the relationship could be managed through a process of internal organization adaptation and modification. To those systems theorists who took a more *open perspective* by acknowledging a multiplicity of issues involved in the relationship. The open systems approach recognizes that there are important environmental factors, beyond the organizational boundary, which may impinge on the operations of the organization by providing both *threats* and *opportunities* to their operations. In order to achieve this, organization decision makers need to develop a meaningful understanding of the organizational/environmental relationship through a process of environmental modelling. A process by which a large complex and uncertain phenomenon can be broken down into a digestible meaningful form.

This interpretation must then be translated into the organization's strategic and operational systems. Systems analysts and designers could play an important part in this process. In some respects they are the conduit between the environment and the organization. Their understanding and perception of what they observe could have an important impact on the outcomes of the system and consequently upon the performance of the organization.

And so the interpretation process continues through the managerial and subordinate structures of the organization. Managerial and subordinate perceptions of the systems similarly are important influences and play a key part in producing both desirable and undesirable outcomes which could affect organizational performance and effectiveness.

Coming to terms with the environment

Many large organizations engage in socially responsible projects and account for them in their annual report to shareholders, and in the case of public quoted companies, the public at large. Whilst social responsibility is primarily concerned with the overall operation of the organization, ethics are contemporary standards or principles of conduct that govern the actions and behaviour of individuals within the organization. Ethics provide a basis for determining what is right and wrong. What is ethical or unethical is complicated because societal values and moral concepts tend to change over time. Acceptable practices are established by society and govern the ethical standard(s) for an industry, a business firm or an individual manager. Laws, government regulations, industry ethical codes, social pressures and conflicts between the manager's personal standards and the need of the firm all affect decisions made by managers involving ethical issues.

In Fig. 4.1. we have sought to address the issue through a framework of analysis, starting with a consideration of the sociocultural expectations – what the environment expects of organizations – and how organizations deal with these expectations through its systems of analysis and design and processes of operation.

> ... a set of elements [factors] and their relevant properties, which elements are not part of the system [organization] but a *change* in any of which can cause or produce a *change* in the state of the organisation. (Ackoff and Emery, 1972)

The environment – a definition

The definition subscribes to the *open systems* perspective by suggesting that the organization exists and depends on the courtesy of a much wider contextual framework. Furthermore, the environment is a changing phenomenon which, again, impinges on the organizational operations. Sociocultural expectations change over time. It is this degree of movement which becomes problematic for organizational decision makers, i.e. the higher the rate of *change* (movement), often manifested by '*exogenous shocks*' – those unplanned, unpredictable changes in environmental elements.

In Figs 4.2 and 4.3, we suggest a process by which such a complex and uncertain phenomenon might be broken down into a more digestible meaningful form. This process of decomposition starts with the general environment.

An environmental model

THE GENERAL ENVIRONMENT

The general environment sets out environmental conditions that involve whole classes of organizations and may be described as those conditions

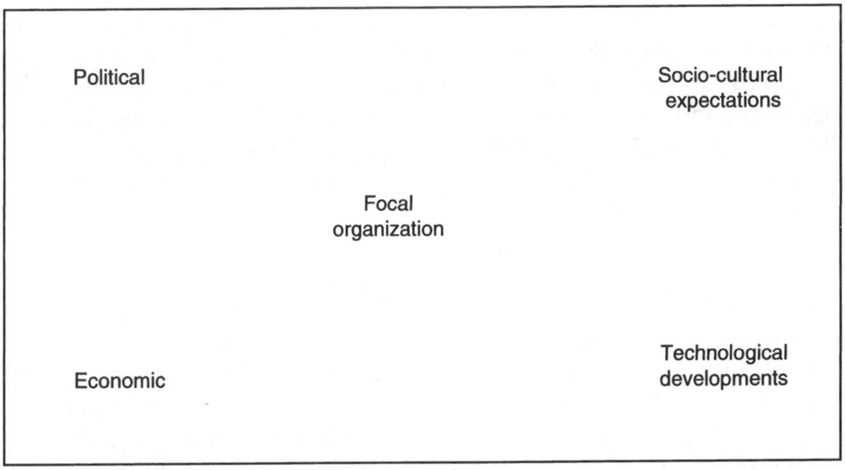

Figure 4.2 An example: the general environment.

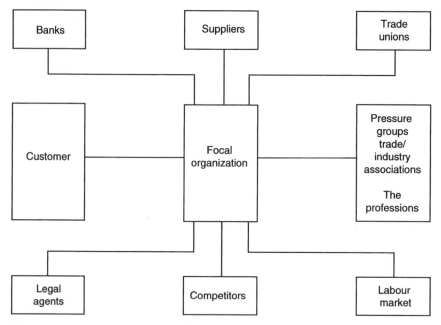

Figure 4.3 An example: the specific environment.

that are *potentially* relevant for the focal organization. Whilst the organization *may not* be in touch with these factors on a day-to-day basis, and as a consequence not particularly well informed about those conditions 'out there', it should instigate environmental scanning and control mechanisms to deal with them.

The political, economic, technological and social environments are almost inextricably linked. They not only impact on the organization, but they impact upon each other. In an environment which is stable and highly predictable there will be well developed rules of behaviour, supported by laws developed in the political sectors that prescribe behaviour and which impose sanctions against those who break the rules. What we have here is a highly predicable organizational/environmental relationship where today is very much the same as yesterday and tomorrow will be like today.

If that organization/environmental relationship becomes disturbed by some unanticipated, unexpected event then the organization is confronted with new situations often not covered by the existing rules, laws and arrangements. Social institutions, i.e. organizations, cannot easily respond overnight to those events – it may take considerable time for political institutions to develop new laws and often requires the demonstration of real harm before they act. In the intervening time organizations are required to act forcing them into a 'grey area' of what is socially acceptable.

THE SPECIFIC ENVIRONMENT

Unlike the general environment, this has more immediate relevance for the focal organization. It represents factors in the environment with which the organization is in *direct* regular, occasional and/or infrequent contact and which constitutes the 'organization-set' (see Fig. 4.3).

It is appropriate to point out here, that each of the factors will have an interest in the focal organization. They will also have expectations which will impinge on the way they deal with the organization and in the way the focal organization deals with them. In other words they become 'stakeholders' in the organization.

Therefore, it could be argued that the organization is better informed, than it might otherwise have been, about this aspect of the relationship between itself and those factors of the environment. In the context of this discussion, the organization is likely to be better informed of what is expected in terms of moral and ethical behaviour and how these expectations match up to its own ethical systems.

Whilst it is not claimed to be the only framework of analysis, the open systems model is useful in that it can be related to a number of references within the business ethics literature concerned with the different 'levels of analysis' contained in the area of interest constituting business ethics. Hoffman and Moore (1990) identify four levels:

Environmental scanning – the open systems approach

1. **The system level**: concerned with the nature of capitalism and the free-market system.
2. **The analysis**: of the nature and role of the business organization within the economic system.
3. **The scanning**: of particular ethical issues as they arise within the course of economic activity; for example recruitment policies, employee rights product safety, etc.
4. **The assessment**: of ethical values which are encapsulated within the structure and nature of business activity; for example freedom of opportunity, economic growth and materialism.

In an earlier paper De George (1987) identifies:

1. The macro-level which considers the economic system of free enterprise.
2. The study of business organizations operating within the free-market system.
3. The morality of individuals operating within the business system.

Epstein (1989), in his study of 'levels of analysis' identified an intermediate level which concerned the conduct of 'collective business actors'; for example, industry and trade associations and which we may take to include professional bodies and institutions which are considered later in this chapter.

The framework of analysis which follows attempts to examine the way and the extent to which these different levels interact with each other in terms of intersubjective understanding; processes and systems of control and ideological legitimation; and the formal and informal exercise of power and influence.

Environmental scanning – the causal texture model

Whilst on the one hand it is helpful for organization decision makers to identify those factors in the general and specific environments which are likely to impinge on its operations, it does not adequately explain the nature of the relationship.

Emery and Trist (1965) sought to explain the organization environmental relationship in terms of the linkages or connections (degrees of connectedness). Understanding the environment, they argue, depends upon understanding the linkages. These are:

1. Internal linkages, here one should consider both the relationship and degree of dependency between internal elements of the organizations. For example, between sales and production, managers and subordinates, etc.
2. External linkages – direct links in and out of the organization. For example, production and a supplier; sales and the customer; professional bodies and individual members of the organization, etc.
3. Causal texture concerns links outside the organization; they are interdependencies (linkages) out there in the environment that can affect the survival of the organization. For example, two suppliers agreeing on price fixing (see the case study later in this chapter). These linkages are less likely to be perceived by the organization and hence they contribute to the degree of environmental uncertainty.

The causal texture model can provide information about the power relationship and the degree of influence the organization may have over the various factors in the environment and vice versa.

Linking the organization to its ethical environment

Understanding the linkage between the organization and its ethical environment may have profound implications on the relationship. In what way and to what extent might the ethical stances of the environmental factors impact on the organization is an important consideration because it could determine the degrees of influence the one has over the other.

A model of an ethical environment – defining the rules of the game

It is true as it is trite to say that organizations are social phenomena, composed of individuals and groups who bear the hallmarks of both strengths and weaknesses of human kind. Similarly, organizations not only exist in a societal framework, which is made up of rules, but by courtesy of that framework who determine whether or not their behaviour, in the light of those rules, is acceptable. Organizations who lose the support of the society in which they operate are in danger of ceasing to exist – unless, of course, they take appropriate action.

It is not intended, neither is it possible, to construct a prescriptive environment. Geisler (1990), for example, points out that many theorists had attempted to describe the basis of right on which rules were defined by society and which are used to develop this discussion (see Fig. 4.4):

❑ Moral right is determined by the one holding power. There could be some connection here with the classical orthodoxy of Taylor, Gilbreth, etc. who postulated that what was good for the organization was good for the people who worked in it – no doubt mindful of the powerful position of the organization in relation to its employees. This opens up the debate of 'managerial prerogative' – the managers right to manage and the subordinates duty to obey – and the inherent values enshrined in the free market economic system (Hoffman and Moore, 1990). An emerging problem with this approach is that it fails to distinguish between *power* and *goodness*, whereupon the issues discrediting this approach arising from the activities of Maxwell, BCCI, Barings Bank, etc. and the *abuse* of power become self-evident.

❑ Morals are the customs of the ethnic. This largely centres around the customs of the community is made up of organizations and the society in which it serves. In other words, because various customs and practices exist then they are right. For example, 'bribes' and 'kickbacks' are not considered wrong in some societies. On the contrary, it is often recognized custom and practice in obtaining lucrative contracts. However, as Geisler (1990) points out this approach produces the

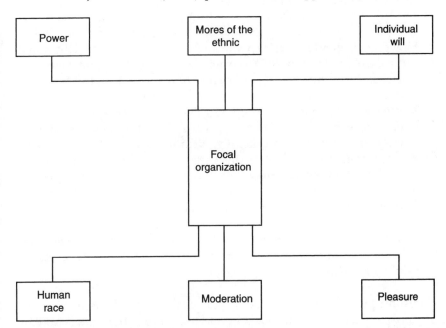

Figure 4.4 An example: a moral environment.

'is-ought' fallacy because 'it-is' cannot be taken to mean 'it-ought-to-be', otherwise groups of organizations, for example cartels, as part of the community could engage in practices detrimental to the society they serve and still be right in terms of their own interests, thereby, producing a situation where two opposites can be right. The problem here appears to be that this approach lacks a system for adjudicating behaviour in the community.

❏ Right is determined by a person's own will. To some extent this relates back to the approach of 'power is right' and bears the hallmarks of anarchy by failing to recognize that what is right for one individual or organization is wrong for another. Similarly, which aspect of human behaviour should be measured? There can be no *community* without *unity*. For example, consider products and services found to be undesirable and which do not comply with societal expectations – although there may be no rule of law to prevent their production.

❏ The human race is the basis of right. This approach seems to suggest that humankind is the measure of all things in that the 'whole' is right for the 'part'. There are hints of democracy in this suggestion in that the majority 'rules OK'. This raises the deep philosophical question as to whether humankind is competent anyway in determining 'right' from 'wrong'. What becomes problematic however, is that what is lacking is a standard 'outside' the human race as a measure of right and wrong. This is an important issue which the Christian and other religious ethics have sought to address.

❏ Moderation is the basis of right. This is often referred to the as the 'golden mean' – the mean between indulgence and insensibility. However, as Geisler (1990) points out in many cases the 'right' thing is the extreme thing to do. For example, wholesale redundancies as a consequence of 'downsizing' or 'right-sizing' might be in the beneficial interests of the organization as a whole. On the other hand a munificent employer should not be prevented from over indulging the workforce in favourable working conditions of employment. At best moderation can only be regarded as a general guide, not a universal ethical law.

❏ Pleasure is the basis of right. In this 'utilitarian' approach, good appears to be defined in terms of most pleasure and least pain – *ergo*, pain is wrong. What seems to have been ignored here is that evil intent is a feature of deviant activity on the part of the miscreant, which can also be defined as wrong. Conversely, warning 'pains' – short-term downturn in orders – can be good if it alerts the organization and the individual to take corrective action thereby, avoiding 'unnecessary pain' by invoking long-term redundancies.

Ethical levels of analysis

Confronted with an ethical situation in an environmental relationship the organization needs to focus the issue and provide a better understanding and rationale for dealing with it. Some examples are given in Table 4.1.

Table 4.1

The focus	The rationale
Identify and clearly describe the facts.	Determine who did what to whom, where, when and how.
Define the conflict.	Ethical, social and political issues concerning higher order values, e.g. freedom, privacy, protection of property rights etc.
Define the dilemma.	Conflict in the means ends relationship.
Identify the stakeholders.	Parties who have an interest in the outcome. Categorize them in terms of power and influence.
Identify options available.	May only be possible to find a 'best' rather than a 'good' ethical solution.
Identify the potential consequences of selected options.	Some options, whilst ethically correct, may only work in the 'short-term'.

The legal framework of an organized society provide rules which are designed to regulate and influence individual and organizational behaviour. There are for instance, those relating to corporate governance (the Cadbury Report), employment, consumer protection, equal opportunities, health and safety, etc. which led the Lord Chief Justice to suggest, in the 1960s, provided us with a 'protective society' in Britain.

Rules as defined by law – absolute or basis

For Friedman (1962) these laws were sufficient for regulating the organization's behaviour in a modern society. When considering the role of social responsibility – the manifestation of good actions – he suggested that there is one and only one social responsibility of business – to use its resources and engage in activities designed to increase its profits so long as it stays within the rules of the game, which is to say, engages in open and free competition without deception and fraud:

> ... few trends could so thoroughly undermine the very foundations of our free society as the acceptance by corporate officials of a social responsibility other than to make as much money for the stockholders as possible. (p. 38)

Others, for example McGuire (1963) and Backman (1975), suggest that the law should be used only as a 'baseline' on which to base *higher standards* of behaviour. A firm is not being socially responsible if it merely complies with the minimum requirements of the law, because that is what any good citizen would do. A profit maximizing firm under the rules of classical economics would do as much. Social responsibility goes one step further. It is a firm's acceptance of a social obligation beyond the requirements of the law.

And so the debate continues culminating in the arguments as to whether an organization should or should not concern itself with ethical issues are illustrated the examples given in Table 4.2.

Table 4.2

The arguments for	The arguments against
It is in the best interests of the organization to pursue ethical objectives	It mis-directs resources and violates sound business decisions that should concentrate on profits.
Organisations have the resources to do so	Costs are excessive relative to the benefits they generate which may bring about price increases
Society reasonably expects organizations to be socially responsible	Corporate management do not have either the resources or the skills to engage in socio-ethical projects
They may generate long-term profits for the organization	It may bring about a degeneration of the full enterprise system
If organizations are not responsive to societal ethical demands, society will press for Government legislation	The market will determine what is acceptable behaviour

Rules of behaviour

In contrasting the two arguments, we have sought to highlight the dilemma facing organizational decision makers as to what is considered permissible and non-permissible behaviour.

Definitions of permissible behaviour can often depend upon the individual or group involved. Schein (1987) suggests using the concept of *vulnerability* to help identify which of the parties should be considered before taking a particular action. If different parties are vulnerable to different courses of action, and in such circumstances it is important to know whose interests one must ultimately protect. Henderson (1982) refers to the *constituency priority* and uses the acronym PWISP – the Party Whose Interest iS Paramount as a means of addressing this dilemma. This would support the contention that the decision-making process, in organizations, is contextually dependent and a reflection of the prevailing distribution of power and political skill – as opposed to being an objective/rational process.

As to which rules one seeks to apply seems somewhat arbitrary. In the previous discussion on 'levels of analysis' the question was raised why and how a specific rule or law was enacted – in whose interests did it seek to represent – which mischief was it seeking to prevent?. Campbell and Connor (1986), in considering the impact of the Data Protection Act, argued that the actual content of the act was the *minimum* required to satisfy Britain's access to European business markets which might have been jeopardized if some form of legislation had not been forthcoming. They also argue that this might explain why the Act has so many flaws regarding safeguards of individual privacy. In the context of this discussion it might be for the organization to choose which rules will best provide a symbiotic relationship with its environment. It is a process of selection. What is fundamentally more complex is understanding the basis on which the rules are established and by whom.

What determines the rules of an ethical environment?

> In the arena of business, no rewards are on offer for effort. (Sir John Harvey-Jones)

Harvey-Jones' statement seems to reflect the conventional wisdom of a contemporary capitalist society whose tendency is to place more emphasis on positive quantitative results rather than the industry and endeavour which went into achieving them. Historically, the fusion of commercial and moral values is not so much a deviation from the 'right path' – as seen in the earlier parts of the century. On the contrary, many entrepreneurs who pioneered industrial production in the eighteenth century were driven by the religious belief that their earthly works would be rewarded in heaven. In the era of the 'manager's right to manage' and the employees 'duty to obey', the rules for ethical and moral responsibility became subsumed in the corporate hierarchical conscience.

On the other hand, organizations who take a more liberal/radical perspective on this issue take a somewhat different view:

> I pay most attention to those outcomes of behaviour which are not capable of quantification. (Chief executive ABB)

The debate centres around the means–ends relationship and the justification, in terms of the right of the one against the other. In ethical terms this is expressed in the deontological approach versus the teleological approach. As Vittell and Davis (1990) point out the fundamental difference between the two are 'specific actions or behaviours' of individuals and groups (deontological) whilst the teleological approach focuses on the 'consequences' of actions. For Hunt and Vittell (1986), the key issue in deontology is the inherent righteousness of a behaviour, whilst the key issue in teleology is the amount of good or harm resulting from the outcomes of those behaviours (see Table 4.3).

For example, an organization who, following a high-risk strategy, as the only possible course of action and in a last ditch attempt to save the business failed to secure the future of the business would, under the teleological approach be regarded as *not* good. The deontological approach, on the other hand, would regard this as a 'right' course of action; in other words righteous behaviour.

Table 4.3

Deontological approach	Teleological approach
Rules determine the result	Result determines the rules
Rule is the basis of the act	Result is the basis of the act
Rule is good regardless of the result	Rule is good because of the result
Results always calculated within the rules	Result sometimes used to break the rules

As with most, if not all theoretical models, individuals and organizations do not neatly fit into either the deontological or teleological approach. Instead individuals and organizations are faced with a mixed system of ethics being neither strictly one or the other.

Incorporating corporate ethics into organizational planning and control systems design – a professional ethical perspective

Whilst traditionalists might argue that business organizations' primary functions are to make profits, it has to be accepted that ethics and values are moving to the centre of the management debate (Drummond, 1994).

Recent privatization of public (not-for-profit) sector organizations has seen an increase in a demand for private (business) sector management techniques. For the newly privatized organization this poses a dilemma in that they are required to be selective in the 'techniques' which they adopt or reject. The new corporate values need to be articulated by the organization before they can be accepted by the individuals who are required to abide by them.

The Cadbury Report on Corporate Governance made the recommendation that companies should draw up a code of ethics to be communicated both internally and externally. In other words it should be incorporated into its systems of planning and control. It has been suggested by some commentators that this was one of the least noticed (and least acted on) parts of the report. However, the need would seem to be confirmed by the behaviour of Maxwell, Barlow Clowes, BCCI, Polly Peck and Lloyds.

The issue of ethics has become an important topic of concern for the information systems profession. In Fig. 4.1 we indicate that the cognitive style, expectations and aspiration of the systems designer is a central element of the ethical interpretative process. Later in the chapter we discuss the potential ethical conflicts that may arise between the systems designer as a 'professional' and the systems designer as a subordinate salaried member of the organization. From a 'traditional' perspective the issue appears to be quite clear. The personal ethical stance of the systems designer is acceptable as long as it is consistent, and subservient, to those of the organization as a whole. For the 'professional' systems designer the situation is less clear. Some balance or agreement has to be reached between the designer's personal ethical stance, those of his or her profession and those of the organization.

A range of potential areas of ethical debate have surfaced among information systems (IS) academics and professionals in recent years (Mason, 1985). This has included wide consideration of the social effects of computerization and information technology (Dunlop and Kling, 1991), consideration of the role of the systems designer in systems development and change (Spedding and Wood-Harper, 1993; Walsham, 1993) and the development of professional standards among the IS community (Anderson et al., 1993; British Computer Society, 1991).

So far, we have explored the general problem of incorporating ethical analysis into managerial systems modelling and the inclusion of a broader social perspective into organization–environment analysis. This section will, specifically, discuss the nature of the ethical dimension in relation to the operation and development of information and control systems in organizations. Control systems are the product of modelling the decision environment and thus their development, and use, can often be at the centre of ethical dilemmas experienced in organizational contexts. We will briefly explore the nature of these dilemmas and draw out implications for the process of systems development and the conduct of systems designers.

Information and control systems pose many potential ethical questions for a range of organizational actors. The model presented in Fig. 4.5 delineates the main dimensions of stakeholder relationships in any IS problem. These may be classified as those responsible for the operation and running of organizations (managers), those responsible for the creation of organizational systems (designers), recipients of systems information (users) and the objects of organizational activities (clients).

Within the model the interests of different participants' in IS is denoted as well as the nature of relationship with each other. Thus, for example, users' interests in systems mainly centre on their information needs and requirement or desire for decision support. Designers are concerned with the functionality of systems and achieving optimum fit with technical criteria that may be of little interest to users. These two requirements may not be, and often are not, mutually compatible in systems development. The relationship between designer and user is based on decisions and

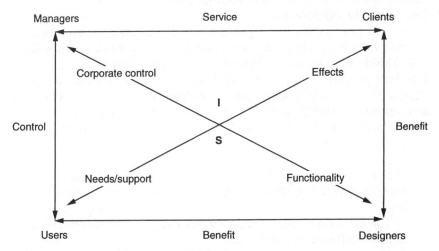

Figure 4.5 Stakeholder relationships in an ethical model of information systems design.

analysis of benefit which is generally the area of negotiation between them. Clearly, the extent to which the systems design process is seen to benefit the user or the designer will form an area of ethical discussion.

This model, thus, represents the major stakeholders in the systems problem and any analysis needs to find ways of depicting the relative merits of their position *vis-à-vis* systems design and operation.

There are difficulties with the construction of any model that seeks to delineate roles and responsibilities in the systems design and control process (as this does) due to the considerable, real and perceived, levels of overlap of activities. For example, managers will in many respects represent and, simultaneously, are major systems users. Similarly, designers can often be drawn as representatives from groups of potential users. A more challenging problem occurs where overlap exists between the effects of systems. A computerized system designed to effect customer service, such as a supermarket checkout facility, not only supports the operators' (user) activities but can also serve to monitor their speed and productivity serving managers interests in corporate control. This poses an interesting dilemma about the purpose, intentionality and use of systems which centres around the question of 'who benefits'?

Nonetheless, it is useful to construct some simple heuristic guide for the broad interpretation of the potential stakeholder map (see Fig. 4.5). This model can be used to understand some of the broad lines of potential difficulties which may be posed by systems in an ethical context. Some of the key areas of these relationships will be discussed here.

Clearly the emphasis and purpose of information needs and use may vary depending where effects and inputs are defined. IS in organizations represent someone's view of reality. The major ethical question in this respect is whose view of reality predominates and how is it represented. Designers, for example, may tend to see systems development as 'a good thing' and positive for the organization. This is not a view necessarily shared by other stakeholders, such as users or even organizational clients.

In this respect issues of control, power and legitimacy are at the forefront in determining the way that information systems are both designed and exploited. Here, power represents the ability of individuals or groups to impose their view of reality upon others, exemplified in the nature and inherent definitions of purpose incorporated into the design of systems features.

> 'When I use a word,' Humpty Dumpty said, in a rather scornful tone, 'it means just what I choose it to mean – neither more nor less.'
>
> 'The question is,' said Alice, 'whether you *can* make words mean so many different things.'
>
> 'The question is,' said Humpty Dumpty, 'which is to be master – that's all.' (Lewis Carroll, Through the Looking Glass, 1872)

Consequently, the ethical position of designers and their willingness to exploit their potential ability to exercise power over users constitutes a key focus of analysis.

There are many grounds for conflict between stakeholders in the systems design process which reflect issues of power between them. The emergence of such conflicts and the nature of their resolution represent items of possible ethical debate. These can be, initially, understood through the dimensions presented in the model. There are six main dimensions:

managers – users
users – designers
managers – designers
designers – clients
clients – managers
users – clients

Difficulties in relation to information systems arise here, mainly out of issues of control. This may be through command and reporting in a traditional hierarchical management structure or, in more complex organizational structures such as a professional bureaucracy (Mintzberg, 1979), through the control and monitoring of resource allocation. Clearly information systems feature heavily in the eyes of users as arenas for the exercise of managerial control over their actions. Not only is this perceived exercise of control through systems a stimulus for resistance and conflicts, it can raise possible ethical difficulties through the clash of values and beliefs that it sometimes produces. These can be seen to reflect conflicts between different sets of assumptions embodied through the various stakeholders.

An example will serve to illustrate this problem.

In the National Health Service the resource management initiative (Buxton *et al.*, 1989) has sought to increase and enhance control over apparently spiralling costs by marshalling improved knowledge about the costs of healthcare actions and interventions. The main route by which this has been achieved is through the creation of a general business management function supported by computerized information systems which allow access to detailed data about episodes of care and the associated expenditure. This has led to many conflicts with the professional clinical groups in hospitals who resent the visibility and control now exercised on their actions by 'unqualified' managers. The business managers are pursuing a goal of greater efficiency and effectiveness in response to an agenda set by a government concerned with the burden on the public purse and a desire of 'value for money'. Professional clinicians, for their part, see their traditional independence eroded and an interference in the previous sanctity of clinical judgement. Moreover, there is an implied fear that clinical decision making will be governed by the needs of the balance sheet rather than the needs of the patient (client).

IS becomes hostage to such ethical dilemmas here and, consequently, implementation often occurs in a highly charged political atmosphere. The conflict of value systems lies between attempts to impose rationally driven management models on human service and notions of client-centred clinical decision making. This can be seen as a clash of rules against rights. In a recent case in Cambridgeshire a child was refused treatment for a life-threatening disease on the grounds that the chances of success against the costs and unpleasantness of the necessary interventions were inequitable. It was interesting to note that in the ensuing public and media outcry concern seemed mainly to centre upon whether this had been a clinical decision or one taken by managers on cost grounds alone. This seems to reflect a fear that systems and decision rules are taking over from human and professional judgement.

The development and use of IS may disturb boundaries of control and lead to conflicts between managers and users. Such disturbance may threaten previously held assumptions about who is in control which reflect social value systems. If these have, themselves, been enshrined into core notions of the organizational mission (such as a hospital) then ethical dilemmas are likely to ensue. Clearly there is a conflict between the value systems of individual clinical decision makers, the business managers who represent a cultural change and the clients whose only concern is with their specific problem.

Any IS would have great difficulty in meeting and satisfying all of these aspirations. The systems designer is placed in a challenging, if unenviable, position in seeking to understand and represent this pinball machine of dilemmas and clashes between values. What, therefore, is the demand on the designer and how should they react?

One response may be to stand on the sidelines with the view that 'it is not our problem' and wait until the others have sorted out their difficulties and are able to bring clear statements of requirements. This ignores two key issues. Firstly, that designers represent a key interest group among stakeholders in any project and cannot thus separate themselves from the problem. Indeed that may be considered unethical. Secondly, there is abundant evidence that designers, themselves, seek to exercise power over users and managers through their professional control of the systems development process (Markus, 1981). Designers need to take into account and be aware of their effects on the systems equation and form views about the ethicality of how design is done.

**Towards ethical
systems design**

In many respects discussions of a more ethical mode of systems design are a return to some well established and long discussed problems in the IS discipline. These include arguments for more human-centred design (Mumford and Weir, 1979) and the notion that achieving wider levels of participation represents best practice in systems analysis and design (Bjorn-Andersen, 1980). Clearly, any design strategy that seeks to illuminate the social dimension within the problem centre of any systems intervention represents a move towards a more ethical stance. A range of methodological approaches, that can loosely be branded 'soft systems', have been developed and utilized to this effect (Checkland, 1981; Wilson, 1984).

Soft systems methodologies (SSM) have greater capacity to move towards a more ethical basis for analysis through their recognition of the pluralist nature of organizations. They are predicated on the assumption that there will be multiple and competing perspectives within any organization. This is in great contrast to the positivistic view associated with structured or 'hard' systems methodologies which adopt a unitarist position about organizations and cannot permit the existence of conflicting views, except as deviant to an accepted norm. From this perspective the analyst's assumption is that what benefits the organization must benefit all the people within it. Consequently it would be very difficult to even surface ethical difficulties or dilemmas. Wilcox and Mason (1987) offer a useful discussion of the relationship of methodological approaches to assumptions about the nature of organization. The use of SSM, therefore, increases the likelihood that analysts may act in a more ethically responsive and responsible manner.

It should be considered, however, that the analysis and expression of a range of value systems and potential conflicts does not *de facto* ensure ethical behaviour in design or development. Criticisms of these approaches centre on the suggestion that they elaborate a social perspective in their analysis but then abrogate any ethical responsibility for the value conflicts inherent in the situation described therein. The inference being that these are political choices to be taken by the actors within the organizational scenario under analysis. This would seem to make major assumptions about the values of the analyst and to ignore the base issue that those who wield greater levels of political power have greater capacity to influence outcomes. Clearly, the analyst in this situation may be more predisposed to those with whom power resides due to the pressure to deliver results. Indeed, SSM and participative approaches in general have been criticized because they do not address issues of power more explicitly and assertively (Coombs et al., 1992).

There is, at present, no clearly defined approach for ethical analysis. It is apparent that the desire is emerging and that the rudiments of such a schema already exist in a conjunction of themes and approaches drawn from organizational development, IS analysis and consulting theory. An ethical approach to information systems analysis and development has been proposed by Wood-Harper et al. (1995) employing a combination of SSM with the stakeholder approach (Mitroff and Linstone, 1993) discussed earlier in this chapter. This includes the construction of an ethical conflict web which is then analysed to identify the significant conflicts. It is proposed that conflict resolution techniques are used to achieve the 'good' in the system. The authors discuss the application of this model to a worked real-world example. Essentially, this approach is an attempt to go beyond the existing descriptive confines of established SSM practice to develop an understanding of why concerns exists and what the value basis of them is.

Whatever framework for systems analysis is developed the responsibility for its execution in an ethical manner rests with the analyst. Modelling ethical dilemmas through stakeholder analysis presents an important first step in surfacing assumptions about value systems. Ultimately, an increased level of self-reflection and a willingness to challenge personal assumptions and belief systems (Schon, 1983) will foster the conditions for ethical analysis to be translated into ethical action. The nub of the question may remain whether existing structures of power and legitimation in organizations will allow that translation to occur.

Structural dimensions of an organizations ethical system – are ethical rules sufficient?

Organizations might point to their 'code(s) of ethics' as evidence of their 'corporate righteousness'. There is an argument that rules (codes) are an important element of control. However, simply having a set of rules does not guarantee that they will be observed by the individuals on whom they are imposed – hence the question 'are ethical rules sufficient'.

Arguments in favour

There is nothing original or novel in the Cadbury recommendations that organizations should construct ethical codes. On the contrary, several writers have argued in favour of the establishment of a code of ethics. Donaldson (1989) suggested that they would act as guides to individual and group behaviour through rules and procedures. For Maitland (1988), the presence of a code of ethics would relieve managers of making subjective judgements concerning the organization's obligations to various stakeholder groups. There is almost a suggestion from Bowie and Beauchamp (1988) that the code might also act as a form of insulation against the need for government regulation. A view supported by Kitner and Green (1978) who argue that codes are an essential ingredient for democratic freedom in that they serve to reduce the need for government intervention which would undermine individual initiative and the free enterprise system. He goes on to observe that having a written code can provide more stability to this aspect of the organization's environment by providing a permanent guide to 'right' and 'wrong' behaviour than could be achieved if left to individual initiative and discretion. Similarly, codes can function as a check on the possible misuse of their power by owners and managers on employees and also act as an independent basis for appeal.

Codes can also serve as a system of communication, not only in establishing the ethical climate within the organization, but as a device for communicating the ethical stance to external stakeholder groups. Molander (1987) takes the argument one stage further with the observation that arguments in favour of codes can be divided into two categories:

(a) those arising from interests external to the business system which tend to concentrate on the weaknesses of the market system and the inadequacy of the law as a means of control, and
(b) those emanating from the parties (environmental factors) within the business system which points to the role of ethical codes in relieving ethical dilemmas for individuals; helping to reduce the incidence of unethical behaviour; and helping to restore public confidence in the business community.

Arguments against codes

There is an argument that if organizations operate in a highly structured manner then individuals will come to rely heavily on the rules and procedures which supports that organizational form. Molander (1987) is more assertive when he notes that expressed codes have so many limitations as to make them almost ineffective in terms of eliminating unethical practices and relieving ethical dilemmas.

Where the organization is driven by ethical rules and procedures there is, *ipso facto*, a constraint placed upon individual initiative and discretion. Therefore, there might be a temptation, on the part of the individual, to believe that anything not covered in the rules is acceptable behaviour.

Stone (1975) further argues that ethical codes can be counterproductive to the extent that they impede the flow of information to top management, particularly information about unethical acts which could seriously harm the organization and the public if it is not acted upon immediately. A criticism of many highly structured systems operating in a dynamic environment.

Similarly, as was suggested earlier, it is doubtful that the adoption of ethical codes alone can assure ethical behaviour. On the contrary, their effect on personal motivation, initiative and discretion should not be ignored. Furthermore, too much attention to codes as ethical rules may divert attention away from the more important activity of raising questions about the underlying moral structure of a decision:

> Managers need more than codes of ethics; they need to ask themselves a few questions to make sure every decision is ethical.
> (Hyman *et al.*, 1990, p. 15)

Finally, there is the spectre of using ethical codes, at the industry level, constructed in such a way as to contravene monopolies and mergers legislation by creating 'barriers to entry' and free competition.

Ethical codes and the corporate conscience

Process re-engineering, for example, has seen layers of the organizational hierarchy removed, organization structures have been redefined, particularly at the middle-management level. The concept of 'empowerment' has been introduced – by which each person is his or her own manager – into the business vocabulary to replace these levels in the organization. The effect in terms of ethical and moral values on the individual is potentially profound. The traditional 'corporate conscience' is being replaced by the 'individual conscience' where individual initiative and discretion plays an active part in organizational activities. The underlying assumption here is that the individual knows what is legitimate corporate ethical and moral behaviour. Individual initiative and discretion does have an important part to play, particularly in a highly dynamic, competitive environment. However, as Drummond (1994) injects a note of caution on the issue of individual discretion:

> ... initiative is all very well ... but unless it is constrained by a knowledge of what is and what isn't legitimate behaviour, it can lead to people trading in what isn't theirs to trade – company reputation.

Competitive information acquisition

In Fig. 4.3, we identified competitors as being a factor in the organization environmental relationship and can influence organizational performance and effectiveness. The current dynamics of the environment have forced many organizations to accelerate their efforts to acquire competitive intelligence (Beltramini, 1986).

Like ethics and morals, information and power become inextricably linked. Communication theorists have pointed out that it is not the acquisition of relevant information, *per se*, that provides the ability to influence behaviour, it is a case of what organizations *do* with it when it comes into their possession.

With increasingly more sophisticated information gathering techniques becoming more readily available, organizations are going to greater lengths to maintain the proprietary nature of any information they develop or acquire. Evidence of this can be found in the recent allegations between Virgin and British Airways. Corporate information espionage is not a new phenomenon, it has probably been in existence for years. What is new is the high level of sophistication and endeavour which has developed within organizations. Beltramini (1986) suggests that

> ... competitive pressures seem to have brought out the worst in businesses as questionable techniques sometimes merged into standard operating procedures.

In other words, it becomes embedded in the corporate conscience as to what is ethically and morally right and legitimizes the behaviour.

The competitive environment has introduced new pressures for information managers in that they 'compete' to develop more ingenious sources before their competitors think of them, and to become more adept at creating new techniques.

The implications of this, again, are profound. If such behaviour is legitimized – either formally or as is more likely informally – then these individuals are again trading with one of the organizations most valuable corporate assets – *the company reputation.*

Information rights concern those rights which individuals and organizations have with respect to information that pertains to themselves.

The ethical concerns that confront individuals in organizations can fall under the following categories.

Moral dimensions and information rights of the individual

1. Privacy: the extent to which personal information collected is used and protected.
2. Integrity: the allocation of responsibility for data integrity and the controls which ensure that integrity.
3. Influence: the extent to which it reduces individual discretion in decision making; the automation of processes in decision making and the results in relation to individual safety and well-being.
4. Impact: the extent to which the IS affects individual up- and down-skilling of work. Also, the possible effects on the workforce due to surveillance, monitoring and measurement of performance.

Table 4.4 seeks to address these issues that encompass situations in the work environment:

Table 4.4

The focus	The rationale
Information rights and obligations.	What rights do individuals and organizations possess with respect to information about themselves? What can they protect? What obligations exist on the parties?
Property rights.	How will they be protected where tracing and accounting for ownership is difficult and ignoring the rights so easy?
Accountability and control.	Who can/will be held accountable and liable for the harm done to individual and collective information and property rights?
System quality.	What standards of data and system quality should be demanded to protect individual rights and the safety of society?
Quality of life.	What values should be preserved in an information- and knowledge-based society? What cultural values and practices are supported by the new information technology?

Clearly, this has implications not only for the management–subordinate relationship but raises ethical concerns that confront information systems designers and professionals.

The individual as a professional – setting the ethical tone

As we discussed earlier, the issue of ethics has become an important topic of concern for the IS profession. These concerns centre around the social implications of computerization and information technology and the role of particular individuals and groups involved in systems design, development and change.

Individuals and groups who take on special rights and obligations which go above and beyond the rule of natural law, by inference, enter into an oblique relationship with employers, customers and society as a whole. They do so on the basis of special claims to knowledge, wisdom and respect. Professional codes of ethics are promises by the profession to regulate themselves in the beneficial interests of society; in return for which they seek to enhance their pay and the respect given their profession.

These professional codes of conduct are rules promulgated by institutes and associations such as Chartered Institute of Secretaries and Administrators, British Medical Association, British Computer Society and so on which take responsibility for the partial regulation of their professions by determining entrance qualifications and competence and behaviour. Most professional bodies enact these regulations through ethics sub-committees, where from time to time their members can appeal for guidance in cases where, for example, they have been compromised by their employers or brought to account when they have broken the ethical code.

Whilst ethical codes will differ in detail between the professions they might include such general moral imperatives as:

❏ contribute to the well being of society
❏ avoid harming others
❏ be honest and trustworthy
❏ respect property rights including copyrights and patents
❏ give proper recognition for intellectual property
❏ access computing resources only when duly authorized
❏ respect the privacy of others.

Desirable/undesirable ethical outcomes – some examples

In the early parts of this chapter we suggested that the organization's observation, perception and understanding of the ethical environment was an important issue. Many organizations have learned to their cost that unethical behaviour impacts upon their performance and effectiveness. Individual personal ethical tensions arising from decision makers as managers and individuals as professionals is often a key issue – unethical behaviour is often a consequence of the ethical dilemmas will be seen from the following examples.

The way and the extent that professional bodies influence the behaviour of its members, in an organizational context is difficult to gauge. Similarly, the extent the individual member can rely upon the professional body for assistance and support, when compromised by their employers or customers, is difficult to measure – the debate seems to centre around determining why people behave the way they do. Werhane (1991, pp. 605–16) summarizes the debate succinctly in her analysis of the behaviour of engineers and managers involved in the *Challenger* disaster:

> How do decent people, people who work for reputable companies engaged in worthwhile projects, people who follow their expertise and their consciences, behave questionably in certain circumstances or produce harmful consequences?

It seems that there were four difficulties associated with this event:

1. Differing perceptions and priorities of the engineers and management of the component suppliers (Thiokol), those of the parent company and the customer (NASA).
2. A preoccupation with roles and role responsibilities on the part of engineers and managers.
3. Contrasting corporate cultures between the supplier organization and its parent company.
4. Failure by both engineers and managers to exercise individual moral responsibility.

The fateful decision appears to have been brought about when the senior engineer, who initially refused to 'sign off' the components as safe, reversed his decision when his line manager (mindful of pressures which had been brought to bear by the customer who were anxious to proceed with the launch of the *Challenger* project) remarked:

> ... take off [your] engineering hat and put on [your] management hat.

What emerges from this is that individuals have different paradigms when faced with difficult situations. Consequently, conflicting priorities of the 'actors' come into play which adds to the problem when decision makers fail to take personal responsibility.

Most research has shown that the ethical tone of a business is set by its management, especially top management. However, as the Vitell *et al.* study found when looking at the role of management information systems (MIS) professionals, there are many opportunities for unethical behaviour. They believe that MIS managers are unlikely to engage in unethical behaviour. They also found that success and ethical behaviour are consistent concepts, and successful managers are perceived as more ethical than unsuccessful ones by the majority of MIS professionals.

The implications of the Vitell study is that unethical practices may be reduced by having codes of ethics and by a top management position that supports ethical behaviour and punishes unethical behaviour.

The van Kirk study (1993) of United Parcel Service in the USA looked at the extent to which companies set out clear policies that inform employees that communications, within their organization, may be monitored. The researchers found that this presented IS managers with an ethical dilemma and the need to balance privacy rights and risks. Although few IS managers want to be in the surveillance business, they are often caught in the conflict between managers charged with safeguarding company assets and users unaware that their electronic mail, hard-disk files and network activities are matters of corporate record. In a recent study, 21.6% of businesses surveyed reported searching employee files, and in nearly half of those organizations, IS managers were granted the authority to do so. Organizations should set up clear policies that inform employees that communications may be monitored and establish procedures for the monitoring process. Many larger organizations are simply ignoring the issue, and smaller firms either conduct no monitoring at all or engage in arbitrary snooping that may be harassing or even illegal.

A US study found that professionals in the information technology field have no single, agreed code of conduct. The codes of behaviour were analysed with regard to the obligations the professional has to society, the employer, to clients, to colleagues, to the professional organization and to the profession. In fact there were four professional organizations promoting four different codes of conduct. A dilemma would appear for an individual who was a member of more than one of the professional bodies.

Conclusion

The nature of a contemporary dynamic environment is characterized by complexity and uncertainty. Sociocultural expectations and behaviours exhibit similar characteristics. Organizations operate in societal framework and exist by courtesy of that framework. The ethical environment is an important component of this framework. We have sought to present a framework of analysis which could be employed in coming to terms with a complex and uncertain environment and which examines some of the ethical issues which exist impinge on both the internal and external elements of the organizational environment. In addition to demonstrating the organization/environment relationship, we have sought to demonstrate how the ethical environment might be interpreted with the use of a systemic model. This interpretation then needs to be translated into a systems design which, cognisant not only of many ethical issues and influences but upon how they will be interpreted and impact on those individuals to whom they apply. The individual, as a 'professional' could be faced with ethical tensions between the organization and the professional body. Ethical codes are a central part of the ethical system, but in themselves they are insufficient. They must be supported by other systems which underpin their operation. Ethical systems – as systems of control – need to be carefully thought out, articulated and understood can otherwise they could produce a strange paradox by which they create a situation they were designed to avoid.

Case study

> **"The Price Fixers" – Causal Texture Example**
>
> A High Street retailer was in negotiation with three of their major suppliers over the annual price review. Unknown to the retailer, the suppliers had met privately as a group and agreed that they should 'stand together' and insist on a 5% increase in prices. The retailer was adamant with the three suppliers that there could be no price rises this year due to the 'downturn' in sales caused by the recession. The suppliers, in turn, were then asked to go away, reconsider their position and return the following afternoon with their decision. Once again the 'three' met in secret and agreed that they would individually hold out for a 2% increase at the meeting the following day. Later that evening, one of the three suppliers, without informing the other two, contacted the retailer and informed them of what the group had agreed in private. Furthermore, the supplier proposed that they would accept a price freeze provided that they were given the combined business of the other two!

Exercises

❑ Using the causal texture model, analyse the situation of the 'price fixers'.
❑ Under which code of ethical behaviour would you seek to justify the behaviour of the 'renegade' supplier?
❑ In what way and to what extent do you consider that a professional code of conduct and standards of behaviour might inhibit the autonomy and flexibility of the professional salaried systems designer?
❑ Critically evaluate the contention that systems designers whose information systems are used to monitor individual performance and behaviour are acting unprofessionally.

Further reading

Dejoie, R., Fowler, G. and Paradice, D. (1991) *Ethical Issues in Information Systems*. Boyd & Fraser. This book focuses on the impact of computer technology on ethical decision making in today's business organizations. It features 25 articles discussing current ethical dilemmas in computing, all by authorities in the fields of computing, education and ethics. Twenty ethical scenarios describing situations in which difficult ethical decisions are required.

Winkler, E.R. and Coombs, J.R. (1993) *Applied Ethics – A Reader*. Blackwell. This volume offers a collection of articles in applied ethics, representing both European and Anglo-American philosophical traditions The essays are concerned with questions about the nature of applied ethics, and with related methodological issues. Taken as a whole, the book advances our understanding of the possibilities and limitations of moral philosophy, and reveals new directions in the exploration of what it means to be rational in moral practice.

Mason, R.O., Mason, F.M. and Culnan, M. (1995) *Ethics of Information Management*. Sage. This book provides ways of thinking about information and the new responsibilities engendered by its acquisition, processing, storing, dissemination and use. It offers a set of concepts, methods arguments and illustrations designed to sharpen the reader's ethical focus.

References

Ackoff, R.L. and Emery, F.E. (1972) *On Purposeful Systems*. Tavistock.

Adams, J.S. (1975) The environmental context of negotiations between human systems. Paper read at the Negotiation Conference, 8 July 1975, Center for Creative Leadership, Greensboro, NC.

Anderson, R.E. *et al.* (1993) Using the new ACM code of ethics in decision making. *Communications of the ACM*, 36(2), 98–107.

Backman, J. (1975) *Social Responsibility and Accountability*. New York University Press, New York.

Beltramini, R.F. (1986) Ethics and the use of competitive information acquisition. *Journal of Business Ethics*, 6, 307–11.

Bjorn-Andersen, N. (1980) *The Human Side of Information Processing*. North-Holland.

Bowie, N.E. and Beauchamp, T.L. (1988) *Ethical Theory in Business*, 3rd edn. Prentice-Hall.

British Computer Society (1991) The British Computer Society Code of Conduct, in *Professional Issues in Software Engineering* (eds F. Bott *et al.*). Pitman.

Buxton, M., Packwood, T. and Keen, J. (1989) *Resource Management: Process and Progress*. Brunel University, Uxbridge.

Campbell, D. and Connor S. (1986) *On the Record – Surveillance, Computers and Privacy – The Inside Story*. Michael Joseph, London.

Checkland, P.B. (1981) *Systems Thinking, Systems Practice*. John Wiley.

Coombs, R., Knights, D. and Wilmott, H. (1992) Culture, control and competition: towards a framework for the analysis of information technologies in organizational settings. *Organizational Studies*, 13(1).

De George, T.T. (1987) The status of business ethics. *Journal of Business Ethics*, 8, 201–211.

Donaldson, T. (1989) *The Ethics of International Business*. Oxford University Press.

Drummond, J. and Bain, B. (eds) (1994) *Managing Business Ethics*. Butterworth-Heineman, Oxford.

Dunlop, C. and Kling, R. (1991) *Computerization and Controversy*. Academic Press, Boston, MA.

Emery, F.E. and Trist, E.L. (1965) The causal texture of organisational environments. *Human Relations*, 18, 21–32.

Epstein, E.M. (1989) Business ethics, corporate good citizenship and the corporate social policy process: a view from the United States. *Journal of Business Ethics*, 8, 583–95.

Friedman, M. (1962) *Capitalism and Freedom*. University of Chicago Press, Chicago, IL, p. 133.

Geisler, N.L. (1990) *Christian Ethics, Options and Issues*. Apollos, Leicester, pp. 17–26.

Henderson, V.E. (1982) The ethical side of enterprise. *Sloan Management Review*, 23, 37–47.

Hoffman, C.W. and Moore, J. (1990) *Business Ethics*, 2nd edn. McGraw-Hill.

Hunt Shelby, D. and Vitell, S. (1986) A general theory of marketing ethics. *Journal of Macromarketing*, Spring, 5–16.

Hyman, M.R., Skipper, R. and Tansely, R. (1990) Ethical codes are not enough. *Business Horizons*, pp. 15–22.

Kinter, E. and Green, R. (1978) Opportunities for self-enforcement of codes of conduct: a consideration of legal limitations, in *Ethics Free Enterprise and Public Policy* (eds R. De George and J Pilcher). Oxford University Press.

Maitland, I. (1988) The limits of self regulation. *California Management Review*, 27.

Mason, R.O. (1985) Four ethical issues of the information age. *MIS Quarterly*, 5–12.

McGuire, J.W. (1963) *Business and Society*. McGraw-Hill, New York.

Mintzberg, H. (1979) *The Structuring of Organizations*. Prentice-Hall.

Mitroff, I. and Linstone, H.A. (1993) *The Unbounded Mind*. Oxford University Press.

Molander, E.A. (1987) A paradigm for design, promulgation and enforcement of ethical codes. *Journal of Business Ethics*, 6, 619–31.

Mumford, E. and Weir, M. (1979) *Computer Systems in Work Design – The ETHICS Method*. Associated Business Press.

Schein, E.H. (1987) *The Clinical Perspective in Fieldwork*. Sage.

Schon, D.A. (1983) *The Reflective Practitioner*. Basic Books, New York.

Spedding, P. and Wood-Harper, T. (1993) Why are ethical considerations important in systems design?, in *Proceedings of the 16th Scandinavian Information Systems Research Seminar*, Copenhagen.

Stone, C.D. (1975) *Where the Law Ends: The Social Control of Corporate Behaviour*. Harper & Row.

van Kirk, D. (1993) IS managers balance privacy rights and risks. *InfWorld*, 15, 65.

Vitell, S.J. and Davis, D.L. (1990) Ethical beliefs of MIS professionals: the frequency and opportunity for unethical behaviour. *Journal of Business Ethics*, 63–70 (1990).

Walsham, G. (1993) Ethical issues in information systems development: the anayst as moral agent, in *Human, Organizational and Social Dimensions of Information Systems Development* (ed. D. Avison *et al.*). North-Holland, Amsterdam.

Werhane, P.H. (1991) Engineers and management: the challenge of the challenger incident. *Journal of Business Ethics*, 10, 605–616.

Wilcocks, L. and Mason, D. (1987) *Computerising Work: People, Systems Design and Workplace Relations*. Paradigm.

Wilson, B. (1984) *Systems: Concepts, Methodologies and Applications*. John Wiley.

Wood-Harper *et al.* (1995) How we profess: the ethical systems analyst. In press.

5 Ethics in marketing

Colin Gilligan

As the part of the organization that is most directly concerned with managing the exchange process and the external profile of the organization, marketing is in a uniquely vulnerable position in any discussion of business ethics. Within this chapter, I therefore focus on the three most significant elements of the marketing and ethics debate, including:

❑ the extent to which ethical issues should be taken into account in the development and, perhaps more importantly, the implementation of a proactive marketing stance
❑ the ethics of market intelligence and the approaches used in its collection and
❑ the ways in which ethical considerations should or might be taken into account in the development and management of the marketing mix.

The criticisms of marketing

Throughout the post-war period, marketing has been subjected to a wide series of criticisms, some of the most common of which are that:

❑ marketing has led to an overly materialistic society and too frequently places emphasis on individual satisfaction at the expense of the overall social good
❑ too many (unnecessary) products are offered
❑ products are often unsafe and of poor quality
❑ it creates an interest in products that pollute the environment
❑ the easy availability of consumer credit makes people buy things they neither need nor can afford
❑ 'middlemen' add unnecessary costs of distribution without adding value
❑ packaging and labelling are too often confusing and deceptive
❑ advertising is too frequently annoying, misleading and wasteful and
❑ marketing exploits the poor.

Although it is undoubtedly possible to find examples that illustrate each of these points to at least some extent, the development of the fabric of consumer protection laws over the past decade has helped to overcome many of the more extreme abuses [see, for example, the Trade Descriptions Act (1968), the Consumer Credit Act (1974), the Sale of Goods Act

(1979) and the Unfair Contract Terms Act (1977)]. At the same time, thinking on the nature and role of marketing has changed greatly, with definitions of marketing having developed to reflect the broader social responsibilities of business. In commenting on this, Kotler (1991, p. 25) has suggested:

> In recent years, some people have questioned whether the marketing concept is an appropriate organisational philosophy in an age of environmental deterioration, resource shortages, explosive population growth, world hunger, and poverty, and neglected social services. The question is whether companies that do an excellent job of sensing, serving, and satisfying individual consumer wants are *necessarily* (my emphasis) acting in the best long-run interests of consumers and society.

Because of a series of shifts in values throughout society, Kotler (1991, pp. 26–7) suggests that the answer to this may well be that marketing as it was traditionally defined and practised is no longer appropriate and that a new definition and interpretation is needed:

> [This] called for a new concept that revised or replaced the marketing concept. Among the proposals are 'the human concept', 'the intelligent consumption concept,' and 'the ecological imperative concept', all of which get at different aspects of the same problem. We propose calling it 'the societal marketing concept.
>
> The societal marketing concept holds that the organisation's task is to determine the needs, wants, and interests of target markets and to deliver the desired satisfactions more effectively and efficiently than competitors in a way that preserves or enhances the consumer's and the society's well-being.

He goes on to suggest that:

> The societal marketing concept calls upon marketers to balance three considerations in setting their marketing policies, namely, *company profits, consumer want satisfaction*, and *public interest*. Originally, companies based their marketing decisions largely on immediate company profit calculations. Then they began to recognise the long-run importance of satisfying consumer wants, and this introduced the marketing concept. Now they are beginning to factor in society's interests in their decision making. The societal marketing concept calls for balancing all three considerations.

But although the societal marketing concept may well have an inherent logic and attraction, being socially responsible can often involve a series of potentially significant and difficult trade-offs, particularly in the short term. In the case of chlorofluorocarbons (CFCs), for example, McCarthy and Perreault (1994, p. 32) suggest that although we now have a far greater understanding of the effects that they have on the environment and the ozone layer, it is not simply a matter of stopping the production of the chemicals, since they are used in several hundreds of products, including refrigerators, air-conditioning systems, fire extinguishers, insulation systems, and electronic circuitry, for which there is currently either no real alternative or one that can be justified on short-term commercial grounds.

By the same token, it is possible to identify a wide variety of other products such as alcoholic drinks, cigarettes, processed foods and soft drinks for which there is now an overwhelming body of evidence to suggest that they harm us in one way or another. Equally, bicycles have been identified by the US Consumer Product Safety Commission as one of the most dangerous products on the market. Given this evidence, the obvious question is whether behaviour that is ethical in an *absolute* sense should be brought into play since if this was to be done, production of these, and indeed numerous other products, would presumably stop. In practice, of course, few would argue for such an extreme step and the question that marketing strategists are therefore concerned with is the far more complex and subtle issue of where the dividing line of acceptability should be drawn. In discussing this, Berkowitz *et al.* (1994, p. 24), pose a question:

> Suppose you buy your fast-food hamburger in a styrofoam warming box and put the box in the restaurant's trash can when you are finished. Is this just a transaction between you and the restaurant? Not quite. Thrown in a dump, the styrofoam hamburger box probably won't degrade for centuries, so society will bear a portion of the cost of your hamburger purchase.

Given this, and indeed numerous other examples, what ethical considerations should consumers take account of when making a purchase?

The nature of marketing ethics

In attempting to come to terms with the nature, significance and implications of ethics in marketing, a useful starting point is the distinction between the legal and ethical nature of marketing decisions and behaviour: a framework for this appears in Fig. 5.1.

The basis of this matrix is straightforward: ethics are concerned with a set of moral principles and values that act as a guide to an individual's conduct, whilst laws represent a society's set of values and standards which are enforceable by the courts. Recognizing this, it seems possible to categorize decisions on the basis of these two dimensions. Quite obviously, the ideal cell in which to operate is cell 4, since the actions here are both legal and ethical.

Equally, cell 1 presents few problems in that the decisions are both illegal and unethical and should therefore be avoided. Problems arise when a decision falls into either cell 2 or cell 3, since in both cases they

	Unethical behaviour	Ethical behaviour
Illegal behaviour	Illegal and unethical decisions and behaviour 1	Illegal but ethical decisions and behaviour 3
Legal behaviour	Legal but unethical decisions and behaviour 2	Legal and ethical decisions and behaviour 4

Figure 5.1 The ethical and legal dimensions of marketing decisions and behaviour. Adapted from Henderson (1982, pp. 37–47).

involve trade-offs between either the legality or the ethicality of the action. For marketing managers, the complexity of this is often increased when operating across market boundaries, since what may be illegal or unethical in the manager's home country may well be legal and/or ethical in another (this is discussed in greater detail in a later chapter in which we focus on ethical issues in an international context). An obvious example of this is the question of payments (i.e. bribes) as inducements to gain business. Whilst in most western nations this is deemed illegal (indeed the United States has passed legislation to prevent this), in many middle eastern and African countries these payments are often standard business practice. The question that therefore needs to be considered is whether a company should behave in line with local expectations and customs by bribing officials in order to secure a contact, or whether it should adhere to home country values. For many managers, of course, the answer may well be determined for them, since levels of competition and local expectations offer little real alternative.

In a broader sense, however, the reconciliation of profit motives and ethical imperatives, be it in a domestic or an international forum, is as Nash (1990, p. 11) has suggested, 'an uncertain and highly tricky matter'. In making this comment, he suggests that there are four systemic factors which constitute to unethical behaviour:

1. The inarguable importance of the bottom line.
2. An overemphasis on short-term efficiency or expediency.
3. The seductive power of ego incentives.
4. The difficulties of personally representing the corporate policy (wearing two hats) (1990, p. 121).

This issue has also been touched upon by Zey-Ferrell *et al.* (1979, p. 568) who have suggested that in the case of marketing managers:

their perceptions of what their peers do and their own opportunity to engage in unethical behaviour that involved others had greater influences on their own unethical behaviour than did either their own beliefs or what they thought management believed. Thus the model for unethical behaviour consists of differential association and opportunity.

This contextualist approach to ethical behaviour has, in turn, been touched on by Jackall (1988, p. 4):

> By occupational ethics, I mean the moral rules-in-use that managers construct to guide their behaviour at work, whether these are shaped directly by authority relationships or by other kinds of experiences typical in big organisations. Given this, and the contemporary pressures confronting marketing personnel in the modern market place; increased competitiveness; the increasing technological complexity of both products and services; and the compression of time through the increasing using use of information technology by marketing personnel, it is not surprising that at times they are confronted by self-doubt and uncertainty regarding what the 'correct' or 'proper' course of action should be.

Reflecting the approach adopted by the book therefore, it is a contextualist approach which is advocated here to determining the ethicality, or otherwise, of any act.

The development of a competitive stance: the ethical conflict

A key element of any marketing strategy involves the development of a clear, meaningful and sustainable competitive stance that is capable of providing the organization with an edge over its competitors. In doing this, organizations have responded in a variety of ways ranging from at the one extreme a series of actions that are both legally and ethically questionable through to at the other extreme an approach that discourages or prohibits doing business with particular customer groups. In the case of the Co-operative Bank, for example, their highly publicized competitive stance has been based on an ethical platform which led the bank to stop dealing with customers deemed to be involved in 'unethical' activities. This policy, which was formulated in 1992, led in the first year to the bank severing its ties with 12 corporate customers, including two fox-hunting associations, a peat miner, a company that tests its products on animals, and a number of others where it took the view that the customer was causing unreasonable environmental damage. The bank has also taken a stand against factory farming.

An ethical dimension was also at the heart of a strategy developed by British Alcan in 1989 to recycle used beverage cans. With the industry suffering in the late 1980s from problems of overcapacity, the price of aluminium on the world markets had dropped significantly and Alcan, in common with other aluminium producers, began searching for ways in which costs might be reduced. The aluminium recycling process offers a number of advantages, since not only are the capital costs of investing in a recycling operation as little as one-tenth of investing in primary capacity, but recycled aluminium also requires only one-twentieth of the energy costs. An additional benefit is that, unlike steel recycling, the recovery process does not lead to a deterioration in the metal. At the same time, however, the company was acutely aware of a series of environmental pressures and concerns and, in particular, the greater emphasis that was being given both by governments and society at large to the issue of finite world resources and to the question of recycling.

Faced with this, Alcan developed a highly proactive stance which involved the development of an infrastructure that was capable of collecting and recycling aluminium beverage cans. The success of the campaign was subsequently reflected by the way in which between 1989 and 1994 the UK's recycling rate of aluminium cans, largely as the result of the Alcan initiative increased from less than 2% to more than 30%. [Editors' note: Alcan's development of their can recycling operation is discussed in detail in a case study by Colin Gilligan which appears in Jobber, *Principles and Practice of Marketing*, 1995.]

An overtly ethical stance has also been pursued by Allied Dunbar and Grand Metropolitan, both of which have become heavily involved in community programmes. In the case of Grand Metropolitan, for example, this has been through the Grand Metropolitan Trust which provides training and sponsorship, as well as financial donations which are channelled to various charitable bodies concerned with employment.

However, for many other organizations the implications of an increasingly demanding and apparently competitively malevolent environment has led to the search for a competitive stance and a competitive edge almost irrespective of the cost. In doing this, the problem that can then be faced concerns the stage at which the need for managers to deliver seemingly ever higher levels of performance leads to actions which subsequently are deemed to be unacceptable, something which the senior management of British Airways (BA) was faced with in the early 1990s.

At the beginning of the 1990s BA was heavily criticized for its supposed 'dirty tricks' campaign against its far smaller competitor, Virgin Atlantic. Virgin, which had been set up by Richard Branson several years previously, had achieved a number of publicity coups, including no-frills, low-cost flights to the United States and then, spectacularly and under the gaze of the world's media, at the outbreak of hostilities between the western world and Iraq, flying out of Baghdad a planeload of British hostages.

Perhaps because of Virgin's small size (it had just eight planes compared with BA's 250) and Richard Branson's apparently relaxed management style, BA had seemingly underestimated the company and the threat that it was capable of posing. However, these became apparent when, in 1991, the Civil Aviation Authority recommended that Heathrow Airport be opened up to a larger number of airlines than had previously been the case. For Virgin, which had been flying from Gatwick, the implications were significant and led Branson to suggest not only that he would be able to cut his already low prices by 15%, but that by 1995 he hoped to capture 30% of the transatlantic market.

Faced with this challenge, BA went on to the offensive with a strategy that involved their helpline team gathering intelligence on Virgin, pursuing a highly proactive public relations campaign which highlighted Virgin's apparent failings, targeting specific routes and, according to Gregory (1994a) obtaining information on Virgin 'by extracting it from BA's own computer reservation system, known as BABS, which it shares with other airlines'. This information was seemingly then used for several purposes including switch-selling whereby passengers already booked on to a Virgin's flight would be approached and encouraged to switch to BA. The ethical significance of using the reservation system in this way was highlighted by Gregory (1994a, p. 10):

> The confidentiality of the information in that system is vital – so much so that it was enshrined in commitments the company had given to the House of Commons transport committee when the system was set up. As it set about using BABS to capture data about Virgin, BA knew that it was straying into the twilight zone of sharp practice and anti-competitive behaviour.

As the details of the BA approach gradually became public, the company was forced on to the defensive as a series of increasingly unsympathetic and revealing articles appeared in the press. This then came to a head when, in 1993, BA was forced into making an humiliating apology in open court to Richard Branson and his company, Virgin Atlantic. Included within this were the words '... they wish to apologise for having attacked the good faith and integrity of Richard Branson', that 'hostile and discreditable stories' had been placed in the press, and that BA's approach gave 'grounds for serious concern about the activities of a number of BA employees ... and their potential effect on the business interests and reputation of Virgin Atlantic and Richard Branson'. (*The Sunday Times*, 27 March 1994, p. 7.)

The BA/Virgin Atlantic story is an interesting one for several reasons, not least because of the way in which it highlights the position that managers can find themselves in when faced with real or imaginary competition. Whilst an aggressive competitive response in these circumstances is both realistic and to be expected, the danger is that of one or more managers resorting to an approach which subsequently becomes difficult to justify either ethically or legally. (A far more detailed treatment of the BA/Virgin Atlantic conflict is the focus of Gregory, 1994b.)

With many markets having grown enormously in their complexity in recent years, so the demand for increasingly detailed and effective market intelligence systems has escalated. Although many of the inputs to a market intelligence system can be obtained through relatively straight-forward and conventional market research routines, the much more strategically useful – and indeed more necessary – information on com-petitors' intentions, capabilities and strategies can, as we saw in the BA example, often only be obtained by radically different approaches. Although the legality of many of these approaches has been called into question, the law, both in Europe and the United States, has in many instances failed to keep pace with the developments that have taken place in information technology and electronic data distribution.

Ethics and market intelligence: the growth of corporate espionage

The implication of this is that whilst the techniques used to gain the more confidential forms of competitive information may not in the strictly legal sense be wrong, the ethics of the approach are arguably rather more questionable and are perhaps an illustration of cell 2 in Fig. 5.1. The net effect of this is that in many companies the search for a competitive edge has led managers to enter what has been referred to as 'the twilight zone of corporate intelligence' in which the traditional boundaries of legal and ethical behaviour are blurred; this is illustrated in Fig. 5.2 which represents a continuum of the types of competitive intelligence that are available, their sources, and the difficulties of gaining access to them.

For many organizations, much of the market research effort over the past two decades, particularly in Europe, has been concentrated towards the upper part of the continuum. However, as competitive pressures grow, so the need for more and more confidential competitive intelligence increases. One consequence of this in the United States, and now increasingly in Europe, has been a growth in the number of agencies which specialize in obtaining the sorts of competitive information that whilst increasingly being seen to be necessary, can only be obtained through what might loosely be termed as unconventional methods. Amongst the more extreme of these is what is referred to in the United States as 'doing trash', something which involves sifting through competitors' rubbish bins, using hidden cameras and listening devices, intercepting fax lines, bugging offices and planting misinformation. Although the leading competitive intelligence agencies have been quick to condemn this sort of approach – and indeed several agencies now publish codes of ethics – the ever greater pressures on managers, parti-cularly in international markets, demand ever more detailed competitive information, little of which may be obtained by adhering to traditional legal and ethical principles.

Because of this, managers are faced with a dilemma, since whilst competitive pressures demand the information, traditional and ethical patterns of behaviour argue against the sorts of actions that will provide it. In these circumstances managers can respond in one of several ways,

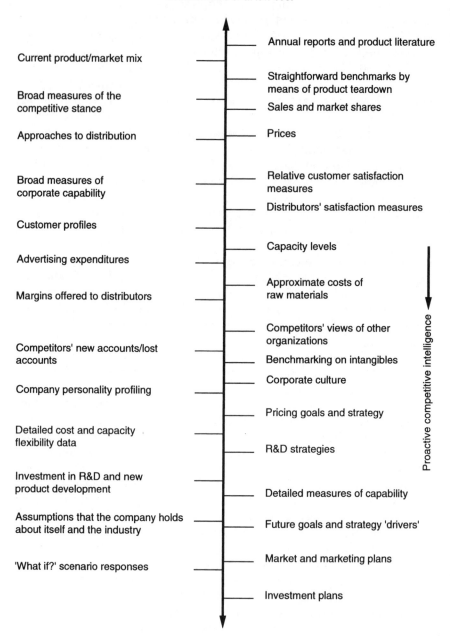

Easily obtainable information that is
available free or at low cost

Current product/market mix — — Annual reports and product literature

— Straightforward benchmarks by
means of product teardown

Broad measures of the — — Sales and market shares
competitive stance

Approaches to distribution — — Prices

Broad measures of — — Relative customer satisfaction
corporate capability measures

— Distributors' satisfaction measures

Customer profiles —

Advertising expenditures — — Capacity levels

— Approximate costs of
Margins offered to distributors — raw materials

— Competitors' views of other
organizations

Competitors' new accounts/lost —
accounts — Benchmarking on intangibles

— Corporate culture
Company personality profiling —

— Pricing goals and strategy

Detailed cost and capacity —
flexibility data — R&D strategies

Investment in R&D and new —
product development — Detailed measures of capability

Assumptions that the company holds —
about itself and the industry — Future goals and strategy 'drivers'

— Market and marketing plans
'What if?' scenario responses —

— Investment plans

Proactive competitive intelligence

Information that can be obtained only with (extreme)
difficulty and at a high cost by using possibly illegal
and/or unethical methods

Figure 5.2 Managerial needs for competitive intelligence. Adapted from Button
(1994).

ranging from an adherence to truly ethical behaviour (and then living with the competitive consequences) through to a pragmatically straightforward belief that the ends justify the means and that without the information the organization will be at a competitive disadvantage.

The work practices of competitive intelligence agencies has highlighted a series of differences between managerial cultures in Europe and the United States, with the general approach of European managers having proved to be far less aggressive and proactive than that of their US counterparts. A Conference Board report in 1988, for example, suggested that only 50% of British managers view the monitoring of competitors' activities as 'very important'. This has, in turn, led to the suggestion by Button (1994, pp. 3–4)

Intelligence gathering and corporate culture

> that there are two major differences between US and European companies. The culture is different, obviously. But also there is a greater degree of loyalty to the corporation in Europe than in the US. One consequence of this, together with the greater frequency of job-moving in the States, is that the incidence of security leaks is greater and US companies are more vulnerable to the corporate spy.

The differences and implications of the two cultures has also been highlighted by McConagle and Vella who have suggested that the ethics of senior UK managers makes them reluctant to engage in 'shady practices or covert operations'. By contrast, corporate intelligence agencies and their clients in the USA, whilst often stressing the ethical and legal standards to which they adhere, are rarely willing to discuss in detail the techniques they adopt:

> Although 'data detectives' don't necessarily lie, they tend not to tell the whole truth either. On the telephone, they regularly identify themselves as industry researchers, without disclosing their affiliation to a specific client. By focusing their introduction on the type of information they need rather than who they are and why they need it, plus an upfront statement that they are not interested in anything confidential or proprietary, interviewees are lulled into a false sense of security. Industry jargon is used with care so as not to appear overly knowledgeable and questions are carefully phrased to avoid suspicion. Ask an interviewee about their employer's weaknesses and they are liable to clam up. But when the victim is protected by their visual anonymity and physical distance from the caller, a question such as 'if you had a magic wand, which three things would you change about your manufacturing/distribution/pricing policy?' often produces the same information, without raising the alarm. (Button, 1994, p. 9)

The significance of industrial espionage and the possible scale of the problem has been highlighted by a series of studies, one of the most useful being that of Johnson and Pound (1992) who found that 40% of large US and Canadian firms had uncovered some form of espionage costing some $20 billion annually. The problems proved to be at their most acute in the high-technology industries where the commercial returns between the leaders and the followers are potentially considerable. Hitachi, for example, pleaded guilty to obtaining confidential documents from IBM dealing with one of its computer systems. However, Berkowitz *et al.* (1994, p. 97) also cite the example of espionage occurring in other less esoteric industries, including the US cookie market with Procter & Gamble claiming that 'competitors photographed its plants and production lines, stole a sample of its cookie dough, and infiltrated a confidential sales presentation to learn about its technology, recipe and marketing plan.' Procter & Gamble took action against the competitor and won $120 million in damages.

In an attempt to overcome the criticisms that have been made of industry practices, a number of competitive intelligence (CI) agencies have published ethics statements which emphasize that they will not lie, bribe or steal in the information gathering process. However, with levels of competition increasing at an ever greater rate, the pressures upon managers, and hence the CI agencies they employ, will invariably become greater. These problems have in turn been highlighted by a series of newspaper revelations concerning the ways in which a number of governmental security services have been involved in commercial espionage for many years. In the case of the old Iron Curtain countries, for example, many of the security agencies, having lost much of their previous role, have now turned their attention to the commercial sector.

Ethical issues and the management of the marketing mix

The marketing mix represents the principal focus of marketing activity. When ethical problems do arise in marketing, they are therefore almost invariably the outcome of decisions relating to the management either of the *individual* elements of the mix (the nature of the product or service; the price or fee; the form of advertising and promotion; and the approaches to distribution that are used), or of the organization's *overall* mix.

THE PRODUCT OR SERVICE

In the case of the product, Dibb *et al.* (1994, p. 619) suggest that:

> Product related ethical issues arise when marketers fail to disclose risks associated with the product, or information about its function, nature or use. As competition intensifies and profit margins

diminish, pressures can build to substitute inferior materials or product components so as to reduce costs. An ethical issue arises when marketers fail to inform customers about changes in product quality; this failure is a form of dishonesty about the nature of the product.

Dibb *et al.* illustrate this by making reference to Shell's launch in the early 1980s of Formula Shell, a new petrol which was designed to improve a car's performance but whose additives subsequently – and unexpectedly – created problems for certain types of engine. Faced with this, Shell was obliged to withdraw the petrol.

Although the cost to Shell was undoubtedly high and can be seen in terms of the loss of a market advantage and the damage to its reputation, these costs pale into insignificance when compared with those incurred in the 1960s by General Motors (GM) with its launch and subsequent marketing of the Chevrolet Corvair. One long-term consequence of this is that GM's Corvair experience is now seen to be one of the major landmarks in the fight against big business for greater levels of consumer sovereignty and contributed greatly to the movements of the 1960s and 1970s.

The Corvair, which was launched in 1959, gave US consumers an affordable sports car reminiscent of those made by the European manufacturers. However, the design proved to have a significant flaw which, in certain circumstances, caused steering difficulties which led to a series of accidents. Although criticisms of the car had begun to mount by the early 1960s as evidence emerged of the design weaknesses, changes to improve safety were not made until 1964. By this time General Motors' legal department was dealing with a series of lawsuits, with several people having been killed. However, the design change, which involved the installation of a stabilizing bar costing about $15 per car, had seemingly been fought by General Motors' senior management for some years because it was 'too expensive'. In 1965, a shareholder in the company asked that the cars made between 1960 and 1963 be recalled for the part to be fitted retrospectively, but seemingly because of the cost ($25 million), GM refused to act.

The next step in the saga was the publication in 1965 of Ralph Nader's book *Unsafe at Any Speed*. In the book, Nader criticized the car industry generally for failing to protect the public from poorly designed vehicles and GM in particular for its 1960–3 Corvair models, accusing the company of 'one of the greatest acts of industrial irresponsibility in the present century'.

GM responded by harassing Nader, an act which led Nader to sue GM for $26 million (Nader eventually accepted an out-of-court settlement of $425,000, the largest such settlement for an invasion of privacy action at the time). However the consequences for GM proved to be far more severe and costly than the settlement alone:

The publicity given to the Corvair case and Ralph Nader brought General Motors a tarnished image and a reputation for deceit, dishonesty and unconcern for customer safety. Sales and profits were affected [see below] and lawsuits by Corvair owners proliferated. (Hartley, 1992, p. 10)

[In 1960, sales of the Corvair stood at 230,000 vehicles. By 1964 they had dropped to 194,000 and in 1965, following Nader's book, fell to 89,000. By 1968 they had fallen to less than 13,000.]

A similar lack of willingness to admit to a weakness in the product characterized Firestone's response to criticisms of its 500 series radial tyres. The company eventually recalled 10 million tyres in October 1978, although this was only after the US National Highway Traffic Safety Administration had received 14,000 consumer complaints, including at least 29 fatal traffic accidents and hundreds of property damage accidents involving cars using the Firestone 500. Throughout the messy episode the company continued to deny, against public anxiety, that there was anything wrong with the product. The US government did not order the recall, and Firestone was perceived to drag its feet. Analysts estimated that the bad publicity that was engendered cost Firestone 3% of its 25% share of the multibillion dollar US tyre market.

Similar mistakes were also made by the A.H. Robins Company who sold the Dalkon Shield, an intrauterine contraceptive device (IUD). Although by 1973 research was beginning to emerge which seemed to link the Dalkon Shield with a variety of medical problems, Robins responded by criticizing the complainants. The US Food and Drug Administration asked Robins to stop marketing the product until tests were completed but by the time this was done in December 1974 Robins was already facing a welter of individual legal actions. In September 1980 the company sent a letter to 200,000 doctors saying the IUD should be removed, although by then the damage to the company's image was irreparable. In 1984 three top executives from Robins were rebuked by a federal judge in Minneapolis, but instead of accepting the judge's remarks, the Robins executives took legal action against the judge – and lost. That same year Robins took an extraordinary charge of $615 million against outstanding claims and later filed for Chapter 11 bankruptcy (Hartley, 1992, Chapter 2).

By contrast with approaches such as these, Perrier, Heinz and Johnson & Johnson all responded far more positively – and ethically – when faced with problems. In the case of Perrier, minute traces of benzene, a carcinogen, were found in bottles of Perrier water in 1990. The company responded immediately and very publicly by withdrawing 160 million bottles of Perrier from shelves throughout the world. The cause of the problem – a faulty filter at the company's Vergeze plant in south-west France – was quickly identified, the public were given unequivocal reassurances of the product's safety, and quality control measures were stepped up. It was the speed of this response and the degree of social responsibility exhibited that was felt to be the principal contributor to the way in which levels of public confidence, and ultimately the sales of the brand, were not weakened (see Wilson and Gilligan with Pearson, 1992, p. 301). By the same token, both Heinz with baby foods and Johnson & Johnson with its Tylenol brand of pain relief, responded quickly and positively to the problems created by product tampering.

Often, however, the legal and ethical dimensions and interrelationships of product decisions are far more complicated. Given the weight of evidence that now exists relating cigarette smoking to respiratory diseases, significant questions can be asked about the ethics of marketing cigarettes, even though they are legal. Equally, dilemmas arise when animals are used quite legally for product testing. Although the weight of public opinion is increasingly against the use of animal testing for cosmetics, the argument for many people is perhaps more complicated when the testing is for medical products, including cancer treatment drugs.

Other types of legal–ethical conflict can arise with products such as carpets and rugs. In a number of countries such as Bangladesh and India, for example, child labour is used to produce the product partly because the costs are lower, but also because of culture and tradition. Knowing that this is the case, marketing managers in this country are faced with a significant problem, since whilst on a personal level they might disagree with the practice of using children as a cheap source of labour, the competitive consequences for the manager's organization as well as the economic consequences for the manufacturing country if a wholly ethical (Western) stance is adopted are likely to be considerable.

PRICING

The four most commonly encountered ethical issues surrounding price as an element of the marketing mix stem from attempts by organizations to **fix prices** by coming to an arrangement with one or more competitors; **predatory pricing** that is designed to force a weaker firm out of the market; **deceptive pricing** in which there is a deliberate attempt to hide the full price of a product by failing to disclose certain elements of the service package or any 'add-ons' which may be necessary; and **price discrimination** in which different buyers are charged different prices for the same product type.

The legality of these practices tends to vary from one market to another and we will therefore limit ourselves to the question of what is meant by 'a fair price'. This is an issue which has been raised on numerous occasions and one which strikes at the very heart of whether organizations should act solely in their own interests or in a broader social context. In discussing this, Berkowitz *et al.,* (1994, p. 392) cite the example of the development by the Burroughs Wellcome Company of Retrovir, a drug found to be effective in the treatment of AIDS.

The initial cost for a one-year patient supply of Retrovir was $8000. According to a company official, the high price was due to the 'uncertain market for the drug, the possible advent of new therapies, and profit margins customarily generated by new medicines'. (The estimated research and development cost of the drug was between $80 and $100 million). A critic countered by saying, 'Burroughs Wellcome has an obligation to give up a significant amount of money to allow people to get access'.

PROMOTION

The promotional element of the marketing mix embraces a spectrum of activities including personal selling, publicity, sponsorship, sales promotion and advertising, and as such is potentially the most controversial single element of the mix.

In the case of personal selling, the difficulty and ethical dilemma stems from deciding precisely what types of sales activity are acceptable. The British pensions, insurance, time-share and double glazing industries, for example, have all been subjected to considerable criticisms because of the ways in which their sales forces, many of which are paid either largely or exclusively on the basis of sales commissions, have put undue pressure on their customers and presented a one-sided view of the product or service. Critics of this have argued that the customer is almost invariably at something of a disadvantage and should therefore be protected. Others however, have argued for the principles of *caveat emptor* to apply and that abuses of this type are generally rare.

The government has, however, responded with a series of legislative moves including the Trade Descriptions Act (1968), the Consumer Credit Act (1974), the Sale of Goods Act (1979), and the Unfair Contract Terms Act (1977), all of which are designed to protect consumers from unfair business practice. One consequence of this is, of course, that as the body of formal consumer protection has increased, so the need – and indeed the scope – for managers and sales staff to make ethical judgements in deciding what is right and what is wrong in the selling situation has been reduced.

By contrast, critics argue, the scope for ethical conflict in what has proved to be one of the fastest growing areas of promotional activity over the past few years, corporate sponsorship, is still considerable. Advocates of sponsorship have pointed to the way in which in the absence of the sponsor's money many activities, but particularly sport, would decline. However, critics of sponsorship have argued that many of the biggest sports sponsors have proved to be the tobacco companies who, faced with significant constraints on their advertising, have shifted funds into a series of high profile and glamorous areas such as motor racing. These critics have given emphasis to the question of the ethics surrounding this, suggesting that whilst this may well be legal, it is largely unethical given the volume of evidence linking smoking and respiratory diseases.

By contrast, sales promotions have proved to be a far less controversial area, although Hoover's experiences proved to be a notable exception. In 1992 Hoover offered any UK customer who spent a minimum of £100 on its products the chance of two free flights to either Europe or the United States. The response proved to be far higher than had been anticipated and the company found itself in the position not only of having to finance an infinitely more expensive promotion than had ever been expected, but also having to respond to many more claimants than their system had been designed to cope with. The immediate effect of this was that the press was full of stories of customers who having bought a Hoover product and filled in the application form, heard nothing from Hoover or its contracted travel agencies for many months. These criticisms were then exacerbated by the way in which those who were offered flights often found that they were at times of the year that were inconvenient.

The consequences for the organization proved to be significant and can be looked at both in terms of the far higher than anticipated direct costs of the promotion and the much harder to quantify indirect costs of the bad publicity engendered by the way in which the problems were handled (the direct costs were highlighted by the announcement at the end of April 1993 that Hoover's parent company, Maytag, had published a net loss of $10.5 million in the first quarter of the year, after having to take a $30 million special charge to cover the unexpected cost of the promotion). Hoover's European president and two senior executives also proved to be casualties of the affair by being dismissed over the offer. The longer-term consequences were then seen in terms of a drop in the company's market share of the upright vacuum cleaner market from 40% in April 1994 to 28% in March 1995 (GFK Lektrak) and from 50% to less than 20% in the premium upright sector. Following this crash in its market share, the Maytag Corporation sold Hoover Europe to Candy for $170 million, a sale price which represented a loss of $130 million for Maytag which bought Hoover Europe in 1989 for $300 million.

The ethics of this promotion proved to be interesting, since Hoover denied for a considerable time that a problem existed and then, in the eyes of many critics, failed to respond in the open way that was needed. Had they responded in this more open and overtly ethical way, it is likely that much of the bad publicity that the promotion attracted would have been avoided.

The final area of the promotions mix to which reference needs to be made – although potentially the most controversial – is advertising. The ethics of advertising have been the subject of considerable discussion for many years and can be traced back to Dr Johnson who suggested that 'Promise, large promise, is the soul of an advertisement.' More recently, Packard, the author of The Hidden Persuaders claimed that:

> ... because of advertising, many of us are influenced and manipulated far more than we realise in the patterns of our everyday lives. Large scale efforts are being made, often with impressive success, to channel our unthinking habits, our purchasing decisions, and our thought processes. (Packard, 1957, p. 7)

Galbraith, in *The Affluent Society* (1958), in a somewhat more succinct comment, argued that the advertising industry 'lends itself to competitive fraud'.

To these claims, one can add the views of many economists who suggest that advertising is an unnecessary business cost which raises prices and hence is a contribution to inflation; that it increases business concentration and opens industries to the abuses of monopoly; that it encourages meaningless product differentiation; that the press is dangerously dependent upon advertising revenue for its survival; and that it detracts from consumer sovereignty. (See, for example, Gilligan and Crowther, 1976, Chapter 3.)

Social commentators have been equally vehement in their criticisms by suggesting that advertising typically exhibits bad taste; that much of it is false and misleading; that it creates a uniformity of values; that it is too persuasive and sells products that people neither need nor want; that much of it is irrelevant; and that it exerts an undue influence upon children (Gilligan and Crowther, 1976, Chapter 4).

Within the space of this chapter it is of course impossible to address all of these criticisms, although it needs to be emphasized that the general weight of evidence suggests that the reality is by no means as stark as the picture that the critics have painted. However, the advertising industry throughout the developed world is very conscious of the strong emotions that advertising appears capable of generating and has therefore moved to control its own behaviour through a series of increasingly stringent codes of practice which reflect a deep-seated awareness of the scope that exists for ethical conflict. In the case of the UK, for example, the Advertising Standards Authority polices its members by means of the code of advertising practice. Equally, throughout Europe, Japan and the United States, advertising is governed by a combination of the law and a series of industry developed and regulated codes of practice that are designed to ensure that abuses do not arise.

Nevertheless, there are numerous examples of advertisements and advertising campaigns that have been the subject of particularly vitriolic criticism, including those by Benetton. Amongst the advertisements to have been criticized on the grounds both of their supposed bad taste and their apparent lack of relevance to the company's principal task of selling clothes are the dying AIDS victim who bore a resemblance to pictures of Christ, the newly born baby with its umbilical cord still attached, a priest and nun who were kissing, and a black woman nursing a white baby. The ethical issues surrounding campaigns such as these are both interesting and complicated. At its most basic it can be argued that the campaign fulfils the essential purpose of advertising in that in a crowded market place it draws attention to the company and that these greater levels of customer awareness will in turn lead to higher sales. The issue then is one of taste and whether at an individual level consumers like or dislike the images portrayed.

In a different circumstance, however, critics seem more willing to accept images that are designed to shock. At the beginning of the 1990s, for example, the RSPCA ran a campaign which featured a pile of dead dogs and a horse suspended by a hook through its throat. These images were justified, it was argued, by the need to illustrate to the public the magnitude of the problems of stray dogs which subsequently have to be put down and the seamy side of the horse flesh trade with France. Ultimately, therefore, it might be that ethical judgements in advertising – whilst obviously personal – are related to the particular situation and raise the question of whether the ends justify the means.

Ethical issues also arose with the Nestlé Food Corporation's advertising in the United States of its Good Start infant formula. Promoted as hypoallergenic, the product was designed to prevent or reduce the colic caused by a baby's allergic reaction to cow's milk. However, some children who were highly milk-allergic experienced serious side-effects after having been given Good Start. Parents and doctors subsequently claimed that the hypoallergenic claim was misleading and the US Food and Drug Administration launched an investigation. Nestlé responded by defending the product claim, saying '[we] don't understand why our product should work in 100 per cent of cases. If we wanted to say it was foolproof, we would have called it allergy-free. We call it hypo-, or less, allergenic' (Freedman, 1989, pp. A1, A6).

DISTRIBUTION

Although relatively less attention has been paid to the ethical dimensions associated with distribution than to the other elements of the marketing mix, the scope for ethical conflict between distribution intermediaries is potentially considerable. Perhaps the most obvious areas for this concerns issues of payment and an abuse of power. Dibb (1994, p. 622), for example, comments that:

Manipulating a product's availability for purposes of exploitation and using coercion to force intermediaries to behave in a specific manner are particularly serious ethical issues in the distribution sphere. For example, a powerful manufacturer can exert undue influence over an intermediary's choice of whether to handle a product or how to handle it.

Other ethical issues in distribution relate to some stores' refusal to deal with some types of middlemen. A number of conflicts are developing in the distribution of micro-computer software. Many software-only stores are bypassing wholesalers and establishing direct relationships with software producers. Some dishonest stores are 'hacking', or making unauthorised copies of software, preventing the producers from getting their due compensation. These occurrences have spawned suspicion and general ethical conflict in the distribution of software.

However, perhaps the most controversial distribution-related ethical issue to have emerged over the past few years concerns the way in which critics have pointed to the scope that exists for large retailers to abuse their power by a series of ever greater demands upon their suppliers. This abuse, it has been suggested, is a direct result of the far higher levels of retail concentration that now exist and is manifested in terms of a threat to delist products (delisting involves the store in taking the product off the shelves) unless the supplier meets the retailer's demands in terms of price levels, packaging, product development/specification, advertising support, order quantities and delivery schedules. The implications of these demands are potentially significant for the vast majority of suppliers, since the largest grocery, do-it-yourself, clothing and electrical retail chains are capable of exerting a huge buying influence. However, despite the criticisms that have been made of these abuses, surprisingly little hard evidence exists to indicate the size or scale of the problem. Although questions have been raised by industry commentators and politicians, few suppliers appear willing to state publicly that they have been subjected to these pressures, seemingly because they feel their organization and its products would immediately be delisted. However, the major retailers have argued that only rarely, if ever, do these abuses exist and that their operating procedures are simply designed to increase levels of market efficiency. In this way, the consumer benefits in terms of a far wider product selection and much lower prices than would otherwise be the case. It follows from this, they suggest, that in so far as ethical factors come into play, they are that the public good far outweighs any problems that an individual (and inefficient?) manufacturer might experience.

The problem of counterfeiting and product piracy

In the mid-1980s, a number of writers drew parallels between business warfare and military warfare [see for example, James (1984) and Ries and Trout (1986)]. This introduction to the business world of the idea of a series of military analogies gave emphasis to the importance of unconventional tactics, with a number of writers suggesting that these unconventional tactics should be constrained only by the commercial reality of the moves and the payoffs rather than anything more fundamental such as ethics.

Amongst the more unconventional methods identified was that of guerrilla warfare using illegal methods such as the pirating of copyrights, patents and trademarks in order to produce counterfeit products. Amongst the products to have fallen victim to this are computer hardware and software, pharmaceuticals, cosmetics, musical recordings, watches, jeans and videotapes. Although counterfeiting can be contained to a greater or lesser extent in the majority of the industrial countries by a series of legal measures and other forms of protection, in parts of southern Europe and in most of Latin America and south-east Asia where the producers of many counterfeit goods are concentrated, controls are far more relaxed. The scale of the problem is perhaps most readily brought into perspective when it is recognized that the trade in counterfeit goods is now believed to be worth some $60 billion a year, or 3% of world trade. Its significance is also brought into sharp relief by the costs involved in containing it. At the beginning of the 1990s, for example, Vuitton, the manufacturers of luxury luggage, were spending more than $1 million a year in an attempt to fight product piracy. Equally, the perfume manufacturers have estimated that in North America alone piracy is running at $300 million annually and is equivalent to 15% of the sales of the leading companies. Because of this, between 1 and 3% of the industry's revenue is spent on fighting piracy. However, it needs to be recognized that different countries often view copying in a very different way from that of most western nations. In Korea, for example, copying is embedded in the country's culture and based on the idea that the thoughts of the individual should benefit society as a whole. Given this, patent infringement is seen in a very different way.

Three forms of product piracy exist: **imitation**, **faking** and **pre-emption**. The first of these, **imitation**, simply involves the copying of an established product and brand name. Thus a Hong Kong-based manufacturer of jeans might produce a relatively poor quality product and put on a Levi's or Calvin Klein label before passing it off as an original product. **Faking** refers to the situation in which the fraudulent product is sold under a similar sounding brand name. Amongst those to have been affected by this are Levi's (Levy's), Reebok (Reabock), and Lacoste (Lacostt). Faking is not however restricted just to fashion products but occurs in virtually every market sector in which strong brand names exist.

The third form of piracy is **pre-emption**, something which is possible in countries which operate with a code law rather than a common law form of legal system. Under the common law system which is used in countries such as the United States, Britain and most of the Commonwealth, the ownership of a trademark is determined by priority of **use**. In other words, the owner of a trademark is the person who is first to use it. However, in code law countries and areas of the world such as South America, ownership is determined by priority of **registration**, even though the trademark may not subsequently have been used. One consequence of this is that multinationals with well-established brand names have found that when they move into a new market subject to code law, these brands may well have already been registered. The firm is then in a position of having to buy back its own brand names from the local owners in order to use them.

Whichever form of piracy is used, the problems for organizations are potentially significant, since not only is there an obvious loss of revenue, but there is also the problem of the pirated product being of a poorer quality and the company's image suffering as a result.

But although most discussions of piracy focus on cheap and poor quality imitations being produced in the Far East, copycatting has emerged over the past few years as a major problem for many companies as the result of the behaviour of British supermarket chains and their development of own-brands. In 1993, for example, Coca-Cola reacted strongly to the launch by Sainsbury's of its own-brand Classic Cola which, Coke argued, was presented in packaging which was too similar to Coke's own. Others to have been affected by the development of own label products which, critics of the approach suggest, owe much of their success to their apparent similarity to branded products include Unilever, Mars, Procter & Gamble, Grand Metropolitan and ICI. In an attempt to fight back, these companies established in 1994 the British Producers and Brand Owners Group. However, the problem faced in Britain in responding to the apparent similarity of an own-label product to an existing brand stems from the difficulty under UK law of winning a passing-off case. At the same time, many manufacturers, including some of the very largest, are only too aware of the buying power of large retail chains and of the consequences of delisting, and appear therefore to have been reluctant to adopt an overtly proactive stance.

Consumers' ethics

Although our discussion so far has focused exclusively on the behaviour of organizations, it is also worth spending a few moments looking at the behaviour of consumers.

The unethical behaviour of consumers represents an area of growing concern for many companies, since the implications for sales revenues and the costs involved in preventing abuses are potentially significant. Amongst the areas affected are:

❑ the filing of warranty claims outside the warranty period
❑ the misredemption of coupons
❑ the fraudulent returns of merchandise

❑ the rerecording of copyrighted music, video cassettes and computer software and

❑ phoney insurance claims.

Although the costs to firms of these abuses are undoubtedly high, arriving at a precise measure of costs is difficult. However, estimates in the United States suggest that in the case of the record industry losses run at around $1 billion annually, a figure which is matched by the costs to firms of falsely redeemed coupons.

In a broader sense, ethical issues and conflicts also arise in terms of consumers' buying patterns. Although the 1980s and 1990s have seen a shift in buying habits as consumers have become far more environmentally aware, it appears that there is a reluctance to pay more than a small price premium for environmentally safer products or indeed to change lifestyles in any truly significant manner; the lack of willingness to move from private to public transport is just one example of this.

Given the nature of our comments so far, it is evident that considerable scope exists for ethical conflicts in marketing; these are illustrated in Fig. 5.3.

The role of ethics in marketing education

It follows from this that ethics should play a role in marketing education. Murphy (1994) argues, however, that a number of problems are likely to be faced in integrating ethics into any marketing curriculum, the most significant of which are the time involved; that marketing staff are not experts in the ethics field; that there may well be problems of integrating the material; that faculty members run the risk of adopting an evangelical tone; that it is a 'soft' area in that it is subjective and unscientific; and that the study of ethics is superfluous.

However, whilst each of these points may well have some validity (although any advocate of ethics would undoubtedly argue that the question of its superfluity is disingenuous), the issue faced by many marketing teachers relates rather more to the broader question of the role that ethical issues should play in management education as a whole. Although as we observed in the introduction to this chapter, marketing is in a uniquely vulnerable position in any discussion of ethics, it needs to be remembered that it is just one dimension of management and, as such, any discussion or treatment of ethics within management education needs to reflect this.

(Note: both the Chartered Institute of Marketing and the Market Research Society have Codes of Conduct, copies of which can be obtained by contacting them).

Summary

We began this chapter by suggesting that marketing is in a uniquely vulnerable position in any discussion of marketing ethics since it is the most obvious and high profile point of interface between an organization

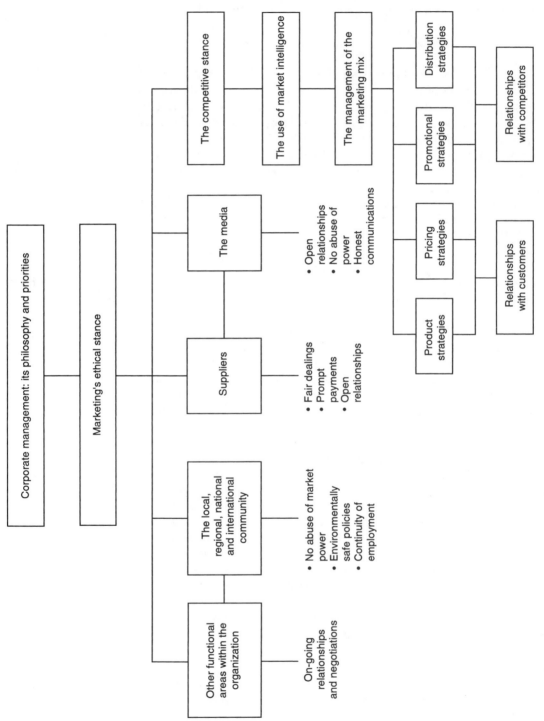

Figure 5.3 The ethical framework of marketing decisions.

and its markets. It should be apparent from the comments that we have made that enormous scope exists for an abuse of this interface and that particularly in highly competitive markets, the temptations – and indeed the corporate pressures – for managers to veer towards decisions and patterns of behaviour that are illegal and/or unethical may be considerable. However, in making this comment we need to emphasize that marketing decisions are not made in a vacuum, but instead are made against the background of a culture within society as a whole and an organizational culture, both of which provides guidelines for what is and what is not acceptable. Recognizing this we can conclude by posing three questions:

1. To what extent is the majority of what is referred to as 'ethical marketing behaviour' actually ethical or simply behaviour tinged with self-interest?
2. There is now a considerable body of evidence to suggest that there is a link between cigarette smoking and respiratory diseases. Although the marketing of cigarettes is not illegal, given the evidence that exists, is it unethical?
3. Is the sale of arms unethical?

Further reading

A number of books on business ethics contain chapters dealing with the ethical aspects of marketing, but there are also a number of specific texts which provide a more detailed discussion for the reader:

Laczniak, G.R. and Murphy, P.E. (eds) (1985) *Marketing Ethics: Guidelines for Managers*. Lexington Books, MA.
Smith, N.C. (1990) Morality and the Market: *Consumer Pressure for Corporate Accountability*. Routledge, London.
Smith, N.C. and Quelch, J.D. (eds) (1993) *Ethics in Marketing*. Richard D. Irwin, Boston, MA.
Chonko, L.B. (1995) *Ethical Decision Making in Marketing*. Sage, London.

References

Berkowitz, E.N., Kerin, R.A., Hartley, S.W. and Rudelius, W. (1994) *Marketing*, 4th edn. Richard D. Irwin, Boston, MA.
Button, K. (1994) Spies like us. *Marketing Business*. March, p. 8.
Dibb, S., Simkin, L., Pride W.M. and Ferrell, O.C. (1994) *Marketing: Concepts and Strategies*, 2nd European edn. Houghton Mifflin.
Freedman, A.M. (1989) Bad reaction: Nestlés bid to crash baby-formula market in the US stirs a row. *The Wall Street Journal*, 16 February, pp. A1, A6.
Galbraith, J.K. (1958) *The Affluent Society*. Hamish Hamilton.
Gilligan, C.T. and Crowther, G. (1976) *Advertising Management*. Philip Allan.
Gregory, M. (1994a) *The Sunday Times*, 13 March, p. 10.
Gregory, M. (1994b) *Dirty Tricks*. Little, Brown & Co., London.
Hartley, R.F. (1992) *Marketing Mistakes*, 5th edn. John Wiley.
Henderson, V.E. (1982) The ethical side of the enterprise. *Sloan Management Review*, 37–47.
Jackall, R. (1988) *Moral Mazes: The World of Corporate Managers*. Oxford University Press.

James, B.G. (1984) *Business Wargames*. Penguin, Harmondsworth.

Jobber, D. (1995) *Principles and Practice of Marketing*. McGraw-Hill.

Johnson, R. and Pound, E.T. (1992) Hot on the trail of trade secret thieves, private eyes fight all manner of snakes. *The Wall Street Journal*, 12 August, pp. 131, B4.

Kotler, P. (1991), *Marketing Management: Analysis, Planning, Implementation and Control*, 7th edn. Prentice-Hall.

McCarthy, E.J. and Perreault, W.D. (1994) *Essentials of Marketing: A Global-managerial Approach*, 6th edn. Richard D. Irwin, Boston, MA.

McGonagle, J. and Vella, C. *Outsmarting the Competition.*

Murphy, P.E. (1994) The expanding role of ethics in the marketing curriculum. *Proceedings of the Marketing Education Group Conference*, University of Ulster, pp. 712–21.

Nader, R. (1965) *Unsafe at any Speed: the Designed – in Dangers of the American Automobile*. Grossman.

Nash, L. (1990) *Good Intentions Aside*. Jossey-Bass, San Francisco, CA.

Packard, V. (1957) *The Hidden Persuaders*. Longmans Green.

Ries, A. and Trout, J. (1986) *Marketing Warfare*. McGraw-Hill.

Zey-Ferrell, K.M., Weaver and Ferrell, O.C. (1979) Predicting unethical behaviour among marketing practitioners. *Human Relations*, 32(7), 557–69.

Wilson, R.M.S. and Gilligan, C.T., with Pearson, D. (1992) *Strategic Marketing Management: Planning, Implementation and Control*. Butterworth-Heinemann.

Constructing organization: technological determinism and ethical choices

6

Sue Whittle

Introduction

This chapter explores the ideology of competitiveness, and its associated technological determinism, as a moral code (Roberts, 1984), intrinsically laudable and the only option for good managers. Its hegemonic character renders other organization logics, other technological choices, inadmissible, dismissed as idealistic, unreal and a guarantee of ruin. The chapter looks at how ethics might enter into the organization design calculus.

Discussions of ethics and technology often relate to high profile 'corporate misdeeds' and to the 'various publics with which a firm is involved' (Hartley, 1993, p. 1). Hartley's book, for example, catalogues a rogue's gallery of technology-linked ethical violations ranging from insider dealing, to the Alaskan oil spill, Bhopal, and the Tylenol drug fiasco. These disasters lead to charges of naivety and negligence and accusations, often, of avarice, exploitation, criminality and inhumanity. They almost invariably result in formal policies and procedures to ensure that the same thing cannot happen again.

Thus, the conventional approach to the ethical management of technology is to produce codes of practice. Unfortunately, this strategy has been heavily criticized as fulfilling symbolic functions but providing little guidance for day-to-day decision making and having little impact on practice (Munro, 1992; Hosmer, 1987).

In a technologically expansive age, our knowledge of the world is becoming less ontological and increasingly epistemological (King, 1994). Our trust in interactive skills is being replaced by a reliance on intellective skills, to use Zuboff's terminology, as experiential knowledge, tacit skills and learned judgement are absorbed by technologies (Zuboff, 1988). We know and relate to the world through VDU's, charts and graphs, dials and gauges, fax machines and robots. It has been argued that this 'degradation' of working lives, through the substitution of people by technology, means that people inevitably become less capable and hence less significant to the performance of manufacturing and commercial processes (Braverman, 1974). People thus have less of a voice in technological decision-making.

Thinking about technology

In the manufacturing world, as in healthcare and financial services, many technological decisions are not recognized as matters of choice. Technological matters are often assumed to be beyond question, beyond doubt, to be value free ... unless something goes wrong.

The literature on technological determinism is well known and readily available (Taylor, 1947; Trist and Bamforth, 1951; Woodward, 1965; Perrow, 1967; Thompson, 1967; Miller and Friesen, 1984; Mintzberg, 1979). As with current discussions in organization culture (Smircich, 1983), works from within this tradition have ranged from perspectives in which organizations 'have' technologies to perspectives on organizations 'as' technologies. Hence, 'technology' has been conceptualized as a whole range of phenomena from physical artefacts, such as machinery and equipment and particularly, now, computers, to 'the sum of knowledge, of received information, which allows things to be done' (Macdonald *et al.*, 1983).

In this chapter a broad definition is used. Technology refers to that

> *knowledge* of cause-effect relationships embedded in machines and methods. (Goodman, Sproul *et al.*, 1990, p. 255)

As such technology is

> the collection of plant, machines, tools *and recipes* available at a given time for the execution of the production task and the *rationale* underlying their utilization. (Woodward, 1965) [my emphasis]

Technology is conceptualized paradigmatically, offering model problems and model solutions through examples, equations and symbolic generalizations (Kuhn, 1962). These constitute models of reality (Kuhn, 1977).

References to recipes, rationales and knowledge as integral to a definition of technology is sometimes received with surprise. Technology is a term often reserved exclusively for physical artefacts such as machines and tools. However, as quickly becomes obvious to anyone who has watched TV programmes in which bygones are presented for identification to invited experts, a tool or machine remains a mystery or bizarre unless knowledge of how to use the machine or tool is available and the purpose for which the tool is intended is recognized as valid. The know-how embedded in a spoon, a thermometer or a factory robot therefore encapsulates only part of their status as technology. The rationale underlying their utilization and knowledge of the effects that they can cause is a prerequisite of their utility.

But are these cause and effect relationships given? Are the applications, the uses to which tools and machinery are put and the behaviours that might be associated with them, determined in perpetuity at invention? Plainly not, as witnessing a child playing drums with a pan and spoon can clearly indicate. Yet the notion of technological determinism, that organization form and human behaviour is, and perhaps should be, dictated by inherent characteristics of technology, is still part of conventional wisdom and informing current thinking on the future of work and organizations.

In characterizing the influence of technology on working life, deterministically inclined texts tend to support one of two opposing view points. They paint portraits of individuals and groups as either (a) liberated from or (b) alienated from their everyday tasks by the technologies deployed in constructing work (Sayles, 1958; Braverman, 1974; Blauner, 1964; Steele, 1989). Within this perspective, technology tends to be cast as either a progressive, beneficial and humanizing force, or as an oppressive, harmful and dehumanizing influence. Discussing technology and ethics may provide an opportunity to break out of these totalizing polarities.

In the manufacturing world, this division into technophobes and technophiles has been evident in writings concerned with improving manufacturing performance and competitiveness through the introduction of just-in-time (JIT), total quality management (TQM), manufacturing resource planning (MRPII), computer-integrated manufacture (CIM) and other 'world-class manufacturing' and 'lean production' technologies (Schonberger, 1986; Oliver and Wilkinson, 1992; Womack *et al.*, 1990). The resulting models of technology management are now being applied to the personal services, in banking, retailing, hospitality management, and the public sector (see, for example, Heskett, 1986; Harvey, 1989; Gummesson, 1990; Morgan and Murgatroyd, 1994).

Two approaches dominate thinking about how to make the right technological choices. These are the Benthamite and the Kantian.

Making technological choices

THE BENTHAMITE CONSEQUENTIALIST OR UTILITARIAN APPROACH

This is essentially an ends-justify-the-means philosophy with the caveat that those ends must maximize the total happiness, welfare or whatever other index of gain is invoked in the decision calculus. Whether technology was ever evaluated in terms of its happiness index is uncertain but today's total gains are measured in

❑ units of time (rate of production per period)
❑ units of quality (defects per million)
❑ units of flexibility (number of product lines per shift), and
❑ units of reliability (downtime/maintenance spend per period).

Whilst the original Benthamite doctrine preached that there is nothing *intrinsically* beneficial (or abhorrent) in an act or practice, and that the relationship between gain and loss must be calculated anew for each context and circumstance, the manifestation of the philosophy in manufacturing management has become simplified, perhaps even caricatured, over time such that there is now held to be a direct, constant and universal relationship between the above measures and corporate gains.

In manufacturing management today, maximizing throughput rates, quality, flexibility and reliability leads to customer happiness, or 'delight' to use Deming's phrase. In turn, according to Deming's virtuous circle, this leads to employee and shareholder happiness (Deming, 1986). The success of this model rests on the identification of the appropriate performance dimensions and their accurate monitoring and measurement. Research council and consultancy funded projects seeking the ultimate calculus are being funded at an increasing rate (e.g. Oliver *et al.*, 1994) and the use of technology for electronic surveillance or work performance is growing a pace (Grant and Higgins, 1989; Lyon, 1994). The quantification of gain into highly measurable units of manufacturing happiness has led to the construction of league tables of manufacturing performance. The premier league is populated by companies known as world-class manufacturers. The first division comprises companies pursuing a lean production approach to manufacturing and the bottom of the league belongs to manufacturers still operating within a mass production system. The production design characteristics vary for each division of the league (Mathews, 1993). Those for lean production are reproduced in Table 6.1.

THE KANTIAN PRINCIPLE-BASED OR DEONTOLOGICAL APPROACH

As a brief reminder, this view prescribes that for decisions and actions to be ethical, they should always comply with general principles or *categorical imperatives* which are *universal* (if they apply to one they apply to everyone) and *reversible* (I must be willing to have my reasons for acting used as rationales for actions taken towards me.) The evaluation as ethical is here not concerned with consequences or outcomes of the action or practice, as in the utilitarian philosophy, but is concerned with rationale – the reasons and motivations for acting. As Kant deems these to be universal, such motivations can be described as maxims or *duties*; that which we must do because it is intrinsically moral. So we should not steal, lie, betray our fellows or be violent towards them. We should be honest, truthful, fair, etc. Since we can only exercise these prescriptions in relation to others, the Kantian philosophy of universal ethical principles presupposes the existence of a moral society – a higher order of humanity.

Table 6.1   The lean production paradigm

Operating assumptions:
❑ Customized mass production (competitiveness derives from price, quality and responsive-
  ness to customers)
❑ Flexibility of manufacturing process (just-in-time organization and quick product
  changeovers)
❑ Flexibility of human labour through multiskilling

Desired outcomes
❑ High quality, low cost products
❑ Functional integration and coordination of human labour
❑ Low inventories and no buffer stocks of raw materials or finished goods
❑ Continuous improvement and sustained competitive advantage

Required inputs
❑ Priority of and high commitment to close customer and supplier relations
❑ Team-based organizational hierarchies
❑ Medium trust industrial relations based on tightly measured performance
❑ High worker commitment to the company and belief in the product.

Adapted from Mathews 1993

Striving to belong to such an order is itself perceived as a moral duty
(Joad, 1936).

In manufacturing management we have seen a drift from Benthamite
to Kantian logic in providing rationales for technological choices.
Returning to the lean production model, it has become the duty of all
manufacturing managers to aspire to membership of this division of their
league and to institute changes in their organizations that will contribute
to its achievement. A concomitant of this has been the need to demonstrate movement towards the ideal through measurement. More and more
organization life is subject to insidious quantification with decision
making by computation subsuming decision making based on judgement
and compromise (Thompson and Tuden, 1959).

**The ideology of
competitiveness**

Petrella (1994, p. 10) argues that the 'ideology of competitiveness' has
become the latest imperative. He laments how industrialists, financiers,
politicians and academics have succumbed to the 'competitiveness credo'
convinced that it is

> the only efficient answer to the problems and challenges that the
> economies and societies of the world are facing. (p. 11)

IMD Lausanne and the World Economic Forum have constructed a 'world
competitiveness scoreboard' which rates countries against six factors that
are held to contribute to their competitiveness [Department of Trade and
Industry (DTI), 1994]. These are: the country's participation in inter-

national trade; its performance in capital markets; its technological capability; the extent to which management is judged to be innovative, profitable and responsible; its infrastructural adequacy; and its people's skills. Out of 22 Organization of Economic Cooperation and Development (OECD) countries, the UK is ranked 13 on the competitiveness scoreboard.

Petrella describes this credo as 'a one-sided vision ... based on a few simplistic ideas'.

The key concept is that societies are engaged in technological warfare with the objective of becoming 'strong enough to defeat the competitor' (Petrella, 1994). The fight for survival is seen to depend on global domination, 'supremacy and hegemony', of know-how, of systems of production, communication and distribution, and of 'mastery' of new technologies (composites, optical fibres, satellites, bio-informatics, and robotics).

The above-mentioned DTI document reports how

> Business is faced with intensifying competitive pressures. The demand for customised solutions, fast delivery and sound environmental performance – all in a global market which is becoming increasingly sophisticated – is growing rapidly. To ensure survival and continued prosperity, business must meet these challenges by providing a constant stream of new and improved products, processes and services. (DTI, 1994, p. 4)

Interestingly, Petrella points out that use of the language of war within economic and industrial activity has coincided with the end of the Cold War.

At a macro-level, Petrella lists the consequences of this ideology for technological research and development (R&D) policy as:

1. Gearing technological developments towards satisfying the needs of the minority of developed countries. To support his case, he quotes the startling statistic that '90% of pharmaceutical R&D expenditure is oriented towards the treatment of illnesses from the aging populations of the richest cities and regions of the world' (Petrella, 1994, p. 12).
2. Emphasizing cost reduction and process innovation to the detriment of worthwhile and significant product innovations. Shortening product life-cycles and increasing obsolescence often means little change for the consumer but big gains for the producer. Consumer electronics is one arena in which producer gains are marketed as consumer benefits. The music industry's increasingly derided compact disk is a topical example.
3. Encouraging the substitution of raw materials from Third World countries by synthetics produced by developed countries for their own consumption. The wealth gap and the consumption index between societies is thus exacerbated.

Research into workers' experiences of the ideology of competitiveness in its manifestation as lean production provides a similarly bleak picture. Garrahan and Stewart (1992) report an arduous and monotonous working regime, leading to aggrieved and disillusioned employees, at Nissan's 'harmonized', 'team-culture' at Sunderland.

Petrella asks whether there any alternatives. In replying 'Certainly there are', he outlines the principles of coexistence, codevelopment and codetermination which, he argues, should inform a global technology agenda in the next decade.[1] But how might this crisis of agreement (Harvey, 1974) on what is held to be progressive in the design and management of production technologies be challenged? How did it come about and why does it persist?

It has become *intrinsically* laudable to be recognized as operating within a lean production philosophy and exalting to have achieved world-class status. Lean production has become virtually a moral code, alternatives being literally unthinkable (Clark, 1985). This is signalled by the difficulties experienced in trying to find non-derisory antonyms for the terms used to describe this model of manufacturing management. (The reader might try to construct viable alternatives to continuous improvement, high quality/low costs, team-based organization, close customer relationships and flexible manufacturing processes.)

Those not striving towards its attainment suffer ostracism, ridicule and pity if, through ignorance for example, their actions are not guided by its precepts. (We see this in attitudes towards east European manufacturing in which many see it as the west's duty to bring advanced manufacturing technologies to these deprived communities. The same logic is also invoked in justifying the export of 'advanced' technologies to the Third World – irrespective of the utility or consequences of their implementation.)

In constructing a typology of ideologies, Geuss describes a total ideology as one which

(a) is a programme or plan of action,
(b) based on an explicit, systematic model or theory of how society works,
(c) aimed at radical transformation or reconstruction of the society as a whole,
(d) held with more confidence (passion) than the evidence for the theory or model warrants. (Geuss, 1981, p. 11)

The essential feature of such an ideology is that its proponents are 'deluded about themselves, their position, their society or their interests' (Geuss, 1981, p. 12). Plainly this would fit Petrella's indictment of the ideology of competitiveness. An aspect of that delusion may be the explanations managers offer for the acceptance by workers of technological change. In this respect 'competitiveness' has shifted from being an effect in search of causal explanation to a causal variable – used to explain and rationalize actions. For example, in explaining how Vickers doubled output per employee over five years, its chairman at that time attributed this success in part to

> investment in more productive equipment ... coupled with the fact that our employees across the company have *a better understanding of the need* to be productive, the need to be competitive and profitable. All this has helped us in some of the more difficult areas where we have had to *reduce headcount*, which we've achieved by negotiation, by collaboration, by *understanding. We've had virtually no difficulty at all in carrying out changes, by being sensitive and by explaining to people this need to be competitive.* (Plastow, chairman of Vickers quoted in Heller, 1987, p. 22)

'Investing in more productive equipment' often means automation, the use of computer-controlled machinery and centralized processing stations. Whilst managers may explain worker acceptance of these new technological forms by reference to the competitiveness imperative, workers themselves can offer other interpretations. In her excellent book on information technology and the future of work, Zuboff records the rationales offered by paper-mill workers themselves to explain their enthusiasm for new technologies.

> I like this job. There are nice control rooms to sit in. You don't have to walk up and down the machines. When everything is running right you don't have that much to do. Its very convenient. I used to be a jet mechanic, but this is better. Its clean and easy. I don't want to turn wrenches any more, or get nasty and greasy. Once I had a taste of this, I didn't want to go back. I enjoy not having to go out and do manual labour. I can just punch in where I want the oil flow to go ... The computer makes our job easier. It takes the pressure off us. You can have a snack, you can talk. (Zuboff, 1988, p. 91)

Challenging the ideology of competitiveness

Gosling argues that

> The hegemony of the discourse of market forces is so complete that [alternative] ideals and values are labelled unrealistic or naive. (Gosling, 1992, p. 121)

How might ethical considerations be introduced into this sealed framework?

Geuss suggests an ideology can be challenged in three ways:

1. *Reveal how it came into existence, its genesis.* Much work on the diffusion of innovations suggests how inefficient and harmful technologies and organization practices can become widely accepted through

the symbolic power of fashion (Abrahamson, 1991). Conformance to the trappings of the innovation (e.g. language and visible artefacts) are more important than any benefits gained from their deployment. Widespread and unquestioning acceptance of forms of technological change are thus indicative of ideological determinism. In Britain, the DTI has institutionalized a commonsense ideology into a formal doctrine through its sponsorship of the 'single recipe' approach to industrial advantage in its innovation programme.

2. *Question its logic.* With reference to the lean paradigm, for example, if everyone follows the same recipe how can it give advantage? Several researchers (Teece *et al.*, 1992; Hayes and Pisano, 1994) have explored the relationship between generic competitiveness recipes such as world-class and lean manufacturing, TQM and JIT, and firm performance and found them wanting. The ideology is flawed.

3. *Show that its claims are not supported by the empirical evidence.* There is considerable evidence to show that lean technologies actually do not deliver competitiveness and improved performance in a law like and predictable way. Throughout the 1980s many manufacturers attempted to rejuvenate their performance by making substantial changes to their manufacturing technology. The implementation of CIM technologies was particularly widespread but adopting companies reported 50% or less successful utilization of their systems' anticipated capabilities (Kearney, 1989). Similarly, Barrar *et al.* (1989) report only 23% of MRPII systems meeting targets fully and on time. TQM tools and techniques also have a less than sparkling track record with Develin and Partners (1989), in a seven-year assessment of quality programmes, reporting only one in three companies achieving increased competitiveness as a result of their total quality investments.

However, whilst these might constitute admirable agenda for academic work and are to be encouraged, they are unlikely to provide viable strategies for influencing technological decisions at the level of the firm. More pragmatically, perhaps, Gosling suggests a procedure designed to raise ethical issues in decision making which can be applied, immediately, to technology choices in organizations. The stages of the procedure are:

1. Identify the stakeholders to the focal issue.
2. Identify the ethical *principles* of concern to each stakeholder for the issue under consideration.
3. Construct alternatives informed by several configurations of principles (a form of scenario planning).
4. Consider the consequences for each stakeholder of the choice of each scenario.
5. Consider the policy implications for the future (other plants, other countries and cultures, other legislation).

6. Decide which principles should take priority, and if contentious, why how, when and by whom they will be reviewed.
7. Explore how compromised principles can be better accommodated next time.

The types of principles and consequences to be considered might include the following.

Is the technology safe, tested, proven, accessible, reliable, affordable, fit for purpose, controllable, profitable, alienating, deskilling, disempowering, dehumanizing, developmental, innovative, the best available, novel, copiable, legal, understandable, green, politically correct, and so on. (Collective terms such as alienating and dehumanizing are offered here for concerns that might include infringements of privacy, loss of dignity and equity. Each needs to be researched individually for any particular context.)

The appropriateness of the principles to each category of stakeholder needs to be established locally and with respect to the particular technology issue at stake. As with any management process, knowing the issues of significance to each stakeholder and in what way they are significant, what they mean to that stakeholder, is a prerequisite for successful management. When this procedure is tried out, we may find some of the boxes are empty, perhaps because we are unaware of what particular issue mean to some stakeholders. The first task then becomes clear – get some information, make contact, find out, start to understand what this or that choice means to people, how it impacts on their working lives.

This method is not about compiling a set of rules, such as might be provided by an expert system. It is a way of constructing a competing values framework (Quinn, 1988) which recognizes the political and negotiated character of organization. Such a phenomenological and contextualist perspective on technology, looking at the forms of life that emerge from technological design decisions, seeks answers to the following questions:

1. Who has access to what technology?
2. Who controls and who can change technology?
3. How is technology evaluated? Who benefits?
4. What technology is acceptable/desirable/taboo?
5. What assumptions and power relationships inform these choices and frame the accepted wisdom, the technological doxa?
6. What is the role for ethics in making these choices?

Much can be revealed by listening to the terms used to describe and explain what different people think is going on, what is important, with regard to the technology in use and the extent to which that is taken-for-granted. For example, John Parnaby, when head of manufacturing technology at Lucas, justified the company's rapid and non-negotiable introduction of Japanese practices in the following way:

> If you go back four or five years ... morale was low. In Britain there were all sorts of tall stores about Japanese success being a consequence of Japanese culture, when in fact its Japanese *professionalism, the use of knowledge* ... Once people get to understand that there is a structured way of solving problems, morale starts to rise. So on the whole, *we are all feeling a lot happier* than we were, now we know ... how to solve our problems. (Parnaby quoted in Heller 1987, p. 55) [my emphasis]

Attention to how technological choices are represented and legitimated, deconstructing the rhetoric, can reveal the competing values (Quinn, 1988) held by various stakeholders and offer the potential for dialogue to construct a negotiated rather than an oppressive order. Conflict of interests is not denied, here, but recognized and the potential for compromise and the emergence of collaborative solutions (Morgan 1986) recognized as valid.

Ethics and technological controls

Using the above framework to capture silenced perspectives and generate novel and ethical options for technological design is now illustrated through some discussion of the issues relating to the use of surveillance technology.

In a recent study on ethics and electronic surveillance, Ottensmeyer and Heroux describe how

> Despite growing evidence that workers dislike it, that expected productivity gains do not occur from it, and that legislatures are interested in regulating it, electronic monitoring and surveillance appear to be on the rise. (1991, p. 519)

The purpose of their study is to understand how this 'irrational scenario' came about and is sustained.

Drawing on Susser, they define electronic surveillance as

> the collection, storage and analysis of information on employee performance using computer and/or telecommunications technology. (Susser, 1988, p. 576)

In the manufacturing world, employees have grown accustomed to having their 'defect rates' publicly displayed, as machines automatically monitor the variability-from-target of components produced. Telephonists and telesales staff accept as a fact of life that their pay depends on achieving an increasing number of contact calls per shift or per hour as monitored electronically. Data-processing workers have had to come to terms with the reality of a working life in which their every stroke on the computer keyboard is monitored – as is every part of a second in which there is no keystroke.

However, it seems that the use of electronic surveillance is not to be limited to shopfloor and clerical staff. In 1989 a US study [Coalition on New Office Technology (CNOT), 1989] reported that four to six *million* employees were known to be subject to electronic surveillance techniques, among them being nurses, pharmacists and stockbrokers (Ottensmeyer and Heroux, 1991, p. 521).

The types of things reported to be monitored were: the number of keystrokes made; time between tasks; number of errors made; time away from workstation; time to complete each task; and total number of tasks completed. The target of monitoring was the individual, rather than a work group, a department or a business process. The appropriate intervention to change the performances monitored was therefore also assumed to be at the level of the individual – through coaching, training, rewarding (in the form of promotion and pay), and punishing (in the form of discipline and redundancy). There was no evidence that the way the technology was used was thought to contribute to the undesired outcomes.

The monitoring technology itself tended to be viewed by managers as simply an automation of a long-established tradition of workplace control. Managing and control tended to be seen as synonymous. A critical issue, therefore, in the ethical management of control technologies, for example, is recognition that there are ethical issues arising from their design and use. Actions are more easily legitimated through the language of control and productivity than they are through the language of ethics. Again, there are no inherent characteristics of the technology that would condemn it as unethical for, as Ottensmeyer and Heroux point out

> Computer monitoring is not universally condemned by monitored workers ... when workers had the opportunity to participate in the design and implementation of computing monitoring systems they were much more likely to focus on the positive aspects of its use. (1991, p. 522)

It is the exclusion of those on whom the technology significantly impacts from involvement in the design process which renders the technology potentially oppressive. Its design is perceived as a non-issue and choices are perhaps not even made. A technological determinism prevails.

In the Ottensmeyer and Heroux case, worker concerns about surveillance technology centred on

❑ fairness (is that which is being monitored, e.g. number of transactions, indicative of performance?)
❑ their ability to still do a good job whilst being computer paced (knowing that failure to keep up with the computer clock means a reduction in pay)

❏ loss of individual control over the management of their working time (some people like to work steadily over the whole shift period whilst others prefer to work in highly active bursts with frequent rest periods. This second pattern, for example, may be construed, under an electronic system, as unproductive 'idle time')

❏ increase in stress and related illnesses such as headaches and depression

❏ loss of autonomy, dignity and privacy (for example, by supervisors listening-in to telephone calls, or auditing electronic communications).

Whilst many of these concerns could perhaps have been predicted, particularly by those with some knowledge of the sociotechnical tradition in organization design (Cummings, 1978; Kamata, 1983; Kornhauser, 1965; Walker and Guest, 1979), their significance lies in reflecting the particular interests of those involved. Methodologically, this implies using techniques such as focus groups and user panels to find out what users think about technological designs and building formal consultative mechanisms into decision-making structures. Eventually, consideration of these matters should be part of everyday management activity and not be separated out into a parallel structure. Many managers, in introducing quality and continuous improvement programmes into their organizations, have unintentionally set-up systems for capturing views on the impact of technological changes on the quality of working life. Unfortunately, the prevailing culture and pressure to perform often leads to the dismissal of ethical issues as unreal (Gosling, 1992).

The extent to which any technological choice incorporates the concerns of various stakeholders can be represented diagrammatically. Figure 6.1 draws on the data in the study outlined above to show how technology design agendas can be rethought to address silent issues. The extent to which any stakeholder concern currently influences the design is indicated by the 'pull' of the map. Pulls towards the external poles of the axes indicate that these concerns exert greater influence in the choice of technological design. Some speculative concerns of a fictitious local community have been added to offer a further set of design considerations.

Which stakeholders are included, the number of axes or concerns per stakeholder and the relative emphasis placed on those concerns are all matters of choice, influenced by political, historical and cultural factors. Changing the shape of the technology map to incorporate concerns not yet addressed is the remit of an ethical approach to technology management.

The phenomenological approach outlined here, in which the essential feature of the ethical management of technology is the enfranchisement of workers (and possibly other stakeholders) into the design process,   **Conclusion**

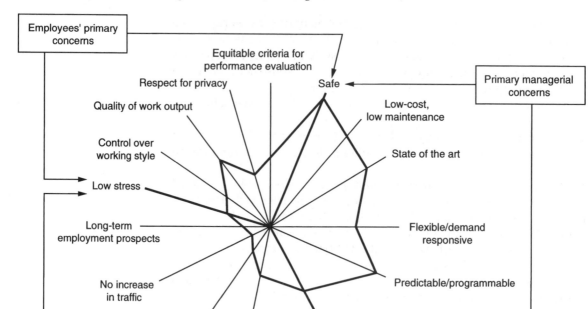

Figure 6.1 A competing values framework for ethical concerns in technology design.

contrasts with the regulatory approach enshrined in the codes of conduct mentality (Munro, 1992). Munro describes such regulatory codes as having the following features:

(a) they are grounded in an authority external to the individual
(b) they are prescriptive and refer to specific issues and values
(c) they tend to be legal in nature
(d) surveillance and sanctions originate from outside the individual
(e) sanctions are external and applied by the corporation such as being fired or demoted. (1992, p. 268)

Universal codes of good or ethical practice can be as alienating and oppressive as anything imposed by management (Whittle *et al.*, 1992). Whilst the use of tools such as formal employee impact statements (Walton, 1982) can stimulate discussion and offer ideas for consideration, they tend to ossify and impose agenda boundaries. Whilst, perhaps inevitably, the introduction of ethical issues into the technology design and management process will start as a formal, clumsy and rather self-conscious activity, as do many organizational innovations, the longer-term aim is to influence the taken-for-granted assumptions, the culture, within which a technological determinism can flourish unchallenged.

This chapter has focused on the dominance of the lean production paradigm, a model which leads to a determinist approach to the management of technology which effectively precludes ethical considerations. Other arenas of working life will have their own doctrines – pervasive ideas that are beyond doubt in structuring decision making. Recognizing and articulating the assumptions, the reifications, informing these models is the first step in challenging their ideological status and thus introducing the possibility for constructing alternative recipes, problems and solutions. This chapter does not offer specific recommendations for designing ethical technology – though such claims to universality are available (Jennett, 1986). The position adopted here is that whilst we can suggest questions to ask we should not provide answers (Munro, 1992). We need to construct principles and ends-means relationships for local contexts, for specific groups at specific times, and these will change. We need local theory (Eldon, 1983) because ethics is a local cultural issue.

Exercises

❑ Consider a recent technological change in your organization. What rationales were used to justify the technological design choices?
❑ Which stakeholders' interests dominated the decision-making process and whose interests were unrepresented?
❑ Can you identify (a) any negative and (b) positive consequences for each stakeholder group arising from the way in which the technological issues were managed?
❑ Are these consequences recognized as legitimate issues for debate and negotiation in your organization?
❑ If not, can you suggest ways in which such debate might be achieved?

Further reading

Delbridge, R., Turnbull, P. and Wilkinson, B. (1992) Pushing back the frontiers: management control and work intensification under JIT/TQM factory regimes. *New Technology, Work and Employment*. Basil Blackwell, Oxford.

Resahef, Y., Stratton-Devine, K. and Bemmels, B. (1994) The impact of manufacturing employees on technological changes. *Economic and Industrial Democracy*, 15(4), 505–30.

Commission of the European Communities, Directorate General Science (1992) What are anthropocentric production systems? Why are they a strategic issue for Europe? Report EUR 13968 EN, Brussels.

Beirne, M. and Ramsay, H. (eds) (1992) *Information Technology and Workplace Democracy*. Routledge, London.

References

Abrahamson, E. (1991) Managerial fads and fashions: the diffusion and rejection of innovations. *Academy of Management Review*, 16(3), 586–612.

Barrar, P., Locket, G. and Tanner, I. (1989) Decision processes in the design implementation and use of CAPM systems in medium sized organizations. Final report to ACME/SERC, Grant GR/E 21278.

Blauner, R. (1964) *Alienation and Freedom: The Factory Worker and his Industry*. University of Chicago Press, Chicago, IL.

Braverman, H. (1974) *Labour and Monopoly Capital*. Monthly Review Press, New York.

Clark, D.L. (1985) Emerging paradigms in organizational theory and research, in *Organizational Theory and Inquiry: The Paradigm Revolution* (ed. Y. Lincoln). Sage, Beverly Hills, CA, Chapter 2.

Coalition on New Office Technology (CNOT) (1989) *Electronic Monitoring in the Workplace: Supervision or Surveillance?* Boston, MA.

Cummings, T.E. (1978) Sociotechnical systems: an intervention strategy, in *Sociotechnical Systems: A Sourcebook* (eds W.A. Pasmore and J.J. Sherwood). California University Associates, La Jolla, CA.

Deming, W.E. (1986) *Out of the Crisis*. MIT Press, Cambridge, MA.

Department of Trade and Industry (1994) *Innovation: The Best Practice*. DTI, London.

Develin & Partners (1989) The effectiveness of quality improvement programmes in British business. London.

Eldon, M. (1983) Democratisation and participative research in developing local theory. *Journal of Occupational Behaviour*, 4, 21–33.

Garrahan, P. and Stewart, P. (1992) *The Nissan Enigma: Flexibility at Work in a Local Economy*. Mansell, London.

Geuss, R. (1981) *The Idea of a Critical Theory: Habermas and the Frankfurt School*. Cambridge University Press.

Goodman, P., Sproul, L. and Associates (1990) *Technology and Organizations*. Jossey-Bass, San Francisco, CA.

Gosling, D. (1992) Is a rational decision procedure possible for business ethics? *Conference Proceedings Business Ethics – Contributing to Business Success*, Sheffield Business School, April, pp. 119–139.

Grant, R. and Higgins, C. (1989) Monitoring service workers via computer: the effect on employees, productivity and service. *National Productivity Review*, 8, 101–112.

Gummesson, E. (1990) *Nine Lessons on Service Quality Implementing TQM: The Best of TQM Magazine*. IFS Publications, Bedford, Vol. 1.

Hartley, R.F. (1993) *Business Ethics: Violations of the Public Trust*. John Wiley, New York.

Harvey, J. (1974) Managing crises of agreement. *Organisation Dynamics*.

Harvey, J. (1989) Just-in-time in health and human services: a client approach. *Public Productivity and Management Review*, 13(9), Fall, 78–88.

Hayes, R. and Pisano, G. (1994) Beyond world-class: the new manufacturing strategy. *Harvard Business Review*, Janunary/February, 77–86.

Heller, R. (1987) *The State of Industry: Can Britain Make It?* BBC Books, London.

Heskett, J.L. (1986) *Managing in the Service Economy*. Harvard Business School Press, Boston, MA.

Hosmer, L. (1987) *The Ethics of Management*. Richard D. Irwin, Homewood, IL.

Jennett, B. (1986) *High Technology Medicine: Benefits and Burdens*. Oxford University Press.

Joad, C.E.M. (1936) *Guide to Philosophy*. Gollancz, London.

Kamata, S. (1983) *Japan in the Passing Lane*. Allen & Unwin.

Kearney, A.T. (Consultants) (1989) Computer integrated manufacturing: competitive advantage or technological dead-end? London.

King, J. (1994) Tools-R-Us. *Journal of Business Ethics*, **13**, 243–57.

Kornhauser, A. (1965) *Mental Health of the Industrial Worker*. John Wiley, New York.

Kuhn, T. (1962) *The Structure of Scientific Revolutions*. University of Chicago Press, Chicago, IL.

Kuhn, T. (1977) *The Essential Tension: Selected Studies in Scientific Tradition and Change*. University of Chicago Press, Chicago, IL.

Lyon, D. (1994) *The Electronic Eye*. Polity Press, Cambridge.

Macdonald, S. *et al.* (1983) *The Trouble with Technology*. Frances Pinter, London.

Mathews, J. (1993) Competing paradigms of productive efficiency – industrial relations and organisation change. Working paper, Centre for Corporate Change, Australian Graduate School of Management, New South Wales.

Miller, D. and Friesen, P.H. (1984) *Organizations: A Quantum View*. Prentice-Hall, Beverly Hills, CA.

Mintzberg, H. (1979) *The Structuring of Organizations*. Prentice-Hall, Englewood Cliffs, NJ.

Morgan, G. (1986) *Images of Organization*. Sage, Beverly Hills, CA.

Morgan, C. and Murgatroyd, S. (1994) *Total Quality Management in the Public Sector*. Open University Press, Buckingham.

Munro, I. (1992) The moral limitations of corporate codes of ethics. *Proceedings of the Business Ethics – Contributing to Business Success Conference*, Sheffield Business School, pp. 260–75.

Oliver, N. and Wilkinson, B. (1992) *The Japanization of British Industry*. Blackwell, Oxford.

Oliver, N. *et al.* (1994) World class manufacturing: further evidence in the lean production debate. *British Journal of Management*, **5**(special issue), June, 53–63.

Ottensmeyer, E.J. and Heroux, M.A. (1991) Ethics, public policy and managing advanced technologies: the case of electronic surveillance. *Journal of Business Ethics*, **10**, 519–26.

Perrow, C. (1967) Framework for the comparative analysis of organizations. *American Sociological Review*, 194–208.

Petrella, R. (1994) Science and technology in the interest of 8 billion people; is it possible? *Proceeding of the DTI's Technology Transfer and Innovation Conference: Identifying and Exploiting Innovation Opportunities*, July, London.

Quinn, R.E. (1988) *Beyond Rational Management*. Jossey-Bass, San Francisco, CA.

Roberts, J. (1984) The moral character of management practice. *Journal of Management Studies*, **21**(3), 287–302.

Sayles, L.R. (1958) *The Behaviour of Industrial Work Groups: Prediction and Control*. John Wiley, New York.

Schonberger, R. (1986) *World Class Manufacturing: The Lessons of Simplicity Applied*. Macmillan, London.

Smircich, L. (1983) Concepts of culture and organisational analysis. *Administrative Science Quarterly*, **28**(3), 339–358

Steele, L. (1989) *Managing Technology: The Strategic View*. McGraw-Hill, New York.

Susser, P.A. (1988) Electronic monitoring in the private sector; how closely should employers supervise their workers? *Employee Relations Law Journal*, **13**, 575–95.

Taylor, F.W. (1947) *The Principles of Scientific Management*. Harper & Row, New York.

Teece, D., Pisano, G. and Shuen, A. (1992) Dynamic capabilities and strategic management. Working paper, Harvard Business School.

Thompson, J.D. (1967) *Organizations in Action*. McGraw-Hill, New York.

Thompson, J.D. and Tuden, A. (1959) Strategies, structures and processes of organisational design, in *Comparative Studies in Administration* (ed. J.D. Thompson). University of Pittsburgh Press, Pittsburgh, PA.

Trist, E. and Bamforth, K.W. (1951) Some social and psychological consequences of the Longwall method of coal-getting. *Human Relations*, **4**, 3–38.

Walker, C. and Guest, R. (1979) *The Man on the Assembly Line*. Arno Press, New York.

Walton, R. (1982) Social choice in the development of advanced information technology. *Technology in Society*, **4**, 41–9.

Whittle, S. *et al.* (1992) The down side of best practice, in *International Operations: Crossing Borders in Manufacturing and Service* (eds R. Hollier, R. Boaden and S. New). Elsevier, Amsterdam.

Womack, J.P., Jones, D. and Roose, D. (1990) *The Machine that Changed the World*. Harper Perennial.

Woodward, J. (1965) *Industrial Organization: Theory and Practice*. Oxford University Press.

Zubhoff, S. (1988) *In the Age of the Smart Machine*. Heinemann, London.

Note

1. The principle of 'coexistence' has been cited recently in a report by the Confederation of Japan Automobile Workers Unions (1992) as a new design principle to overcome some of the problems associated with lean production. Particular aims include: reducing working hours; decoupling assembly from a single production line; decreasing noise levels; increasing space and layout ratios; lengthening model change cycles. [Source: *European Industrial Relations Review*, **223**, 15 (1992).]

Ethics and human resource management

7

Peter Cooke and John Shipton

We explore the phenomenon of human resource management (HRM) in this chapter to determine if it represents a 'new orthodoxy' for managing people in the UK and whether it is based on any moral or ethical principles. We stress the enigmatic quality of a notion that has promised to provide public and private organizations with the capacity to survive demanding market conditions and satisfy the needs and wants of a sophisticated labour force. We argue that a defining characteristic of HRM is its strategic approach to managing people. In a number of respects this strategic focus represents the major difference between the core concerns of business strategy and scholars from the disciplines of business ethics and industrial relations. A paramount crusade for the business strategist is that of understanding the behaviour and methods of organizations which have achieved success in a given market place.

In contrast, the dominant focus of ethics and industrial relations is the study of the moral worth, on the one hand, and the utilitarian value on the other, of human conduct and understanding the rules and principles which do and ought to govern it. We suggest that it is possible, and perhaps even desirable, for a model of HRM to possess ethical foundations or characteristics. However, it is also our contention that an ethical dimension is not a necessary condition of most normative or empirical models of HRM. The employment contract is pivotal to any analysis of HRM, and in our opinion, the degree of ethicality in a particular situation will be influenced, if not determined, by the capacity and willingness of the primary stakeholders to give due consideration to each other's needs and interests as well as those of other stakeholders. We nevertheless recognize that there are few easy answers in business ethics or in HRM! As Dachler and Enderle (1989) emphasized, the existence of HRM in any objective sense is problematic, 'HRM cannot be known independently of the observer who is trying to understand and deal with it'. Finally and paradoxically, we suggest that there may be a higher correlation between success in the market place and a relationship based on fairness and respect than with one which is characterized by its strategic approach to managing people.

The development of HRM

In retrospect, the mid-1970s can be viewed as a watershed period for most of the Organization of Economic and Cooperation and Development (OECD) countries. In the following 15 years the 'rules' of international capitalism were radically transformed as a consequence of the increased pace of technological change and a shift in the centre of gravity of manufacturing output to the newly emerging industrialized centres on the Pacific rim.

The older industrialized countries responded to these pressures in different ways, but the most significant reaction in the UK and the United States was that of deregulating internal labour and product markets. One of the principal repercussions of implementing this 'free market' policy or ideology was the destabilization of some of the traditional systems for providing social cohesion and economic order. By the early 1990s it was debatable whether the UK's 'old orthodoxy' for managing people was in terminal decline or undergoing a period of adjustment, and if the former, could we discern the shape and qualities of a new order?

During this period in the United States and the UK there was clear evidence of economic change, some of which could be determined as progress and development. However, we were also becoming more aware of an enlargement in the level of social and economic inequality within the UK which was partly a consequence of the economic conditions and the 'free market' policies of successive right-of-centre governments. The paradox of the 1980s lay in the contrast between the belief, the rhetoric and for some the actuality that we were witnessing a new dawn for the British economy while the experience of others was that of minimal hope and limited options. The optimists perceived radically new methods and approaches for management which recast the employment relationship and transformed the capacity and performance of organizations. The perceptions of the less fortunate stakeholder of the 'revolution' could have been influenced by being on the wrong end of a plant closure, downsized workforce or a re-engineered organization. A further paradox in the dialogue and practice of managing people at work is the gap between what is advocated as contemporary wisdom and actual behaviour. For example, most theories associated with the 'enterprise' culture advise that the various interests in an organization should harmonize and base their rewards on individual or group performance, if they wish to succeed under current market conditions. However, the authority of the revelation depreciates, if not appears trite, if there is evidence to suggest that the enhanced rewards of senior managers bear little, if any, relationship with the performance of the enterprises which they are managing (London School of Economics, 1992).

Throughout the1980s printing presses were busy producing a plethora of publications which provided recipes for managing high performance and change in organizations. Most of the assessments anticipated the collapse of traditional orthodoxies and paradigms for managing people in organizations and acquainted us with their transformational successors. A common feature of many of the 'new wave' management theories (Wood, 1989) was the significance given to the management of people and the social system. Peters and Waterman believed that excellent companies 'are the way they are because they are organized to obtain extraordinary effort from ordinary human beings'. Managers, in such high-performing organizations, need to be super-heroes and champions who 'engender, enthusiasm and intensity of effort' from their employees by helping them to find meaning in their lives. 'New wave' theorists emphasized the need to manage meaning by the use of language, stories, symbols, rituals, etc. Peters and Waterman believed that excellent companies could and should transform the employee into a hero, cast, family or crew member, associate or just a special and important individual which provided a sharp contrast to the traditional image of the employee as a cost, potential trouble, statistic or union member.

Although most representations of HRM are somewhat less sanguine than Peters and Waterman in proposing that the business enterprise should be the appropriate site for a moral order, they do share the characteristic that the management of people should be holistic, strategic, flexible and possess a hard and soft edge. A number of HRM models and Peters and Waterman imply that they are the appropriate options for organizations whose competitive strategy is based on quality, the market, innovation and high productivity. The standard representation of HRM found visionary leaders less appealing. However, they do pay more attention to operational-level processes and systems for managing people, such as performance management techniques, methods of selection, etc. HRM models and 'new wave' management theories imply that their respective approaches have the intent and the capacity to adapt to the changing needs and interests of the various stakeholders, including employees. For instance, it was not exceptional during the 1980s for the US business press to 'report' that organizations are becoming more 'caring and concerned', that adversarialism is giving way to trust, and that managers are learning to be 'aware' of the whole employee.

'New wave' management theories and HRM have been the focus of considerable controversy regarding the origins, consistency, and validity of their models. To illustrate the point; two years after the publication of *In Search of Excellence*, it was dismissed by Peter Drucker as a 'book for juveniles', a fad that would have a short shelf-life. This verdict was subsequent to the book selling, in 1985, some one million copies, in 15 translations. The Japanese edition sold 300,000 copies in six weeks (Silver, 1987). Equally, evaluations and descriptions of HRM have ranged from 'old wine in new bottles', mere hype to a lean, strategic and flexible model, which promises organizational survival and growth under the rules of competition in the global and 'postmodern' economy. Most of the empirical studies of HRM in action (Storey, 1992; Guest and Hoque, 1994; Fernie *et al.*, 1994) offer a somewhat enigmatic picture of the use of the model by British companies. Indeed Keep and Mayhew (1994) argue that British manufacturing industry suffers from a number of 'deep seated, interacting structural characteristics' that counteract attempts to introduce pure HRM approaches to managing people.

Barbara Townley argues that HRM is a diverse, if not *ad hoc*, collection of activities. Traditionally, the subject area has obtained its theoretical coherence from the implicit organizing principle or analytical focus of a system's maintenance or functionalist perspective. Townley proposes the employment relationship as an alternative underpinning for HRM which she derives from the work of Michel Foucault on the process of power-knowledge in organizations and society. The fitting paradigm for the employment relationship is seen to be transaction, 'supplying a satisfying exchange relation which is part of the economic problem, and broadly construed, has special relevance where the employment relationship is involved'. However, the institutional symbol of the relationship, the contract of employment, is inadequate because it only describes in very general terms the nature of the services to be provided by the employee, referring vaguely to issues such as commitment, effort, behaviour, etc. (Townley, 1994).

A contributory factor to the imperfections in the contract are deficiencies in the standards of language and skills used for completing complex contracts. Townley, draws upon the Foucauldian perspective to offer an analysis of the employment exchange focusing on, firstly the 'relational' nature of exchange, transaction, or contract and, secondly on the unavoidable uncertainty of ordered social relations. This different way of seeing the subject area offers the possibility that HRM performs the function of bridging the 'gap' between the promise of labour power and the performance of labour and thereby 'creates' the human resource that 'fits' internal and external market conditions. The strength of this perspective is that it highlights the possibility that an employer may utilize methods and styles for HRM that are ostensibly in the spiritual and material interest of the employee, but may prove, on closer inspection, to be the opposite. In some circumstances, employers could manipulate individual employees, with the use of symbols, language, sentiment, processes and systems, into a mendacious 'psychological contract' which might become a more potent form of control and exploitation. However, the weakness of the approach is that, as with the traditional industrial relations position on managing people at work, it does not address a significant influencing variable in the relationship, namely, how does the organization compete effectively in the product market? (Beaumont, 1990).

If we accept the Aristotelian assumption that the human is essentially a political and social creature then the primary focus of ethical studies is to reflect on the essence of a 'good' relationship between people in different contexts and situations. In these circumstances it would seem reasonable to suppose that there should be a modicum of common ground between the interests of business ethics and HRM. However, things are never what they seem so we need to resolve a number of quandaries regarding the essence of business ethics and HRM before searching for possible symbiotic areas to the relationship.

Firstly, it is doubtful whether the proponents of business ethics and HRM would develop a fruitful dialogue if it is assumed that, in a business context, the only worthwhile values are the pursuit of narrow self-interest, giving total priority to the principal stakeholder, responding only to short-term market pressures and minimal legal regulation. Not surprisingly, in these circumstances, the employee is perceived as a factor of production with a value and worth determined solely by his or her marginal product and the condition of product and labour markets. In contrast, Charles Handy (1994) is of the view that Adam Smith's ideas have been misinterpreted, and in particular, the precept that by purely looking after our particular interest an 'invisible hand' will, in the long run, arrange the best of all circumstances. In the absence of a 'duty to consider one's neighbour and grandchildren' or some compassion for the less fortunate then individual rights and freedoms become mere licence and egoism. Handy maintains that Adam Smith was first and foremost a professor of moral philosophy rather than a scholar of the 'dismal' science of economics. Prior to writing his well-thumbed *Wealth of Nations* he produced the *Theory of Moral Sentiments* in which he argued that a stable society was based on sympathy, a moral duty, to have regard for your fellow citizens. The market? That is a mechanism to differentiate between the efficient and the inefficient and not therefore a substitute for moral responsibility. Karl Marx and Peter Drucker, however, would, no doubt, subscribe to the view that to be effective in a competitive market system, which is underpinned by private ownership and profit, managers are not and should not be restricted by moral duties and responsibilities. Therefore, business ethics become a 'contradiction in terms'. There is, moreover, the question of which particular set of values and interests do we use to create and support the moral order? Ordinarily, in society and organizations the dominant values are shaped by those with the greater access to the resources of power!

A further reason why the areas of business ethics and HRM have experienced a somewhat arrested discourse stems, partly, from the fact that many of the advocates of HRM have been more enthusiastic to show that the primary qualities of the model are those of managing change and improving performance and partly because the business ethicists have been, arguably, somewhat aloof from the concerns of managers operating in a business environment.

Ethics and HRM: the possibilities for a dialogue

During the last 15 years, in the United States and latterly in the UK, the field of business ethics has become 'big business'. The initial interest in ethics and business originated, at the turn of the century, from the evident imperviousness of the large corporation to the pressures from the 'invisible hand'. This awakened interest in exploring a broader view of a business enterprise's obligations in society and the subsequent appearance of the corporate social responsibility school. They believed that big business should have wider responsibilities than attention to the immediate bottom line, maximizing shareholder equity and conforming with (or evading) the legal minimum. They argued that senior managers should voluntarily operate from a basis of enlightened self-interest and develop standards that are in advance of the current dictates of the market and the law. Although this approach may prove costly in the short-term, it would pay off in the longer term because the market will reward prescient and socially responsible behaviour. Apart from the absence of a primary value or system of beliefs, a significant weakness of this optimistic *Weltanschauung* lay in its neglect of managers who were attempting to incorporate an ethical dimension into their everyday decisions. Nevertheless, it did direct our attention to the potentially critical role of the chief executive officer (CEO) and senior managers in inculcating ethical, and other, values and standards into the modern organization.

A more recent upsurge of activity and interest in business ethics sprang, in part, from a spate of business and political scandals on both sides of the Atlantic (for example, Watergate, the Iran–Contra affair, the Iraqi supergun, Maxwell and the British Airway's subterfuge) and partly from the uncertainties induced by the accelerating pace of economic, scientific and technological change. The form of the upsurge in the 1980s was driven by the moral philosophers who moved into a 'gap in the market'. At this time their methodology was based on applying general principles, derived from religious beliefs or rationality, to specific situations, through the use of deductive logic. The method paid scant attention to the 'real' world of organizational life and their early findings gave little support to the principle of enlightened self-interest. Moreover, contrary to the expectations of 'enlightened' business managers, ethical behaviour was not always in the company's best interest. This assertion no doubt caused dismay to those responsible for 'minding the conscience' of the organization. However, their less sensitive colleagues in the corporate world could well have been dumbfounded on receiving proclamations that 'to behave ethically can cost dearly', and 'to be ethical in business because it may increase your profits is to do so for entirely the wrong reason. The ethical business must be ethical because it wants to be ethical'. The gulf between ethicists and the 'typical' business manager, grappling to survive in a war of all against all, could only widen when offered the absolutism and solace that, 'if in some instance it turns out that what is ethical leads to the company's demise' then 'so be it' (Stark, 1993).

The objective or absolutist school of business ethics were equally un-compromising when they addressed a central question of HRM; namely what is the basis for a 'good' relationship between the employer and employee? Freeman and Gilbert (1988) develop, to its logical conclusion, the religious or Kantian principle, that *Homo sapiens* should be regarded as moral entities and therefore ought to be treated as ends and not as means. Business enterprises that wish to be considered to be genuinely ethical when managing the 'human resource' need to expel all the methods that they employ to *externally* motivate the individual. To be ethically correct, the contract of employment must be based on consent and the job tasks should be compatible with an employee's 'own personal goals'. Any element or form of coercion should be spurned as a means of influenc-ing the employee's behaviour and therefore an individual's motivation would be totally dependent on *internal* stimulation. There are, no doubt, 'enlightened' HR managers who would advocate that the management of people in their organizations should be characterized by moral probity and who would warm to the spirit of 'renaissance man' but still argue for conditional rights for the employee and the retention of a wide range of managerial prerogatives. Certainly, the biographies of business leaders illustrate that there are many who ignored 'one-dimensional market rationality' and introduced policies and practices that provided a sense of dignity and fairness for working people. In a number of cases, such as J. Arthur Rank, Cadbury. Lord Nuffield, the motivation and idea for their 'philanthropic' attitudes arose from the codes of conduct which originated in their church and/or family. Incidentally, this also applies to many past (and some present) leaders of the labour movement. What we are less confident about, however, is the precise factor which activated the behaviour of particular individuals! Macfarlane (1993) contends that 'the instincts of Victorian paternalism have been customized into an essen-tially amoral caring corporatism and ... in the new age of individualism there is a notable absence of the restraining forces of religion, family and strong secular moral codes'. He believes that in these 'postmodern conditions' the 'possessive' individual is more likely to have mixed motives for his or her behaviour and is more likely to be motivated by one or a mixture of guilt, prudence, fear, pride, shame, or the search for esteem, love or respect.

One of the integral features of both HRM and 'new wave' management theories is the promise of a panacea for managing change and achieving corporate success under contemporary market conditions. There is, however, an inkling in the literature that HRM, in particular, may be more congruent to situations where organizations are responding to mar-kets which demand not only cost competitiveness, but also emphasize quality, innovation, flexibility and customer sensitiveness. In the majority of the HRM models it is claimed that the critical resource is people: 'our

HRM: the new panacea?

most valuable resource'. This raises a number of issues regarding the images and the inherent assumptions of people and management within the human resource metaphor and HRM models. Firstly, in comparison with scientific management and bureaucracy, the images and potential of people are decidedly more heroic. The individual has the capacity to be a committed, rational, energetic, innovative, creative, flexible, cooperative and sociable employee who also possesses the additional strength of being able to learn and develop. Nevertheless, the extent to which any of these capacities and qualities are recognized and used is not, within the models of HRM, determined by reference to any 'abstract' or 'concrete' moral foundations. It is more contingent on variables such as the condition of product and labour markets, the competitive strategy of the enterprise, the philosophy or fancy of the CEO, etc.

Boxall (1993) believes that two broad strands of meaning can be discerned from the sometimes heated debate, by theorists from competing disciplines, into the meaning and significance of HRM. The first, sees HRM as a particular management strategy, based on the commitment of the employee and unitarist in essence because it views labour unions as being unnecessary. The second meaning views HRM as a broad theoretical development with a central concern of building links between the business disciplines of HRM and the field of strategic management. In Boxall's opinion the second strand of meaning carries more significance if there is a desire and need to develop theory and research possibilities of HRM. From this perspective, the subject area (and functional specialism) should be theoretically grounded in a branch of strategic management. The outcome for business managers would be the provision of a range of options from which to choose the most appropriate HRM strategy for their particular circumstances. In these conditions a primary goal for HRM research could be identifying and analysing the relationship between different strategic options and the subsequent commercial results. This new orthodoxy offers a sharp contrast with the moribund traditions and techniques of the 'one best way' of personnel management.

Storey (1992) has developed a useful typology which 'maps' the various meanings that HRM represents and indicates the strategies for managing people in the workplace (see Fig. 7.1). The strong axis provides a focus for most of the HRM prescriptions which have arisen, although, arguably, the weak axis is just as prescriptive. Three elements emerge:

1. HRM is integrated with the organization's business strategy.
2. HRM applications emphasize the careful planning of human resources (not necessarily always employees).
3. HRM is concerned with developing employees in both abilities and commitment to the organization.

Storey's map points at the role of the personnel profession which has been seen historically as a sort of repository of the organizational con-

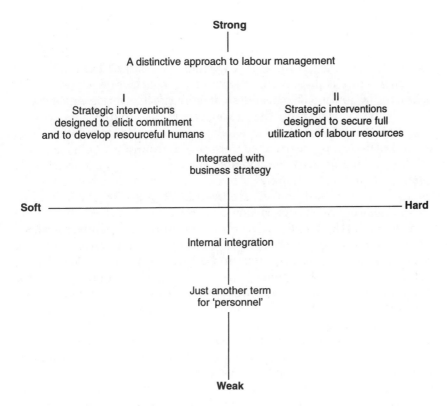

Strong

A distinctive approach to labour management

I
Strategic interventions
designed to elicit commitment
and to develop resourceful humans

II
Strategic interventions
designed to secure full
utilization of labour resources

Integrated with
business strategy

Soft ——————————————————————————— **Hard**

Internal integration

Just another term
for 'personnel'

Weak

Figure 7.1 HRM 'mapping' of various meanings.

science. A survey by the University of Westminster reinforces this view by placing the personnel profession second only to the clergy in terms of ethics (*PM Plus*, January 1993). Personnel specialists, therefore, appear to be significant stakeholders in the HRM/ethics arena.

Professional bodies [and the Institute of Personnel Development (IPD) is no exception] argue that a major *raison d'être* is to regulate standards of behaviour of their members. Codes of practice are one of the ways in which this regulation is carried out and IPD/Institute of Personnel Management has issued around 15 codes to date. However, the development of codes of practice reflects a set of prescriptions from a relatively small, if senior, group of practitioners and their effect in protecting employees might be overdone. Fletcher (1992), for instance, reports in a study of ethics in the job interview, that support for the acceptability of asking questions about political beliefs and the candidate's spouse and family was *stronger* among candidates than among interviewers.

Arguably, the IPD, more than most other professional bodies, is concerned with squaring the ethical circle in that its stated aims over many years have included the need to promote both organizational efficiency *and* organizational justice. In discussing the then IPM's mission, for example, Whittaker (1992) states that the Institute is for 'all those responsible for the optimum use of human resources to the mutual benefit of the enterprise, each person and the community at large'. The implication of such a stance is that an efficiency/justice reconciliation is possible.

The realization and demonstration of more effective management could, in itself, be viewed, from some perspectives, as ethically and morally beneficial. For example, Alan Flanders was strongly of the opinion that 'the claim for management to be treated as a profession could have little validity so long as it has no accepted standards of conduct which fully define its moral responsibilities'. For example: 'the underemployment, by its wholesale waste of human resources, offers a glaring example of an irresponsible use of managerial power' (Cressey *et al.*, 1985). There could be many in the UK's traditional centre of manufacturing who may reflect, from a utilitarian perspective, upon the long-term economic and social costs associated with the decline of the indigenous car and motorcycle industry. They may also ponder on the possibility that in both cases the causation was the same unholy trinity of poor management and control, dreadful industrial relations and harmful government policies. In a number of respects the 'old orthodoxy' of British industrial relations was an example of 'arrested' development in a relationship. In too many situations the parties to this 'collective consensus' conspired to retain a *status quo* which displayed little interest in the wider and deeper needs of the respective parties. The relationship was frequently focused on a narrow range of short-term issues and contained too few examples of the parties exploring possible areas for longer-term cooperation and risk taking. Relationships within the manufacturing sector especially were saturated in the traditions of the British class culture so the degree of respect between employer and employee tended to be low and the relationship was impregnated with low trust, reactive, uncooperative and adversarial attitudes and behaviour. Not surprisingly, in these circumstances, the parties had limited expectations for the pay-offs from the relationship. The central goals were built around maintaining the traditional order of authority, status, occupational structures and differentials/relativities. There was a system of order to control labour but it was not always a moral order!

Stephen Dunn (1992) contentiously employed the root metaphor of 'trench war' to illustrate a view of the scholarship and the conduct of British industrial relations of the 'old orthodoxy'. The combatants, observing each other from a distance, were engaged in a relationship which had limited horizons and objectives. The boundaries and frontiers for the relationship were preserved by the tacit 'agreement to live and let live' and maintained within a procedural consensus. The adjectives closed, static and pessimistic that were used to describe the qualities of the traditional approach vividly contrasted with the hopefulness and sense of progress which was generated by HRM's metaphor of 'becoming'.

What were the prospects, however, for a model, which emphasizes the value of individualism, flexibility, strategic integration and commitment, becoming the 'new orthodoxy' for managing people within organizations? A number of questions arise. Firstly, when compared with the 'paradigms' of the 'old orthodoxy', would a model of HRM provide an adequate foundation for developing viable research and scholarship in subjects associated with the employment contract? Secondly, will HRM deliver its promise to be a more effective approach to managing people at work in the present market conditions? Thirdly, will the positive qualities of the 'old orthodoxy', namely, providing the opportunity for employees to have an effective voice via trade union organization and democratic practices and procedures, be retained in the new order? Fourthly, will HRM offer additional values and standards for supporting an effective and ethical relationship between people in employment? Fifthly, will HRM models in action deliver a higher level of individual freedom (from and to) for employees? Finally, will the application of a HRM model enhance the dignity of the individual by terminating discriminatory practices and minimizing the degrees and area of inequality between people?

We argued earlier in the chapter that one of HRM's most significant features was its strategic dimension and that Boxall was of the view that in order to develop the subject and functional area it should be lodged in the stable of business strategy rather than those of, say, accountancy or organization behaviour. This, however, raises certain difficulties if we wish to retain the integrity, consistency and impartiality of the subject area so that it provides an 'even playing field' for handling the conflicting interests of both employer and employee. Meyer (1991) highlights a number of advantages that business strategy has gained from offering itself as a 'pluralistic meeting ground where different disciplines, theories and methods compete to find answers to important questions for organization and societies'. He argues that business strategy's development as an inter-disciplinary arena was facilitated by concentrating on an exclusive focus for research and by gathering their empirical work around a single question. The challenge for business strategists was to discover how particular organizations and enterprises constantly prospered, relative to their rivals, in the market. Hallier (1993) points out that a guiding research question for HRM needs to extend beyond business strategy's concentration on the single issue of competition. Success in the market place and the 'notion of competitiveness' may be a pre-eminent issue for business strategists, but HRM needs to consider all aspects of the employment relationship and give equal priority to the interests of the employer and the employee. In order to promote HRM research and scholarship, Hallier (1993), suggests that the pertinent question should be: Is, and, if so, in what circumstances, the management of the workplace compatible with the mutual achievement of long-term employer and employee objectives?

The strategic dimension

Storey and Sisson (1993), using the Workplace Industrial Relations Survey to track the record of HRM in the UK reach the conclusion that despite the substantial razzmatazz and hype that has accompanied the arrival of HRM on this side of the Atlantic, there are relatively few circumstances where a comprehensive model is in operation. There is, however, ample evidence of the introduction of changes to management in a piecemeal fashion and employing some of the methods that are strongly associated with HRM. Guest (1990) is critical of this *ad hoc* innovation rather than 'integrated' strategic changes. Boxall (1993), however, supports this 'Fabian' tactic, in asserting that a form of 'creative incrementalism' could well achieve change in contemporary conditions and might also fit with an aspect of 'strategic learning' (Johnson and Scholes, 1988). Paradoxically, the circumstances where all or part of the HRM model is most likely to be discovered alive and well are in those companies which have recognized and have developed a working relationship with trade unions. The implication of this is that non-union companies who are unlikely to have any alternative formal system for managing people are the least probable site for HRM. So why has HRM failed to make a more emphatic impression on UK employers when, in theory, it promises the panacea for achieving success in the marketplace and fulfilling the needs and wants of the employees?

One reason is related to HRM's possible incompatibility with existing management priorities and beliefs! In this scenario the CEO consciously or unconsciously responds to external pressures on the existing system by employing a cost-cutting exercise with a consequential zero investment in the human resource. For example, Keep and Mayhew (1994) are of the opinion that Britain's shortage of human resource skills in manufacturing industry is only partly caused by an inadequate supply. They argue that it is also created by the low demand from many employers and therefore some of the attempts to improve the skills of the labour force in many areas of the economy could prove disappointing, if not wasteful. Undoubtedly, given the current conditions in international markets, there are some difficulties with the quantity and quality of skills and education in the UK labour force. Keep and Mayhew assert, however, that it may be a fallacy to assume that employers are behaving illogically, if not unethically, in damaging the long-term interests of the company by not investing in improving the stock of human resource skills. Management's response is deemed to be entirely rational given that within the UK economy there are 'a series of deep seated, interacting structural characteristics which militate against an increased demand from employers for skills'. In their evidence to the House of Commons Select Committee on competitiveness in manufacturing industry they perceived the principal restraining forces to be; firstly, the failure of many firms to adopt HRM systems congruent with a high-skill strategy which was reflected in the inability of companies to capture the motivational benefits of training, the lack of internal labour market structures and opportunities for progression and development. Secondly, they cite the short-termism in the British economy which influenced behaviour within the company by giving priority to cost-control, management accounting structures and reward systems. Thirdly, there are the difficulties of labour poaching caused by the overdependence of companies on the external labour market. Fourthly, they point to the dwindling importance of the UK as a market and as a production base for many large companies; and finally, the high volatility of the British economy compared with other developed countries.

One salient issue that arises from the above discussion is the extent to which an individual employee should be deemed dishonourable and unworthy because of engaging in behaviour which has been adjudged, at the place of work, to be in some respect 'unethical'. It may be argued that in the majority of situations, when decisions are being made in organizations, the individual will possess some area of autonomy and a modicum of discretion. If these circumstances hold it would follow that the decision makers ought to be responsible, at least to some degree, for the decision and the repercussions. An alternative viewpoint highlights the possibility that decision making in business and other contexts forms part of a wider system which could seriously inhibit the freedom of the individual to make moral or ethical judgements. The individual in question may not in fact be conscious of any ethical ramifications to the decision because it was perceived as routine and 'normal'. Accordingly, behaviour that might be evaluated by an outsider as reckless, self-regarding and harmful to other interests could well be classed as typical and functional by those cooped-up in the 'psychic prison' that has been created by the systems and culture of a particular organization.

Badaracco and Webb (1995) in an attempt to explain why companies deviated from a code of ethical standards interviewed younger managers who had studied business ethics as part of their master of business administration (MBA) degree and about half of whom worked at companies with a formal ethics programme. They concluded that the ethical ambience of the organizations in the study was 'extremely fragile' because in too many companies behaving 'ethically' was construed as performing successfully, competently and pledging loyalty and allegiance to the company. Managers, on the lower rungs of a career ladder were discouraged from becoming overcommitted to, and in some cases concerned with, ethical benchmarks. Although, successful managers refrained from breaking the law, they interpreted the ethical conventions of the company in a liberal and flexible manner and tended to have little respect for whistleblowers. It was stressed that because junior managers were operating in highly competitive markets, managing under intense business and personal pressure, including the threat of 'downsizing', they could not engage in 'avoidance behaviour' if a clash occurred between the demands of business and ethics. At this critical stage in the decision-making process first line and junior managers looked for mentors and guidance from middle and senior managers who interpret and set the ethical code. The outcome? Not surprisingly, strong signals to put business first, especially in situations were companies grappled with the need for lower costs and faster decisions. Badaracco and Webb suggest that if the principal stake-holders in companies wish to raise ethical standards they might, firstly, support the code of ethics with investigatory powers and tough sanctions and secondly make sure the chiefs lead by example!

Earlier in the chapter we argued that the majority of the 'new wave' management theorists placed much emphasis on the potential of the employee to generate added value to the organization. Most concentrated on the 'resource' and, with a few exceptions, they gave less significance to the 'human' dimension. 'New wave 'theorists acknowledged that a style of management which derived its authority largely from coercion or sys-tems was in crisis. Despite this awareness, they reconceptualized the employee from a passive instrument of production, with some sort of needs-driven mechanism, a rational and avid maximizer of profits, a resource to be exploited into a rational, feeling and choice-making human being; then impounded him or her within the traditions and frameworks of utilitarian functionalism and neo-classical economic thought (Artouf, 1992). The theories and models of HRM and 'new wave' management have been described as revolutions or transformations in how people are managed within organizations. It would seem, however, that to radically change the relationship there is a need, in theory and practice, to give greater credence to the employee, as a human being, which implies assign-ing greater respect for his or her interests and autonomy. There are examples of successful commercial companies who base their manage-ment style on the idea of the 'humanized firm' (Artouf, 1992). Ricardo Semler the CEO of Semco on taking over the company from his father dismantled the corporate hierarchy and redesigned the company as a double circle, with a group of counsellors (directors) in the middle and all the associates (including partners and coordinators) in the outer space which was held together in smaller circles by coordinators. Partners (senior managers) have to set their own salaries and bonuses and the associates determine their own hours, productivity targets and evaluate the partners. Handy (1994) submits that a challenge for Ricardo Semler is to contend with the rising expectations stimulated by the new titles and re-organization while operating without any change to the legal owner-ship of the company. If he can survive and develop in the difficult condi-tions of the Brazilian economy then 'it must be possible elsewhere'.

The UK-based John Lewis Partnership is unique because the structure is built on the assumption that in some respect the organization belongs to its members, who receive dividends from the profits, but do not own shares that can be sold. Although the company is organized and managed with conventional structures and roles, the employees are provided with open information and the opportunity to give their views on strategic and operational issues. Artouf offers an example of commercially viable organizations which operate outside the functional–consensual tradition and in different ways have developed open, frank and mature relationship with their employees. Storey and Sisson (1993) point to the experience of the Rover car company. Although much more mainstream in its style of management, it has dramatically improved the performance of the organization in the marketplace by developing a close working relationship with local unions and the employees.

A pivotal element of most HRM models is the development of a control system founded on self-control and a psychological contract based on commitment rather than compliance. Oliver and Lowe (1989) believe that the idea of commitment in the HRM and other literature is laden with conceptual and empirical difficulties. It is generally and loosely considered as an attitude with three basic components: firstly, a belief in the goals and values of the organization; secondly, a willingness to exert effort and, thirdly, a desire to stay with the corporation (Mowday *et al.*, 1982). In a piece of research into examples of an espoused swing from control to commitment strategy within two companies in the UK, (one US and one Japanese owned), Oliver and Lowe (1989) identified much of the HRM symbols, language and initiatives. Both companies had distinct corporate and management philosophies, which were epitomized by one of the mission statements: 'We shall strive to be a good company, trusted in every part of the world, by placing the customer *first*, respecting the *individual* and displaying *collective strength*'. The structures of both companies diverge from the traditional hierarchy, one into a matrix and the other claiming to be 'anti-hierarchical, anti-structure, anti-status, with a flexible, change and individual orientation' (Oliver and Lowe, 1989). Both companies possessed strong cultures and used highly developed methods for recruitment and selection and related the management of people to the goals of the organization. One of the companies claimed to operate a sophisticated human resources function which gave prominence to individual empowerment whereas the other company placed more emphasis on group processes. Both companies operated in a fast-moving market and, in the opinion of the authors, the employees demonstrated a high level of commitment by investing 'extraordinary amounts of time and effort' into their work. However, Oliver and Lowe indicated that it was less apparent why people were so 'committed'. 'Our respondents were clearly struggling for attributions for their own behaviour; most appeared to have difficulty in distinguishing between their own identity and that of the organization'.

Conclusions

HRM and business ethics came to prominence during the early 1980s and produced a 'theory of the firm' based on a more absorbing and complex model of the individual than that found in the traditional paradigms of economic or organization theory. Both HRM and business ethics offered a vision, which if realized, could transform the orthodox approach to managing people and decision making in business organizations. From an optimistic interpretation of the respective constructs it could be argued that they possessed the necessary qualities to eradicate apparently insoluble contradictions between, on the one hand, business efficiency and virtuous behaviour, and on the other, the conflicting interests of capital and labour. However, from a more sanguine perspective, the prominence of HRM and business ethics could also signify a crisis of confidence in the established modes, ideas and institutions of control in western business organizations. These recent innovations were perceived more as palliative than the radical reconstruction of decision-making systems required to incorporate some form of ethical principles or to base the management of people on a balance of compassion and efficiency! The recent captivation of business and management education with business ethics could be interpreted as a search for an alternative 'spiritual underpinning' for the market system to replace the now defunct 'Protestant work ethic'. However, the outlook is not entirely promising for securing a synthesis between ethical thinking and business behaviour. Business ethics does not provide easy answers for managers trying to reconcile conflicts between an ethically sound and a commercially viable decision. Moreover, there is evidence which indicates that, in the absence of external regulation, the CEO will carry substantial responsibility for creating and maintaining a system which is capable of making 'good' as well as effective decisions in the organization!

The literature and research on HRM suggest that the CEO will also have a prominent role to play in supporting a system and strategy which both promise success for organizations that are operating in turbulent product markets and fulfil the multifarious needs of *Homo sapiens*. The development of a strategy to elicit a high level of commitment from individual employees to organizational goals and values is the principal HRM thrust for closing the 'gap' in expectations between those of the employer and the employee. We have indicated, however, that a substantial degree of ambiguity surrounds the precise meaning of HRM in general and the idea of employee commitment in particular. There is abundant case study and survey evidence to confirm that, during the past decade, there have undoubtedly been changes in the methods used for managing people within organizations. What is less clear, however, is the extent to which these changes are strategic in kind and based upon a wider recognition of the qualities of 'renaissance man'. Or perhaps they are merely an illustration of the management of meaning in a 'postmodern' society? We also stressed the point that there are conditions which seem to be more or less favourable for introducing a strategic approach to managing people and developing 'ethical' standards in the employment relationship. For instance, Keep and Mayhew (1994) argued that there are structural flaws within the UK which militate against the improvement of skills in the labour force. One of these, the shortage of structures and systems which foster the motivational benefits of training and development, could also impede a strategy for increasing the level of employee commitment to the goals of the organization. Finally, it seems that in the short to medium term, the prospects in the UK look somewhat gloomy for basing the contract of employment on either the philosophies and practice of HRM or on a construct of business ethics. We arrive at this less than cheery conclusion primarily because it appears excessively demanding to sustain a decent and longer term relationship in circumstances where the stakeholders are in pursuit of wholly short-term, narrow and self-regarding goals. Charles Handy (1994), in an uncharacteristically sombre tone, observes that it is difficult, given the present climate and the structure of the capital market, to envisage the stakeholders within publicly quoted companies successfully reaching an agreement on longer term goals. He recognizes that the owners of public companies are mostly institutions who 'have no direct involvement with the business. They do not manage or work in it. They do not know those who do. They are not locked in [because] the average shareholding by the large institutional investors in Britain is held for [only] four years.'

❏ Is there an identifiable set of human rights applicable to all employees in all organizations?   **Exercises**
❏ Is it possible for a company to pursue a short-term cost leadership/ reduction strategy and employ ethical standards or use a HRM model for managing people?
❏ In what circumstances, if any, can you preserve ethical standards for managing people by introducing a professional code of practice?
❏ Consider the view that, in the end, what is good for the organization is good for its employees.

Handy, C. (1994) *The Empty Raincoat*. Hutchinson.   **Further reading**
Stark, A. (1993) What's the matter with business ethics? *Harvard Business Review*, May/June.
Townley, B. (1994) *Reframing HRM: Ethics and the Subject of Work*. Sage.

Artouf, O. (1992) Management and the theories of organisations in the 1990s: **References**
towards a critical radical humanism? *Academy of Management Review*, 17(3).
Badaracco, J. and Webb, A. (1995) Business ethics: the view from the trenches. *California Management Review*, 37(2).
Beaumont, P.B. (1990) *Change in Industrial Relations: the Organization and Environment*. Routledge.
Boxall, P.F. (1993) The significance of human resource management: a reconsideration of the evidence. *International Journal of Human Resource Management*, 4(3), September.

Dachler, P.H. and Enderle, G. (1989) Epistemological and ethical considerations in conceptualizing and implementing human resource management. *Journal of Business Ethics*, 8, 597–606.

Dunn, S. (1992) Root metaphor in the old and new industrial relations. *British Journal of Industrial Relations*, 28, 1–31.

Fernie, S., Metcalfe, D., and Woodlands, S. (1994) Does HRM boost employee–employer relations? CEP Working Paper 548, February

Fletcher, C. (1992) Ethics and the job interview. *Personnel Management*, March.

Freeman, R.E. and Gilbert Jr, D.R. (1988) *Corporate Strategy and the Search for Ethics*. Prentice-Hall.

Guest, D. (1990) Human resource management and the American dream. *Journal of Management Studies*, 27(4).

Guest, D. and Hoque, K. (1994) The good, the bad and the ugly: employment relations in new non-union workplaces. *Human Resource Management Journal*, 5(1).

Hallier, G. (1993) HRM as a pluralistic forum: assumptions and prospects for developing a distinctive research capacity. *International Journal of Human Resource Management*, 4(4), December.

Handy, C. (1994) *The Empty Raincoat*. Hutchinson.

Johnson, G. and Scholes, K. (1988) *Exploring Corporate Strategy*. Prentice-Hall.

Keep, E. and Mayhew, D. (1994) The competitiveness of UK manufacturing industry. Evidence to the Select Committee for Trade and Industry, HMSO, London.

London School of Economics (1992) Economic performance, the disappearing link between director's rewards and corporate performance.

Macfarlane, B. (1993) Business ethics and the role of pride. *Management Education and Development*, 24(4).

Meyer, A.D. (1991) What is strategy's distinctive competence? *Journal of Management Studies*, 17(4).

Mowday, R.T., Steers, R.M. and Porter, L.W. (1982) *Employee–Organization Linkages: the Psychology of Commitment, Absenteeism amd Turnover*. Academic Press.

Oliver, N. and Lowe, J. (1989) New look employee relations: the view from the inside. Paper to Conference on Strategies for Managing People, Cardiff Business School.

Silver, J. (1987) The ideology of excellence: management and neo-conservatism. *Studies in Political Economy*, 24, Autumn.

Stark, A. (1993) What's the matter with business ethics? *Harvard Business Review*, May–June.

Storey, J. (1992) *Developments in the Management of Human Resources*. Basil Blackwell, Oxford.

Storey, J. and Sisson, K. (1993) *Managing Human Resources and Industrial Relations*. Open University Press.

Townley, B. (1994) *Reframing HRM: Power, Ethics and the Subject of Work*. Sage.

Whittaker, J. (1992) The pivotal role of the personnel professional in business ethics – contributing to business success. Sheffield Business School, April.

Wood, S.J. (1989) New wave management. *Work, Employment and Society*, 3(3), September.

Part Two
Contemporary critical issues in business ethics

The management control of ethics: the case of corporate codes

8

Phil Johnson, Catherine Cassell and Ken Smith

Phil Johnson, Catherine Cassell and Ken Smith

This chapter is concerned with a fundamental aspect of all organizations – the processes through which an organization's membership determine what, and how, things get done. As many commentators have noted (e.g. Gouldner, 1959; Silverman, 1971; Johnson and Gill, 1993), everyday organizational life must be seen as a continuous process of conflict, negotiation and, indeed, cooperation between people who have a multiplicity of goals perceived interests and purposes. It is in this context that managers undertake what has been called their 'quintessential role' (Storey, 1983, p. 96) of attempting to exercise control over both human and inanimate resources. Here our intention is to consider one aspect of this role: the means by which senior management might attempt to purposively influence, or control, the ethical dimensions of members' organizational behaviour. However, such processes are inherently problematic since any attempt to control any dimension of members' behaviour is

Introduction

> ... a complex and ill understood activity precisely because it involves an attempt to control a complex network of self-controlling human beings. (Emmanuel and Otley, 1985, p. 10)

In considering these significant issues this chapter examines the question of the relationships between ethics and different forms of management control. Using the case of corporate codes of ethics as an illustrative example, these different forms of control are assessed. The question is then raised about the impact of these relationships on the everyday 'ethical' behaviour of organizational actors. Finally the chapter outlines the utility of a contextualist approach in aiding the understanding of what are complex organizational issues.

As was indicated in the introduction to this book, some commentators claim that business and ethics are either incommensurable, or that there is a difference between the often implicit moral rules within the workplace and how one should behave outside (Carr, 1968). In contrast, others have maintained that there is an 'ethics of the workplace' and that there is a need to avoid the all too prevalent 'moral muteness' so as to legitimize the discussion of ethical issues within the organization (Bird and Waters, 1989). Intriguingly, McHugh (1988) has argued that business ethics in the twentieth century has become to be perceived as being predominately a managerial matter. These observations imply that the ethical dimension to members' organizational behaviour, while often 'mutely' guided by informal norms, can, and should, be formally specified, reinforced or modified through the creation of systems of management control (Jensen and Wygant, 1990).

Empirical evidence suggests that there are many ways in which management may choose to purposively exert control over the ethical dimension to members' behaviour. These include ethics training (e.g. Snell, 1990; Stead *et al.*, 1990), the establishment of ethics committees (Feldman *et al.*, 1986) and modifying an organization's information and reporting systems (McCoy, 1985). However, the most important way by which management have attempted to 'institutionalize ethics' has been through the development of a corporate code of ethics (e.g. Mathews, 1988; Schlegelmilch and Houston, 1989; Sims, 1991; Manley, 1992; Webley, 1988, 1992). In effect a corporate code provides a visible and public statement of ostensible organizational values, duties and obligations. As such they can both play a role in controlling members' behaviour and present a particular public image of the organization to stakeholders (Mathews, 1988). But understanding how such attempts at specifying and controlling the ethical dimension of behaviour actually operate in practice simultaneously requires an understanding of how individuals make choices regarding ethical issues in an organizational setting. This entails an analysis of how the various control influences in an organization, that might derive from senior management or elsewhere, also impact upon the individual and thereby mediate the influence of a code of ethics or any other ethics intervention. These considerations focus attention on how members might attempt to regulate their own behaviour, and that of colleagues, in ways that might be either commensurable with or antagonistic to the injunctions of a corporate code of ethics.

The nature and prevalence of ethical codes

It is evident that the nature and content of codes vary in terms of issues they purport to concern themselves with and how they are designed. Taking the case of Britain, until recently it was possible to maintain, for a variety of reasons, that an interest in corporate codes was limited (Epstein, 1976, 1977; Schlegelmilch and Houston, 1989). But in the last five or so years it would seem that both business ethics and corporate codes of ethics, have received an increasing amount of study and research (see, for example, Donaldson, 1989; Schlegelmilch and Houston, 1989, 1990; Jennings, 1990; Chadwick, 1992; Munro, 1992; Webley, 1988, 1992; Manley, 1992). It is difficult to measure this increasing concern with any degree of accuracy, partly because of the lack of any commonly accepted criteria, or definition of what precisely constitutes a code, and also because one would have to distinguish between the different types of codes – industry, trade association, professional, and international. Melrose-Woodman and Kverndal (1976) found that even those codes created by an individual business organization could take a variety of forms, which makes precise enumeration difficult. Schlegelmilch and Houston (1989) noted that in only four of their 31 cases of companies having a code was it actually referred to as a 'code of ethics', it variously being referred to as a 'code of conduct', 'operating principles' or 'company objectives'. For example, Touche Ross have a 'statement of intent'; Hewlett Packard have 'the HP way' and Prudential: 'a code of conduct and mission statement', all of which seek to encapsulate the company's values as well as providing guidelines for appropriate and inappropriate conduct.

As well as the variety in titles, codes also differ considerably in terms of their content. Indeed such variety in content is not surprising given that codes are supposed to uniquely reflect an organization's values and goals. There are, however, sets of recommendations about what should be contained within a code which provide useful summaries of key content areas. Webley (1992) outlines ten areas to be covered in an illustrative code. The first concerns relations with customers and typically focuses on such issues as confidentiality of customer information, quality and reliability of products/services, and gifts for customers. For example, part of Thomas Cook's code suggests:

> We will develop customer relationships that inspire trust … Every encounter between ourselves and our customers will enhance the trust that our customers place in us. For in these encounters we will consistently deliver the values of reliability, responsibility and knowledge.

The second area of illustrative content is relations with shareholders and other investors where content focuses on issues of accountability to shareholders and investors. Thirdly, Webley outlines the area of relations with employees. Manley (1992) suggest that codes need to be very explicit with regard to the rights of employees and this section of a code will cover a wide range of issues including general principles of interaction between employer and employees, together with more specific statements about company responsibilities with regard to such issues as health and safety, or training and career planning. Some even contain contingency plans for organizational decline. Scott Bader for example suggest:

> we try to be open and frank in our relationships with our fellow workers, to face difficulties rather than avoid them and to solve problems by discussion and agreement rather than through

reference to a third party. We are agreed that in the event of a downturn in trade we will share all remaining work rather than expect any of our fellow members to be deprived of employment, even if this requires a reduction in earnings by all.

Relations with suppliers is another key issue covered by codes. A range of ethical dilemmas can face organizational actors in this arena. Consequently code content in this area covers a range of thorny issues from the payment of suppliers to receipt of gifts. A typical example is that of United Biscuits:

UB's size gives it considerable power as a purchaser. This power must never be used unscrupulously ... Employees must not allow themselves to become in any way beholden to a supplier. They must avoid doing anything which might create the impression that a supplier has a 'friend at UB' or that any special influence may have been exerted upon a suppliers behalf.

Increasingly organizations are becoming more aware of their relationships with the local community and environmental policies in particular are consequently commonplace in many ethical codes. As Manley (1992) suggests, one of the most important issues facing firms in the 1990s is balancing economic growth and respect for environmental concerns. Links with the community cover such issues as the extent to which a company supports the community in which it is located, both in terms of employment opportunities and activity in local affairs. The sixth of Webley's areas is relations with competitors. Quaker Oats code is typical in that it covers the area of gaining and using information about competitors:

As a competitor in the marketplace, we continually seek economic knowledge about our competition. However, we will not engage in illegal or improper acts to acquire a competitor's trade secrets, customer lists, information about company facilities, technical developments or operations. In addition, we will not hire competitors' employees to obtain confidential information or urge competitive personnel or customers to disclose confidential information.

Issues to do with international deals are also typically covered in codes. This section usually deals with respecting the traditions of different cultures, international pricing policies and cartels, and, in some cases, discussions about dealing with countries with oppressive human rights regimes. The final two content areas in Webley's illustrative code are behaviour in relation to mergers and takeovers and ethical issues concerning directors and managers. Within this latter category the principle usually outlined is that the company will conform to the major guidelines of the Cadbury report on the financial aspects of company governance. So the content of a code of ethics can focus on a wide range of issues.

Recent research all tends to point to a growing concern with ethical codes in British organizations. In questioning why such codes have been seized on by organizations, it is clear that the perception must be that there are business benefits associated with the adoption of such codes. Manley (1992), as a result of research with top executives of 145 British and multinational companies, identifies 18 primary benefits of an ethical code all of which are seen as integrally linked to organizational performance and success. These include providing guidance for employees about organizational values and culture. As Manley argues 'It is critically important that firm's values are inculcated in employees, especially managers' (p. 5). Other benefits are 'sharpening and defining the company's policies and unifying the workforce', 'improving bottom-line results', 'promoting excellence', 'realizing company objectives' and 'strengthening the British free-enterprise system'.

Our concern here is the extent to which ethical codes can become mechanisms for management control. It would seem that clear links between codes and controls must exist, given the range of benefits perceived to be associated with the effective implementation of a code. How else could such benefits be achieved without some form of control over the behaviour of employees? In order to further this discussion the next section considers the links between different types of organizational controls and corporate codes of ethics.

Forms of control

Regardless of content, an ethical code might be seen as a formal attempt to purposively influence, or control, dimensions of members' organizational behaviour. But the design and implementation of a code does not take place in a social vacuum, indeed it is unlikely that it is going to be the only formal control operating in any organizational context. Inevitably there will be a variety of other formal controls *in situ*. Although their terminology varies, several writers (e.g. Dalton, 1971; Hopwood, 1974; Mintzberg, 1979; Child, 1984) have all attempted to develop conceptual schemes which identify the different types of formal control processes. However, both Hopwood and Dalton are careful to show how such controls are embedded in organizational contexts from which derive alternative, and often competing, modes of influence that have arisen spontaneously out of members' everyday social interactions. Such 'informal' or 'social' controls arise as groups attempt to regulate the behaviour of their memberships according to various mores, norms and values which have become socially established and sanctioned in different intra-organizational contexts. Thus *all* formally designed control mechanisms are designed and applied in social contexts that mediate their content and functioning. Not only are formal controls social constructions in terms of being vehicles for the values and beliefs of the designers, in their application they also confront spontaneously arising informal social controls that groups have developed so as to regulate the intragroup behaviour of members. Moreover, both of these types of control, ultimately, can only be implemented through the personal agency of self-controlling individuals. The result is that the behavioural impact of a ethical code can only be fully understood and explained through reference to the interaction of these three forms of control.

FORMAL CONTROLS

Codes of ethics may be seen as a type of these organizational phenomena in that they are purposively designed to bring particular norms to bear, on members' everyday organizational behaviour, by formally specifying notions of what is taken to be right or wrong and often by being reinforced by procedures for monitoring and sanctioning compliance with those provisions. Indeed Webley (1992) in his illustrative code suggests that 'strict adherence to the provisions of the code is a condition of employment in the company' (p. 10). An important aspect of the organizational context of an ethical code will be its interaction with other extant formal controls which may not be necessarily commensurable with the former's aims and objectives. We shall discuss the dilemmas raised by the issue of commensurability as we identify the various forms which such formal controls might take.

At a general level the most pervasive manifestation of such formal control strategies is the use of rules and procedures, which Mintzberg (1979) categorizes as an attempt to standardize and prespecify work processes. This immediately raises an important contextual question with regard to the behavioural impact of an ethical code: to what extent are the norms and values encoded into an organization's bureaucratic apparatus commensurable with those expressed by the code of ethics? If they are commensurable the bureaucratic apparatus is more likely to reinforce the desired behaviour expressed by the code. In contrast if they are not commensurable, the behavioural outcomes may become dependent on members' evaluation and comparison of the various intrinsic and extrinsic rewards they attach to the different courses of action that are sanctioned by the conflicting controls (see Lawler and Rhode, 1976; Raiborn and Payne, 1990). The situation is further compounded by the possibility that bureaucracy can create resistance to change particularly when those who have developed it have an interest in maintaining the *status quo* (Walsh and Dewar, 1987).

For many commentators, due to some of the basic characteristics of the work being done (e.g. complexity and unpredictability), it is not always possible to predict what work behaviour should be and thereby preprogramme it (Perrow, 1967; Simon, 1977; Ouchi, 1978). This situation leads us to one of the domains of an alternative form of formal control that might coexist with an ethical code – output control. Output or 'cybernetic' (Otley and Berry, 1980) controls, since they focus on the 'after effects' (Ouchi, 1978, p. 175) of behaviour rather than the actual behaviour itself, can ensure control while leaving the everyday accomplishment of tasks to the judgement and discretion of members. Many types of formal control that are common in modern organizations, (e.g. budgets, management by objectives and some forms of payment system) rely largely upon these processes and mechanisms of output control.

For Thompson (1987, pp. 534–6), output controls may be seen as systems of signs that convey meaning. That is, they are signifiers that have been 'stabilized' by being inserted into a particular 'gaze' so that they are congruent with particular interests. This 'gaze' gives prominence and visibility to particular aspects of organizational life, and thereby makes them available for inspection and evaluation. They may be seen as epistemic structures that create and express expectations which are encoded into objectives and measures that shape members' perceptions of what is important by defining 'success' and 'failure'. So by highlighting certain aspects of organizational reality, output controls exclude and deny possible alternatives by casting them into shadow. The question that is raised by these processes is to what extent are the norms encoded into an ethical code revealed, or cast into shadow, by any output-based controls that are simultaneously operating? If such ethical norms are built into such objective setting processes it is more likely that they will be behaviourally reinforced. But if they are cast into shadow by the output control, their behavioural impact may again be dependent on members' evaluation and comparison of different sets of perceived intrinsic and extrinsic rewards and sanctions.

In general, individuals will often concentrate their attentions upon those actions which are formally assessed and rewarded. Moreover, McDonald and Zepp (1989) report that the setting of unrealistic targets and evaluation schemes can exert considerable pressure on individuals to behave in an unethical manner so as to achieve the specified performance levels. Thus, Nash (1990) maintains that the importance attributed to the 'bottom-line' combined with an emphasis upon short-term efficiency and expediency, by performance evaluation and control systems, significantly contributes towards the creation of unethical behaviour towards both organizational colleagues and customers. So it is hardly surprising that a variety of commentators have argued for the need to develop more comprehensive information and control systems that take into account, and thereby institutionalize, ethical issues (e.g. McCoy, 1985; Stead et al., 1990).

Ouchi (1978, 1979, 1980) has observed that, where controllers have neither the expert knowledge about how tasks should be performed, nor the ability to measure the outputs of members' task performance, the only viable means by which formal control might be established is through members' commitment to the collectivity on the basis of shared beliefs and values – 'clan controls'. Instead of overtly focusing on members' actual behaviour, or the outcomes of that behaviour, these formal controls focus upon the basic **value premises** which surround members' behaviour and decision making. That is they attempt to ensure that subordinates internalize, or have already internalized, the values, beliefs and attitudes which are supportive of the goals and objectives set by hierarchical superiors.

There is evidence to suggest that, following established practices in the USA and Japan, there is a shift in the UK towards using more sophisticated and systematic procedures during recruitment and selection in order to **pre-emptively** ensure the attitudinal and behavioural characteristics of members (Townley, 1989). Townley argues that this changing 'locus of control' (pp. 101–3) is a movement towards developing more flexible and adaptive organizations.

For Pascale (1985), recruitment and selection is only the first of a series of steps by which such control may be established. Research has noted the malleability of people in the early stages of their organizational membership (Katz, 1967; Brim, 1968; Berger and Kellner, 1981; Knights and Collinson, 1987; von Zugbach de Sugg, 1988). Writers have noted the critical importance of the first year of organizational membership (Berlew and Hall, 1965) for it is during this 'initiation stage' (see Schein, 1965) that these new members are placed on training and development programmes. These processes, in conjunction with recruitment and selection, have been identified by Hellreigel and Slocum (1978) as an important strategy through which control is established by ensuring the transmission of 'appropriate' attitudes and values – something which is facilitated by the primary concern of a neophyte to 'seek safety' (Hall and Nougain, 1968) by demonstrating their organizational competence by learning and publicly adhering to the values displayed by experienced members in new and uncertain social settings (Van Maanen and Schein, 1979).

Thus management may attempt to influence the value premises of members' behaviour by trying to **restructure** (see Wood, 1986) their attitudes and beliefs. So it is hardly surprising that writers have argued that the enforcement of codified ethical standards may be achieved through recruitment and selection (Stead *et al.*, 1990), systematic training and the symbolic communication of established ethical codes through the public activities of established ethical committees (Sims, 1991). Indeed Manley suggests that the use of performance evaluations and incentive systems is a spur to effective implementation. He recommends that ethical behaviour in line with a code should be clearly tied in to recognition and rewards, including pay and promotion. His research provides the example of Norwich Union where senior executives have used performance evaluation to create support for their ethical code amongst management.

However, this current vogue of trying to eradicate cultural plurality, and establish management control through cultural homogenization, may be undesirable. Sinclair (1993, pp. 66–8) points to how such 'management of meaning' is thought to influence the ethical aspects of members' organizational behaviour. She demonstrates how such culture management is thought to be achievable through the translation of a clearly formulated corporate strategy, philosophy or mission into a statement about organizational values articulated and communicated through a code of ethics. For Sinclair, although the role of output based and bureaucratic controls are important for reinforcing this ethical dimension, it is evident that one of the keys to culture management is the importance of senior managers as role models for others. But there is an alternative to such an integrationist (i.e. homogenizing) strategy.

By commencing with a recognition of the inevitability of cultural plurality, Sinclair (1993) argues that organizations should tolerate diversity and can also benefit from the discourse about ethics that will develop. Although she feels that this could lead to the anarchic proliferation of diverse ethical values that might leave no basis for consensus; it does avoid the hazards of frustrating creativity and change through the intolerance of deviancy that an integrationist strategy might encourage. So instead of trying to impose ethical values that derive from senior management, the task of management becomes one of understanding the configurations of extant subcultures and their areas of potential consensus that could form the basis of a core of organization-wide ethics. By fostering and sponsoring subcultural coexistence, Sinclair argues that management could unleash the moral commitment of subcultures towards goals determined through consensus.

This approach eschews the imposition of putatively privileged management-derived ethical codes. Instead it encourages members' reflexive and critical thought processes which entail self-scrutiny and debate prior to action. According to Sinclair (1993, pp. 69–70), it is through such thought processes that members weigh-up personal and organizational obligations and responsibilities before finally applying the resultant decision standards and making a decision – for Sinclair the key to ethical behaviour.

In sum it may be argued that the enforcement of codified ethical standards may be achieved through recruitment and selection, systematic training and the symbolic communication of established codes. But such commensurability may not be easily achieved. Besides the important issues around members' participation and consensus raised by Sinclair, a lot might be dependent on the perceived importance of the code by senior organizational members. As Manley (1992) states: 'No critical factor for successful code implementation is more important than support by top executives' (p. 90).

Generally where there is a lack of commensurability between a code and the various formal organizational contexts reviewed above, the behavioural impact of that code may well be compromised as members attempt to resolve the conflicting demands that have been created.

SOCIAL CONTROLS

The domain of social, or informal, control adds a layer of complexity to the processes which influence how members actually behave in everyday organizational situations. Many decisions in organizations are not taken by individuals in a state of social isolation. This implies that the management of ethical issues needs to be firmly located in an understanding of the informal interpersonal processes which spontaneously operate in any organizational context.

Here we are mainly concerned with the informal socialization processes (see Van Maanen, 1976) by which members induct one another into membership of particular cultures. In any social context within an organization, those members who are successful in passing on to others their particular culturally derived renditions of reality, in effect, thereby socially validate those portrayals by gathering further social support and sanction (Berger and Luckmann, 1967, p. 92).

Our understanding of ourselves is, according to Mead (1934), a reflection of the standpoint of other people who are significant in our lives. Particularly important 'significant others' in these processes may be the 'reference group', for whom the actor renders a performance which have a role as sources of, or references for, ways of thinking, feeling, perceiving and evaluating – they may be audiences which are physically present or absent in any interaction, but towards whom an actor orientates his or her conduct. Van Maanen (1976) (see also Van Maanen and Barley, 1985) illustrates the importance of these social networks in socialization and notes the link between an individual's acceptance of a particular subculture and his or her involvement in social networks composed of people who share a set of experiences and problems. However, an individual's direct involvement with a particular social network does not mean that it automatically becomes a reference group for that person. The possibility of such displacement may depend on the extent to which the group, as symbolized by its dominant members, 'serves as a positive point of reference' (Newcomb, 1966, p. 262).

So as Jackall (1988) has observed about managers, their stances may be ever changing, relative and situation specific. This is because

... morality does not emerge out some internally held convictions

or principles, but rather from ongoing albeit changing relationships with some person, some coterie, some social network, some
clique that matters to that person. (p. 101)

Jackall argues that managers bracket, or suspend, the moralities that
they adhere to privately and instead follow the 'prevailing morality of
their particular organizational situation' (p. 6). For most managers this
enables them to perform their work roles through the pursuit of a strategy
based on a morality that prioritizes their personal survival and
advancement by doing what is 'right' for the organization in terms of the
'fealty and alliance structure' that characterizes the organization's
hierarchy (p. 45). So Jackall emphasizes how managers play a role within
an organizational arena that entails the careful presentation-of-self to
significant others.

Although primarily concerned with managers, Jackall's work lends
force to the view that the various complexities arising at the social 'level'
in organizations influence not only how formal controls are designed and
applied, but also how they are perceived and responded to by members.
The behavioural implications of the social dimension to control adds a
layer of complexity to the everyday behavioural impact of formally
constituted ethical codes. Given the probability of the existence of a
cultural plurality in any organization, how members respond to the
injunctions articulated by an organization-wide code may be mediated by,
and dependent on, the nature of established customs, values and mores
of the groups of significant others with whom any individual interacts.
Again, where commensurability exists reinforcement is likely, but where
the formal and informal are incommensurable the behavioural outcome
may depend on the individual's evaluation of the subsequent rewards and
sanctions that might be exercised at both levels.

PERSONAL-SELF CONTROL

The notion of self-control focuses on the processes that underpin
individual behaviour. For Hopwood (1974, p. 31), in order for social and
formal controls to be an effective influence on members' behaviour, they
must become expressed through the actions and attitudes of individual
managers and employees. They must operate as 'self-controls' – the
controls that people exert over their own behaviour. This highlights the
importance of Phillips' (1991) observation that only individuals behave
ethically or unethically – that the ethical behaviour of an organization is
only the sum of the actions, of self-controlling individuals.

However, self-controlled conformity to the injunctions of any social or
formal control may be underpinned by variable psychological
orientations. For instance Kelman (1961) argues that 'compliance' is a

mode of conforming behaviour of a person who is motivated by a desire to gain a reward or avoid a punishment. Such behaviour lasts only as long as the promise or threat of sanction exists. On the other hand 'identification' is a conforming response to social influence brought about by a desire to be like the people who are exerting the influence on the individual. It therefore involves emotional gratification through emotional attachment to 'significant others'. In contrast to 'internalization', 'identification' does not involve the development of internal moral imperatives within the individual. However, such imperatives may develop as the individual adopts the beliefs, norms and values of the significant others in their perceptual world, thereby producing what Kelman specifically defines as 'internalization'.

The sources of social influence which the individual might (variably) conform to, or might deviate from, vary in that they can derive from either formal or informal organizational contexts. Some evidence suggests that where there is a conflict between those values held by the individual and either those formally articulated by an organization, or informally by a peer group, it is the individual's values which become subordinated (England, 1967; Harrison, 1981; Jackall, 1988). However, in a study of unethical behaviour amongst marketing practitioners, Zey-Ferrell *et al.* (1979) observed that peer group pressure on an individual may be sufficient to ensure that he or she complied with group norms without having internalized them. But the cognitive dissonance created by such compliant behaviour may eventually impel an individual to adapt his or her personal values to fit external demands – a process often reinforced by perceptions of self-interest (Harrison, 1981). Thus Liedtka (1991) concluded that many of the managers within her study found themselves forced to choose between preserving their relationship with the firm (operating in a political model) versus following their own values (using the value-driven mindset). As she notes, these decisions were often extremely painful for the managers involved and tended to be made in isolation with little support or acknowledgement in the corporate cultures within which they occurred.

Linking codes with behaviour

While a number of writers (e.g. Melrose-Woodman and Kverndal, 1976; Molander, 1987; Webley, 1988; Manley, 1992) provide guidelines for managers wishing to construct a code of ethics, the eventual content can be expected to be a reflection of the preferences and cognitions of those participating in the design process. This emphasizes the importance of locating an understanding of the design process within a contextual framework, in that the prevailing culture(s) of the organization in question will play an important part in influencing the actual process of the design, its subsequent content, as well as its implementation and enforcement.

Designers are faced with the dilemma that corporate codes are both mechanisms of formal control and culturally derived ethical statements.

Quite how these two attributes are balanced in terms of the design and content of the code are important in terms of its impact and effectiveness. While Raiborn and Payne (1990) suggest that the qualitative characteristics of a code should be clarity, comprehensiveness and enforceability, there is a potential danger that the pursuit of clarity results in a prescriptive list of 'do's' and 'don'ts'. So while Robin *et al.* (1989) note that the codes which they studied tended to be somewhat 'legalistic', Molander (1987) observed that where a code is too specific and prescriptive, there is a danger that the code becomes relatively inflexible and inapplicable in situations not expressly foreseen in the code content. Where such a scenario develops, the assumption may be made that whatever is not explicitly prohibited by the code is therefore acceptable. Hyman *et al.* (1990) indicate this potential danger when they observe that simply providing a list of rules to memorize and obey will not necessarily create moral employees.

In other respects the eventual effectiveness of the code will not depend solely on the culturally derived ethical principles which it enshrines, but also on how it is perceived and evaluated by those whose behaviours it is intended to influence (Molander, 1987). This raises issues with regard to the extent to which members feel that they were stakeholders in the formulation of the code in the first place. It also raises the issue of how members perceive the implicit and explicit motives of those involved in the actual design process. Finally it is important to emphasize that these perceptual processes take place in the formal, informal and self-control contexts described above.

To summarize, there is an implicit assumption in many of the writings on corporate codes that such codes have an 'actual effect' on members' behaviour. This tends to be something which is taken for granted but is not empirically validated by subsequent investigation (Stevens, 1994). In this chapter we have illustrated that, within any organizational context, a number of factors can mediate the effects a corporate code. Firstly, there is the 'nature of the code' which comprises its content and the processes by which it has been designed and implemented. Secondly, there are the organizational control mechanisms (both formal and social), and thirdly, individual influences which focus on perceptual and self-control processes. Thus the context which mediates the behavioural impact of an ethical code may be represented by the interaction of these phenomena. This is illustrated in Fig. 8.1.

Conclusions

This contextualist model represented by Fig. 8.1 is useful in that it highlights the interactions between a number of different interrelated individual, group and organizational factors that impact on ethical behaviour. As such the model raises a series of questions that anyone concerned about the effective implementation of a code must ask.

1. What are the implications of the design processes for members'

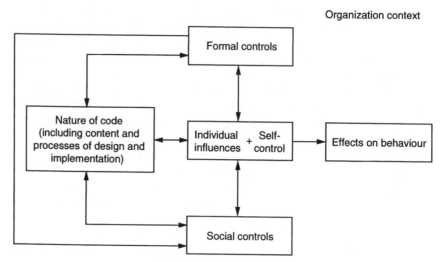

Figure 8.1 A conceptual model of the factors that influence the relationship between corporate codes and organizational behaviour.

perceptions of ownership of the code?

2. Given the design process and subsequent content of the code, what systems and processes are needed to effectively and efficiently enforce the code?
3. Are the demands of the code supported and reinforced by existing formal control systems?
4. How might the existing various informal organizational contexts affect the operation of the code?
5. How do individual members perceive and understand the content of the code and its relevance to their job performance?
6. Will, and if so in what circumstances, members deviate from the code?

So when applied to specific instances this checklist can aid the pinpoint-ing of why ethical or unethical behaviours (in terms of the specifications articulated in the code) occurred. Some explanations might arise from an examination of the content of the code and the processes by which it was designed. For instance, there is a need to consider which stakeholder groups the code is intended to address and the implications that this may have for both the tone, style of the code, its content and means of enforce-ment. Furthermore an analysis through the model can demonstrate to what extent the code content has implications for the existing control mechanisms already in use in the organization. To what extent does the code fit in neatly with the formal organizational context? Therefore it may be used as a means of re-appraising existing mechanisms of organizational control and the various informal social contexts known to exist in the organization in the light of how individuals are interpreting and responding to the code. Finally the model also provides the basis for change. Its specification of the key elements which mediate the links between codes and behaviour highlight areas which can be examined for the purpose of facilitating or encouraging change.

In this chapter we have provided a model which examines the factors that influence the relationship between corporate codes and organizational behaviour. The model is context based and consequently focuses on the importance of the organizational context(s) within which a corporate code of ethics is implemented. It therefore relates the issues surrounding the implementation of corporate codes to broader questions of management control. It is thus interdisciplinary in that it is based on the integration of a range of material from a number of social science disciplines. The model can be used as an explanatory tool in understanding critical incidents in relation to ethical behaviour. It can also be used as a pointer for highlighting the key factors that impact upon ethical behaviour. Finally it can also lead to the development of insights into organizational processes generally since corporate codes both express and impact on other organizational phenomena.

While a corporate code might specify notions of ethicality in an organization, alone it does not necessarily create ethical behaviour. As we have argued, any corporate code of ethics may be seen as an attempt at controlling the ethical dimension of members' behaviour. As such, a code will inevitably confront other existing modes of management control and social influence. Therefore the everyday ethical dimension to members' behaviour has to be understood and investigated within this context.

❑ How and to what extent might members' participation in the design **Exercises**
processes of a corporate code of ethics mediate their attitudes towards
that code?
❑ It could be argued that the introduction of a corporate code of ethics
is just another way of exercising tighter management control over the
ways in which members go about their work. To what extent do you
agree with this contention and why?
❑ Identify the different codes which exist in your organization (e.g. equal
opportunities, ethics, professional). Taking one code as an example:
(a) assess the extent to which it has an actual impact on your own
behaviour and that of colleagues
(b) identify the factors that mediate its impact on your own behaviour
and that of colleagues.

Manley (1992) and Webley (1992) both give accessible overviews of code content **Further reading**
and design issues which should be read in conjunction with Stevens' (1994)
critical analysis of studies of corporate codes. Jackall (1988) presents a vivid
empirical account of the 'moral mazes' in which members' everyday behaviour
is embedded while Johnson and Gill (1993) provide an extensive theoretical
analysis of the behavioural context of management control systems and processes.

References

Berger, P.L. and Kellner, H. (1981) *Sociology Reinterpreted*. Penguin, Harmondsworth.

Berger, P.L. and Luckmann, T. (1967) *The Social Construction of Reality*. Penguin, Harmondsworth.

Berlew, D.E. and Hall, D.T. (1965) The socialization of managers: effects of expectations upon performance. *American Sociological Review*, 21, 341–7.

Bird, F. and Waters, J.A. (1989) The moral muteness of managers. *California Management Review*, Fall, 73–88.

Brim, O.G. (1968) Adult socialization, in *Socialization and Society* (ed. J. Clausen). Little, Brown, Boston, MA.

Carr, A.Z. (1968) Is business bluffing ethical? *Harvard Business Review*, January/February, 143–55.

Chadwick, R.F. (1992) The function of corporate codes of ethics, in *Conference Proceedings Business Ethics: Contributing to Business Success*, Sheffield Business School, Sheffield.

Child, J. (1984) *Organizations: A Guide to Problems in Practice*, 2nd Edn. Paul Chapman, London.

Dalton, G.W. (1971) Motivation and control in organizations, in *Motivation and Control in Organizations* (eds G.W. Dalton and P.R. Lawrence). Richard D. Irwin, Homewood, IL.

Donaldson, J. (1989) *Key Issues in Business Ethics: A Critical Assessment*, Academic Press, London.

Emmanuel, C. and Otley, D.T. (1985) *Accounting For Management Control*. Van Nostrand Reinhold, Wokingham.

England, G.W. (1967) Personal value systems of American managers. *Academy of Management Journal*, 10, 53–68.

Epstein, E.M. (1976) The social role of business enterprise in Britain: an American perspective: part 1. *Journal of Management Studies*, 13, 213–33.

Epstein, E.M. (1977) The social role of business enterprise in Britain: an American perspective: part 2. *Journal of Management Studies*, 14, 281–316.

Feldman, J.D., Kelsay, J. and Brown, H.E. (1986) Responsibility and moral reasoning: a study in business ethics. *Journal of Business Ethics*, 5, 93–117.

Gouldner, A.W. (1959) Organizational analysis, in *Sociology Today* (ed. R.K. Merton). Basic Books, New York.

Hall, T. and Nougain, K.E. (1968) An examination of Maslow's hierarchy of needs in an organizational setting. *Organization and Human Performance*, 3, 12–35.

Harrison, E.F. (1981) *The Managerial Decision-making Process*, 2nd edn. Houghton Mifflin, Boston, MA.

Hellreigel, D. and Slocum, J.W. (1978) *Management: Contingency Approaches*. John Wiley, New York.

Hopwood, A. (1974) *Accounting and Human Behaviour*. Prentice-Hall, London.

Hyman, M., Skipper, R. and Tansey, R. (1990) Ethical codes are not enough. *Business Horizons*, March/April, 15–22.

Jackall, R. (1988) *Moral Mazes: The World of Corporate Managers*. Oxford University Press, Oxford.

Jennings, M. (1990) *The Guide To Good Corporate Citizenship*. Director Books, London.

Jensen, L.C. and Wygant, S.A. (1990) The developmental self-valuing theory: a practical approach for business ethics. *Journal of Business Ethics*, 9, 215–25.

Johnson, P. and Gill, J. (1993) *Management Control and Organization Behaviour*. Paul Chapman, London.

Katz, D.(1967) The motivational basis of organization behaviour, in *Readings in Organization Theory* (eds W.A. Hill *et al.*). Allyn & Bacon, London.

Kelman, H. (1961) The processes of opinion change. *Public Opinion*, 25, 57–78.

Knights, D. and Collinson, D. (1987) Shop floor culture and the problem of management control, in *Business Case File in Behavioural Science* (ed. J. McGoldrick). Van Nostrand, London.

Lawler, E.E. and Rhode, J.R. (1976) *Information and Control in Organizations*. Goodyear, London.

Liedtka, J. (1991) Organizational value contention and managerial mindsets. *Journal of Business Ethics*, 10, 543–57.

Mathews, M. (1988) *Strategic Intervention in Organizations*. Sage, London.

Manley, W.W. (1992) *The Handbook of Good Business Practice: Corporate Codes of Ethics*. Routledge, London.

McCoy, C. (1985) *Management of Values*. Harper & Row, New York.

McDonald, G.M. and Zepp, R.A. (1989) Business ethics: practical proposals. *Journal of Management Development*, 8(1), 55–66.

McHugh, F.P. (1988) *Keyguide to Information Sources in Business Ethics*. Nichols, New York.

Mead, G.H. (1934) *Mind, Self and Society*. Chicago University Press, Chicago, IL.

Melrose-Woodman, J. and Kverndal, I. (1976) *Towards Social Responsibility: Company Codes of Ethics and Practice*. Management Survey Report No. 28. British Institute of Management, London.

Merton, R.K. (1957) *Social Theory and Social Structure*. Glencoe, New York.

Mintzberg, H. (1979) *The Structuring of Organizations*. Prentice-Hall, Englewood Cliffs, NJ.

Molander, E.A. (1987) A paradigm for the design, promulgation and enforcement of ethical codes. *Journal of Business Ethics*, 6, 619–31.

Munro, I. (1992) The moral limitations of corporate codes of ethics, in *Conference Proceedings Business Ethics: Contributing to Business Success*. Sheffield Business School, Sheffield.

Nash, L.L. (1990) *Good Intentions Aside: A Manager's Guide to Resolving Ethical Dilemmas*. Harvard Business School Press, Boston, MA.

Newcomb, T.M. (1966) Attitude development as a function of reference groups: the Bennington study, in *Readings in Social Psychology* (eds E.E. MacCoby *et al.*). Tavistock, London.

Otley, D.T. and Berry, A.J. (1980) Control, organization and accounting. *Accounting, Organizations and Society*, 5(2), 231–44.

Ouchi, W.G. (1978) The transmission of control through organizational hierarchy. *Academy of Management Journal*, 12(2), 173–92.

Ouchi, W.G. (1979) A conceptual framework for the design of organizational control systems. *Management Science*, 25, 833–48.

Ouchi, W.G. (1980) Markets, bureaucracies and clans. *Administrative Science Quarterly*, 25, 129–41.

Pascale, R. (1985) The paradox of corporate culture: reconciling ourselves to socialization. *California Management Review*, 27, 26–7.

Perrow, C.A. (1967) A framework for the comparative analysis of organizations. *American Sociological Review*, 32, 194–208.

Phillips, N. (1991) The sociology of knowledge: toward an existential view of business ethics. *Journal of Business Ethics*, 10, 787–95.

Raiborn, C.A. and Payne, D. (1990) Corporate codes of ethics: a collective conscience and continuum. *Journal of Business Ethics*, 9, 879–89.

Robin, D., Giallourakis, M., David, F.R. and Moritz, T.E. (1989) A different look at codes of ethics. *Business Horizons*, January/February, 66–73.

Schein, E.H. (1965) *Organizational Psychology*. Prentice-Hall, Englewood Cliffs, NJ.

Schlegelmilch, B.B. and Houston, J.E. (1989) Corporate codes of ethics in large UK companies: an empirical investigation of use, content and attitudes. *European Journal of Marketing*, 23(6), 7–24.

Schlegelmilch, B.B. and Houston, J.E. (1990) Corporate codes of ethics. *Management Decision*, 28(7), 38–43.

Senge, P.M. (1990) *The Fifth Discipline: The Art and Practice of the Learning Organisation*. Century Business, London.

Silverman, D. (1971) *The Theory of Organizations*. Heinemann, London.

Sims, R.R. (1991) The institutionalization of organizational ethics. *Journal of Business Ethics*, 10, 493–506.

Simon, H. (1977) *The New Science of Management Decision*. Prentice-Hall, Englewood Cliffs, NJ.

Sinclair, A. (1993) Approaches to organizational culture and ethics. *Journal of Business Ethics*, 12, 63–73.

Snell, R. (1990) The manager's development of ethical awareness and personal morality. *Personnel Review*, 19(1), 13–20.

Stead, W.E., Worrell, D.L. and Stead, J.G. (1990) An integrative model for understanding and managing ethical behaviour in business organizations. *Journal of Business Ethics*, 9, 233–42.

Stevens, B. (1994) An analysis of corporate ethical code studies: where do we go from here? *Journal of Business Ethics*, 13, 63–9.

Storey, J. (1983) *Managerial Prerogative and the Question of Control*. Routledge & Kegan Paul, London.

Thompson, G. (1987) Inflation accounting in a theory of calculation. *Accounting Organizations and Society*, 12(5), 523–43.

Townley, B. (1989) Selection and appraisal: reconstituting social relations?, in *New Perspectives on Human Resources Management* (ed. J. Storey). Routledge, London.

Van Maanen, J. (1976) Breaking in: socialization to work, in *Handbook of Work, Organization and Society* (ed. R. Dubin). Rand-McNally, Chicago, IL.

Van Maanen, J. and Barley, S. (1985) Cultural organizations: fragments of a theory, in *Organisational Culture* (eds P.J. Frost, L.F. Moore, M.R. Louis, C.C. Lundberg and J. Martin). Sage Publications.

Van Maanen, J. and Schein, E.H. (1979) Toward a theory of organizational socialization, in *Research in Organization Behaviour* (ed. B.M. Straw). JAI Press, Greenwich, CT.

Von Zugbach de Sugg, R.G.L. (1988) *Power and Prestige in the British Army*. Avebury, Aldershot.

Walsh, J.P. and Dewar, R.D. (1987) Formalization and the organizational life cycle. *Journal of Management Studies*, 24(3), 215–31.

Webley, S. (1988) *Company Philosophies and Codes of Business Ethics*. Institute of Business Ethics, London.

Webley, S. (1992) *Business Ethics and Company Codes: Current Best Practice in the United Kingdom*. Institute of Business Ethics, London.

Wood, S. (1986) The cooperative labour strategy in the U.S. auto industry. *Economic and Industrial Democracy*, 7(4), 415–48.

Zey-Ferrell, M., Weaver, K.W. and Ferrell, O.C. (1979) Predicting unethical behaviour among marketing practitioners. *Human Relations*, 35(7), 587–604.

9 Business ethics and discriminatory behaviour in organizations

Catherine Cassell

Introduction

The area of discrimination within organizational life has been a rich source of debate and controversy in Britain over the past 30 years. This chapter outlines the meaning of discrimination, considers the nature and prevalence of discrimination within British organizations today and examines the extent to which it is an important issue for those concerned with studying or implementing business ethics. It is argued that a full analysis of the way in which discrimination functions in everyday life requires a contextualist approach where the focus is on looking at the organizational context in which such behaviour takes place. A key element of such an approach is on the interpretative and evaluative processes of organizational members in terms of how they make sense of discrimination and discriminatory processes within the given organizational context. Such an approach enables a focus on the ways in which discrimination is socially constructed. This chapter examines some of the measures that have been taken with the aim of reducing discrimination at work, and analyses some of the key ways in which managers can address this issue.

Within the literature on business ethics, discussion of discrimination and its implications is prevalent. Most of the US textbooks on business ethics (for example, Iannone, 1989; Shaw, 1991; Velasquez, 1992) have chapters on discrimination and occasional papers on discrimination can be found in the current journals within the area. Concerns about discrimination also occur in the practitioner literature. Studies of corporate codes that seek to institutionalize ethical principles and encourage ethical behaviours within organizational life usually have some reference to discriminatory issues (Webley, 1992). These codes focus on an individual's right to be treated and respected as an individual regardless of any characteristic along which they can discriminated on, for example: age, race or sex. Additionally, many organizations now have codes to deal with issues of specific discrimination such as sexual or racial harassment. The last 20 years have seen an increased awareness of the characteristics along which individuals discriminate, the consequence being the proliferation of codes in some organizations. A particularly pertinent issue at time of writing is that of the health of individual employees. Recently a number of codes have been developed in response to increased awareness of HIV/AIDS in the United States and Britain (Adam-Smith and Goss, 1993). Discrimination then is a typical and insidious feature of organizational life and is clearly an issue for those interested in the area of business ethics.

JOB DISCRIMINATION

What is job discrimination? Velasquez (1992) points out that the root meaning of the term 'discriminate' is 'to distinguish one object from another' (p. 311). As such it is a morally neutral term. In current usage however, the term has come to mean an unfair practice particularly within the employment arena. Discrimination is interpreted as making an adverse decision against an employee or potential employee on the basis of some characteristic that distinguishes them from others, for example, sex, race or age. Therefore although many organizational practices are based on managers discriminating between individuals, what is important is the nature of the criteria used and their appropriateness. Velasquez therefore suggests that discrimination in employment must involve three basic elements. Firstly, it is a decision that is not based on the individual merit of an employee (or potential employee). Secondly, the adverse decision arises from some kind of prejudice or stereotypes held by the decision maker about a characteristic that the individual has (e.g. being a member of an ethnic minority group). Thirdly, the decision is seen as having a harmful impact on the individual.

To illustrate, in a recent piece of research conducted by the author (Walsh and Cassell, 1995) a female manager in a large organization was turned down for promotion to the board of directors at the third time of trying. In her view this had nothing to do with her work experience or qualifications which on paper were considerably better than other colleagues in the promotion race, but was instead a result of two factors: her age and gender. When interviewed, she expressed a belief that the company view of a successful director was of a relatively young ambitious male prepared to dedicate his life to the firm. In contrast at the age of 38 and female, she was perceived as unable to fit into the appropriate mould, and was declined the promotion that she felt she rightly deserved. So in her view she had been discriminated against: firstly the decision was not based on her individual merits; secondly, it was based on stereotypes about age and gender; and thirdly, the decision clearly had a harmful impact on her career. It was how age and gender were constructed in the minds of those involved in the selection process that impacted on her chances of promotion.

It is important here to make a distinction between direct and indirect discrimination. Direct discrimination emerges when an individual is treated unfairly as a result of a particular characteristic. Indirect discrimination is more hidden. In a selection process for example it may be that applying a certain criterion for success is more achievable by a specific group of candidates. In the example outlined above, if an expectation is that the successful candidate will devote most of their life to the company at the expense of a home life then this indirectly discriminates against women, who traditionally bear the brunt of caring for children or other dependent relatives. Using continuous length of service as a criteria for compulsory redundancy, for example, is also indirect discrimination. In a similar vein, Velasquez (1992, p. 311) makes the useful distinction between discriminatory behaviours according to the extent to which they are intentional and isolated (or non-institutionalized), and the extent to which they are unintentional and institutionalized. Where behaviour is intentional and isolated it is usually the behaviour of a single individual who discriminates as a result of their own prejudice. Evidence suggests that it is foolish to underestimate the impact that a prejudiced individual can have on decisions regarding recruitment and promotion (Cockburn, 1991; Collinson *et al.*, 1990). This is particularly relevant when that individual holds a position of considerable power within an organization. Collinson *et al.*'s (1990) work, for example, demonstrates a variety of reasons why individual personnel managers discriminate against women in selection processes, ranging from their concern to protect their own identity within the organization to a desire for conforming with the views of the panel as a whole. On the second dimension, a discriminatory act can be intentional but also institutionalized, that is where a group or an organization actively seek to discriminate as a result of their collective prejudices. As Barnes (1992) outlines, the findings of a government survey of a representative sample of 1160 employers found that the majority of employers described most of the work in their establishments as unsuitable for disabled workers, especially in terms of what they described to be 'vital abilities to do the job'. This can be interpreted as institutionalized and intentional discrimination. The view is based on an unquestioned assumption or prejudice about the abilities and potential of disabled workers. Thirdly Velasquez suggests that discrimination can be both isolated (the behaviour of an individual) and unintentional, where an individual can reflect the prejudices of society without clearly thinking about it. An interviewer who assumes that an ethnic minority manager will not be as effective in communicating with clients is a good example here. Finally, a discriminatory act may be unintentional and institutionalized, that is, it is part of the way in which the organization has always worked, perhaps integral to the culture, and therefore unquestioned. Assumptions about what is appropriate work for women or men are pertinent in this context. As a number of authors have commented that women in organizations are often expected to do 'emotional labour' or 'emotion work' (Hochschild, 1983), the significance of which is rarely recognized or rewarded (Parkin, 1989; Savage and Witz, 1992; Hearn *et al.*, 1989). Such gender assumptions that women will do the 'care' work are located deeply within organizational cultures and often remain unchallenged. Even if there is no intention of discrimination, it still reflects the prejudice on which such an assumption is based. This categorization by Velasquez is useful in that it highlights the subtle and sometimes hidden way in which discrimination operates. Despite being unintentional, it can have harmful effects. The importance on focusing on the covert as well as the overt is something that will be returned to later where the role of organizational factors in facilitating discrimination are considered.

DISCRIMINATION AND EQUAL OPPORTUNITIES

Within Britain evidence suggests that a variety of groups are discriminated against within organizations. Although publicly very few people would now defend discriminatory practices against certain groups, a number of commonly held stereotypes still exist that facilitate the maintenance of discriminatory practices. In Britain a lot of research has focused on discrimination faced by women (Cockburn, 1991; Firth-Cozens and West, 1991; Collinson *et al.*, 1990) ethnic minority groups (Jones, 1994) and the disabled within the labour force (Barnes, 1992) yet increasingly it has been demonstrated that individuals are also discriminated against on a range of factors: their age (Taylor and Walker, 1993; Dhooge, 1994); sexuality (Hall, 1989; Colbert and Woofford, 1993); and any previous criminal behaviour (NACRO, 1988) being just three of many.

Within Britain the context for examining discriminatory practices has long been associated with the philosophy of equal opportunities. The basic premise of equal opportunities is that talent and ability is equally spread through all groups including between men and women; able-bodied and people with disabilities; all ethnic groups and so on (Coussey and Jackson, 1991). Therefore, equal opportunities policies and codes of practice (in theory) are aimed at ensuring that organizations make the most of a diverse workforce rather than losing those talents through discriminatory processes. Today many employers in Britain refer to themselves as 'equal opportunity employers' implying that they are keen to disassociate themselves from discriminatory practices. In practice minority groups of employees within those organizations can still experience considerable discrimination as many studies show (Walsh and Cassell, 1995; Cockburn, 1991; Aitkenhead and Liff, 1991). The movement towards such equal opportunities programmes in Britain is clearly linked to the development of equality legislation in Britain since the 1970s (Cockburn, 1991). Currently within the UK there are laws legislating against sex and race discrimination (and religious discrimination within Northern Ireland only). The Equal Pay Act in 1970 outlawed the practice of paying men and women different salaries, the Sex Discrimination Act in 1975 gave rights to both sexes to be treated equal. A Race Relations Act was introduced in 1976, which built on early legislation and outlawed the discrimination in employment and other situations on racial grounds. Despite the initial high expectations of such legislation, in comparison to other equality legislation in Europe and the United States, it has been found to be lacking for a number of reasons. As Cockburn (1991) points out the Sex Discrimination Act is seriously limited by its design. As a law it does not give rights to women as a disadvantaged group, but to both sexes. Indeed, interestingly 40% of complaints to the Equal Opportunities Commission (the body set up to review the workings of the equality legislation) are now lodged by men. This is not surprising given the nature of the equal rights the act provides for: equal rights for the privileged and the disadvantaged. There is no provision within the Act for positive discrimination or affirmative action as it is called in the United States; the concept of 'equal value' is very difficult to enforce and women's experiences of tribunals have been quite distressing. A case of sexual harassment can, for example, lead to front-page headlines for those involved, with little compensation for the victim, and little harm to the protagonist. Indeed, the ceiling of £11,000 on compensation in discrimination cases under the Sex Discrimination Act has recently been ruled illegal by the European Court of Justice who ruled that awards must reflect the extent of the damage caused. The race relations legislation, despite having some provision for positive discrimination in providing members of particular ethnic groups with access to education, training or welfare, has also demonstrated itself to be a 'flimsy tool that activists have found frustrating to use' (Cockburn, 1991, p. 34). The Commission for Racial Equality, a similar body to the Equal Opportunities Commission, has very few sanctions when employers blatantly or indirectly use discriminatory practices. Moreover such legislation will do little to rectify the more indirect forms of discrimination as by their very nature they do not appear discriminatory but rather as part of normal everyday working patterns.

ETHICAL APPROACHES TO DISCRIMINATION AND EQUAL OPPORTUNITIES

In understanding the extent to which discrimination is a pertinent issue for business ethics it is important to consider the approach taken to discrimination from a variety of ethical standpoints. This section considers approaches to discrimination from the perspective of utilitarianism, rights and justice.

Utilitarianism

Very briefly, the underlying theme of utilitarianism is that any action or policy should be evaluated on the basis of the benefits or costs that that action has for society as a whole. Consequently in any situation where a practice is being assessed, the 'right' or most 'moral' line of action is the one that will produce the most 'utility' for the majority. When this approach is applied to issues of discrimination, the analysis is initially straightforward. Given that different individuals have different skills and abilities, and that different jobs require different abilities, in cost-benefit terms, the approach that produces the most utility is for individuals to be in the jobs which most suit their skills and abilities, regardless of any other characteristic. This approach would be the most productive for organizations at large.

A set of problems emerge however when we consider that individuals and groups have very different interpretations of what is best for society and what creates the most utility. One could argue for example that as women are the childbearers of society it makes the most sense in terms of society's productivity for women to spend their time working in the home childrearing: bringing up the families of the future, rather than attempting to have an active role in the labour market. Such discrimination is therefore legitimate. This highlights how the operationalization of utility is problematic and always implicitly value-laden. The key question is whose values are perceived as appropriate?

An interesting perception of the utilitarian approach in this context is that framed in a different way it has provided the basis for much of the literature on the management of diversity (Thomas, 1990; McEnrue, 1993) where the emphasis is on how in *economic* terms it is crucial that organizations make the most of the skills and talents of the whole workforce regardless of the nature of the composition of that workforce. The 'business case' for including a variety of diverse groups at all organizational levels effectively operates on a similar cost-benefit analysis, where it is argued that it is better for the organization as a whole that everyone's skills and abilities are utilized. In itself the notion of 'the organization as a whole' causes problems. Essentially a unitarist conception, it assumes that interests are shared by all groups within the organization, rather than recognizing that some stakeholder groups have more influence than others.

Rights

Rights focus on individuals and their life experiences rather than taking a societal focus as utilitarianism does. Kant's categorical imperative, for instance, suggests that everyone should be treated as a free person equal to everyone else. From the perspective of considering discrimination, one could argue that individuals have the positive right not to be discriminated against in their organizational life, and that others have a duty to provide an individual with that right. Velasquez (1992) suggests that discriminatory behaviours violate this principle in two ways. Firstly discrimination is based on the view that one group is inferior to another, for example that older workers are less competent than younger workers, or that women are less ambitious than men. Such stereotypes can undermine the self-esteem of such groups and therefore violate their right to be treated as equals. Secondly, discrimination places members of discriminated groups in lower economic and social positions whereby opportunities are considerably less than their counterparts. This again contravenes the right to be treated as a free and equal person. In asking the question whether it is morally right or wrong to discriminate against others, Kantian theory presents two criteria for determining a moral right: universality and reversibility. Universality suggests that an individual's reasons for acting in a particular way must be reasons that everyone could act on, whereas reversibility is the extent to which an individual would be happy to have others treat them in the same way. Clearly individuals would not want their own discriminatory behaviour universalized, they would not want to be discriminated against themselves, consequently discrimination from this perspective is morally wrong.

Again a critique of such an approach needs to consider differences in individuals interpretative frameworks in terms of how they view their own organizational life. A woman manager could, for example, discriminate against a female subordinate as a result of the stereotypes she holds about women's commitment to work. She may also agree that it is right that she has been discriminated against herself. In this example discriminatory behaviour would be seen to be morally right, a clear problem for this approach.

Justice

The extent to which discrimination is perceived as injustice is the focus of this approach. Justice and fairness are concerned with the comparative treatment given to groups. Distributive justice focuses on the fair distribution of society's benefits and burdens: in this case discrimination clearly contravenes that principle. Another approach is to see justice as equality, the argument being that as all people are equal, everyone should be treated equally. As Velasquez (1992) states, discrimination in employment is wrong because it violates the basic principle of justice by differentiating between people on characteristics (e.g. race or sex) that are not pertinent to the job they are to perform. Despite the attractiveness of this egalitarian approach, clearly every selection and assessment process within an organization is about discriminating on the basis of certain characteristics, for example, aptitude, experience or potential. Individuals are not generally all equal on those kind of characteristics. The key question here therefore is how does one determine what are the relevant characteristics to discriminate on: it is the criteria for discrimination that are important.

Despite the prevalence of equal opportunities philosophy in Britain and the insights provided by ethical theories into the rights and wrongs of job discrimination, discriminatory practices are still rife within organizational life, some more easily recognizable than others. The most researched and commented on are those associated with selection and assessment in organizations which are briefly outlined below.

Discriminatory practices in organizational life

RECRUITMENT PRACTICES

Recruitment is the process through which organizations create a pool of potential job candidates. The pool needs to have sufficient numbers of high-quality individuals to enable selection to take place. There are a number of aspects of recruitment that concern activists within the area of equal opportunities. Coussey and Jackson (1991) suggest that many of the traditional channels that organizations use for recruitment tend to be a channel for only attracting one kind of applicant. An example of a traditional channel is word-of-mouth recruitment. There is considerable evidence that employers in Britain are increasing their use of such informal recruitment channels (Collinson *et al.*, 1990), with the inevitable result that the composition of the workforce is reproduced. Evidence also conclusively suggests that individuals are keen to recruit and select those they see as like themselves, therefore informal methods of recruitment tend to generate a pool of candidates who replicate the sex/ethnic mix of the current workforce. Other aspects of recruitment that are important, are the nature of job advertisements for example the language used and the places where jobs are advertised.

SELECTION PROCESSES

There is countless evidence to demonstrate how discrimination occurs within all selection processes. Alimo-Metcalfe (1993) describes a 'kaleidoscope of concerns' around psychometric testing which focus on how women can be indirectly discriminated against. She suggests that one of the ways of designing an instrument to select good managers is to look at the skills and behaviours that define 'good managers'. These scales are then standardized on other 'good managers'. However, in practice this approach means that as most of Britain's managers are male (Davidson and Cooper, 1993) the instrument will reflect how male managers go about their work and consequently men will be more likely to fit the ideal profile. Often the discriminatory nature of such instruments are so deeply embedded within selection practices that they remain taken for granted and unquestioned (Townley, 1994). Other studies have demonstrated how the use of psychometric testing can actively disadvantage ethnic minority groups. An interesting case emerged in 1990 when eight guards at London's Paddington station took British Rail to court (with the support of the Commission for Racial Equality) over alleged racial discrimination after failing the train-driver assessment process (Kellett *et al.*, 1994). The selection process included a variety of techniques including personality measures; an interview; vigilance and attention tests; and psychometric aptitude tests. A review of test performance of white and ethnic minority candidates demonstrated that the aptitude tests, particularly that of verbal comprehension, were a source of adverse impact. British Rail reached an out-of-court settlement with the guards before the tribunal date. Part of the settlement involved the British Railways Board agreeing to review the assessment processes and implement an improved one, a task now clearly in progress (Kellett *et al.*, 1994). Research about interviews also highlights similar discriminatory processes though it still remains the most widely used method of selection (Arvey and Campion, 1982).

One of the problems in the consideration of discrimination in selection situations is that the context created is one where stereotypes are rife. Rosen and Jerdee (1976), for example, found that a number of stereotypes exist about older employees: they are seen as more resistant to change; more rigid and less creative; are less likely to take risks; have fewer physical abilities and tend to avoid learning new things. The stereotype of women as indecisive, passive and too dependent considerably inhibits their progression in management posts (Fagenson, 1989). Despite the move to increasingly systematized and structured methods of selection (Townley, 1989), individual agency still impedes the process of 'fair' decision making. Collinson *et al.* (1990) for example explain some of the reasons why individuals make decisions that may not necessarily follow from structured processes. They outline how branch mangers in the insurance industry were found to invest their identity as competent selectors in their decision making such that the perceived risk attached to appointing a woman as a salesperson was magnified:

> A concern with personal status and career was also found to condi-
> tion both personnel managers' compliance with line managers
> informal and sex-discriminatory practices and their own reproduc-
> tion and rationalisation of job segregation. (p. 198)

Selection decisions therefore cannot fail to be influenced by the stereo-types held by those involved in making the decisions.

PERFORMANCE APPRAISAL AND PROMOTION

Within most organizations in Britain the highest profile and most prestigious jobs are taken by white men. This is reflected in the annual pay bill for male and female employees. Women still earn less than 70% of men's wages and a fair distribution of pay between men and women would require the transfer of £21.22 billion in earned income from men to women. Discrimination clearly occurs within the promotion process. In relation to women, the glass ceiling is a key concept that has emerged over the last few years. The glass ceiling is an invisible barrier that confronts women when they come to enter, or attempt to enter positions of power. The metaphor is based on the notion that women can look upwards and see those in power, they can see what it takes to get there, and although they may have those qualities, a barrier is preventing their progression upwards. As Davidson and Cooper (1992) say, although invisible, it is a very real barrier that most women come up against in their careers 'often requiring a sledgehammer to shatter!' (p. 15).

Where women have made it to top positions they have interesting views about the underlying causes of discrimination in organizations. A survey of 200 female members of the Institute of Directors (Nelson, 1992) found that the most common reason given for the perceived lack of equal opportunities for women in career positions was male attitudes towards women (37%). Other reasons given were the difficulties that women had returning to work due to childcare commitments (18%) and the view that it was more difficult for women to prove themselves in the workplace (14%). Individuals from ethnic minority groups are even less likely to achieve positions of power within organizational life. As Jones (1994) outlines: 'a recurring theme of all previous studies of ethnic minorities in the British labour market is their relative concentration in the lower level and more poorly-paid jobs compared to the white labour force' (p. 68).

The nature of overt organizational discrimination has been well documented. Recently there has been more interest taken by both academics and practitioners alike about the more covert forms of discrimination. Covert discrimination, by its very nature is difficult to observe, decipher and analyse. Yet such discrimination can be very significant.

The pervasive nature of organizational discrimination

Covert discrimination is often found in the things we take for granted or are usually left unquestioned in organizations, that are a normal part of everyday life. This links into the importance of examining the contextual factors that impact on discrimination within the workplace. An interesting example can be found around assumptions and notions about sexuality in organizational life. Displays of sexuality such as sexual innuendo in conversation, flirting and the existence of sexual relationships between individuals are regularly part of organizational life (Korda,1979;

Burrell, 1984; Hearn and Parkin, 1983; Hearn *et al.*, 1989), yet are rarely explicitly recognized as an organizational phenomenon. Research is beginning to emerge that demonstrates the persistence and privileging of men's sexuality in organizations (Marshall, 1992). Males express their domination over females and also over other males, through expressions of their sexuality (Hearn *et al.*, 1989; Hearn and Parkin, 1983; Collinson and Collinson, 1989) and through sexual discourse. Cockburn (1991) argues that male bonding or sociability is cemented by male sexual discourse, to the exclusion of women. Recent debate has also focused on different types of masculinity and male power in organizations (Hearn and Morgan, 1990). The complex relationships between sexuality, gender and power, played out within organizations can produce discrimination. Apart from the most obvious example of sexual harassment (DiTomaso, 1989; Stockdale, 1991), the privileging of heterosexuality within organizational life has an impact on homosexual employees. First there is the overt discrimination that can occur for those open about their sexuality, more covertly the implicit message of much sexual banter in organizations is that homosexuality is at best, out of place, leading to those who define themselves as gay being effectively excluded or developing a range of strategies in order to 'manage' their sexuality at work (Hall, 1989; Sheppard, 1989). The whole issue of whether or not to 'come out' to workmates creates many dilemmas for gay employees given the risks of the consequences of their sexual orientation being made explicit. Indeed Palmer (1993) in a survey of 2000 lesbians and gay men found that one in 12 had been dismissed due to their sexuality whilst 48% had experienced harassment at work. Two-thirds of those working found it necessary to conceal their sexuality in order to avoid discrimination. Pringle (1989) describes how daily life in the office is 'relentlessly' heterosexual (p. 164). It takes place in concrete social practices ranging from managerial policies through to everyday informal conversations (Hearn and Parkin, 1987), yet is rarely openly discussed. Perhaps the classic example is that of secretaries. As Pringle points out:

> Male bosses can decide for themselves the extent to which they will keep their public and private lives separate. Secretaries do not have this luxury. Male bosses go into their secretaries offices unannounced, assume the right to pronounce on their clothes and appearance, have them doing housework and personal chores, expect them to do overtime at short notice and ring them at home ... Secretaries would rarely ring bosses at home or intrude on their privacy. On the other hand men 'invade' women's private space all the time and women have to defend it. The sexual metaphor is apt. (p. 169)

Witz *et al.* (1994) in three case studies of a local government office, a hospital ward and bank branch examined the sexualized discourses and practices within everyday organizational life. They suggest that despite important variations in the form and extent of the masculinization of the culture, the variations lie within the bounds of a 'hegemonic masculinity, the central feature of which is its heterosexism, and emphasized femininity' which is all tied in with accommodating the interests and desires of men. In essence such sexualized practices and discourses underpin gendered hierarchies and patterns of control in the workplace. Such is the nature of covert discrimination, it is submerged deep within organizational assumptions about appropriate modes of behaviour and engagement.

ORGANIZATIONAL CULTURE

In understanding the more covert forms of organizational discrimination, it is important to examine the cultures of organizations. Schein (1984) produces a formal definition of culture which is useful in outlining its component elements:

> Organizational culture is the pattern of basic assumptions that a given group has invented, discovered, or developed in learning to cope with its problems of external adaptation and internal integration, and that have worked well enough to be considered valid, and, therefore, to be taught to new members as the correct way to perceive, think and feel in relation to those problems. (p. 3)

Culture adds an additional arena within which to examine the more subtle ways in which discrimination works. Schein (1984) distinguishes between the visible artefacts of organizational culture, such as architecture, dress codes, prizes, office layout, etc.; the values; and the underlying basic assumptions such as 'normal' hours of working and communication patterns. Basic assumptions are taken for granted and invisible. They are about the very nature of human activity and organizing. An organization may therefore have a number of visible prodiversity and antidiscrimination strategies such as an equal opportunities policy and an espoused commitment to the development of minority managers, whilst still having a set of underlying assumptions which reflect the interests of more dominant groups. As they are 'invisible' and unsaid, they are very difficult to challenge.

The role of culture is a key theme within the management of diversity literature (Thornburg, 1994, Thomas, 1990; McEnrue, 1993) where the emphasis is on creating an 'inclusive' organizational culture where each individual employee feels involved with the organization, that is they have a place and an important part to play. In examining culture from this perspective however, it is crucial to recognize that culture is not a unitary phenomenon. Of key importance is the need to take into account the differentiated, or sometimes ambiguous nature of culture in organizations, rather than focusing on an integrationist approach (Meyerson and Martin, 1987). The important issues are how individuals and groups interpret the messages of the culture that they exist in and how this interpretation impacts on their everyday organizational behaviour. An example comes from an interview study conducted by Walsh and Cassell (1995) about the barriers to the progression of women into senior management. In an interview study of 60 people in the publishing industry, both male and female managers interviewed reported that they had never seen any obvious cases of discrimination in their organizations. Under the surface, however, they perceived various hidden or covert barriers within the culture of their organizations that prevented the progression of women up to board level. One barrier, for example, was related to perceptions surrounding women having children. The women interviewed experienced a clear conflict between company entitlements and policies regarding maternity leave and the organizational messages about having children and their consequent impact on career development. Indeed despite equal opportunities policies there was evidence of an implicit discouragement of women who became pregnant. Indeed one interviewee described his organization as having a 'culture of restricted fertility', where despite the existence of positive policies people knew that having babies was frowned on. Getting pregnant therefore had an extremely negative impact on a woman's career. Such ambiguous organizational messages left women unclear about how their contribution was valued. Alvesson and Due Billing (1992) argue that culturally defined norms and values that produce such messages are significant components of stereotypical categorizations about race and gender but these categories can vary considerably between organizations.

Therefore in order to understand the more subtle or covert ways in which discrimination operates within organizations some analysis of organizational culture and the context in which discriminatory behaviour takes place within an organization is a key issue. This approach emphasizes the ways in which discrimination is individually and socially constructed and should therefore provide clues as to how discriminatory stereotypes are produced and reproduced in organizations.

Interventions designed to address discrimination

Given the pervasive nature of organizational discrimination a number of interventions have been made that attempt to address the issue of discrimination in organizational life. This section examines three different approaches that have been taken, based on legislation, affirmative action, and the management of diversity.

LEGISLATIVE INTERVENTIONS

As outlined earlier legislation exists in Britain to offset discrimination on the grounds of race, sex, or religion (in Northern Ireland only). Despite questions about the utility of such legislation in practice, there is still a debate as to whether other groups who suffer discrimination should also be protected in a similar way, rather like in the United States where comprehensive legislation protects a variety of 'disadvantaged' groups. Handley (1993) argues that despite the emergence of various campaigns and initiatives regarding age discrimination in employment, persuasion and voluntary effort in itself will not be enough to eliminate it. Consequently he argues, legislation is necessary. Such legislation would firstly raise the prominence of age discrimination; secondly demonstrate a moral disapproval of such behaviour; thirdly, provide a means of influencing those who do discriminate against older workers; fourthly, empower those discriminated against to take action and finally, improve organizational effectiveness by offsetting the costs incurred through the loss of skilled employees. Though Handley is referring directly to issues to do with age, similar arguments could be put for any group who find themselves discriminated against.

An alternative view which is particularly pertinent in relation to business ethics suggests that legislation in itself will not stop discriminatory behaviour and consequently the implementation of equal opportunities policies and codes should be pursued with employers as an ethical issue. Rennie (1993) suggests that the issue of disability and employment highlights some of these issues. Currently there is no law in Britain to prevent discrimination on the basis of disability, yet many organizations do have equal opportunities policies which make provision for staff with disabilities. Rennie argues that as the motivation is not a fear of legal prosecution then the aim of such policies must be about promoting a positive organizational image to the public at large, or of promoting ethical behaviours at work.

An additional question concerns the scope of potential legislation with regard to the discriminated groups catered for. A couple of examples from the United States demonstrate some of the complex ethical issues that may arise. Legislation designed to protect unborn children has led to a number of organizations introducing foetal protection policies (Sprotzer and Goldberg, 1992). These policies typically exclude all fertile female employees from jobs that expose them to hazardous chemicals. Such exclusionary policies clearly discriminate against women, but the key question is whether such discrimination is justified given the 'rights' of unborn children. Faludi (1991) outlines the impact this has had on some female employees who in a number of cases have sought 'voluntary' surgical sterilizations in order to keep their jobs. Another example comes from Crow and Payne (1992) who point out that until recently discrimination against 'physically unattractive' people in employment has not been perceived as a moral or ethical issue. The recent introduction of the Americans with Disabilities Act has, however, provided a potential way in which such discrimination can be challenged. The attractiveness of job candidates is often seen as legitimate by employers, for example for reception work (Biswas and Cassell, 1994). In Britain 10% of vacancies in job centres require applicants to appear 'clean and tidy' or be of 'generally good appearance' (Jones and Longstone, 1990), indeed Barnes (1992) suggests that such criteria can often discriminate against disabled people as disability is often viewed as unattractive.

When discussing legislation with regard to discrimination then, the key issues are does it work and how wide should the scope be? Evidence suggests that in other parts of Europe and the United States legislation has had a positive effect on the working lives of some disadvantaged groups. In Britain however, current antidiscriminatory legislation seems toothless in comparison. Given the significance of the covert under-pinnings of discrimination outlined above, it is very difficult for legislation to comprehensively address such issues.

AFFIRMATIVE ACTION AND TARGETS

Policies of affirmative action remain a key way in which discrimination is addressed within the United States. However, there has been a consider-able debate as to the merits and consequences of such policies and prac-tices. Affirmative action programmes have arisen as a direct response to the discrimination that groups have suffered in the past. They therefore represent a positive step to eliminate the effects of past discrimination. Affirmative action is sometimes confused by the use of the label 'reverse discrimination'. In practice this label is incorrect, affirmative action policies do not suggest that a certain group (white males) deserve unequal treatment or are inferior, rather that women and ethnic minorities need an additional set of opportunities in order to compete on a level playing field.

The theory and practice of affirmative action generates a number of ethical issues which have been discussed within the ethics literature. Exponents of affirmative action suggest that it is based on the concept of compensatory justice in terms of correcting wrongs that have been done to particular groups in the past. It is also seen to encourage fairer competi-tion by, for example, compensating for the disadvantages that ethnic minority workers might have been exposed to earlier in their lives as a result of discriminatory activities in education. Those who argue against affirmative action suggest that today's white males should not be made to suffer as a result of the sins of their fathers. Indeed such actions, it is argued, violate the rights of white men to be treated as individuals. They also argue that affirmative action in itself is a discriminatory practice and violates general principles of equality. At the theoretical level these arguments have generated much discussion, but it is important to consider the impact that affirmative action policies have actually had in challenging discrimination in practice. Within the United States affirmative action programmes have enabled the access of a number of minority individuals into organizations but there have been a number of problems, the recognition of which has partly contributed to the move towards diversity management as a more wide-ranging tool with which to address the problem. Too often minority individuals are recruited into organizations only to meet the view that they are just there to make the numbers up, a view reflected in the common experience of still facing the same discrimination when attempting to climb the promotion ladder. A focus on numbers also detracts from a focus on the quality of work experience.

Whereas affirmative action is illegal in Britain, a number of organizations have set targets for attracting numbers of employees from traditionally disadvantaged groups. This is usually linked to a 'monitoring' process where an organization's on-going equal opportunities practices are continuously assessed. The Disabled Persons Employment Act (1944) requires employers to ensure that 3% of their workforce are disabled. In practice however, many employers never meet this target and there is evidence that the figures are getting worse. A recent study found that for the last 15 years there has been a steady decline in the number of disabled people employed by local authorities, only 15 local authorities now meet their quota for disabled people compared with 64 in 1979 (Gladwin, 1973). The definition of targets is nevertheless perceived to be a way forward by some organizations. In 1991 a British government-sponsored scheme, Opportunity 2000, was set up to try and increase the representation of women in the higher positions in organizations. Those companies who subscribed to the campaign had to outline what measures they were going to take in order to improve the position of women in their organizations. A number chose to set targets for the number of women in managerial positions, for example the BBC aimed to have 30% of its middle management as women by 1995.

In theory affirmative action and the setting up of targets all serve to increase the numbers of those from traditionally discriminated groups in organizations. The problems emerge however when targets are used in isolation without any complementary interventions aimed at changing the organization's culture. There is some notion that the situation for such groups within organizations will improve, just by an increase in their numbers. There is however no evidence that this is the case. An 'add women and stir' approach for example does not necessarily improve the position of women in an organization as a whole (Cassell and Green, 1994). In order to understand that position the whole nature of an organization's context: its cultures, structures and power relationships need to be addressed and understood. Just being part of the game doesn't amount to much when you don't understand the rules and nobody passes you the ball. Rather the introduction of targets can only be effective as part of a far-reaching strategy of organizational change in this direction.

THE MANAGEMENT OF DIVERSITY

A more recent set of organizational interventions focuses on the organizational level and presents a business case for moving towards a diverse workforce where the skills of all groups are recognized. The argument is that given the current shortage of skilled labour (particularly in the United States) the effective use of diverse skills within an organization makes good business sense. Diversity management is particularly popular in the United States where the skill shortages are more pronounced than in Britain. Management of diversity in based on the notion of difference and the effective management of difference. Valuing difference is seen as an important concept because it is specifically linked to organizational culture and values. A key element is to move towards 'cultures of inclusion' (Thomas, 1990) recognizing that various organizational practices often lead to certain groups feeling left out or unwelcome. Exponents of the management of diversity (McEnrue, 1993; Thornberg, 1994) argue that all differences must be valued including those of white males. The benefits of the successful management of diversity are seen to be very rich, Cox (1991) for example describes them as 'better decision-making, greater creativity and innovation, and more successful marketing to different types of customers' (p. 34).

Thornberg (1994) outlines three phases which represent a company's evolutions towards a more diverse heterogeneous culture. The first is to bring in more women and minorities, the second to emphasize working on problems of individual and group behaviour associated with race and gender, that is to begin to understand how people are different and why; and the third a focus on company culture which involves evaluating all of the organization's policies and procedures. There is an abundance of anecdotal evidence from the USA that demonstrates that successful diversity programmes do have an impact on organizational success. There is, as yet, little empirical evidence of a direct link, though to make the most of an organization's skills and talents is clearly important as an human resources management (HRM) policy. What is less clear is how easily the principles behind the management of diversity translate into British organizations where the composition of the labour force is quite different. Although such interventions question the nature of existing organizational cultures, it is not clear exactly how they seek to change them and how 'successful organizational change' is defined. Just how such programmes will address the taken for granted assumptions that underlie much covert discrimination is unclear. Inevitably any intervention based on a 'business case' is open to alteration when economic conditions change.

Although discrimination is initially presented as a moral issue, its consequences extend beyond the ethical. In describing and analysing various sources of discrimination and a number of interventions that can address such issues it is evident that discrimination is costly in both individual and organizational terms. It is also apparent that the most pervasive forms of discrimination are not always overt, yet may be subtly hidden within the cultures of organizations. So what does the manager do in order to address the issue of discrimination in organizational life? Within this chapter it has been argued that it is important to take into account the contextual factors that impact on discrimination. Individual organizations therefore need to design appropriate organizational strategies to tackle the issues. The previous analysis suggests that discrimination is a multi-faceted process, consequently any strategy needs to address potential discrimination at all levels: the individual and the organizational. As Cockburn (1990) suggests in order to understand barriers to equal opportunities there needs to be an understanding of the relationship between individual agency and organizational structure: 'The powerful act both face to face as individuals (with a passing sneer about homosexuality, for instance), and through systemic processes (stacking recruitment interviewing panels with white men)' (p. 85).

Discrimination: implications for managers

Initially then, a strategy designed to address some of these issues through, for example, designing an appropriate equal opportunities or diversity code of behaviour needs to contain an element of research into the distinctive discriminatory practices of the organization. Given that discriminatory behaviours can take different forms in different organizations, it is important to examine what specific processes, procedures and practices exist within an organization in order to proceed. Initial research could focus on the notion of culture audits or equal opportunity monitoring (Gladwin, 1993). Equal opportunities monitoring focuses on all the elements of an organization's selection and appraisal procedures. Monitoring in itself can enable an organization to do a range of things including identifying discriminatory employment practices; measuring change and progress towards equality; and complying with the codes of practice the organization subscribes to. Such monitoring or workforce audit can provide important information about the diverse groups that work in an organization and the levels at which they are based. A cultural audit takes as its focus a different level of analysis. Rather than focusing on numbers, the aim is to investigate how the culture of the organization is interpreted by those within the organization, particularly in relation to issues regarding discrimination. A variety of questions can be asked of individual employees as to how they experience the organization and their views as to the values and assumptions which guide organizational behaviour. Such research is a prerequisite for the successful design and implementation of a code.

The key question that now emerges is will such a code be effective in addressing discriminatory behaviour? Given the framework outlined earlier, the success of the implementation of such codes in relation to actually significantly addressing discrimination needs to be treated with caution. As outlined earlier, evidence suggests that the implementation of equal opportunities codes and policies have often failed to meet the expectations of both the organizations involved and equal opportunity activists (Cockburn, 1991; Aitkenhead and Liff, 1991; Walsh and Cassell, 1995).

Why is this the case? In assessing how such codes have an impact on behaviour the model described in Chapter 8 outlines the important contextual factors that need to be taken into consideration. The processes through which a code is designed and implemented will impact on how an organization's members interpret and act on the code. Also important is the extent to which the code is commensurable with other formal and informal control mechanisms in the organization. An individual's own previous experience of discrimination and other psychological factors will also impact on potential behaviour and behaviour change. From that model a number of recommendations can emerge about the issues that need to be considered when attempting to develop more effective codes and policies. Assessing and reflecting on the taken for granted assumptions within an organization's culture is a starting point for examining why equal opportunities codes and policies don't work in practice, and challenging some of those reasons. It is crucial that an approach is taken that questions and challenges such assumptions so that double-loop learning can occur. Such assumptions are about asking questions about how groups experience an organization: what messages exist about success in this organization; what meanings exist around being black, being older, being a mother, being disabled, etc.; what expectations do we have about how people do their work, what norms do we expect them to fit into? An understanding of these assumptions helps to demonstrate how discrimination within the organization is socially constructed. The design process is key, to what extent do individuals feel they have some commitment to the values within the code? In assessing how a code ties in with formal control mechanisms, the important question is are individuals held accountable for their discriminatory behaviour? Are managers rewarded, for example, for their awareness of the needs of, and support for, those groups traditionally discriminated against? In examining informal modes of control, what assumptions form the basis of group behaviour in relation to any policy or code? What is the role of subcultures and groups with the organization as a whole? Finally how do individual members perceive and understand the code and its content and relevance to their job performance. Where individuals perceive no clear link, this needs to be made more explicit by the organization, alternatively training interventions can be designed to address such issues as the nature of discrimination. Examining the design and implementation of a code in this way is a starting point for organizations to address the nature and existence of discrimination in organizational life. It remains to be seen however, whether such interventions can ever fully challenge the ingrained attitudes and assumptions that underpin discriminatory behaviour.

Summary and conclusions

This chapter has examined the nature of discrimination within organizations in Britain today and has argued that in order to fully understand how such behaviour is produced and reproduced within individual organizations an understanding of its social construction through the organizational context is required. This is not to detract from the key significance of societal structures in the production and reproduction of discrimination. Rather in order to understand the experiences of individuals within a specific organization a detailed analysis of the organizational practices and processes is required. In particular such an analysis needs to focus on the more covert nature of discrimination and the taken for granted assumptions that provide the basis of it.

Given the extent of discrimination in Britain today and the implications it has for those discriminated against, it is clearly a significant issue for those interested in the area of business ethics. It also represents a big challenge for those concerned with encouraging ethical behaviour within organizations, one which needs to be centre stage in any programmes or developments designed to address ethical issues. Without this prominence the field and practice of business ethics will lose the key opportunity of challenging some of the most unethical practices in British organizations today.

Exercises

❏ Thinking of your own organization, what examples are there of direct and indirect discrimination? To what extent is such discrimination institutionalized?

❏ In understanding examples of discrimination how useful are utilitarianism, rights and justice? Which is closer to your understanding of why discrimination exists?

❏ What initiatives would you recommend to assess whether the recruitment, selection and appraisal procedures in your organization contain discriminatory elements?

❏ Design a research project to explore the existence of covert discrimination based on age within your organization.

❏ Evaluate the various interventions that have been designed to address discrimination within British organizations. How successful have they been?

❏ You have been given the task of designing an ethical code of conduct about discriminatory behaviour within your organization. What are the key issues in the design process and how would you resolve them?

Further reading

A number of business ethics textbooks have chapters within them which apply various ethical theories to discrimination, for example:

Shaw, W.H. (1991) *Business Ethics*. Wadsworth, San Francisco, CA.

Velasquez, V.E. (1992) *Business Ethics Concepts and Cases*, 3rd edn. Prentice-Hall, London.

Iannone, A.P. (1989) *Contemporary Moral Controversies in Business*. Oxford University Press, Oxford.

A useful introduction to the issues surrounding equal opportunities is:

Coussey, M. and Jackson, H. (1991) *Making Equal Opportunities Work*. Pitman, London.

For a clear and useful overview of the issues involved with the management of diversity try:

Kandola, R. and Fullerton, J. (1994) *Managing the Mosaic: Diversity in Action*. Institute of Personnel and Development, London.

Finally a useful guide for managers in the issues surrounding the implementation of equal opportunities from an ethical perspective is found in a chapter in:

Clutterbuck, D., Dearlove, D. and Snow, D. (1992) *Actions Speak Louder: A Management Guide to Corporate Social Responsibility*. Kogan Page, London.

References

Adam-Smith, D. and Goss, D. (1993) HIV/AIDS and hotel and catering employment: some implications of perceived risk. *Employee Relations*, 15(2), 25–32.

Aitkenhead, M. and Liff, S. (1991) The effectiveness of equal opportunities policies, in *Women at Work: Psychological and Organizational Perspectives* (eds J. Firth-Cozens and M. West). Open University Press, Milton Keynes.

Alimo-Metcalfe, B. (1993) Gender, leadership and assessment. Paper presented to the *British Psychological Society Annual Occupational Psychology Conference*, Brighton, January.

Alvesson, M. and Due Billing, Y. (1992) Gender and organizations: towards a differentiated understanding. *Organization Studies*, 13–14, 73–102.

Arvey, R.D. and Campion, J.E. (1982) The employment interview: a summary and review of recent literature. *Personnel Psychology*, 35, 281–32.

Barnes, C. (1992) Disability and employment. *Personnel Review*, 21(6), 53–73.

Biswas, R. and Cassell, C.M. (1994) The persistence of gender segregation in the service sector: implications for strategic HRM. Paper presented to the *Strategic Direction of HRM Conference*. Nottingham Trent University, 15–16 December.

Burrell, G. (1984) Sex and organizational analysis. *Organization Studies*, 5(2), 207–28.

Cassell, C.M. and Green, E. (1994) New opportunities for women?: The role of information technology in facilitating equal opportunities. Paper presented to the *British Psychological Society Annual Occupational Psychology Conference*, Birmingham, January.

Cockburn, C. (1991) *In the Way of Women: Men's Resistance to Sex Equality in Organizations*. Macmillan, London.

Colbert, C.R. and Woofford, J.G. (1993) Sexual orientation in the workplace: the strategic challenge. *Compensation and Benefits Management*, 9(3), 1–18.

Collinson, D. and Collinson, M. (1989) Sexuality in the workplace: the domination of men's sexuality, in *The Sexuality of Organization* (eds J. Hearn, D.L. Sheppard, P. Tancred-Sheriff and G. Burrell). Sage, London.

Collinson, D.L., Knights, D. and Collinson, M. (1990) *Managing to Discriminate*. Routledge, London.

Coussey, M. and Jackson, H. (1991) *Making Equal Opportunities Work*. Pitman, London.

Cox Jr, T. (1991) The multi-cultural organization. *Academy of Management Executive*, 5(2), 34–47.

Crow, S. and Payne, D. (1992) Affirmative action for a face only a mother could love? *Journal of Business Ethics*, 11(11), 869–75.

Davidson, M.J. and Cooper, C.L. (1993) *Shattering the Glass Ceiling: The Woman Manager*. Paul Chapman, London.

Dhooge, Y. (1994) Over 40's need not apply. *Training Tomorrow*, May, 25–7.

DiTomaso, N. (1989) Sexuality in the workplace: discrimination and harassment, in *The Sexuality of Organization* (eds J. Hearn, D.L. Sheppard, P. Tancred-Sherif, and G. Burrell). Sage, London.

Fagenson, E.A. (1989) At the heart of women in management research: theoretical and methodological approaches and their biases. *Journal of Business Ethics*, 9, 267–74.

Faludi, S. (1991) *Backlash: The Undeclared War Against Women*. Chatto & Windus, New York.

Firth-Cozens, J. and West, M.L. (1991) *Women at Work: Psychological and Organizational Perspectives*. Open University Press, Milton Keynes.

Gladwin, M. (1993) *We're Counting on Equality: Monitoring Equal Opportunities at Work in Relation to Sex, Race, Disability, Sexuality, HIV/AIDS and Age*. City Centre, London.

Hall, M. (1989) Private experiences in the public domain: lesbians in organizations, in *The Sexuality of Organization* (eds J. Hearn, D.L. Sheppard, P. Tancred-Sherif, and G. Burrell). Sage, London.

Handley, K. (1993) The case for legislation on age discrimination. *Personnel Management*, 5(21), 4.

Hearn, J. and Morgan, D.H.J. (1990) *Men, Masculinities and Social Theory*. Unwin Hyman, London.

Hearn, J. and Parkin, W. (1983) Gender and organizations: a selective review and a critique of a neglected area. *Organization Studies*, 4(3), 219–42.

Hearn, J. and Parkin, W. (1987) *Sex at 'Work': The Power and Paradox of Organisation Sexuality*. Wheatsheaf, Brighton.

Hearn, J., Sheppard, D.L., Tancred-Sheriff, P. and Burrell, G. (eds) (1989) *The Sexuality of Organization*. Sage, London.

Hochschild, A. (1983) *The Managed Heart*. University of California Press, Berkeley, CA.

Iannone, A.P. (1989) *Contemporary Moral Controversies in Business*. Oxford University Press, Oxford.

Jones, T. (1994) *Britain's Ethnic Minorities: An Analysis of the Labour Force Survey*. PSI Research Report No. 721. Policy Studies Institute, London.

Jones, A. and Longstone, L. (1990) *A Survey of Job Centre Vacancies.* Department of Employment, Employment Services, Sheffield.

Kellett, D., Fletcher, S., Callen, A. and Geary, B. (1994) Testing in the workplace: the Paddington guards. *The Psychologist: Bulletin of the British Psychological Society*, **7**(1).

Korda, M. (1979) *Power in the Office.* Weidenfeld & Nicolson, London.

McEnrue, M.P. (1993) Managing diversity: L.A. before and after the riots. *Organization Dynamics*, **21**(3).

Marshall, J. (1992) Organization cultures: attempting change often means more of the same. *The Journal: Women in Organizations and Management*, **3**, 4–6.

Meyerson, D. and Martin, J. (1987) Culture change: an integration of three different views. *Journal of Management Studies*, **24**, 623–47.

NACRO (1988) *Education and Training in the Resettlement of Black Offenders.* National Association for the Care and Resettlement of Offenders, London.

Nelson, T. (1992) *Women's Participation in the Labour Force: Institute of Directors Members' Opinion Survey.* Institute of Directors, London.

Palmer, A. (1993) *Less Equal Than Some.* Stonewall, London.

Parkin, W. (1989) Private experiences in the public domain: sexuality and residential care organizations, in *The Sexuality of Organization* (eds J. Hearn, D.L. Sheppard, P. Tancred-Sherif and G. Burrell). Sage, London.

Pringle, R. (1989) *Secretaries Talk: Sexuality, Power and Work.* Verso, London.

Rennie, S. (1993) Equal opportunities as an ethical issue. *Equal Opportunities Review*, No. 51, 56.

Rosen, B. and Jerdee, T.H. (1976) The influence of age stereotypes on managerial decisions. *Journal of Applied Psychology*, **61**, 428–432.

Savage, M. and Witz, A. (eds) (1992) *Gender and Bureaucracy*, Blackwell, Oxford.

Schein, E. (1984) Coming to a new awareness of organizational culture. *Organization Dynamics*, Autumn, 24–38.

Shaw, W.H. (1991) *Business Ethics.* Wadsworth, San Francisco, CA.

Sheppard, D.L. (1989) Organizations, power and sexuality: the image and self-image of women managers, in *The Sexuality of Organization* (eds J. Hearn, D.L. Sheppard, P. Tancred-Sheriff and G. Burrell). Sage, London.

Sprotzer, I. and Goldberg, I.V. (1992) Fetal protection: law, ethics and corporate policy. *Journal of Business Ethics*, **11**(10), 731–5.

Stockdale, J.E. (1991) Sexual harassment at work, in *Women at Work: Psychological and Organizational Perspectives* (eds J. Firth-Cozens and M. West). Open University Press, Milton Keynes.

Taylor, P. and Walker, A. (1993) Employers and older workers. *Employment Gazette*, **101**(8), 371–8.

Thomas Jr, R.M. (1990) From affirmative action to affirming diversity. *Harvard Business Review*, March/April, 107–17.

Thornberg, L. (1994) Journey towards a more inclusive culture. *HRMagazine*, February.

Townley, B. (1989) Selection and appraisal: re-constituting 'social relations'?, in *New perspectives on Human Resource Management* (ed. J. Storey). Routledge, London.

Townley, B. (1994) *Reframing Human Resource Management: Power, Ethics and the Subject at Work.* Sage, Beverley Hills, CA.

Velasquez, V.E. (1992) *Business Ethics Concepts and Cases*, 3rd edn. Prentice-Hall, London.

Webley, S. (1992) *Business Ethics and Company Codes: Current Best Practice in the U.K.* Institute of Business Ethics, London.

Walsh, S. and Cassell, C.M. (1995) *A Case of Covert Discrimination: The Women into Management Study*. Book House, London.

Witz, A., Halford, S. and Savage, M. (eds) (1994) Organised bodies: gender, sexuality, bodies and organisational culture. Paper presented at the *BSA Conference on Sexualities in Social Context*. University of Central Lancashire, March.

10 Leadership and ethics

John Gill

Introduction

This chapter first reviews the main approaches to the study of leadership – the 'trait', 'style', 'contingency' and 'charismatic' approaches and takes the position that all are fundamentally different ways of controlling and coercing subordinates and that this of course poses ethical dilemmas.

The social construct of leadership on the analysis presented here is viewed in the nature of a myth to reinforce different social beliefs about leaders in organizations. Accordingly it will be argued that the consequences of the leadership myth will result in alienation characterized by intellectual and emotional deskilling and gamesmanship. Reframing socially constructed meanings of leadership will emphasize awareness of covert and undiscussable power and authority dynamics in organizations.

The chapter will conclude that forms of distributed leadership and self-leadership in the context of a democratic ethics may provide one solution to the management of complex organizations in rapidly changing environments. It may also help address some alienating consequences of current practice and unethical leadership behaviour often encountered in organizations.

The evolution of the concept of leadership

In most texts leadership is defined as a process of social influence whereby a leader steers members of a group towards a goal. Indeed Smircich and Morgan (1982) consider leadership situations to be those in which there exists an obligation or a perceived right on the part of certain individuals to define the reality of others. Such definitions imply deeply ingrained cultural assumptions that leaders are unquestionably necessary for the functioning of organizations and have considerable power over subordinates. Issues such as why leaders are necessary or what existential problems the concept of the leader is expected to address are usually absent from the organizational behaviour literature as also for the most part are the ethical dilemmas which might arise (Enderle, 1987).

The persistence of attempts to determine the nature of effective leadership is probably accounted for by subconscious psychodynamic forces of the sort hinted at above. As Smith and Peterson (1988, p. 11) discuss 'there has been a period of about 70 or so years during which researchers into leadership acted as though they were mediaeval alchemists in search of the philosopher's stone.'

In a later section the leadership myth and its function in organizational life will be explicated but for the moment we trace the development of leadership theory. Such a history reinforces the belief that what we term the leadership myth functions as a social defence whose main aim is to repress uncomfortable needs and emotions that emerge when people endeavour to work together.

Leadership theory and the continuing fascination of managers with what makes an effective leader has also reinforced the belief that much of managing is concerned with directly and closely controlling subordinates. Thus there seems to be some support for the view that the leadership concept may function as a social construct to reinforce existing managerial beliefs and structures about the necessity as a control device of hierarchy and leaders in organizations (Gemmill and Oakley, 1992). All this seems more evident when we briefly review some approaches to leadership.

THE TRAIT APPROACH

The trait approach was the first systematic attempt to research the nature of leadership by seeking to establish the personal characteristics of leaders which distinguished them from followers. Traits which have been researched are physical factors such as height, weight and appearance; abilities such as intelligence, scholarship and knowledge; and personality variables such as conservatism, dominance and emotional control.

However influential reviews of the trait research especially by Stogdill (1948) failed to find evidence to suggest that personal factors played a part in who became a leader. Despite a mild resurgence of the trait approach bound up with the current focus on the charismatic leader, studies such as Stogdill's led to searches for alternative approaches and in the 1950s the emphasis turned to a concern with leadership style or behaviour.

THE STYLE APPROACH

Classic studies of leadership as a universal behavioural style were carried out by Lewin *et al.* (1939) who examined the impact of three different leadership styles in boy's clubs.

During the 1950s and 1960s many attempts were made to define effective leadership styles by using research designs which took data by questionnaires from managers and subordinates in actual organizations. Perhaps the largest project of this kind was that based at the Ohio State University. This work which became known as the Ohio State leadership studies (Stogdill and Coons, 1957) described leadership style as varying on two dimensions called 'consideration' and 'initiating structure'.

Consideration was defined as behaviours such as consultation which encouraged mutual trust between leader and led, and initiating structure which included behaviours which directly resulted in speedy completion of tasks such as defining and ordering. Thus effective leaders were those who behaved towards others in a considerate manner but who also provided appropriate structure to enable tasks to be completed expeditiously.

However these early studies failed to take into account the circumstances or contingencies in which leadership acts occurred and accordingly the same criticisms of universality levelled at the trait approach were also made in the case of behavioural approaches to leadership style.

THE CONTINGENCY APPROACH

One of the earliest contingency theories of leadership effectiveness was put forward by Fiedler in 1967. His measure of leader personality is constructed around the 'least preferred coworker' scale which rests on the assumption that the person with whom the leader has most difficulty working reflects a basic leadership style. Fiedler's second assumption is that the leader's implicit behavioural style that contributes most to group performance varies according to the nature of the situation which is held to change according to three factors. These are the quality of the leader's relationship with subordinates, the leader's formal position power, and the degree of task structure, the last two variables being the direct exercise of managerial control. Task-oriented leaders will do best they believe in situations which are highly favourable and also in situations which are very unfavourable. In intermediate situations the relationship-oriented leader is expected to do better.

Whilst there is some empirical support for Fiedler's theory many consider he relies on a personality measure which is of doubtful validity and indeed that his findings are somewhat ambiguous (Feldman and Arnold, 1986).

Subsequently path–goal theories of leadership (House, 1971) have been developed which assert that leaders must first ensure that subordinates understand how to accomplish leaders' goals and then that as far as is possible subordinates achieve their personal goals in the process. The leader's task is then very directive and high on control in that he or she ascertains the task environment and then selects those behaviours which will ensure that subordinates are motivated towards organizational goals. However, empirical tests of the path–goal model in different work situations have produced findings which are highly variable and have yielded mixed support for the model (Schriesheim and von Glinow, 1977).

More recently House (1984) has attempted to widen the scope of contingency theories by drawing on work of contingency theorists more broadly in the field of organizational behaviour. On this basis House makes 60 propositions about the personal and organizational circumstances which would cause a particular leader to choose a specific style. Of significance to our discussion of ethical issues House suggests that a principal factor in the leader's choice of style are expectations about how subordinates will respond to them.

This is also evident in Vroom and Yetton's (1973) work on decision making. Here a contingency theory of decision making is presented which focuses on leadership acts in settings which require explicit decisions including the extent to which subordinates should be involved in the process. Heilmann *et al.* (1984) when testing the Vroom–Yetton model found that it was supported when students took the perspective of the manager but not when they took that of the subordinate. Further subordinates apparently preferred to participate in all decisions regardless of their nature.

In general then leadership theorists have taken what might be termed a strongly managerialist position. Traditional leadership theory has thus focused at least in part on the leader as controller over aspects of the followers' environment such as rewards and punishments and authority relations.

THE CHARISMATIC APPROACH

The disillusionment with the confusion inherent in earlier approaches to the study of leadership has to some degree led to a revival of Weber's (1947, p. 328) notion of charismatic leadership. This relies on the personal qualities of the leader 'resting on devotion to specific and exceptional sanctity, heroism or exemplary character of an individual person, and of the normative patterns or order revealed or ordained by him.'

In the late 1970s House (1977) and Burns (1978) revived this focus. For his part House (1977) offers seven propositions about aspects of charismatic leadership in complex organizations. Amongst these are that charismatic effects are dominance and self-confidence, need for influence and a strong conviction of the moral righteousness of their beliefs. Further the more favourable the perceptions of the potential follower towards a leader the more the follower will model the values of the leader.

On the other hand Burns' (1978) analysis was based largely on the study of major political leaders and his primary interest was in what has become to be known as transformational leadership which he contrasts with transactional leadership. In transactional leadership a mutual exchange is judged to take place between leader and follower as long as both derive benefit from it; in other words the subordinate agrees to accept leadership in exchange for extrinsic rewards. Burns (1978, p. 20) contrasts this with transforming leadership within which 'leaders and followers raise one another to higher levels of motivation and morality'. Further it is suggested that transformational leaders go beyond basic emotions such as fear and greed to appeal to such ideals and moral values as justice and liberty.

The charismatic leadership theories thus focus on the emotional and motivational arousal of followers by engaging the followers' self-esteem and confidence in the leader, all values that are important to followers' intrinsic motivation. The Burns' study has been instrumental in leading to many others, described by Kets de Vries, (1990, p. 755) 'as a movement back to basics, i.e. a renewed interest in the observation of leaders in action'. Accordingly there have been a large number of recent studies of the charismatic leader in context (Bennis and Nanus, 1985; Tichy and Devanna, 1986; Kotter, 1988; Conger and Kanungo, 1988; and a useful summary review by Bryman, 1992).

Typical of such studies is that by Tichy and Devanna, (1986) who refer to the accelerating rate of change and the key to global competitiveness being the ability of companies to continually transform themselves. In order to achieve this they see a need for transformational leadership at all levels of the organization. Their work draws on Zaleznik's (1989) comparison of managers and leaders, their study being based for the most part on interviews with 12 leaders in a wide variety of organizations (Tichy and Devanna, 1986). Tichy and Devanna's (1986) analysis is then typical of many recent books written primarily for managers in that the data are presented in an attractive, albeit racy, style and their prescriptions are based on limited data.

In concluding Tichy and Devanna (1986) review the common characteristics that differentiate their sample of transformational from transactional managers. These they believe are the conscious identification of themselves as change agents; their courage; their clear articulation of their value position and its congruence with their behaviour; their view of mistakes not as failures but as learning experiences; their ability to deal with complexity, ambiguity and uncertainty, and their sense of vision. Similarly Enderle (1987) and Badaracco and Elsworth (1989) take the view that the complexities involved in taking leadership decisions are at base a matter of integrity in perceiving, interpreting and creating reality.

These are clearly all-important concerns but they all implicitly suggest superhuman and magical qualities and overdependence of subordinates on the leader. This may pose ethical dilemmas and induce a lack of employee creativity and initiative and excessive dependence. It may also present succession and survival problems when the leader is no longer around. Ludwig and Longenecker (1993) further suggest that many ethical violations by senior managers are the consequence of successes rather than competitive pressures. Success they believe may allow managers to become complacent; have privileged access to information and people; and increasingly unrestricted control of organizational resources.

Finally they believe success may inflate a manager's belief in his or her ability to manipulate outcomes. They suggest that even individuals with a highly developed moral sense may be seduced by the convergence of these dynamics.

The evolution of leadership theory therefore portrays successive attempts to account for the factors which give rise to effective leadership. Effectiveness may be judged by the needs that are served by leaders and these may include what is described in the following section as providing social defences against the anxieties of organizational life.

The leadership myth as a social defence

The notion of social defences arises out of the British object relations tradition of enquiry into psychodynamic processes. For example Jaques (1955) shows that one of the elements binding individuals into cohesive human associations is that of defence against painful anxieties.

Menzies (1960) first used the term 'social defence' in the context of the stresses which arise in fulfilling the nursing role. In a leadership context Jaques (1955) provides as an example the relationship between captain and first mate on ships at sea. In this case the sailors maintained a collective defence system in which they protected themselves from ambivalent feelings towards the captain, on whom they were very dependent for their safety, by projecting their negative feelings on to the first mate who thereby acquired a very negative image.

The leadership myth thus functions as a social defence for when members of an organization are faced with uncertainty regarding its direction they often feel anxiety, disappointment and hostility and dispel these feelings by projecting them on to the leader role. These projections allow organizational members to avoid confronting these emergent emotions and by not thinking allow regression into a form of mindlessness. These consequences are perpetuated by the undiscussability of the leader myth and so its alienating effects are based in forces which regard leadership as a healthy concept. Thus leadership in Morgan's (1986) terms becomes a psychic prison, created by people's mental constructs. It would also seem that much of the current theorizing on charismatic leadership stems from a deepening sense of social despair and may help account for the wish for a messiah and magical rescue.

Krantz and Gilmore (1990) also regard the splitting of management into what they call managerialism and heroism (or charismatic leadership) as ways in which managers in our increasingly turbulent organizations cope with their anxieties. Managerialism they believe results when the same methods and techniques that have been used to accomplish the social purposes of organizations are elevated to ends in themselves.

Here we are reminded of Kets de Vries and Miller's (1984) speculative typology of neurotic styles and organizational dysfunctioning and in particular of their compulsive organization; here there is an emphasis on formal controls and information systems to ensure the organization is operating smoothly. However, things are so programmed in these organizations that bureaucratic dysfunctions, inflexibility and inappropriate responses become common. The organization becomes to be poor at managing differences as such behaviour requires flexibility and the capacity to cope with ambiguity. Managers in such situations are likely to become alienated because initiatives are stifled and they lack influence and discretion.

The second manifestation of this splitting according to Krantz and Gilmore (1990) results in the lionization of the heroic or charismatic leader. Here we are presented with saviours who through force of vision will lead our organizations back to dominance by overcoming inertia and bureaucracy.

Similarly Pauchant (1991), whilst reminding us that research on charismatic leadership is sparse and inconclusive, suggests that it has its 'darker' side.

Pauchant constructs a hypothesized typology of 'transferential' leadership dependent on a complex of leader–follower attributes and relationships. He concludes that 'one of the most destructive potentials of this type of leadership seems to emerge from the psychic unit where the leader is self-inflated and the followers self-deflated' (Pauchant, 1991, p. 523).

He therefore cautions against too ready an acceptance of the notion of the beneficial effects of charismatic leadership especially as he cites evidence (e.g. Rogers, 1980) of self-deflation in our organizations and society. He also suggests on the other hand that self-inflated managers seem to be gaining positions of power in our organizations. Such views are supported for example by Lasch (1979) and Gill and Whittle (1993).

The result of the introduction of charismatic leadership on this analysis may therefore be an excessive reliance on the leader and a consequent stifling of creativity and initiative in subordinates. Such dynamics are cyclic and self-supporting for as social despair, helplessness and anomie increase so the need for a messiah and magical rescue by an heroic leader become more pressing. We agree with Gemmill and Oakley (1992) and Krantz and Gilmore (1990) that the significance of the charismatic as a leadership style may be in its meaning as a social delusion and maladaptive response in conditions of uncertainty and turbulence that allows followers to escape responsibility for their own actions and inactions. As such charismatic leadership poses serious ethical problems and demands a more constructive alternative to the dilemmas inherent in managing organizations. We now turn to some possible remedies.

Towards self-controlling organizations

In this concluding section we explore the possibility of moving towards the concept of the commitment-based self-controlling organization and examine the effect of doing so on leadership, management and business ethics.

Management has rightly been considered to be obsessed with control (Mintzberg, 1989), control which paradoxically is in any case probably illusory (Dermer and Lucas, 1986). Mintzberg (1989) describes the final chapter of his book as a pessimistic polemic in which he contends that the structural form which he has earlier labelled the machine bureaucracy dominates our thinking about how organizations should be constructed. The central driving force in these structures he describes as an obsession with controlling leadership.

Mintzberg then goes on to argue that professional management has been dehumanized and in turn has dehumanized their organizations by making them so 'rational' and efficient that they cease to function effectively as by emphasizing calculation they drive out commitment.

The conventional managerial control model assumes that control involves the exercise of leadership to achieve compliance and that management is the dominant controlling force. 'Strategy expresses management's expectations which in turn serve as a reference point for management control' (Dermer, 1988, p. 26).

By contrast with the conventional approach, an approach termed consensual (e.g. Tannenbaum, 1968) differs in that the expectations on which control is determined are arrived at by interdependent relationships rather than by a unidirectional imposition of authority by leaders. Thus the consensual approach emphasizes the sharing of control and the building of a consensual organization through various forms of participative management. The autonomous activity engaged in by stakeholders is a means of reconciling the contradictions they perceive between management strategy and actual conditions in practice. Accordingly then the traditional management model based on functionalism, strategy and cybernetics needs on this argument to be augmented with an approach which recognizes the importance of the autonomous activity of self-interested and self-led individuals.

This latter position moves closely to that which we go on to advocate here, that of commitment based self-controlling organizations based on intrinsically motivated individuals supported by a carefully constructed external organizational environment; an environment in which managerial leadership and control is based not on control through command and authority but in more supportive processes which encourage employees to lead and control themselves. Such a prescription entails the democratization of work organizations and this is clearly rather a tall order but we feel in the long run inevitable. For as we have argued not only are attempts to rely solely on unilaterally imposed, external controls dehumanizing, bureaucratizing and ethically suspect but all this effort as a sure means of control is in any case probably illusory.

However, the advocates of commitment-based self-control as a form of self-leadership (e.g. Mills, 1983; Manz and Sims, 1989; Manz, 1991, 1992) suggest that there are organizational conditions which when present will have a strong possibility of resulting in self-motivating individuals. Importantly this is likely to result in a more committed, productive and creative workforce and pose fewer ethical dilemmas for managers.

Whilst we caution against a normative and universal approach to human motivation as propounded by the neohuman relations school (Johnson and Gill, 1993) it does nevertheless seem to be the case that trends which we outline below may be reinforcing approaches to control based on commitment-based self-control. The crucial point in this regard is to view the self-influence system as the ultimate system of leadership and one with which other control systems are compatible and supportive. Recognizing and facilitating employee self-regulating mechanisms suggests a more realistic view of leadership than that based solely on external influence. Furthermore overreliance on external leadership and control as we have seen may lead to dysfunctional, rigid bureaucratic behaviours, an alienated workforce and give rise to ethical dilemmas.

The self-management literature has been developed from at least three other main sources. First it has originated from social learning theory and related work (e.g. Bandura, 1969; Mahoney and Thoreson, 1974); secondly in the organization literature, specifically that concerned with self-managed or autonomous work groups or teams (e.g. Luthans and Davies, 1979; Andrasik and Heimberg, 1982; Manz and Sims, 1987); and thirdly it has been stimulated by recent advances in technology and consequent structural changes.

Work redesign programmes largely focusing on the individual or the group were introduced in the 1960s, 1970s and 1980s throughout the developed economies of the west and in Japan. Trist (1970) and others interested in the impact of technology on organizational structure have considered that the shopfloor worker has a new role, primarily as fact finder, interpreter, diagnostician, judge, adjuster and change agent. Clearly the role of management may change in these circumstances to 'more of a process than a role filled by a group of people' (McWhinney and Krone, 1972, p. 7). Further Trist believes that 'the autonomous work group ... would appear to be the organizational paradigm which matches ... the information technology. The advance of technology itself has reversed the world of Frederick Taylor' (Trist, 1970, p. 28). Many examples of experiments involving autonomous work groups seem to be employing a highly participative, team approach designed to create a significant degree of decision-making autonomy and behavioural control at the level of the work group.

The self-managed group apparently results in a shift in focus from individual methods of performing work to group methods on the basis that the group can more effectively allocate its resources when and where required than can an aggregate of individuals. As we have hinted the role of management will in such circumstances probably change significantly and it seems likely that management as a process might be undertaken spontaneously and informally by a wide variety of individuals at various levels rather than formally and more permanently through the organizational hierarchy. These conditions are to be found in a wider organizational context in matrix organizations or, in Mintzberg's terms, 'adhocracies' (Mintzberg, 1979).

A number of different strands accordingly seem to be coming together for not surprisingly the conditions we describe are also predicted for the manufacturing organizations of the future on the basis of research work undertaken in British manufacturing industry into appropriate manufacturing organization for computer-integrated technology (Smith *et al.*, 1991). It was predicted from the literature at the outset of this research that the work organizations of the future would display increasing integration of tasks; teamworking and role sharing; semi-autonomous work groups; cellular manufacturing; flexible teams, multiple roles and skilling; increasing local discretion; alternative payment systems, e.g. for team output and quality; and leadership as a resource rather than as a controller. Similarly it was suggested that control was more likely to be exercised by informal mechanisms and to be self-organized within a broad framework rather than by formal rules and procedures. Further bureaucratic lines of control were likely to be replaced with more flexible control systems and a hierarchical power structure with simultaneous centralization (tight controls) and decentralization (loose controls). Communication in such organizations were it was suggested likely to be by networking in flat structures with few levels. At the same time control of work was predicted to change from formalized standards controlled by appraisal by superiors to various forms of self-assessment. These predictions whilst not particularly novel, in that they were essentially and in outline the findings of the research by Burns and Stalker (1961) in the early 1960s and as we have seen have been elaborated by others since. Nevertheless they were in large part confirmed by empirical work undertaken in a number of cases of the introduction of computer integrated technology in British manufacturing industry.

Given these findings drawn widely from a number of sources it seems reasonable to predict that the roles of supervision and management and their control functions may change substantially in future in terms of their leadership styles. Some evidence in this regard is reported by Manz and Sims (1987) who identified salient leader behaviours in one medium-sized, small-parts manufacturing plant that had been operating for several years under a system of self-managed work teams. The investigation focused on the external leaders of these work groups the objective being to identify leader behaviours in such situations. Specifically the researchers wished to discover what behaviours were used by leaders, who were called coordinators, within the self-managed work groups and how this compared with leadership behaviour in other contexts. They were especially interested to discover the relationship between certain leader behaviours and their effectiveness and hypothesized that leaders who encouraged employee self-management would be particularly effective.

The small-parts engineering plant was situated in the southern United States and employed about 320 employees. It was organized from the start on a self-managed work team basis each work group being assigned to a sequence of interdependent, related tasks.

Organizationally the plant was structured in three hierarchical levels. Upper plant management, known as the support team, taking many of the traditional plant management responsibilities and being responsible, for example, for planning production and dealing with clients. The support team, as its title suggests, attempted to work as a team and played a supportive rather than a directive role.

The work team coordinators formed the middle layer in the organization and were the main focus of the study; they acted in a supportive role to the work teams themselves. Most work teams had between eight and 12 members and each had an elected team leader who for the most part performed the same work as other members of the team. Apart from performing routine work, teams met on a regular weekly basis to engage in problem-solving discussions to improve work performance. External co-ordinators did not attend meetings routinely but might often be invited, for example, to help team members deal with a particularly difficult problem.

As we have mentioned the focus of the study was on the coordinator role which was external to the teams; a role which clearly poses contradictions and ambiguities for those performing such roles in organizations with self-management philosophies. Coordinators were observed carrying out supportive roles in relation to problem-solving activities, and training activities to encourage groups to undertake self-evaluation. There was an absence by them of direct commands and instructions to the teams rather an encouragement to teams to question their own activities and practice team and self-control.

In summarizing their findings Manz and Sims (1987) contrast them with the work of Schriesheim *et al.* (1976) and Lord *et al.* (1984), research which was designed to examine aspects of traditional leader behaviours. Despite the differences in the period in which these researches were undertaken the findings of all the studies were similar. Both regarded leaders in the traditional fashion as those who do something to influence others directly on the assumption that power, initiation and control is entirely with the leaders.

By contrast, self-management leader behaviours in the case presented by Manz and Sims (1987) were designed to encourage self-reinforcement; self-observation, evaluation and control; self-expectation and goal-setting; and rehearsal and self-criticism.

Self-management strategies advocated by, for example, Mahoney and Arnkoff (1979) and Manz and Sims (1989) provide a number of approaches to self-leadership derived from their application in clinical contexts. These include the development of self-leadership through modelling; self-goal-setting and productive thought patterns; self-reward and reprimand; and cueing strategies which are all covered in detail in Manz and Sims (1989) and Manz (1992).

Conclusion

The argument has been advanced that many of our organizations are overmanaged and overcontrolled. A case has been made for a different and ethically more justifiable form of managerial leadership. Developments in a number of directions seem to support these trends.

It is contended that a reduction in close control will help create self-controlling organizations based on the intrinsically motivated individual. Managerial leadership in such organizations is likely to be based not on control through command and authority but in more supportive behaviours which encourage employees to control and lead themselves. For individuals working in organizations the promise is of a more ethical and a less exploitative relationships between leaders and led.

As we have argued not only are attempts to rely solely on unilaterally imposed controls likely to be dehumanizing, bureaucratizing and alienating but all this effort as a means of control is probably wasted. We therefore might hopefully predict a reduction in the number of managers in the organizations of the future and a change in the leadership roles of those that remain.

Finally we end on a cautionary note. Such developments would seem in part to depend on a supportive environment characterized by the democratization of the wider society and its institutions. At the present time there would not seem to be cause for a great deal of optimism in this regard; however times may change.

Exercises

❏ How far do you believe that alienation in work organizations is largely the consequence of a predominantly directive and controlling leadership style?
❏ Leadership has been described above as a mythical concept. How does the myth arise and what needs does it serve?
❏ How might a more reality-based leadership perspective be developed?
❏ What environmental supports are emerging for approaches which are described above as 'self-leadership'.
❏ How far do you believe 'self-leadership' will result in more motivated and less alienated employees and more ethical working relationships?

Further reading

A recent collection of articles which question the implicit assumption that leaders are naturally 'ethical' can be found in a special issue of *Business Ethics Quarterly* [5(1), 1995]. Similarly, articles by Ludwig and Longenecker (1993) and Sankowsky, (1995) provide interesting reading. Badaracco and Ellsworth's (1989) book provides the reader with another account of the subject.

References

Andrasik, F. and Heimberg, J.S. (1982) Self-management procedures, in *Handbook of Organizational Behaviour Management* (ed. L.W. Frederikson). John Wiley, New York.

Badaracco, J.L. and Ellsworth, R.R. (1989) *Leadership and the Quest for Integrity*. Harvard Business School Press, Boston, MA.

Bandura, A. (1969) *Principles of Behaviour Modification*. Holt, Rinehart & Winston, New York.

Bennis, W. and Nanus, B. (1985) *Leaders: Strategies for Taking Charge*. Harper & Row, New York.

Bryman, A. (1992) *Charisma and Leadership in Organizations*. Sage, London.

Burns, J.M. (1978) *Leadership*. Harper & Row, New York.

Burns, T and Stalker, G.M. (1961) *The Management of Innovation*. Tavistock, London.

Conger, J.A. (1990) The darker side of leadership. *Organization Dynamics*, **19**(2), 44–55.

Conger, J.A. and Kanungo, R.N. (1988) *Charismatic Leadership: The Elusive Factor in Organizational Effectiveness*. Jossey-Bass, San Francisco, CA.

Dermer, J.D. (1988) Control and organizational order. *Accounting, Organizations and Society*, **13**, 25–36.

Dermer, J.D. and Lucas, R.G. (1986) The illusion of management control. *Accounting, Organizations and Society*, **11**, 471–82.

Enderle, G. (1987) Some perspectives of managerial ethical leadership. *Journal of Business Ethics*, **6**, 657–63.

Feldman, D.C. and Arnold, H.J. (1986) *Organizational Behaviour*. McGraw-Hill, London.

Fiedler, F.E. (1967) *A Contingency Theory of Leadership Effectiveness*. McGraw-Hill, New York.

Gemmill, G. and Oakley, J. (1992) Leadership: an alienating social myth? *Human Relations*, **45**, 113–29.

Gill, J. and Whittle, S. (1993) Management by panacea: accounting for transience. *Journal of Management Studies*, **30**, 81–295.

Heilmann *et al.* (1984) Reactions to prescribed leader behaviour as a function of role perspective: the case of the Vroom–Yetton model. *Journal of Applied Psychology*, **69**, 50–60.

House, R.J. (1971) A path–goal theory of leadership effectiveness. *Administrative Science Quarterly*, **16**, 321–8.

House, R.J. (1977) A 1976 theory of charismatic leadership, in *Leadership: The Cutting Edge* (eds J.G. Hunt and L.L. Larson). South Illinois University Press, Carbondale, IL.

House, R.J. (1984) Power in organizations: a social psychological perspective (unpublished paper). Faculty of Management, University of Toronto.

Jaques, E. (1955) Social systems as a defence against persecutory and depressive anxiety, in *New Directions in Psychoanalysis* (eds M. Klein, P. Heimann and R.E. Money-Kryle). Tavistock, London.

Johnson, P. and Gill, J. (1993) *Management Control and Organizational Behaviour*. Paul Chapman, London.

Kets de Vries, M.F.R. (1990) The organizational fool: balancing a leader's hubris. *Human Relations*, **43**, 751–70.

Kets de Vries, M.F.R. and Miller, D. (1984) *The Neurotic Organization: Diagnosing and Changing Counterproductive Styles of Management*. Jossey-Bass, San Francisco, CA.

Kotter, (1988) *The Leadership Factor*. Free Press, New York.

Krantz, J. and Gilmore, T.N. (1990) The splitting of leadership and management as a social defence. *Human Relations*, **43**, 183–204.

Lasch, D. (1979) *The Culture of Narcissism. American Life in the Age of Diminishing Expectations*. Warner Books, New York.

Lewin, K., Lippitt, R. and White, R. K. (1939) Patterns of aggressive behaviour in experimentally created social climates. *Journal of Social Psychology*, **10**, 271–99.

Lord, R.G., Foti, R.J. and De Vader, C.L. (1984) A test of leadership categorization theory, internal structure, information processing and leadership perceptions. *Organizational Behaviour and Human Performance*, **34**, 343–78.

Ludwig, D.C. and Longenecker, C.O. (1993) The Bathsheba syndrome: the ethical failure of successful leaders. *Journal of Business Ethics*, **12**, 265–73.

Luthans, F. and Davies, T. (1979) Behavioural self-management: the missing link in managerial effectiveness. *Organizational Dynamics*, **8**, 42–60.

McWhinney, W. and Krone, C. (1972) Open systems planning. Unpublished manuscript available from Enthusion, Venice, CA.

Mahoney, M.J. and Arnkoff, D. B. (1979) Self-management theory, research and application, in *Behavioral Medicine: Theory and Practice* (eds J.P. Brady and D. Pomerleau). Williams & Wilkins, Baltimore, MD.

Mahoney, M.J. and Thoreson, C.E. (eds) (1974) *Self-control: Power to the Person*. Brooks/Cole, Monterey, CA.

Manz, C.C. (1991) Leading employees to be self-managing and beyond: towards the establishment of self-leadership in organizations. *Journal of Management Systems*, **3**, 15–24.

Manz, C.C. (1992) *Mastering Self-leadership: Empowering Yourself for Personal Excellence*. Prentice-Hall, Englewood Cliffs, NJ.

Manz, C.C. and Sims, H.P. (1987) Leading workers to lead themselves: the external leadership of self-managing work teams. *Administrative Science Quarterly*, **32**, 106–28.

Manz, C.C. and Sims, H.P. (1989) *Superleadership: Leading Others to Lead Themselves*. Prentice-Hall, Berkeley, CA.

Menzies, I.E.P. (1960) The functioning of social systems as a defence against anxiety. *Human Relations*, **13**, 95–121.

Mills, P.K. (1983) Self management: its control and relationship to other organizational properties. *Academy of Management Review*, **8**, 445–53.

Mintzberg, H. (1979) *The Structuring of Organizations*. Prentice-Hall, Englewood Cliffs, NJ.

Mintzberg, H. (1989) *Mintzberg on Management*. Free Press, New York.

Morgan, G. (1986) *Images of Organization*. Sage, London.

Pauchant, T.C. (1991) Transferential leadership. Towards a more complex understanding of charisma in organizations. *Organization Studies*, **12**, 507–27.

Rogers, C.R. (1980) *A Way of Being*. Houghton Mifflin, Boston, MA.

Sankowsky, D. (1995) The charismatic leader as narcissist: understanding the abuse of power. *Organizational Dynamics*, **23**(4), 57–71.

Schriesheim, C.A. and von Glinow, M.A. (1977) The path–goal theory of leadership: a theoretical and empirical analysis. *Academy of Management Journal*, **20**, 398–405.

Schriesheim, C.A., House, R.J. and Kerr, S. (1976) Leader initiating structure: a reconciliation of discrepant research results and some empirical tests. *Organizational Behaviour and Human Performance*, **15**, 297–321.

Smircich, L. and Morgan, G. (1982) Leadership: the management of meaning. *Journal of Applied Behavioural Science*, **18**(3), 257–73.

Smith, P.B. and Peterson, M.F. (1988) *Leadership, Organizations and Culture*. Sage, London.

Smith, J.S., Tranfield, D.R., Ley, D.C., Bessant, J.R. and Levy, P. (1990) Changing organization design and practices for computer integrated technologies. *Proceedings of the Operations Management Association Conference on Manufacturing Strategy: Theory and Practice*, London, 26–27 June, pp. 862–73.

Stogdill, R.M. (1948) Personal factors associated with leadership: a survey of the literature. *Journal of Psychology*, **25**, 35–71.

Stogdill, R.M. and Coons, A.E. (eds) (1957) *Leader Behavior: Its Description and Measurement*. Bureau of Business Research, Ohio State University, Columbus, OH.

Tannenbaum, A.S. (1968) *Control in Organizations*. McGraw-Hill, New York.

Tichy, N.M. and Devanna, M.A. (1986) *The Transformational Leader*. John Wiley, New York.

Trist, E. (1970) A socio-technical critique of scientific management. Paper presented at the *Edinburgh Conference on the Impact of Science and Technology*, May.

Vroom, V. H. and Yetton, P. W. (1973) *Leadership and Decision-making*. University of Pittsburgh Press, Pittsburgh, PA.

Weber, M. (1947) *The Theory of Social and Economic Organization*. Free Press, Glencoe, IL. (First published 1924.)

Zaleznik, A. (1989) *The Managerial Mystique*. HarperCollins, New York.

Ethical issues in the management of change

11

John McAuley

Change gives a sharper focus to many of the ethical issues that are faced in day-to-day management because the turbulences encountered in periods of change amplify the impact of organizational processes on members and external stakeholders. I shall explore ethical issues that lie in front of some of the philosophical positions to which change agents have recourse at either conscious or preconscious levels. These positions are discussed with some degree of separation, but in the awareness that in many situations they might well run concurrently with different degrees of emphasis and covertness as part of the dialectical process within the arena – the 'organizational reality which both shapes and is shaped by organizational members' (Phillips 1991, p. 787).

In this chapter I shall look at some of the issues of change that are encountered in the relationship with external stakeholders. I shall than look at ethical issues associated with some of the approaches to, and processes of, the management of change. Because the scope of this topic is so wide I have not explored the impact of the interplay of economic, social or technological change.

Introduction

The relationship between the organization and what is identified as its environment is mediated through the meanings that the key actors give to it. An examination of the ethical issues managers face in their relationship with their environment is usefully undertaken through use of Mitroff's (1983) stakeholder analysis. What he stressed was the nature of the psychological (and we would add sociological) relationship between 'the organization' and the groupings which constitute the external meaning structures within which the organization is placed – the customers, suppliers and competitors.

These stakeholders exercise some claim on the organization at manifest or latent levels – 'the first [of these terms] referring to those objectives for [the organization] ... which contribute to its adjustment and were so intended; the second referring to unintended and unrecognized consequences of the same order' (Merton (1968, p. 117). The ethical issues are concerned with the ways in which, in managing change, relationships

Ethical issues of change and external stakeholders

with these different stakeholders are gauged. For example, the presence or absence of discrepancies between the organization's claims to be ethical and the ways in which it deals with different stakeholders can give its audience strong signals about the 'reality' of the organization's ethical relationship with all its stakeholders. In relation to customers the ways in which the organization selects some as their customer base and marginalizes others has ethical implications as does the ways in which the organization treats its suppliers in relation to the specification of standards of performance and the creation of a relationship which is experienced by the supplier as equitable.

Some of the ethical issues in the supplier/customer relationship involved in change management may be illustrated through the example of healthcare delivery within the UK National Health Service. As Johnson and Scholes (1993, pp. 218–19) point out, 'the policies of the government towards the … Service were seen quite differently by supporters and opponents'; this is an arena in which there are competing basic assumptions (Schein (1991, p. 15) of members about the nature of healthcare, about its organization, and the relationship of these to external stakeholders.

From the supporters of the change the legitimating philosophy has been, basically, utilitarian in character which gives rise to a managerialist (Pollitt, 1993) approach to its management. Stripping this philosophy bare, its principle axiom, in relation to public services, is that they exist to achieve the greatest happiness of the greatest number – although, given the problematic nature of that state of being, maybe we need to echo Freud's definition of the psychoanalytic cure, which was that it enables very unhappy people to achieve a state of 'normal unhappiness'.

Williams (1972) suggests four major aspects of utilitarianism that give it appeal as an ethical position. The first of these is its secular, non-transcendent, nature; it is grounded in the pragmatic world of everyday 'reality'. In the hands of a radical agent, 'utilitarianism promises more radical change' (p. 97) than would be possible if its hands were tied by a transcendent morality in which there may be appeals to a 'higher authority' such as professional allegiance or a sense of vocation. This legitimates *inter alia* the replacement of 'professionals' (e.g. medical staff) by 'managers' in the management of change.

The second feature is that utilitarianism 'is a *minimum commitment* morality … given … a willingness to consider other people's wants as well as one's own, utilitarianism can get going on this spot' (p. 99); in organizational change there is no need to erect major codes of ethics or indeed be too troubled by ethical issues as long as this minimum commitment is present. One aspect of this is that ends can be used to justify the means. An example is the concept of 'tough love' – which is used to legitimate policies in which new and higher demands are made on customers or suppliers. We could suggest that 'tough love' can be seen as an ethical stance if it used as a means by which one party can, within the boundaries of mutuality, take a responsible stance in relation to the self and others; it is unethical where it is an agency of oppression, where, as Seligman (1993) suggests, a protected group can tell others 'this will hurt, but it is for your own good'.

Williams suggests that the 'third attraction is that moral issues can, in principle, be determined by empirical calculation of consequences.' (1972, p. 100). Williams asserts, and Praill and Baldwin (1988, p. 3) demonstrate, that there are difficulties in achieving this quantitative control of the world and its presentation to stakeholders. The latter write of the use of uncoordinated 'assessment' and 'evaluation' procedures, adherence to 'meaningless statistics', and the invention of 'cosmetic indicators for monitoring standards'. For example, a patient attending a hospital in the UK can according to the 1994 Patients Charter anticipate that the length of time between seeing his or her general practitioner and his or her first visit to the specialist can be time regulated, the patient can feel some assurance that the reception staff will handle the conversation efficiently and that the wait in the hospital reception will be of a certain duration: what cannot be guaranteed is the quality of interaction with the patient's clinician will be of a type that he or she can be assured that he or she has been well treated. However, this principle justifies, in the management of change, the setting up of 'a quasi-competitive framework' with an emphasis on cost-control and a managed service (Pollitt, 1993, p. 49) in order to deliver services. A utilitarian approach to change enables 'providers [i.e. internal stakeholders] of the service to add value, and for buyers [i.e. external stakeholders] of the service to seek better value' (Johnson and Scholes 1993, p. 239) in ways that are amenable to calculation.

The fourth of the principles mentioned by Williams is that 'there can be no coherent idea of a right or wrong thing to do, other than what is, or is not, *the best thing to do on the whole* ... ' (1972, p. 99). In organizational terms, utilitarians would argue that as long as the change processes are seen to be 'rational' and in accord with the logics of efficiency, we are, ethically, home and dry. There is here an interesting ethical paradox. On the one hand the utilitarian stance could encourage a stance that since change is 'the best we can do under the circumstances'. They could anticipatedly admit to failure, that the 'best' can turn out to be 'not good enough', or that it was only the 'best' in the sense that it created the greatest happiness at that time. In this sense there could be an ethic that sees change as non-linear, that not all change is for the best in the long run. On the other hand an ethic such as this could be seen by utilitarians to smack of weakness, a lack of determination to achieve utilitarian outcomes and it also runs counter to notions of utilitarian rationality – that if we act think and rationally then we can determine quality outcomes. This stance provides additional legitimization for the management of change through 'strong' management. Since choice is made through informed judgement calls, conflict over means and ends is inefficient and choice is best exercised by those in closest strategic contact with stakeholders. This legitimates, as we shall discuss in more detail later, management privilege in decision making and a safe haven for them in the 'hierarchy of credibility' (Becker 1977, p. 129) – such that management accounts of the world are taken to be more amenable to belief than those of other stakeholders whether internal or external.

What we have tried to do in the above is to take seriously the hint provided by Warnock (1994) that when we are looking at ethical issues we need to be able to understand the underpinning philosophy – and to be able to comprehend our own philosophical presuppositions when we comment on what we perceive to be the stance of others. As she suggests, 'in the context of real choices or real arguments, almost every word that is uttered contains some hidden value judgement'. She goes on to suggest that a key task facing the moral philosopher is to assist those with different perspectives to achieve some sort of consensus. Perhaps, in the absence of such august persons on an everyday basis, this becomes a key task for managers in their exploration of the relationship between the themselves and their environment.

An example of interaction between internal and external stakeholders might be that of provision of hospital care for women and by women professionals. In the late 1970s a London hospital, the Elizabeth Garrett Anderson, was threatened with closure and became something of an icon for those who, coming from a feminist/distributive stance, felt that medical care for women should, as of a right, be delivered by women. The threat to closure was withdrawn. It is perhaps interesting to note that the bases of closure was based on an appeal to 'efficiency', but at a time when the new-right (Pollitt, 1993) philosophy was less coherently articulated than became the case by 1992 when the local health authority again decided on closure. This time the appeal for closure is clearly articulated around market, utilitarian philosophical bases and also around an expressive structure of 'providers' and 'suppliers'. According to a senior manager: '... the hospital provides a valuable service, but it has a large cost implication' (Brindle, 1992, p. 7), Thus, closure can be justified on the ethical basis that the current arrangement does not provide the 'greatest good for the greatest number'. The ethical objection to closure – that a perceived to be vulnerable group of people (in this case women who do not want to be treated by male professionals for reasons of privacy or whatever) was met by the provision of beds – albeit smaller in number than presently – which 'would be reserved for women patients who could opt to be treated by women doctors' (Brindle, 1992, p. 7).

It would appear (for there may well be much that is not reported) that in this case the change agents have attempted to understand what different stakeholders really want, that they are transparent with regard to their own stance but have also recognized that the stance of others in relation to complex issues of the distribution of scarce resources has an ethical basis. An ethical relationship with stakeholders – whether suppliers, competitors, or customers – is negotiated in the sense that although the rules of stakeholder relationship and the boundaries of responsibility and decision making well understood this is within a context of potential renegotiation through engagement in '... the most intense and sensitive interaction ... that means as close to the border between what insiders and outsiders want' (Stacey 1991, p. 390).

There is an assumption embedded in much of the literature on change and its management that there are actors who need to mediate between the environment and the organization and as a consequence of this mediation, undertake change within it. For example Gioia and Chittipeddi (1991) suggest that 'the initiation of strategic change can be viewed as a process whereby the Chief Executive Officer makes sense of an altered vision of the organization and engages in cycles of negotiated social construction activities to influence stakeholders and constituents to accept that vision' (p. 434).

Transformational change through leadership

In this tradition of change management, the heroic transformational leader has a powerfully personal vision of the future organization. Within this perspective,

> strategic [transformational] leaders believe they can have a major impact on the organization by empowering organization members to realize the leader's long-range organizational vision ... The approach emphasizes leader personal characteristics, organizational settings within which visionary leaders act and specific actions that they take to build vision and future. (Hunt, 1991, p. 195)

This view of the nature of change management has interesting ethical outcomes. If there is an acceptance of Nietzschean philosophical presuppositions, with their respect for the ameliorative power of those 'who can sublimate and control their passions, employing them creatively' (Urmson and Ree, 1989, p. 224), then there is legitimization for a dominant élite because it is assigned superiority in practical affairs, in aesthetic matters or in the life of the spirit – all of which may well be involved in ethical approaches to the management of change.

For example, the visionary leader provides a holding environment for organizational members; they can see within the overall mission and vision that is personified by the leader a notion of safety that will take them through troubled times ahead – a womb with a view, so to speak. Citing the work of Burns (1978), who claimed that the relationship between transformational leader and led is one in which 'leaders and followers raise one another to higher levels of motivation and morality', Dunham and Klafehn (1990) go on to suggest that this type of leadership enables staff to 'see the meaningful interrelationship of both the vision and their work and understand how their work contributes to the successful accomplishment of the vision'.

Assertions that change management through transformational leadership is essentially ethically sound is reinforced by the view that 'symbolic managers influence cultural and ethical values by articulating a vision for organizational values that employees can believe and by engaging in day to day activities that reinforce these values ...' (Daft, 1992, p. 330). This relationship between the transformational leader, the management of change and the accomplishment of an organization which achieves ethically good organizational objectives through its workforce is neatly summarized by Clampitt when he suggests:

> The challenge for the manager is to transform [the manager's] power into duty and [employee's] conformity into desire ... The culture holds the organization together in the absence of threats and rewards. Without a healthy culture we are merely beasts. (1991, p. 54)

Underlying the notion of the transformational leadership is a unitarist, monolithic understanding of the nature of change. It could be argued that this position is not in itself ethically problematic; where it becomes so depends upon the context of commitment that the transformational leader expects of employees. Kanter (1968, p. 501) usefully distinguishes three levels of commitment – instrumental compliance (which I summarize as 'I am paid to believe in the change, and I will be punished if I do not, therefore I give it my commitment), or because of an affective link to the transformational leader ('I love my leader therefore I will follow'), or because the followers have truly internalized the values and beliefs of the transformational leader ('my leader and I are as souls intertwined').

All three of these have ethical gains and losses. As far as the first level is concerned we could suggest that the ethical issues are located around the degree of choice within the marketplace members have, their freedom to remove themselves to other work if they cannot tolerate the leader's expectation of compliance. In the other two levels transformational leaders, in their management of change, rely on symbols; the 'charisma' of the leader figure may be presented as a potent symbol of the change process and its agency. This can lead to feelings of 'organizational seduction [the company's attempts to make the employee choose to act in a certain way, when in reality he or she has no other choice] ...' (Alvesson and Berg, 1992, p. 172).

There is, however a more intransigent ethical issue attached to the enactment of transformational leadership. Wilson (1992, p. 125) points out that if the visionary leader/sponsor departs from the organization there is a sense that the centre can no longer hold and the change programme collapses; the members of the organization have become dependent on the leader. This issue is also illustrated by instances where the personal vision becomes distorted by the onset of such phenomena as *folie à grandeur* on the part of the leader, where the leader's 'unresolved sense of self or unrealistic idea of potency, can affect the working of an organization' (Kets de Vries, 1993, p. 32) creates as a dynamic within it very high states of dependency on the part of key staff. Both these instances illuminate a broader ethical issue which involves the state of dependency which is part and parcel of transformational leadership; it comes to represent, as Anzieu points out, in the context of group life, a 'regression to early childhood situations ... [It] corresponds to an eternal group dream, the dream of a good, strong, intelligent leader who assumes responsibilities in their stead' (1984, p. 111).

To push this a little further, dependency represents a denial of individual responsibility. This happens when boundaries are unmanaged and where expectations of commitment have become collusive so that members become unable to handle conflict, to express dissent (Harvey, 1974). This is particularly the case when the transformational leader projects a powerful message that is messianic in its thrust – 'that all is for the best in the best of all possible worlds'. The invitation that the transformational leader issues to members of the organization with which to cooperate is that the future organization represents an ego ideal – 'the committed person's idea of the organization'. Schwarz suggests that this ideal represents what 'the organization is supposed to be and would be except for the bad aspects of the world, and what he or she accepts as an obligation to help bring about' (Schwarz, 1990, p. 19). He suggests that because members become colonized by the organizational ideal they lose their own identity to be replaced by the narcissistic fantasy that – because they are so closely identified with it – they live within the fantasy being of their organization. Hirschorn (1988) points to the pain of managing change in circumstances where the transformational leader fails to acknowledge, because of the seduction of the fantasy, real difficulties encountered by members as the change is happening because of discrepancies between the vision as ideal and as enacted – the double bind of charismatic change.

This ethical issue can be resolved at least to some extent if there is embedded into the organization culture and structure boundary management so that there is autonomous (rather than compulsive) assent to the symbolic nature of the transformational leader – there is a high level of reflexive self-consciousness such that members know what they are doing when they are doing it. This accords with the view expressed by Bate who suggests that 'the guiding philosophies of the ethical leader are asceticism, humanism but especially scepticism' where this last quality is one in which the leader is 'critic, interrogator and whistleblower all rolled into one, a disturbing force that will not ... take itself too much for granted' (1994, p. 274).

Habermas expresses a much more astringent ethical view. He argues in a societal context, that there has been the emergence of rule by élites within the democratic context. In an organizational context, transformational leaders empower those who are managed to undertake that which the leader wants to have happen; they do not characteristically empower those who wish to defeat the visionary paradigm. Accordingly, '... the conditions under which all legitimate interests can be fulfilled by way of realizing the fundamental interest in self-determination and participation are no longer understood' (Habermas, 1976, p. 123). All this points to the mutuality of the ethical exchange. Just as, as we have seen, the leaders need to be able to exercise scepticism about their relationship to themselves and their organization, so members have ethical responsibilities. Camus somewhat rhetorically asked, and then answered in a gender specific way:

> What is a rebel? A man who says no: but whose refusal does not imply a renunciation. He is also a man who says yes as soon as he begins to think for himself. A slave who has taken orders all his life, suddenly decides he cannot obey some new command ... The slave asserts himself for the sake of everyone in the world when he comes to the conclusion that a command has infringed on something inside him that does not belong to him alone, but which he has in common with others ... (1953, pp. 20–2)

It is clear that there are, where transformational leadership is seen as the way forward in the management of change, some powerful ethical issues. The transformational leader creates and sustains for members through personal symbolization and through culture management a holding environment in times of major change. The key ethical issue is that within the holding environment there needs to be an awareness of the shadow such that the oppressive elements of the holding environment are well contained through the development within the organization of an awareness of the dynamics of this approach to change, a voluntaristic assent to it.

This vision thing

We have seen that the transformational leader has particular ethical responsibilities. Not all managers with a responsibility for the management of strategic planned change enact their role in this charismatic manner; indeed Johnson and Scholes suggest that texts which emphasize the need for charismatic change management can be misleading 'because they fail to identify the context in which change agency occurs ...' (1993, p. 411). The key feature that transformational leaders and what we shall call mundane managers with responsibility for change have in common is a notion of some idea of a future state. In the case of the former this is the outcome of a personal vision; in the latter it is claimed to be the outcome of a rational exploration of the future, such that a morally better world can be achieved through management of change geared towards the achievement of efficiency and effectiveness in an ordered, managed manner. It should be mentioned that 'mundane' management appears in several guises, each of which comes from somewhat different but interlinked philosophies, but with a common core that is concerned with 'a set of broad assumptions about the unique potentials and rights of management' (Pollitt, 1993, p. 11). We have already looked at some of the features of 'managerialism', which, in the spectrum of approaches to management 'is ... a much more specific set of models of efficient organizational functioning and techniques through which smooth functioning may be realized' (Pollitt, 1993, p. 11) – it is 'management' with attitude; in the discussion which follows we shall refer to a generic model of management.

In many organizations the statement of the ultimate ends of the change process is captured by processes of corporate strategy of greater or lesser sophistication. In his exploration of the underpinnings of different approaches to strategic thinking, Gilbert suggests that there are two features that can render them ethical in nature. The first is that the approach to strategy in the organization *'celebrates the possibility that a person can grow* [Gilbert's italics] through by her chosen purposeful actions at the corporation' (1992, p. 150). By this he is referring to the idea that members are able to find some sort of meaning in their relation to the workplace, what Senge refers to as the '... connections between personal learning and organizational learning, in the reciprocal commitments between individual and organization, and in the special spirit of an enterprise made up of learners' (1990, p. 8). The second feature that he would look for is the extent to which the strategic process *'celebrates the distinctions among persons* [Gilbert's italics] who seek to enact lives that they prefer ... the criterion admits men and women to a worldly story on the basis of their preference for acting purposefully' (1992, p. 150). In what follows it would perhaps be useful to take these criteria as useful underpinnings in the discussion of change by mundane managers.

As far as that aspect of strategy which is concerned with the management of change there is characteristically some statement of superordinate goals (Waterman *et al.*, 1980) or mission statement or corporate plan. This is the key identifier of management values both for the outside world and (perhaps even more potently) for insiders. In creating a portrait of the future of the organization, senior management is also, *inter alia*, identifying their moral stance towards change by indicating what it is that they will and will not (by implication) stand for. Clearly the ethical issue that is most readily identified here is that of the extent to which vision statements represent, in Argyris' (1990) sense, espoused values which mask over what he characterized as values in use – a compromising of the espoused.

At a deeper level, there are ethical issues in the very attempt of management's attempts to define and shape for the future both the organization and the future (and the lack of it for individual members, given the tendencies towards downsizing in many planned change efforts) of its members. The core of legitimacy in a moral sense for mundane management was described and analysed wonderfully by Weber in his discussion of the 'ideal type' bureaucracy (Weber, 1912, pp. 196–204). More recently Jaques (1990), in an attempt to rebut some of the more fashionable ways of organizing people, suggests that in periods of change, hierarchical arrangements need to operate successfully because these enable members to exist within boundaries which enable them to function effectively. Managers' assertion that they should be at the pinnacle of the hierarchy arises 'from the belief that managerial authority and power are justified because managers possess an ability to put skills and knowledge to work in the service of achieving certain ends' (MacIntyre, 1981, p. 72). These core assumptions enable managers to legitimate, be seen to be ethical in, their claim to optimism in the management of change.

This may be illustrated through the sorts of competence that are apparently required of managers acting as change agents. As exponents of an essentially rationalist approach to organizational change, Johnson and Scholes discuss attributes such as '… *clarity of direction and vision* … someone who can perceive the nature of planned change, able to employ an appropriate *style* of managing change … ability to use political and symbolic processes [as] levers …' (1993, p. 411). Contrastively Stacey writing of what he characterizes as open-ended change situations – by which he is referring to what he feels is the emergent postmodern situation with its connotations of chaos theory in which organizational end-states are unknowable – discusses such behavioural attributes as being able to identify *'what questions to ask'* the ability to generate 'new mental models', the ability to deal with 'conflict and interpret what is going on', accept the implications of the 'unknowable future' and to be able to deal with the essential tensions and ambiguities that this generates – what he calls 'extraordinary management' (1993, p. 256).

These very different approaches to change and change management place significance on the role of management in undertaking strategic change. There is, however a contrary view. Writers such as MacIntyre (1981) suggest that managerial belief in their own activity is in itself a grand illusion, that it is philosophically an unjustifiable activity. In this light it is perhaps somewhat disconcerting to note that on the bases of their research Buchanan and Boddy concluded that 'the competencies of the change agent are easily identified and unremarkable …' (1992, p. 7). As things stand, however – radical issues such as this not having reached the ears of most managers – enactment of the management of change gives the manager a particular claim to 'moral agency' (MacIntyre, 1981, p. 30).

In addition, MacIntyre asserts that managers base their claim to organizational dominance because of their claim to moral neutrality (1974,

p. 70). He relates this to the emergence of 'management science', and to the manager's claims to understanding the 'facts' of the matter. What often appears to happen is that management theorists seem to translate with a dreadful literalness – that is without irony, awareness of metaphor – the magnificent theorizing of the natural sciences. Thus many traditional versions of planned change are based on a literal translation into human affairs of the physical sciences; newer theories represent a 'translation' of chaos theory. Characteristically, as Huczynski (1993) shows, versions of this magnificent theorizing are disseminated to managers in search of a solution by the 'management gurus' to form the 'new belief' of management and change management.

If managers translate naively these mythologies [presented in the guise of a claim 'to create order out of disorder' and the provision to managers 'with new systems of coherence and continuity' (Huczynski, 1993, p. 198)] seriously into organizational action there are a number of ethical issues. The first is concerned with the imposition on organizational members of 'recipes' that are frequently short-termist where the underlying issues are not. The second issue is that adherence to recipes leads to an idealization of the change management process, and an idealization of the 'heroic' managers role which leads to a diminution of difficulty, complexity and the personalization of opposition – the organizational snakepit (Schwarz, 1990). We would suggest that there is ethical clarity when the relationship between the and the 'guru' are transparent both to themselves and to organizational members and so that there is clear boundary management in their relationship and in their contribution to the change management process.

We would also suggest that there is ethical responsibility under way when these recipes are voiced modestly so that members are given choice and autonomy. In this way, the key movements in management thinking – classical management, human relations, scientific management, postmodernist chaos theory and so on – are understood to be 'significant sets of *design criteria* which are used to structure work' [my italics] (Huczynski, 1993, p. 215) rather than organizational saviours.

The ethical issue is the degree to which claims are made for their essential 'rightness' or moral neutrality in managing change. We would suggest that in an ethical sense these are competing organizational rhetorics (Roy, 1955) in which the major themes in managing change – incremental change, radical change, open-ended change or whatever are understood to be more or less successful design criteria. Additionally, even if MacIntyre may be felt to be overemphasizing the invalidity of management as an activity, his writing pushes managers towards the need for development of the habit of self-reflexiveness, a detached sense of self irony, and an ability to communicate options for the management of change without, at the same time neutralizing the manager's ability to manage change.

If, however, advocacy of change methodologies is made either with the authority of an appeal to morally neutral science or with the imperatives of management's claims to sole effectiveness in the management of change then the ethical issues become located around inequitable distribution of power; management is attempting to impose what it presents as deterministic, 'only way', solutions. In this section I have tried to show that management claims to hold the appropriate vision of organizational end state, and their claims to particular psychological and social competencies in relation to the management of change are based on somewhat shifting sands, and that these claims have ethical consequences.

The Yellow Brick Road   In the last section we have explored some of the ethical issues involved in management's rights to claim ownership for the management of change; in this section we shall look at some of the issues involved in managements' attempts to undertake the processes of change.

Pared down to their essence, the majority of conventional change models are derived from the work of Lewin (1951) and, as Wilson (1992) suggests, the use of force field analysis as a core methodology. Underlying Lewin's practical theory of change lies a metaphor derived from the natural sciences which suggests that phenomena rest in a state of quasi-stable equilibrium at any one moment and that state depends upon the forces at play on it. Some of those forces may be seen as hindering forces in the sense that they are preventing the phenomenon from achieving its potential indeed may contain premonitions of entropy; others may be helping forces which may enable the phenomenon to develop and move synergistically. In the world of natural science the assumption is that these forces can be identified and relative weighting assigned to them.

At its heart the process, when the theory is presented as a device for managing change, is relatively simple. It depends on a diagnosis of the present state (the state of quasi-equilibrium), define the desired future state, define the helping (i.e. forces which will militate for the change) and resisting forces (i.e. forces which militate against the change) that are present in the situation, reduce the resisting forces and emphasize the helping forces and *et voila* we are managing change. As it is conventionally used, it plays to a model of change management that is essentially linear, deterministic and amenable to enactment by the individual manager. In this light, Burrell suggests that '... if we analyse linear versions of time they are often associated with notions of progress, where what is contemporary and fashionable is claimed to represent a "higher" level of development ... This assumption ... rests heavily upon ... a belief that the rationalistic management of change is possible' (1992, p. 168).

The author sometimes presents this as a methodology to research scientists undertaking a management development process. In doing so he will present to his audience his understanding (the essential truth being more significant than the mundane biography) that Lewin started off his professional life as a physicist and then (somewhat self-deprecatingly) the author will suggest that Lewin mixed with bad company and became a social scientist. We then have gently derisive comments from the physicists about the rigour of Lewin's theorizing although the biologists will usually come to his defence. Doing it this way gets the author off an ethical hook – he is not presenting it as serious science but rather as a modest device, as a way of getting some grasp on the nature of complex reality, but still allowing it to be complex – not everything can be covered in force field analysis (Wilson 1992, p. 50). When, however, devices like this are used as serious features of symbolic management – such that the force field analysis becomes a potent symbol of the will to change it generates a ' "false" conception of reality [creating] a pseudo-world which replaces the otherwise complex and confusing reality' (Alvesson and Berg 1992, p. 172).

The second aspect of Lewin's (1947) understanding of the change process also pervades much conventional thought about the dynamics of change and its management '... has proved to be highly useful to action-oriented mangers and other employees' (Hellriegel et al., 1995, p. 667). Basically what is suggested is that when a phenomenon is in quasistable equilibrium there is a need for a trigger – what he refers to as unfreezing – to shift it into a potential change state. For example, based on their research into advanced manufacturing technology, Tranfield and Smith wrote: 'taken for granted assumptions form the basis of how people think and act. In our experience changing tfg's is central to the successful management of technological and organizational change ...' (1986, p. 8). There then needs to be a process of movement. This process represents a shift towards the 'desired future state'. Once this sublime state is reached there is then a process of refreezing which signifies the institutionaliza-tion of change. There are many formulations of this process and a more detailed account may be found in Schein (1987).

If we take this as a fundamental model of change (McAuley, 1994; Stacey, 1993, p. 135) then the ways in which it is applied in the manage-ment of change poses a number of ethical issues. If we take, for example, the unfreezing stage there is, in many presentations of it an air of drama in its task of the destabilization of organizational members, as in the following:

> Successfully unfreezing the forces maintaining old behavior often requires shock treatment: disconfirming feedback about the efficacy of current behavior that is so direct and threatening that it pierces any perceptual defenses and overrides the effect of reinforcements for current behaviors. To stimulate major organizational change, managers might develop dissatisfaction with the status quo among stakeholders ... . (Organ and Bateman, 1991, p. 635)

The ethical issues are heightened during the movement phase when senior management becomes benign in the interest of developing 'new behaviours, values and attitudes through changes in organizational structures and processes ...' these being managed through 'empathy and support ... communication ... participation and involvement' (Hellriegel *et al.*, 1995, p. 669). Through these softer methodologies the 'dominant managerial task ... of persuading individuals to accept and support the change' and convincing others 'of the utility of the reorganization' (Wilson, 1992, p. 10) is achieved.

To make claims as to the ethical inappropriateness of management-driven change through this process would be to whistle in the wind; what is at issue is the way in which it is undertaken. The sorts of ethical issue that can take on significance include a clear understanding on the part of the change agents of power and control issues. This may be illustrated through the ways in which matters such as secrecy/openness about the process, the dynamics of inclusion/exclusion in the change-making process, and the empowerment/disempowerment of members to influence the change process and at centrality/marginality of the level of influence (Fisher, 1993, p. 498).

For example, it could be argued it can be ethical that the dynamics of change – especially unfreezing – should not in all circumstances be revealed to all members of the organization. We can suggest three reasons why this position could be seen as ethical – and there may be more. One is that 'telling the tale' will impair the dynamics because it will result in a lessening of the pain; this accords with a philosophical presupposition – which we might suggest comes from the Protestant work ethic – that where there is no pain there is no gain. The second is that these processes, where the change is unwanted, have an air of deterministic inevitability (Fink *et al.*, 1971) and that for people to survive the change process they must go through each step of the process and that although there needs to be psychological safety nets, explanation of the process would not be comprehended. The third reason is that in the turbulence of the unfreezing process much of the anxiety and blame generated by the process can be projected on to senior management. Such hate in the transference (McAuley, 1989) may be seen as ethical in the sense that it is part of the holding environment [what Schein refers to as the 'psychological safety net' (1987, p. 99)] in that management becomes a source of focused resistance within which unfreezing can begin because, it is claimed, the focused resistance lowers dependence and causes members to develop self-understanding. However, it is axiomatic that both for practical and ethical purposes this negative transference needs careful boundary management.

We could go further and argue that the drama of the undisclosed dynamic of change has ethical legitimacy in at least three circumstances. One is where there are, amongst organizational members 'coping patterns [which are] extremely dysfunctional' (Tichy, 1983, p. 148) at the level of understanding the issues that confront the organization where it may be that the shock of the new is appropriate in circumventing compulsive behaviours. The second circumstance could be the case of an organization which is undergoing radical change, where '... the frame of reference for the organization [is broken], often creating new equilibrium because the entire organization is transformed ... Radical change is important especially when an entire industry is undergoing upheaval' (Daft, 1992, p. 253). The third circumstance may be when there is an issue of organizational survival and where leakage of information, such as a major restructuring, would be commercially very risky. Proponents of covert methodologies both in organizational change and in psychiatry would argue, that objections to their attempt to treat members as 'cultural' or 'psychological dopes' (Garfinkel, 1967) comes from an humanistic aesthetic and is not properly to be considered in the ethical frame.

In going down the route of radical management change an ethically significant feature, however, is that those managers whose desire to be seen as people of action do not confuse their need to be seen as proactive and the concomitant compulsive drive towards radical change with a situational need for the gentler climate of incremental change – 'a series of continual progression that maintain the organization's general equilibrium ...'(Daft, 1992, p. 250) – and that those managers who feel unable to confront difficult situations collude with gradualism when drama is required.

Clearly, in a management driven process of change there are issues about rights, equity and the use of power. There are also issues concerned with the assumptions of management 'superiority' in the creation of *de haute en bas* structures and culture such that members are potentially cast into an anomic situation (Merton, 1968) that is designed to produce conforming behaviours. These effects are inevitably reduced dramatically and organizational members are ethically encouraged when they have a clear understanding that managers themselves are deeply involved in the processes of change themselves. For example, if the undisclosed psychodrama of the change dynamic is enacted with organization development consultants clearly identified as the change agency and that management are themselves undergoing unfreezing, the dynamic is still uncomfortable but maybe experienced as ethically equitable.

Ethical issues and consultants in the management of change

An approach to this can be seen in ways in which the organization development process can operate. Many writers in this tradition attempt to establish clarity in the nature of the psychological contract (Tranfield and Smith, 1991) such that there is established, either explicitly or implicitly, an ethical equity as between management and workforce in change situations and that there can be an exploration of these deeper issues in the organization. As matters of both practical and ethical necessity the need for good boundary management is even more important when consultants are working within the framework of organization development.

The key concern of organization development is to generate, using consultants, a 'conscious effort on the part of top management' (French and Bell, 1990, p. 232) to undertake such processes as to develop the scope by which members can be empowered, by which management can become 'more responsive' to organizational data and be able to 'legitimate conflict as an area of collaborative management' (1990, p. 233), and to be able to 'examine its own leadership style and ways of managing' (1990, p. 233). Clearly these statements of developmental intent need to be more than 'apple pie' sentiments of a general good. In his discussion of management responsibility for unfreezing – which he refers to as diagnosis – Tichy (1983, p. 151) establishes clearly the boundaries of management, its responsibilities, and its involvement in this process: overall he presents a picture of deep management involvement in the pain of the change process. Similarly Argyris (1990) describes well the ways in which the consultant works with senior management in ways that unfreeze them from what he characterizes as 'single loop' learning (that is ways of responding to change that are based on habituated panic and emptiness presented under the guise of rationality) to a situation where they feel able to unlearn their commonsense understandings of the very nature of management.

What then becomes possible is that ethical practices become embedded into the very fabric of the organization and its management of change. This accords with the view that 'The truth about business ethics is that an attempted intervention will not survive if it receives only lip service or compliance training support ... There must be true commitment of resources [time–money–people] equal to the other priorities in the organization' (Axline, 1994, p. 317) Sharma (1993) showed how, in working as a consultant for a professional organization she was able to move them from traditional approaches (i.e. training courses and/or the distribution of manuals of 'good practice') to the development of equal opportunities policies into an extensive exploration at all levels in the organization of key issues of change. What she did was to transform an important substantive ethical issue into a trigger for change which involved all members in reflective and then action-oriented activity. In this case what was undertaken was to get members – including managers at all levels – '... to accept that ethics is a way of proactive thinking and acting – not a set of codified procedures conveniently organized into a desk reference or crisis manual' (Axline, 1994, p. 322).

For these processes to be enabled to happen there are important preconditions in the development of an ethical relationship between the consultant and the client. French and Bell (1990, p. 232) cite particular ethical guidelines which relate to issues of task and process – interestingly in relation to the issue of disclosure of process they suggest that the 'client system should be *as informed as is practical* about the nature of the process' (my italics) (1990, p. 232).

Lying beneath these are two key ethical issues in the relationship. One is the primary need for clarity about the nature of the boundaries between client and consultant. Nevis suggests 'The most useful stance implies a balance; one affiliates with the system yet is clearly autonomous and apart' (1987, p. 179). The other concerns depth of intervention – that approaches to the management of change through consultancy interventions are not 'seen as an end in themselves without reference to the context in which they operate' (Wilson, 1992, p. 125), there is an understanding shared between both consultant and client that 'effective organizational change is unlikely to be brought about by the traditional "quick fixes" '(Kets de Vries and Miller, 1984, p. 154) so that neither seduces the other into quick conclusions when the going gets rough.

This accords with a view that change management is much more complex than the simplicities of transformational management or mundane management would allow. Within this complexity, senior managers are members of an arena in which the end states of the change process cannot be determined in advance, where change 'is the result of the interplay of history, economics, politics, business sector characteristics [for example]' (Wilson, 1992, p. 10). Within this postmodern framework there is a 'a climate of some uncertainty which seems unlikely to diminish in the foreseeable future ... Relevant theory [of the management of change] must develop from the recognition that social arrangements are artifacts ... Moreover it should develop an action-oriented perspective' (Blacker, 1992, p. 292).

Postmodern approaches to the management of change

The development of such a theory needs also to take in the ethical considerations that are at play in this environment of uncertainty, an environment in which features of chaos theory come into play. Stacey characterizes this as a situation in which it is 'difficult to know what questions to ask ... Open ended change ... causes insecurity, conflict and confusion. But it is also characterized by the repetition of similar qualitative patterns at a general level – history repeats itself' (1991, p. 34). This invites the development within the organization of a wide understanding of 'issues of time and history and individuality and their interconnectedness' (Burrell, 1992, p. 182) in ways that make them a collective endeavour.

The ethical issue for managers may well be that they need not only to hold on to their own view of change and direction, but also, rather like Warnock's moral philosophers, be able to achieve a consensus among the internal and external stakeholders as to ways forward. In this complex organization there would be experienced a diversity of competing ethical issues because of diverse priorities and purposes and a 'plethora of competing values of subcultures' which, if they are not managed could leave members 'unable to find a common basis on which to proceed' (Sinclair,1993, p. 71). The result would be a situation of ethical muddle, giving those who shout loudest (or with the most articulate rhetoric) making gains for their ethical stance.

The ethical issue for members is that they assent to the degree of ambiguity that is a prerequisite of this more radical view of organization and also assent to the need on practical grounds for decisions to be made, for difficult issues to be resolved, for there to be a locus of voluntaristic commitment within the organization to its purposes.

Concluding remarks

In the management of change it is clear that all the approaches discussed in this chapter can work and work well. It is likely that as agencies for change all three of the approaches discussed in this chapter – and more, for we have left some things not discussed – will work together in the same organization in more or less complex ways. Indeed in a paper which looks only at two of the dynamics for the management of change discussed here – leadership and mundane management, Krantz and Gilmore suggest that there are inherent practical dangers in the 'splitting apart of [different approaches to managing change], with the concomitant idealization of one and denigration of the other' (1990, p. 202). The ethical issue here is that splitting leads to delusory fantasies of heroes and villains, recipes of 'best practice' in the management of change, and ideological fixation which preclude the exercise of reflective understanding and judgement.

In this chapter we have focused on the role of management in the change process. There is a sting in the tail for organizational members. Sinclair suggests that if '... being ethical requires a level of reflexivity and on-going self-inspection, then it is not enough to adhere simple-mindedly to standards of behaviour prescribed by others ...' (1993, p. 70), or we would add, in the matter of change, to standards that do not take account of new circumstances. Nevis (1987) has suggested that on practical (and, we would suggest, ethical) grounds managers should not indiscriminately use labels like 'resistance to change', but should rather take issues raised by 'resistors' on board. By the same token we would suggest that there is a need for reciprocity here, that resistors need to be clear about the nature of their resistance and its expression. Clearly it is management's ethical (and practical) responsibility to articulate and enact a culture in which members feel able, through the articulation of the outcomes of their own 'processes of self-inspection, critique and debate' (Sinclair, 1993, p. 71) to enter the arena of change in their organization; the ethical responsibility of members is then to become a part of the change management process.

Exercises

An underlying view taken in this chapter is that, whatever the ethical issues involved, change can 'be managed'. Another view is that it cannot, and claims to human agency in the matter are fundamentally flawed and indeed unethical in that claims to manage change legitimate power relations. You are invited to discuss this radical view.

In this chapter we have explored some of the major processes by which change is managed and hinted at some of the outcomes of the managed change process. What do you understand to be the critical features of an ethically managed process of change, and how are these best to be expressed to engage the attention of change agents?

Further reading

Some of the books which I found useful in an exploration of some of the issues are listed below.

It has become conventional to see culture and culture change as a major driver in the overall management of change. Bate (1994) goes further than any other currently available to explore in real depth the implications of culture management and regards many of the means adapted with a sceptical view. The book is particularly strong on the identification of ethical issues and points to an ethical way forward.

In this chapter we have mentioned the ways in which consultants can be used either to promote a particular view of change in the organization or as 'honest brokers' in organization development. Nevis (1987) takes a profoundly ethical view of the way in which the change agent can work in the organization. Although the term 'ethics' is not actually used it permeates insights about such issues as an understanding of the underlying issues of change, intervention by the consultant, and a deep understanding of issues of 'resistance' to change.

Although some readers may find the tone of Senge (1990) to be somewhat messianic and prescriptive, it both points to ways of designing that meet both organizational needs and human needs. It focus on the idea of managing change so that all members of the organization are members of what Senge characterizes as the learning organization – a process of managing change that meets human aspiration to be and develop.

Although not explicitly about the role of the transformational leader in the management of change, Kets de Vries (1993) helps an exploration and understanding of the nature of the transformational leader and the dynamics of collusion that can occur between the leader and the idealizing staff. It is a reminder that where leaders are attempting to lead and change, both they and the people who work with them need to develop lifetime habits of scepticism.

References

Alvesson, M. and Berg, P.O. (1992) *Corporate Culture and Organizational Symbolism*. Walter de Gruyter, Berlin.

Anzieu, D. (1984) *The Group and the Unconscious*. Routledge & Kegan Paul, London.

Argyris, C. (1990) *Overcoming Organizational Defences: Facilitating Organizational Learning*. Prentice-Hall, New York.

Axline, L. (1994) Business ethics and OD: organization development or decay?, in *What is new in Organization Development?* (eds D.W. Cole, J.C. Preston and J.S. Finley). The Organization Development Institute, Chesterland, OH.

Bate, P. (1994) *Strategies for Cultural Change*. Butterworth–Heinemann, Oxford.

Becker, H.S. (1977) *Sociological Work: Method and Substance*. Transaction Books, New Brunswick, NJ.

Blacker, F. (1992) Formative contexts and activity systems: postmodern approaches to the management of change, in *Rethinking Organization: New Directions in Organization Theory and Analysis* (eds M. Reed and M. Hughes). Sage, London.

Brindle, D. (1992) Women-only hospital hit by market forces. *Guardian*, 5 June.

Buchanan, D. and Boddy, D. (1992) *The Expertise of the Change Agent: Public Performance and Backstage Activity*. Prentice-Hall, London.

Burns, J.M. (1978) *Leadership*. Harper & Row, New York.

Burrell, G. (1992) Back to the future: time and organization, in *Rethinking Organization: New Directions in Organization Theory and Analysis* (eds M. Reed and M. Hughes). Sage, London.

Camus, A. (1953) *The Rebel*. Hamish Hamilton, London.

Clampitt, P.G. (1991) *Communicating for Managerial Effectiveness*. Sage, Newbury Park, CA.

Daft, R.L. (1992) *Organization Theory and Design*. West Publishing, St. Paul, MN.

Dunham, J. and Klafehn, K.A. (1990) Transformational leadership and the nurse executive. *Journal of Nursing Administration*, **20**(4).

Fink, S.L., Beak, J. and Taddeo, K. (1971) Organization crisis and change. *Journal of Applied Behavioral Science*, **7**(1), 15–37.

Fisher, D. (1993) *Communication in Organizations*. West Publishing, St. Paul, MN.

French, W.L. and Bell, C.H. (1990) *Organization Development: Behavioral Science Interventions for Organization Improvement*. Prentice-Hall, Englewood Cliffs, NJ.

Garfinkel, H. (1967) *Studies in Ethnomethodology*. Prentice-Hall.

Gilbert Jr, D.R. (1992) *The Twilight of Corporate Strategy: A Comparative Ethical Critique*. Oxford University Press, New York.

Gioia, D.A. and Chittipeddi, K. (1991) Sensemaking and sensegiving in strategic change initiation. *Strategic Management Journal*, **12**, 433–88.

Habermas, J. (1976) *Legitimation Crisis*. Heinemann, London.

Harvey, J. (1974) The Abilene paradox – the management of agreement. *Organizational Dynamics*, **3**(1), 63–86.

Hellriegel, D., Slocum, J.W. and Woodman, R.W. (1995) *Organizational Behavior*, 6th edn. West Publishing, St. Paul, MN.

Hirschorn, L. (1988) *The Workplace Within: Psychodynamics of Organizational Life*. MIT Press, Cambridge, MA.

Huczynski, A.A. (1993) *Management Gurus: What Makes Them and How to Become One*. Routledge, London.

Hunt, J.G. (1991) *Leadership: A New Synthesis*. Sage, London.

Jaques, E. (1990) In praise of hierarchy. *Harvard Business Review* January/February.

Johnson, G. and Scholes, K. (1993) *Exploring Corporate Strategy*, 3rd edn. Prentice-Hall, London.

Kanter, R.M. (1968) Commitment and social organization: a study of commitment mechanisms in utopian communities. *American Sociological Review*, **33**(4), 499–517.

Kets de Vries, M.F.R. (1993) *Leaders, Fools, and Imposters: Essays on the Psychology of Leadership*. Jossey-Bass, San Francisco, CA.

Kets de Vries, M.F.R. and Miller, D. (1984) *The Neurotic Organization*. Jossey-Bass, San Francisco, CA.

Krantz, J. and Gilmore, T.N. (1990) The splitting of leadership and management as a social defence. *Human Relations*, **43**(2), 183–204.

Lewin, K. (1947) Frontiers in social science. *Human Relations*, 15–41.

Lewin, K. (1951) *Field Theory in Social Science*. Harper & Row, New York.

MacIntyre, A. (1981) *After Virtue: A Study in Moral Theory*. Duckworth, London.

McAuley, J. (1989) Transference, countertransference and responsibility. *International Journal of Psychotherapy*, **19**(4), 283–97.

McAuley, J. (1994) *Managing Your Enterprise: Managing Change*. Open University (Mesol).

Merton, R.K. (1968) *Social Theory and Social Structure*. Free Press, New York.

Mitroff, I.D. (1983) *Stakeholders of the Organizational Mind*. Jossey-Bass, San Francisco, CA.

Nevis, E.C. (1987) *Organizational Consulting: A Gestalt Approach*. Gardner Press, New York.

Organ, D.W. and Bateman, T.S. (1991) *Organizational Behavior*, 4th edn. Richard D. Irwin, Homewood, IL.

Phillips, N. (1991) The sociology of knowledge: toward an existential view of business ethics. *Journal of Business Ethics*, **10**, 787–95.

Pollitt, C. (1993) *Managerialism and the Public Services*, 2nd edn. Blackwell, Oxford.

Praill, T. and Baldwin, S. (1988) Beyond hero-innovation: real change in unreal systems. *Behavioural Psychology* **16**(1), 3–13.

Roy, D. (1955) Efficiency and 'the fix'; informal intergroup relations in a piecework machine shop. *American Journal of Sociology*, **60**, 255–66.

Schein, E.H. (1987) *Process Consultation, Vol. II: Lessons for Managers and Consultants*. Addison-Wesley, Reading, MA.

Schein, E. (1991) The role of the founder in the creation of organizational culture, in *Reframing Organizational Culture* (eds P.J. Frost, L.F. Moore, M.R. Louis, C.C. Lundberg and J. Martin). Sage, Newbury Park, CA.

Schwarz, H.S. (1990) *Narcissistic Process and Corporate Decay*. New York University Press, New York.

Seligman, D. (1993) Loving toughly. *Fortune*, **128**(15), 194.

Senge, P.M. (1990) *The Fifth Discipline: The Art and Practice of the Learning Organization*. Century Business, London.

Sharma, M. (1993) An account of OD consultancies in public sector organizations. Unpublished dissertation, Sheffield Business School.

Sinclair, A. (1993) Approaches to organizational culture and ethics. *Journal of Business Ethics*, **12**, 63–73.

Stacey, R.D. (1991) *The Chaos Frontier; Creative Strategic Control for Business*. Butterworth–Heinemann, Oxford.

Stacey, R.D. (1993) *Strategic Management and Organizational Dynamics*. Pitman, London.

Tichy, N.M. (1983) *Managing Strategic Change: Technical, Political and Cultural Dynamics*. John Wiley, New York.

Tranfield, D. and Smith, S. (1991) *Consultancy Skills Manual: How to Manage Clients Effectively*. Technical Communications.

Tranfield, D. and Smith, S. (1986) Culture change approach to managing technological innovation. Research Paper 1, Sheffield Business School, Sheffield.

Urmson, J.O. and Ree, J. (1989) *The Concise Encyclopedia of Western Philosophy and Philosophers*. Routledge, London.

Warnock, M. (1994) On ethics and moral philosophy. Lunchtime lecture, Royal Geographical Society, London.

Weber, M. (1912) Bureaucarcy, cited in Gerth, H.H. and Mills, C.W. (1948) *Max Weber: Essays in Sociology*. Routledge & Kegan Paul, London.

Williams, B. (1972) *Morality: An introduction to Ethics*. Cambridge University Press, Cambridge.

Wilson, D.C. (1992) *A Strategy of Change*. Routledge, London.

Ethics in international business

12

Robin Lowe

In international business, ethical considerations take on additional and particularly significant dimensions, partly because they do not simply involve judgements based on the attitudes, opinions and perceptions prevalent within a society dominated by a single culture, but also because they are concerned with the differences in culture which exist between trading nations.

For many firms, one of the most critical steps that they take is in making the decision to invest resources in another country. This investment may range from a small firm committing marketing resources in another country to a multinational enterprise (MNE) setting up a full-scale manufacturing and marketing subsidiary. As a firm takes further steps towards internationalization, it becomes increasingly exposed to the fundamental tensions that exist because of the different and opposing demands and expectations of commercial, domestic and host country stakeholders, shown in Fig. 12.1, which are central to the issue of ethics in international business.

In this chapter we focus on the implications of the decisions that MNEs take in addressing these tensions by discussing a number of specific issues, including:

❑ the factors that have heightened the importance of business ethics as a consideration for international businesses
❑ the effect of cultural differences on decision making
❑ the implications of the decisions made by MNEs for governments, the public and for individuals both as employees and consumers
❑ the measures that are being taken to curb the undesirable behaviour of MNEs and
❑ the ethical challenges facing managers within transnational businesses both on an occasional basis (examples of this include the *Exxon Valdez* and Bhopal incidents) and on a day-to-day basis, such as the payment of bribes and incentives.

In discussing the ethical issues which affect MNEs, Donaldson (1989) highlights eight areas of concern:

Introduction

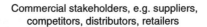

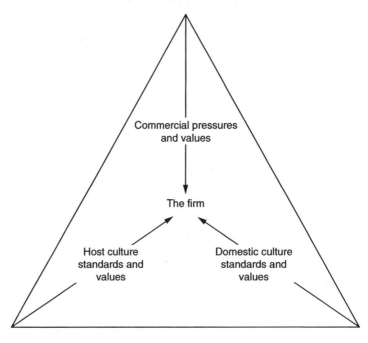

Figure 12.1 The stakeholder demands of the firm.

1. bribery and corrupt payments
2. employment and personnel issues
3. marketing practices
4. the impact of the multinational on the development of host countries
5. effects on the natural environment
6. cultural impacts of multinational operations
7. relations with host governments
8. relations with home countries.

The relative importance of each of these categories in international business is dependent on the standpoint being taken and a number of these issues such as employment and personnel issues, marketing practices, and the potentially adverse effects of production processes and the firm's facilities on the natural environment in their domestic context have been discussed at length in earlier chapters. In this chapter, therefore, we focus on those issues particularly affected by the *international* dimensions of business.

Before focusing in detail on the increasing attention that is now being given to the subject of ethics in international business, it is worth reflecting on the major differences between domestic and international operations. These are summarized in Fig. 12.2 and illustrate the more fragmented, less predictable and higher risk nature of international business.

The ethical dimensions of international businesses

The moment a firm begins to operate in a new country it is faced with a different cultural environment in which many of the beliefs and assumptions on which the society is built will differ from those of its home country. Because these beliefs and assumptions lead to different values and perceptions about what constitutes acceptable business behaviour, the firm faces the problem of deciding to what extent it should conform on the one hand to the values and demands of its domestic stakeholders, and on the other to its host-country stakeholders. Business practitioners frequently must choose between deciding what is commercially viable and what may be desirable for their host country stakeholders. An example of this occurred when British Airways (BA) recently withdrew its service to the Ivory Coast. Whilst the service itself was not profitable and the contribution it made to the wider BA network was insignificant, the decision needs also to be seen from the viewpoint of the Ivory Coast since it was likely to have a considerable impact there through the loss of an important communications link and the prestige associated with it.

The question that therefore needs to be considered is whether when making decisions, consideration should be given to the social implications for the host country or whether they should be based solely on commercial factors. If the answer to this is that host country social factors should be taken into account, the question that then arises is to what extent this should be done. In doing this however, recognition must be given to the

Domestic operations	Factor	International operations
predominantly single	culture	multicultural
more homogeneous	market	fragmented and diverse
usually available and accurate	data	difficult and expensive to obtain
lower risk	politics	high risk of interference
relative freedom to operate	government	strong influence on operations
coherent structure	company	highly distorted organisational structure
stable and more predictable	economy	high risk of instability
uniformity of operations	finance	variety of methods used
single	currency	differ in stability and value

Figure 12.2 The differences between domestic and international operations.

fact that the commercial factors themselves usually reflect the values and ideology of western economies in general and the domestic country commercial ethos in particular.

Following on from this, thought needs also to be given to the extent to which policies, corporate values and operations can – and indeed should – be standardized within and across the various countries in which the firms operate. Small firms usually have relatively few options and their scope for standardizing a variety of activities such as products and services, advertising messages, selling techniques and employment methods between home and host country are often restricted, this is shown as a continuum in Fig. 12.3. However, the scope for an MNE operating globally to influence rather than be influenced by its environment is potentially considerable. This influence is typically derived from the investment, employment and marketing power it is often capable of wielding within the societies in which it operates, and has contributed to the way in which the international aims and activities of MNEs are often viewed with suspicion and why it is often argued that host governments have a responsibility to exert greater control over them.

THE POWER OF THE MNES

Table 12.1, which compares the gross domestic products (GDP) of some countries with the revenue of the largest multinational corporations, illustrates the significance of the multinationals on the world stage.

Figure 12.3 The international standardization continuum.

The issue of the power of the multinational corporations and the consequent scope for its abuse is not, however, new. Multinational trading companies have wielded power for hundreds of years, Barnett and Muller (1974), for example, note that the British East India Company backed up its trading activities with the largest standing army in the world, deployed 40 warships and was the strongest single influence on the development of the subcontinent with its then population of 250 million people.

It is, however, during the last 30 years that the activities of the firms have developed most rapidly in size and international influence. The reasons for this include:

❑ the rapid growth of large organizations
❑ the search for economies of scale which has led to the search for new markets
❑ the rising labour costs in the developed countries

Table 12.1(a) The world's top ten industrial companies

Company	HQ	Business	Sales £bn	Profits £bn
1 Itoh (c)	Japan	Sogo shosha	86.6	2.2
2 Mitsui	Japan	Sogo shosha	84.7	2.2
3 Sumimoto	Japan	Sogo shosha	81.4	2.4
4 Mitsubishi	Japan	Sogo shosha	80.2	2.7
5 Marubeni	Japan	Sogo shosha	79.5	2.4
6 General Motors	US	Automobiles	65.9	1.3
7 Exxon	US	Oil and gas	61.6	5.1
8 Shell	Netherlands/UK	Oil and gas	58.1	6.1
9 Nissho Iwai	Japan	Sogo shosha	55.6	1.2
10 Ford	US	Automobiles	47.3	3.6

Source: The Times 1000 1992–3.

Table 12.1(b) Typical country population and Gross National Product (GNP)

Country	Population (millions)	GNP £bn	GNP per capita £
USA	250	3,683	14,738
Japan	124	1,974	15,981
UK	57	657	11,456
Denmark	5	83	15,975
China	1,139	246	216
Thailand	56	53	943
Indonesia	179	68	381
Greece	10	44	4,335
New Zealand	3	29	8,437
Mexico	86	117	1,358

Source: IMF international financial statistic yearbook 1992.

❑ the significant cost savings to be gained in locating manufacturing operations in Third World and developing nations
❑ improvements in communication and transportation
❑ the rising and increasingly similar patterns of world-wide consumer demand and
❑ the formation of strategic alliances between existing MNEs in order to achieve the global distribution necessary to satisfy these global consumer demands.

It can be argued that the MNEs themselves through strategic distribution alliances contribute significantly to encouraging standardization of demand with typical examples being fast food, cars and alcoholic drinks. Together, these factors have encouraged firms to spread their purchasing, component sourcing, assembly, marketing and sales, and administration across an increasingly wide range of locations. The rationale for this is based on the theory of comparative advantage, developed by the classical economist David Ricardo, which at its simplest suggests that trade between countries takes place because one country is able to produce a product at a lower cost than is possible elsewhere. Because of this, firms are able to threaten to transfer operations (and jobs) to a lower labour cost location in another country and so are able to increase their sphere of influence and thus exert greater power over governments in the various countries in which they operate.

Whilst Table 12.1 shows the size of multinationals relative to the economies of the countries, the influence they exert is dependent to a much greater degree on the extent to which their activities and the sources of their competitive advantage are concentrated. A multinational can exert the greatest power if, for example, it is a major employer using a poor small country as a low-cost manufacturing base, has a significant lead in a critical technology, such as arms, or by means of advertising is able to influence the culture, beliefs and values of a country. MNEs are most in danger of abusing their power when they are dealing with the less-developed countries (LDCs) which can only negotiate from relatively weak positions but which need MNEs for the employment and status they bring.

Given this, De George (1993) has identified seven guidelines which, he suggests, MNEs should follow when dealing with LDCs in order to prevent abuse of power:

❑ do no intentional direct harm
❑ produce more good than harm for the host country
❑ contribute by their activity to the host country's development
❑ respect the human rights of their employees
❑ respect and work with the local culture provided it does not violate ethical norms

❏ pay their fair share of taxes
❏ cooperate with local government in developing a sound infrastructure.

Whilst these guidelines might be reasonable and acceptable in concept, many MNEs are likely to regard them as largely theoretical in nature and apply them only at the margins of their business activity and then only if it is in their interest. It can be argued that there is some justification for MNEs being sceptical about the practicability of such guidelines because of the problems that arise in deciding, for example, whether a single action might produce more good than harm. There have been many occasions when short-term expediency has proved to be harmful in the long term. For example, 7000 shoemakers were replaced by 40 injection-moulding machine operators in one African country and, whilst the industry itself was more efficient in that it could produce potentially exportable goods, dependence switched from local raw materials to imported machinery and raw materials, so seriously affecting unemployment and the balance of payments.

THE EFFECT OF CULTURAL DIFFERENCES ON THE ACCEPTABILITY OF BUSINESS PRACTICES

Pervading every aspect of international business is the issue of culture. Culture is particularly difficult to define but can be regarded as essentially being the way people live together in society. Because it is affected by many different factors, such as religion, education, the traditions of the country, the family and the stage of economic development, it is unique to a particular country or region. It is the ways in which culture is expressed, such as the values and norms, and in artistic expression that the differences emerge.

If we trace the first steps of firms in international business, it is apparent that for the smallest scale companies the most commonly adopted approach is 'when in Rome, do as the Romans do', since they typically have little scope to influence the behaviour of the host country. For multinational companies operating throughout the world, the principal problem is in deciding if the system of values used in the home country can be standardized throughout the organization and so be imposed on the host country operations, or if it should be adapted for each individual country operation. Ethnocentric MNEs, such as Coca-Cola, McDonalds and Kentucky Fried Chicken have exported not only products, but also their home-country cultures and business practices.

Although many multinationals from north-western Europe or the USA claim that home-country standards are usually higher than those of the host country and should therefore be adopted, this is an ethnocentric rather than a universal morality. Problems occur in a wide variety of areas such as the acceptability of dress at work, images and lifestyles portrayed in advertising, and businesses involved in controversial medical practice, which might be regarded as controversial, for example, abortion clinics.

The varying economic circumstances which exist in a particular country are often the most significant factors in setting standards locally. For example, in a poor society the need for income and employment is likely to be seen in some situations as even more necessary than maintaining higher safety standards. Whilst child labour in factories is condemned as unacceptable in well-developed countries, it is quite common in some less well-developed countries such as Bangladesh. Whilst western-dominated pressure groups might call for a boycott of products made by firms employing such labour, the consequences for the children employed, their families and the community may well be catastrophic. As a result, consumers in advanced nations are left not knowing whether continued purchase of the products contributes to the economy of the country or simply prolongs an unacceptable way of life. MNEs marketing the products are much more likely to be perceived to be exploitative rather than contributing positively to the local economy as comparisons will inevitably be made with home country standards.

This example points to the fact that individual societies view moral acceptability differently and their views change over a period of time. Sorrel and Hendry (1994) note that for Aristotle slavery was morally acceptable, and releasing someone from slavery was, in general, morally wrong. Today it is possible to perceive considerable differences between the way that different cultures deal with such wide ranging issues as moneylending, sexual relations, birth control, social status, treatment of the elderly and the consumption of drugs, alcohol and even certain foods. Moreover, equal treatment of men and women is of increasing importance in western societies, but is still considered to be of less concern in Islamic society.

The assumption might be made that each different set of values can be justified on the basis of the circumstances that exist in a particular society although this would imply that moral values are linked directly to the stage of development of a particular society and, by implication, to the market in which an MNE operates. However, a comparison of the values of some of the most economically advanced nations such as the USA, Japan and Germany suggests that even here there are considerable differences in the way that ethical issues such as equal opportunities, employee involvement in decision making, tax evasion and marketing practices are dealt with in similarly developed countries. These situations need to be considered against the background of the issue of ethical relativism, because there is no universal agreement on which moral values society should strive for or even accept as a minimum standard. Percep-tions about what is and is not acceptable are conditioned by the circumstances both of the individual observing and the situation being observed, and both of these are clearly affected by the prevailing culture.

CULTURE AND ETHICAL DILEMMAS

Sorrell and Hendry (1994) suggest that there are three types of ethical dilemmas that arise between different cultures. They occur when:

1. There are different but culturally acceptable standards. One culture might believe it is morally better at dealing with such issues as employment where the opportunity for promotion might depend on any of a variety of criteria such as ability, seniority, gender, caste or status.
2. Practices are ethically unacceptable in the home country but acceptable and perceived to be morally sound in the host country. This includes such issues as questionable payments to individuals, attitudes to alcohol, drugs, sexual morality and standards in dress.
3. There is no moral conflict, but differing circumstances lead to alternative views of what is and is not acceptable practice. These might include safety standards in mining and manufacturing industry, and pollution and environmental damage. Within this category too might be included a number of situations relating to the illegal and unethical supply of goods which are likely to be used later against a nation's interest such as 'arms to Iraq' in the UK and 'Irangate' in the United States.

Whilst the tensions caused because of the cultural differences between the host and domestic country pose significant ethical problems for the organization operating internationally, it is when commercial pressures are applied too that ethical problems take on an additional dimension.

In attempting to avoid this dilemma many MNEs base their operational decision making on considering factors which are largely internal to the organization, using in their defence Milton Friedman's argument that 'there is one and only one social responsibility of business – to increase profits'. He does acknowledge that the firm should stay within the rules of the competitive game, but, bearing in mind our earlier suggestion that commercial factors express the values and ideology of western economies, this suggests an ethnocentric approach towards business organization and shows little sensitivity to the different cultural issues in international business.

In practice, many firms acknowledge the desirability of recognizing the standards and values of the host and domestic cultures, but are much more likely to believe that their success is primarily dependent on simply giving existing and potential customers the best possible value for money. Increasingly, however, MNEs are recognizing the importance of the stakeholders model in guiding their actions. Figure 12.4 shows some typical stakeholders of an MNE and by considering their individual expectations it becomes obvious that many of their demands will be conflicting. The critical question is one of deciding to what extent the firm should utilize the stakeholder model as against the profit argument when making decisions.

It can be argued that it is the change in the demands and expectations of better educated consumers who are also better informed as a result of more effective global communications that is driving MNEs to give greater consideration to their stakeholder demands and world-wide corporate ethical image, particularly relating to ethical behaviour. However, the question remains as to whether this is simply a further result of western values being imposed on others or more widespread demands for MNEs to address these issues. The implications of the stakeholder model are illustrated in Fig. 12.5 which demonstrates the link between commercial, host and domestic country cultural characteristics and the firm's behaviour which leads to the emergence of a number of ethical issues.

The implications for MNEs of ethical issues

It is when the firm makes a more permanent investment in another country that these ethical issues become increasingly significant. The different cultural standards and values, and the different stages of economic development of the host country can, on the one hand, create

Figure 12.4 Some stakeholders of MNEs.

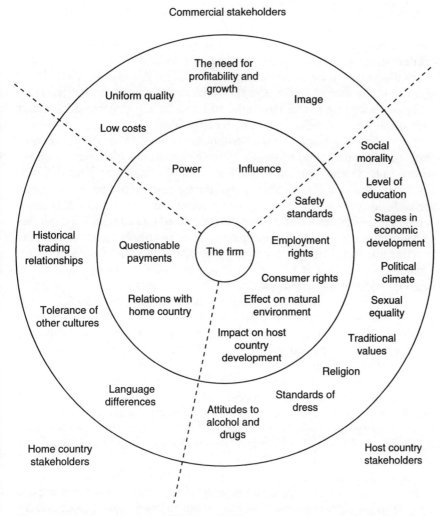

Commercial stakeholders

The need for profitability and growth

Uniform quality

Image

Low costs

Power   Influence

Social morality

Level of education

Safety standards

Historical trading relationships

Questionable payments

The firm

Employment rights

Stages in economic development

Consumer rights

Political climate

Relations with home country

Effect on natural environment

Sexual equality

Tolerance of other cultures

Impact on host country development

Traditional values

Religion

Language differences

Standards of dress

Attitudes to alcohol and drugs

Home country stakeholders

Host country stakeholders

Figure 12.5 Some commercial, host and home country cultural characteristics and their impact on MNE behaviour.

barriers to the firm's growth plans, but on the other, can create opportunities for exploitation by unscrupulous firms.

BRIBERY AND CORRUPTION

Bribery and corruption are, perhaps the highest profile areas of international business ethics and are the result of firms and individuals choosing expediency in response to commercial pressures rather than making a response based on ethical considerations, and Donaldson (1989) suggests that a distinction should be drawn between petty bribery and more serious corruption. However, this raises the question of when does petty bribery change to become more serious corruption and who is the arbiter of the acceptability of such business practices? Whilst this might point to the use of corporate codes of conduct it can also be argued that this is equally unacceptable and the only stance which can be defended is that of adopting moral absolutes and concluding that anything other than totally ethical behaviour is unacceptable.

Petty bribery is usually linked to countries with lower levels of economic development and is considered to be necessary to conduct business successfully in the host country. For example, in a number of South American countries it appears to be almost impossible to move goods through customs without giving the customs official a small and often standard payment to avoid undue delays caused by red tape. The salaries of these officials appear to be set perhaps in acknowledgement that the practice goes on. Bribery on a larger scale, however, has more significant implications because it is a serious violation of the fundamental international right of fair competition.

Kakuei Tanaka, the Japanese prime minister from 1972 to 1974 was given a four-year suspended sentence for taking a £1 million bribe from Lockheed Aircraft Company. Whilst Lockheed claimed that this was accepted in Japan and indeed, even in 1994 a survey suggested that nearly one in ten Japanese politicians had been caught taking illegal donations, the public were shocked at the revelation. The issue, perhaps, is more to do with the publicity and enforcement of ethical codes – the general public cannot demonstrate their reaction if they are unaware of the scale of the activities. It might be concluded that international firms too easily accept that bribery and corruption is commonplace and so encourage the practice by their actions.

There are some apparent commercial benefits to the firm of paying bribes, for example, to avoid red tape delays or ensure that contracts are not lost to competitors who offer bribes, but the very existence of bribery demonstrates that there are inefficiencies in the market and this usually leads to distrust and cynicism amongst consumers of the motivation of MNEs often resulting in damage to the market in the longer term.

The response of different countries to bribery varies considerably. The US Foreign Corrupt Practices Act makes it illegal for US companies to bribe an official of a government or political party whereas in Germany bribes are tax deductible, providing that evidence of the payment is available to the authorities. In some countries paying bribes is justified on the grounds of expediency. Bribes are not regarded as providing the firm with a competitive advantage but instead simply ensure that business practices, which occur without additional payment in other countries, take place in the normal way. Failure to pay bribes under these circumstances means a failure to do business.

Clearly if products are demonstrably superior, the marketers and distributors of US products can use the law as justification for avoiding such payments, and they can therefore benefit financially from not paying bribes. However, where there is little difference in product performance, firms have to find alternative ways of securing the sale. A common practice for MNEs who do not wish to be directly involved in bribery is to distance themselves from their independent distributors who are expected to make 'unauthorized' payments from a high built-in profit margin.

It is often in linked complex deals where there is a greater opportunity for hiding or disguising questionable payments. An example of the potential difficulty this can cause was demonstrated when, to the embarrassment of a number of UK ministers, a contract for the Pergau Dam project in Malaysia was shown to have been linked to overseas aid provided by the UK government. Questions, too, were asked about the substantial payments made to Mark Thatcher, the son of the then prime minister Margaret Thatcher, in respect of a major arms deal with Saudi Arabia. Although no allegations of corruption were made, it was suggested in the media that benefiting in this way was unethical.

Waterhouse (1994) reports that western countries have been unwilling to penalize firms paying bribes, instead preferring to prosecute government officials such as Gordon Foxley of the British Ministry of Defence, who accepted at least £1.3 million of bribes from three European companies to award them ammunition supply contracts. This might imply that firms have not been expected to give recognition to the moral status of their transactions. Now, after a four-year inquiry, the 25 members of the Organization for Economic Cooperation and Development (OECD) have recommended that the payment of overseas bribes should be made illegal and questionable payments should no longer be allowable business expenses. OECD intends that after a three-year trial period, these measures should become mandatory. Such action should be welcomed by individual managers. In the past inadequate host government laws have been regarded as a defence for wrongdoing by international firms and so the unethical firms have not been penalized. If the MNEs were held responsible for their unethical actions a likely result would be that competition should be fairer.

CONTRIBUTING TO POLITICAL PARTIES AND LOBBYING

Contributions are made by businesses to the funds of a particular political party in their domestic country usually because of the political allegiance of the senior executive in the business but contribution to the funds of a political party in a host country with which the firm would be expected to have little political affiliation must be regarded as highly questionable.

In the late 1980s the Conservative party in the UK benefited from payments made by senior company executives, including from Asil Nadir, who fled the UK to Cyprus to escape fraud charges over the failure of Polly Peck.

Whilst bribery and corruption tend to be linked to specific deals, contributing to political parties and lobbying governments is used to attempt to persuade politicians and civil servants to favour particular industries or firms. This issue became the subject of debate in the UK in 1995 with the government setting up the Nolan Committee to enquire into standards of public life.

The application of pressure by lobby groups and individual firms to encourage politicians to support desired legislation is backed by considerable resources and is carried out to extreme lengths in the USA. Lobbying is, for example, frequently cited as an important reason why the sale of firearms in the USA is almost unrestricted. Against a background of adverse balance of payments with the Pacific Rim countries the tobacco lobby in the United States persuaded the US trade and industry department to apply pressure to these countries to allow wider promotion of US tobacco products, including the Philip Morris 'Marlboro' brand, for example, on television and at pop music concerts.

The strategy of using contacts and influence for competitive advantage is providing increasingly lucrative incomes for ex-government ministers and civil servants that are well known and respected internationally. The Carlyle group set up in 1987 with a seed capital of $5 million has gone a stage further. The group has as its key players Frank Carlucci, a former defence secretary, James Baker the former secretary of state and other high-ranking politicians. By 1994, Alexander (1994) reports that it had taken over businesses with sales of $6 billion and was one of the top 25 defence contractors in the world. Whilst this is not illegal there is the suggestion that it is unethical to use political influence in this way.

MARKETING PRACTICES

For many MNEs the marketing practices which they pursue are the source of major tension between the commercial pressures and the host and home country expectations (illustrated in Fig. 12.1). If an MNE is accused of marketing malpractice or deception, its mistakes are capable of becoming increasingly visible to its consumers around the world causing immense damage to its reputation and image. In an increasingly competitive environment, MNEs are aware of the impact of their world-wide corporate image on revenue and brand value in each individual country. Because of this, a considerable part of the public relations activity of the firm is concerned with the management of situations which are potentially damaging – the golden rule being that the firm should act before the media or government forces it to do so – in order for it to be perceived by its customers to be behaving ethically.

The cost of damage limitation can be extremely high. Johnson & Johnson withdrew the drug Tylenol before the government acted after seven deaths were linked to it in Chicago in 1982. The cost was estimated at $100 million plus the loss of future product sales. Perrier withdrew all their bottled water from around the world at a cost of $140 million when traces of benzene were detected in Canada in 1990. Perrier acted quickly because of the potential damage to its image of providing a 'pure' product although the risk of ill effects was extremely low.

Sometimes there is pressure on firms from different sources to sell into LDCs products which have reached maturity or decline in their life cycles in developed country markets. The consumption of tobacco products is in decline in Europe and the USA due to the greater awareness amongst smokers of potential health risks and this, together with fierce price competition has forced the major tobacco product suppliers to look towards LDCs to maintain the flow of profits. It is unlikely that in LDCs the customers are fully aware of the proven risk to smokers.

It can be argued, however, that some products prohibited in developed countries can benefit LDCs. Selling products which have previously been shown to be potentially damaging would usually be considered to be exploitation, but this can sometimes be justified. For example, DDT is the only chemical capable of removing malaria-bearing mosquitos and it can be argued that for LDCs this benefit outweighs the side-effect of the ground eventually becoming contaminated. A number of drugs and veterinary products which have been withdrawn in developed countries because of their side-effects and superseded by improved but much more costly drugs still offer benefits to LDCs which are unable to afford the new product.

Often products are developed within an environment where they are expected to be used but problems can occur when legitimate products are used incorrectly because of the different circumstances of use or a lack of knowledge or resources of the consumers. If managers could predict that this misuse is likely to occur, marketing the product would be unethical. One of the most widely publicized examples of this was Nestlé who sold powdered milk in LDCs without considering the full implications for the mothers and babies who did not have the necessary availability of clean water, money or training. An extensive campaign by pressure groups, and subsequent investigation led to Nestlé being accused first, of misrepresentation, and changing the indigenous behaviour to the detriment of the health of the population, second, giving promotional samples of the product to mothers in hospital which led to the mothers' milk drying up so that they would be forced to use the product, and third, that they carried on these practices in the knowledge that the mothers could not afford the product and as a result babies would receive insufficient nourishment and suffer from malnutrition. A world-wide boycott was introduced and lasted for seven years and the case resulted in new guidelines drawn up by the United Nations (UN).

There are a number of government policies on marketing practice which other countries and their MNEs consider to be unethical. By comparison with the openness of western markets, the Japanese market is largely closed to foreign goods. The reasons for this are partly historical, because the Japanese have a long tradition of buying domestically produced goods which they usually regard as being superior to foreign goods, but it is protectionist too. The Japanese government, for example, have taxed imports prohibitively, limited the distribution of foreign goods by raising non tariff barriers on a wide range of products from rice to cars and have been accused, for example, of deliberately delaying planning permission for international discount retailers to build supermarkets in order to protect local and largely inefficient shops.

Product dumping is a second area of questionable intercountry marketing and occurs when products, produced in one country, are offered for sale in large quantities in international markets at very low prices. This is often due to state subsidies or debt write-offs and occurs frequently in industries with high exit barriers such as the steel, shipbuilding and airline industry. When dumping occurs it is argued that businesses and jobs are put at risk in one country by state supported, non-viable jobs in another. For example, it has been claimed that the French government has subsidized Air France heavily over the last few years at a time when there was substantial overcapacity in international air travel.

By contrast, particularly low labour or material costs, extremely low-cost production methods or the need for foreign exchange are used as justification for the dumping of cheap goods from LDCs, for example, shoes from eastern Europe and clothes from the Pacific Rim countries into the UK. Given that jobs are created in the LDCs and low-priced products become available in the west, there are strong arguments in favour of this type of dumping, but these must be set against the loss of many thousands of jobs in the textile and shoe industries in the west.

Taking this one stage further, counterfeiting provides some short-term benefits in the form of low prices for consumers and jobs in counterfeiting firms. It is a growing problem and is more prevalent in luxury goods markets where many product copies originate from LDCs. Essentially the copying firm violates the patent or copyright of another but many consumers welcome the opportunity to purchase a copy of a luxury product at a fraction of the cost. Of course, this very act helps to diminish the value of the original product whose image has been built at considerable cost. As with many other ethical issues, there is too, a fine line between acceptable and unacceptable practice. In the fast moving consumer goods market in the USA and UK, some would argue that private label goods approach the category of counterfeiting too. Sales of own brand products by major food retailers is growing and increasingly the gap between the design of branded and own brand products is being reduced. Recently Sainsbury, the UK food retailers, produced a cola pack so similar in design to that of Coca-Cola that after being accused of copying they were persuaded to make modifications.

A further problem facing international marketing companies is that of parallel importing or grey marketing, which involves the importing and selling of products through market distribution channels which are not authorized by the manufacturer. It occurs when there are significantly different market prices for the same product in different countries because of variations in exchange rates, local rates of taxation and different market cost structures which allow an unauthorized dealer to purchase branded products intended for one market at a low price and then sell them in a higher-priced market. The particular problem for the manufacturer is that this can result in their authorized distributors losing motivation and, if the problem becomes serious, the practice can ultimately lead to loss of markets. Whilst it can have detrimental effects on the market and the consumers, who often receive much lower service levels and guarantees, it is not considered to be illegal. It is another example of a practice on the edge of what is legal, unethical and acceptable. However, ethical issues were raised when Superdrug, the UK drugstore chain, sold perfumes, obtained through unauthorized distribution channels at heavily discounted prices in competition with the authorized retailers. In 1992 the *Financial Times* reported Superdrug's attempt to obtain supplies directly from the perfume houses. The case was referred by the Office of Fair Trading to the Monopolies and Mergers Commission (MMC) but Superdrug lost the case because the MMC ruled that a major factor of the appeal of the perfume was its exclusive image which would not be enhanced by mass distribution.

Since the restrictions on the quantity of goods imported by individuals from one European Union (EU) country to another have been removed a considerable amount of alcohol is being bought by UK day-trippers to France for home consumption. The UK brewing industry is particularly concerned with the resulting loss of UK sales and the resulting job losses.

EFFECT ON HOST-COUNTRY DEVELOPMENT

Growth in the prosperity of a country is dependent on increasing international trade and for many LDCs lacking skills and resources, the solution has been to encourage foreign inward investment. However, a number of the marketing and investment practices adopted can have a detrimental effect on the development of the host country, as the reason for the investment is usually based on the MNE benefiting from low labour costs or locally available resources. Many of these investments are considered to be exploitative. In agriculture, for example, land is bought by MNEs for growing cash crops for export rather than food crops for the indigenous population. Whilst this might seem on the surface to be unethical, in practice it could be desirable to generate foreign currency and so develop the economy provided, of course, that the population has enough to eat and has the opportunity to work. In these circumstances it is necessary for the host country to manage the industry or agricultural sector by ensuring that balance is achieved in land use and that taxation is sufficient to ensure that a significant proportion of the income is retained in the host country. In extraction industries too, it is necessary for the government to ensure that MNEs are prevented from transferring raw materials at low prices to a processing plant in another country where major profits might be made.

Whilst the effects that we have so far discussed have been and continue to be immensely damaging to LDCs it is, however, the effects of banks on the development of host countries that have over the last few years been most detrimental. De George (1993) maintains that banks in general have had few beneficial effects on LDC economies. Their operations in LDCs have led to few jobs because the financial investment has normally gone to government projects rather than to support entrepreneurial business. Lax control of financing has led to huge debts and, moreover, banks often act as a conduit for flight capital – the transfer of investment capital from less developed countries to more secure destinations often to secret accounts.

De George argues that the development of the country is not the same as the development of the people and banks have usually lent to the governments of LDCs and the élite. Although this policy is less risky for the banks, the finance has not usually been used for the general good of the people in the country. LDC debt has usually resulted from poorly considered loans, lack of control over the money loaned, variable interest rates and unrealistic future projections. In many cases it has been necessary to use all the hard currency obtained from exports to service the country's debt with the result that no more loans could be granted leading to a reduction in the standard of living.

Whilst it is typically the leading politicians in LDCs, such as Saddam Hussain and Imelda Marcos that are able to obtain bank loans, it is they who usually place the substantial sums of money that they acquire in Swiss bank accounts rather than invest it in their own country. In this way much of the money loaned to LDCs has simply been recycled back into the multinational banks without benefiting the LDC. It is now well accepted that banks knowingly or unknowingly have laundered substantial amounts of money resulting from the proceeds of drug trafficking and other illegal activities. It is claimed that a number of banks operate fraudulently, for example BCCI, chartered in Luxembourg and Cayman Islands, is alleged to have stolen $5 billion from depositors in Cameroons,

Nigeria, Sierra Leone, Botswana and Zimbabwe.

The World Bank has recently acknowledged the inadequacies of banking policy in LDCs and a panel formed from members of industrialized nations is looking at bank reforms. De George (1993) suggests that banks in the future should:

❏ practice restraint in lending to governments and individuals in LDCs
❏ support entrepreneurial projects rather than just major investments
❏ should not issue loans which might be used for exploiting the people.

The issue of bank loans to LDCs provides a powerful argument for the stakeholder model as a basis for decision making because the profit motivation of banks, whilst leading to profits in the short term, has ultimately resulted in considerable losses during the late 1980s as LDCs have defaulted on loan repayments. It might be argued, therefore, that banks should adopt strategies which take into account the longer-term implications of their actions, not only for the benefit of those taking loans, but ultimately for their shareholders too.

CULTURAL IMPACTS OF MULTINATIONAL OPERATIONS

In addition to the direct commercial impact, some MNEs also have a less overt but equally significant impact on the LDC. The most obvious form of this is 'Coca-colonization' of various countries, in which the American lifestyle has been exported to the four corners of the globe by strongly ethnocentric firms such as McDonalds, Coca-Cola and Kentucky Fried Chicken. The impact of importing a foreign culture can create significant tensions within the host country society. France and Germany have at different times attempted to preserve their language from imports of foreign words and, for example during the General Agreement on Tariffs and Trade (GATT) talks, French frustration with the all pervasive American culture lead to attacks on McDonald's restaurants in Paris. In January 1994 a law was passed in France to restrict popular music radio stations to no more than 40% of American output. The Pacific Rim countries too have seen Japanese culture in the form of music and lifestyle become increasingly popular amongst the young. This is resented by older people who remember with some bitterness being forced to learn Japanese during the Second World War.

Host-country emotions can run high when the country's industrial heritage is perceived to be sold off to MNEs. There was considerable anger when parts of the UK car industry were being sold off to the US and European manufacturers and despite their free market stance, Americans resented the take over of Columbia Pictures by Sony and Universal Pictures by Mitsubishi at a time when Japanese purchasing of US assets appeared to have reached unacceptable proportions.

The impact of foreign companies on the local culture is not always predictable even when the intentions appear to be exemplary. Anita Roddick, the owner of Body Shop, has specifically searched the world for sources of naturally occurring products as ingredients for a range of toiletries and cosmetics, and in so doing has attempted to bring prosperity to poor areas. The Kayapo Indians of Brazil have provided naturally occurring materials for Body Shop products, but the Kayapo leaders have tended to spend their income on western-style luxuries rather than on addressing social needs such as the high infant mortality rate. They have also continued with deforestation activities, which work contrary to the Body Shop ethos.

THE MEASURES BEING TAKEN TO CONTROL MNES

So far in this chapter we have discussed the ethical dilemmas and problems that businesses from the smallest exporter to the largest multinational enterprise face largely arising because of the cultural diversity of trading countries. We have also identified the ethical issues which arise as firms respond to the commercial pressures and seek to exploit opportunities in other countries.

It is against this background and in response to the growth of multinationals since the war that guidelines have been introduced in an attempt to influence the development of MNEs particularly in such areas as employment relations, consumer protection, environmental pollution, participation in political activity and basic human rights through a large number of intergovernmental agreements, compacts, accords and declarations. The most important of these bases of transcultural corporate ethics appear in Fig. 12.6 and have been interpreted by a number of international organizations in the form of codes of conduct which might be used to develop the various relationships which MNEs form with their major stakeholders.

The other main influence in controlling the operations of MNEs has been the growth of the big trading blocs. A large free internal market such as the EU is intended to create MNEs sufficiently powerful to operate globally. However, in the EU, for example, to ensure that these MNEs are genuinely competitive and do not exploit their larger home market, considerable effort has been expended on legislation which has been developed, among other reasons, to prevent anticompetitive actions, achieve greater equality, control environmental pollution, and protect consumer and employee rights.

Frederick (1991) has identified significant sources of moral authority for laying down the guidelines for the formulation of multinational policies on ethical behaviour. The guidelines are based on the concepts

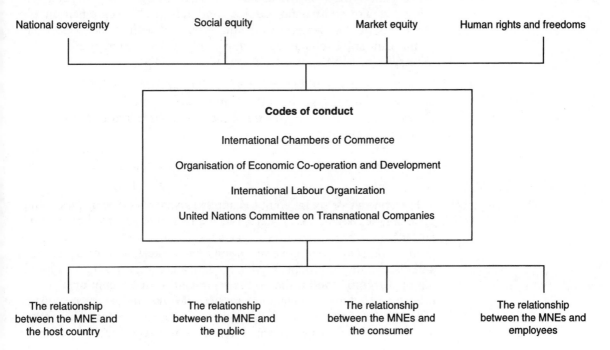

Bases of the guidelines

United Nations Declaraction of Human Rights (1948)

The European Convention on Human Rights (1950)

The Helsinki Final Act (1975)

The OECD Guidelines for Multinational Enterprises (1976)

The International Labour Office Tripartite Declaration of Principles Concerning MNEs and Social Policy (1977)

The UN Code of Conduct on Transnational Corporations (incomplete)

Sources of moral authority

National sovereignty   Social equity   Market equity   Human rights and freedoms

Codes of conduct

International Chambers of Commerce

Organisation of Economic Co-operation and Development

International Labour Organization

United Nations Committee on Transnational Companies

| The relationship between the MNE and the host country | The relationship between the MNE and the public | The relationship between the MNEs and the consumer | The relationship between the MNEs and employees |

Figure 12.6 The measures taken to control MNEs.

of national sovereignty, market integrity, social equity and human rights and freedoms. However, whilst these concepts can be defined relatively easily, their implementation is much more difficult, because in many cases the concepts offer contradictory guidelines.

At the basis of national sovereignty is the belief that each nation should not infringe on the sovereignty of its neighbours and should be committed to preserving the integrity and self-interest of that neighbour. However, the real significance of country borders is increasingly being challenged. As regional trading blocks such as the EU develop closer intergovernment relationships with increasing political and economic ties, fierce debates have ensued over the trade off in benefits between national sovereignty and achieving closer partnership between countries. The changing relationships between the member countries have considerable implications for international business. In the case of the EU, for example, we have witnessed, among others, conflicts on fishing rights, support for agriculture, and mutual recognition of product and service standards.

National sovereignty is challenged too because country borders do not prevent the impact of one country's actions being felt by another. The effect of major construction projects and industrial development involving rivers, major deforestation and problems with nuclear electricity plants cannot be contained within a particular country and so it is necessary for MNEs to:

❏ be aware of the cross border effect of their own activities
❏ respect the aims, goals, cultural and historical traditions
❏ respect the direction of the host country's economic and social development and
❏ not interfere in the internal political affairs of the host country through improper political activity or making questionable payments to public officials.

The concept of social equity is applied to many situations including, for example, pay between sexes, racial and ethnic groups, host country nationals and parent country expatriates, professional and occupational groups, indigenous employees and migrant workers, and the advantaged and disadvantaged groups. Equity, Frederick argues, should also apply in job opportunities and training, the treatment of the unemployed and to other work-related benefits and services. MNEs, however, are able to offer considerable justification for maintaining differentials in employment conditions because of the different commercial value of particular skills and knowledge.

Market integrity is a source of guidelines on restrictive business practices, the cross border flow of capital, repatriation of profits and rights of ownership. The GATT, which has now evolved into the World Trade Organization (WTO) is instrumental in this area by working to reduce protectionism and promote multilateral trade by the use of 'most-favoured nation status' which obliges each signatory to the GATT treaty to grant the same treatment to all other members on a non-discriminatory basis. Whilst this might be welcomed in the ethical context, critics of GATT argue that the circumstances of LDCs often mean that they are likely to lose out to the developed countries in a better position to take advantage.

The most substantial source of moral authority for corporate guidelines is that of human rights and freedoms which place the human person as the fundamental of moral authority, but this is inevitably in conflict with some issues of national sovereignty, social equity and market integrity. Human rights are in practice conditioned by political, social and economic values and are challenged by the concept of market equity which leads to the relocation of production from a high wage to a low wage area, and so to arguments against minimum wages and in favour of breaking the restrictive practices of trade unions on the grounds of 'market forces'. Many measures which seek to enhance national and corporate productivity in the short term, can deprive workers in the long term of jobs, living wages, and security in retirement.

In developing codes of conduct it is important first to recognize the unique position of MNEs. They are expected by their various stakeholders to balance often conflicting demands, for example they need to:

Codes of conduct

❑ meet the needs of their customers, but in doing so recognize that whilst the customers have similar characteristics and expectations of products and services, they may experience great differences in lifestyle and personal circumstances
❑ invest in areas and operations in which stakeholders can expect a return on their investment and involvement and manage the risks associated with their activities
❑ efficiently manage their finances including their tax structures and
❑ compete effectively in their chosen markets.

Companies need to regularly reassess their manufacturing facilities and capacities and make new investment decisions based on the performance of individual plants. Their decisions are driven by the need to be competitive rather than by the likely adverse impact that closing a plant would have on a particular country or region.

Diffuse, contradictory or unclear company aims and objectives lead inevitably to the decline of the firm and so MNEs focus primarily on the growth and development of the business. For this reason the main thrust in setting up the codes of conduct has come from outside agencies. Four codes of conduct have been developed by the International Chamber of Commerce, the OECD, the International Labour Organization and the UN Committee on Transnational Companies.

Getz (1990) suggests that at the heart of these codes of conduct are the implications that they have for the relationships between MNEs and their important stakeholder groups, namely host governments, the public, consumers and employees and that they increase in importance as the market entry involves more commitment by the MNE within a particular country.

THE RELATIONSHIP BETWEEN THE MNES AND THE CONSUMER

In Chapter 5 we dealt with a number of marketing issues affecting the relationship between the firm and the consumer and earlier in this chapter we have discussed the international dimension – that the marketing activity should respect the laws and regulations of the host country in regard to consumer protection rights, and ensure the health and safety of consumers. Product liability, for example, has become a major reason for litigation in the USA and this has had substantial implications for the development of new products particularly in potentially life threatening situations such as pharmaceutical. Such legislation might also have the effect of discouraging some smaller firms from exporting to the USA simply because they cannot afford the risk of litigation.

MNEs would be expected to avoid the exploitation of weaknesses in legislation in particular countries by selling products which are banned in others and instead assist governments to prevent the marketing of unsafe products. However, problems may arise if MNEs become closely involved in advising governments in specific areas of expertise where the government is not as technically capable as the firm. The firm may well have the opportunity to gain competitive advantage by persuading the government that their product specification is the most suitable one to adopt.

It is not only with the product itself where there is an issue of ethics. Advertising should not be misleading and the methods of selling should be appropriate for the situation. Differences of culture and circumstances too give rise to ethical problems in marketing prompting the need for sensitivity to local needs in product and process design, and communications. For example, the ingredients of McDonalds and Burger King are beef and pork which are not acceptable in certain countries.

THE RELATIONSHIP BETWEEN MNES AND EMPLOYEES

In earlier chapters of this book we have discussed the relationship between the management of firms and their employees. Employees of an MNE have a right to expect that they will have safe and fair working conditions, a reasonable degree of economic security, the opportunity to be represented by trade unions and acceptable living standards when in retirement. In addition, as human beings they have a right to freedom of expression relating to social, cultural and personal values.

In international business, employees make comparisons of their situation not only with workers from other firms in the host country, but also with employees in other parts of the firm and in other countries. The environments within which the employees work are usually so different that judgements become difficult to make about the value that should be and is placed on the work of a particular employee and so it is highly unlikely that the views of employees from different parts of a firm can be reconciled.

As might be expected the emphasis which companies place on these codes of conduct in respect of the relationship they have with their employees varies considerably between organizations and also between different countries, particularly in such areas as the provision of stable employment, giving priority to the employment and promotion of employees of the nationals of the host countries and paying a minimum basic living wage.

The power and influence of MNEs with many of their stakeholders is increasing, but as competition becomes more fierce for all businesses and the effects of macro changes on political, cultural and economic conditions appear to be more dramatic so stability is becoming more elusive. In the past many MNEs have appeared to offer job security and better conditions for their host country employees, but they cannot easily provide guaranteed jobs to workers. Even in Japan, workers no longer can expect a 'job for life'. The relationship between many MNEs and their employees is therefore developing within a much more uncertain business environment where working patterns, tasks and responsibilities, and management methods are changing ever more rapidly.

THE RELATIONSHIP BETWEEN MNES AND HOST GOVERNMENTS

The success of this relationship is primarily dependent on the MNE having respect for the national sovereignty of the host government. Any activity which might adversely affect the political autonomy, economic or social development of the country should be avoided, and this includes, for example, not adversely affecting the balance of payments or currency exchange rates of the host countries. It is not only in LDCs where MNEs operate and profit from the fluctuations in currency markets for which they are in part responsible. It is, perhaps, more lucrative for foreign exchange dealers to 'play the market' in developed countries where exchange rate speculation is often overshadowed by political debate and is not, therefore, subject to the intense scrutiny on ethical grounds that might be expected.

MNEs might also be expected to conform to local taxation laws and regulations and avoid using accounting practices, such as transfer pricing policies which are designed to modify the taxation basis on which they are assessed in order to reduce the amount of tax they must pay. It is often extremely difficult for governments to prove tax avoidance because of the complexity of international business transactions. The situation is becoming worse particularly because of the expansion of the international trade in services. Increasingly the most valuable commodity, information, is transferred by telecommunications and is not, therefore, subject to taxation.

We have, so far, concentrated on the unethical behaviour of MNEs but governments too participate in activities against MNEs which many would consider to be unethical particularly if a major investment has been made in a host country. During the 1960s and 1970s, too, a number of host countries particularly in Latin America and in Arab countries expropriated firms, by taking over their local assets and operations without compensation. This phenomenon is now less common perhaps reflecting changes in politics, less confidence in the ability of local ownership, the increased power of MNEs, the greater care taken by MNEs when investing in politically risky areas and the power of developed countries to protect their MNEs from the action of unscrupulous governments. Indeed the current trend is towards privatization of state assets, but this too is subject to allegations of favouritism and corruption.

Further illustration of the diversity of potential ethical problems occurring is the involvement of government in developing international business through ensuring that its own MNEs have a powerful home base and cooperate with each other in international markets to develop competitive advantage. The Japanese government has used these methods over many years to strengthen the power base of its own industrial firms and severely restrict the activities of foreign MNEs in its own markets, something which has been the source of considerable conflict between Japan and the west, notably the USA.

THE RELATIONSHIP BETWEEN MNES AND THE PUBLIC

This relationship focuses on the rights of the public in the host country to obtain the technology needed for economic development and a clean environment in which to live. The ethical principles on which this is based are that the public have the right to expect economic development. Whilst no direct link between technology transfer and economic development is made, it is implied, and it is based on the concept that greater and more productive use will be made of local resources and personnel with the result that the economy will improve.

The contentious issue associated with technology transfer, however, is that whilst attempts are made to ensure that less developed countries should obtain favourable treatment in obtaining technology, there must also be the recognition that MNEs transfer technology not as charity or out of a sense of duty, but rather on the expectation that they will receive payment. Whilst MNEs are prepared to commit resources in a host country for the purposes of presenting a more acceptable face to the local community they are unlikely to give away potential competitive advantage. Many firms tend to be over cautious with releasing old technology because, in reality, the commercial value of the technology is dependent on the value that customers place on the uses to which the technology is put rather than its apparent intrinsic worth. The transfer to India, for example, of some relatively old motor vehicle technology has been successful because of the simplicity of the design which is better suited to the country's infrastructure and usage conditions.

Technology transferred from developed countries to LDCs is not automatically beneficial. It must be appropriate to the needs of the country and respect the host culture. After the famine of the 1980s in the Horn of Africa, 40,000 nomads were airlifted to a fertile plain in Somalia, where brick-built homes and sophisticated farming machinery were provided. Ten years later the nomads had returned to their old way of life and millions of pounds worth of machinery remained idle and corroded.

In this chapter we have discussed the issues which provide the background for the development of codes of conduct for MNEs. Whilst we have discussed the complex nature of international business and its ethical implications, in practice the dilemma for most managers is how to balance the firm's objectives, the principal one of which is making profits, with the expectations of the firm's stakeholders.

The challenge for international business managers

In a study of 160 Australian firms, Armstrong and Everett (1993) concluded that there was no significant relationship between the perceived importance of the problems, the perceived extent of ethical problems and the perceived managerial actions, with the implication that managers do not adjust their policy in response to the frequency of ethical problems. In the absence of appropriate action, this suggests that an organizational code of ethics is necessary. Armstrong and Everett also conclude that the extent of ethical problems increases with greater international involvement and, perhaps unsurprisingly, that all respondents considered themselves to be very ethical.

The development of codes of ethical practice in international business is particularly challenging because of the complexity resulting from cultural differences and the wide range of stakeholders that have expectations about the way the business operates. International managers must manage the issue of ethics within the overall context of the job and so before discussing the ethical issues it is necessary to consider the increasingly competitive business environment in which the international manager operates.

During the past 30–40 years the world economy has moved from a situation in which there was unsatisfied demand for the majority of the goods in which MNEs trade to one in which there is excess supply with the result that competition is intensifying in virtually every industry sector throughout the world. The pressure on managers is becoming greater as businesses become increasingly concentrated with fewer larger opportunities to sell products. Marketers are required to strive to make their product or service offer more attractive by driving down costs and convincing the buyer that this is the most competitive deal on offer. Success for international managers is largely measured by financial performance and it is inevitable that against this background some managers will be tempted to use unethical behaviour to gain advantage over competitors.

Consumers increasingly have greater expectations of products and services and, partly due to greater equity ownership, are increasingly knowledgeable about the performance and behaviour of businesses. Pressure groups act to make changes in many areas of environmental concern, consumer protection and employee rights by operating internationally. The influence for example of environmental groups, such as Greenpeace, has widened, and the Green Party achieved representation in the European parliament some years ago.

Within an environment in which the various internal and external pressures must be balanced, individual managers find themselves in the unenviable position of being unable to meet their own short term targets because of the unethical behaviour of their competitors. In such circumstances and even with codes of conduct in place, senior managers may well turn a blind eye to the questionable practices of junior staff. However if these practices become public knowledge it is usually the junior staff that are sacked to preserve the reputation of the company and its senior managers. By contrast if the case reaches the courts, senior managers are usually considered to be responsible for the actions of junior managers as was the case in the Zeebrugge ferry disaster when the court of investigation found that they had failed to assign responsibility for safety through the absence of planning (Boyd, 1990).

The conclusion, that follows from this therefore, is that managers should take responsibility for the consequences of their own individual and collective actions. They should also take the lead in setting standards where unsatisfactory standards exist but this then leads to a debate about the moral status of the corporation and where responsibility for decision making is situated and exercised within the MNE. This begs the ultimate question as to whether the MNE has the courage to lose revenue in the short term but speak out about the unacceptable behaviour of those competitors using unethical practices and whether its individual managers are prepare to 'blow the whistle' on unacceptable behaviour that occurs within the firm. In practice only a minority of managers are likely to have the courage to take decisions which, at least in the short term, are likely to be commercially damaging for the firm. However, as MNEs become more powerful and benefit from increasing international business it is inevitable that the international authorities will hold them culpable to an ever increasing degree when they cross the line into unethical behaviour, particularly in such areas as bribery and corruption, environmental pollution and consumer protection.

We are entering the age of the transnational international business which in concept has allegiance to no specific country and no ethnocentric codes of ethical behaviour but has immense power. Transnational firms are ideally placed to play a leading role in setting ethical codes because they are not overly dependent on a particular country, official or group of customers and can use improved communication to explain their position to their consumers. Unacceptable behaviour on their part will damage their prestige and integrity with their own stakeholders. In balancing their diverse stakeholder expectations, MNEs must aim to satisfy acceptable basic moral values, be open and honest about their operations, be prepared to create and operate rules, when none exist in LDCs by using the best knowledge available to them for the benefit of both the country and the MNE.

Ethical considerations will become increasingly important in the strategic and operational development of MNEs. In responding to this, managers will need to base their ethical decisions on personal integrity. Within the international context, it is essential that this is done with sensitivity to the culture of the host country and an appreciation of the country's short- and long-term needs. In future it will be those managers that possess these attributes that will be successful internationally.

Exercises

❏ What justification might be offered in support of firms being prevented from contributing to the funds of political parties in a host country whilst allowing the practice in a domestic country?
❏ Can the stage of economic development of a country be used by a firm as a defence for its unethical practices?
❏ How effective are the measures to curb the undesirable behaviour of MNEs likely to be?
❏ Which questionable business and marketing practices might be acceptable and under what circumstances?
❏ To what extent can social and business culture be used to defend what might be perceived to be questionable practices?

Further reading

Craig-Smith, N. and Quelch, J.A. (1993) *Ethics in Marketing*. Richard D. Irwin, Homewood, IL.

References

Alexander, G. (1994) How Reagan's aids rescued Euro Disney. *Sunday Times*, 12 June.
Armstrong, R.W. and Everett, J.E. (1993) Managerial perceptions of ethical

problems in international marketing: Australian evidence. *Asian Journal of Marketing*, December.

Barnett, R. and Muller, R. (1974) *Global Reach: The Power of Multinational Corporations*. Simon & Shuster, New York.

Boyd, C. (1990) The responsibility of individuals for a company disaster: the example of the Zeebrugge car ferry, in *People in Corporations – Ethical Responsibilities and Corporate Effectiveness*. Kluwer, Dordecht.

De George, R.T. (1993) *Competing with Integrity in International Business*. Oxford University Press.

Donaldson, T. (1989) *The Ethics of International Business*. Oxford University Press.

Frederick, W.C. (1991) *Journal of Business Ethics*, **10**, 165–177.

Getz, K.A. (1990) *Journal of Business Ethics*, **9**, 567–577.

Waterhouse, R. (1994) War declared on corruption. *Independent on Sunday*, 5 June.

Sorrell and Hendry (1994) *Business Ethics*. Butterworth–Heinemann.

Conclusions: accounting for the field of business ethics

13

Ken Smith and Phil Johnson

The previous chapters in this book have indicated the complexity and the **Introduction** relevance of business ethics in an era of on-going organizational and societal change. The contributors have demonstrated that it is overly optimistic to believe that the field of business ethics can supply unambiguous solutions to the various problems and dilemmas that organizational members regularly confront. In doing so, contributors have themselves taken a variety of different approaches to investigating the ethical dimensions of their particular subjects of interest. In this, the concluding chapter of this book, we shall argue that such variability is only to be expected in the field of business ethics due to the social context in which any ethical discourse is located.

That business ethics cannot provide any guarantees of success is indicative of the complexity and uncertainty of the contemporary business contexts within which it is applied.

In a period of rapid technological, organizational, and social change, it would be naive to assume that organizational members can ever be certain that their decisions will necessarily have the intended outcomes, or that the benefits will always outweigh the costs. Incorporating a conscious and deliberate ethical debate into organizational decision-making processes and control influences cannot guarantee 'ethicality', but it may provide a potential safeguard against overly precipitative action by facilitating members' critical self-reflection.

However there is the need to acknowledge that just as business activity has become synonymous with change and uncertainty, so has business ethics. Indeed Lewis (1985) has noted that there are over 300 different definitions of business ethics available in the literature which implies that there is little consensus regarding what constitutes 'business ethics' (see also Derry and Green, 1989; Robertson, 1993). Meanwhile, other writers (e.g. McHugh, 1988; De George, 1987) have argued that the evolution and growth of business ethics has occurred in phases, each phase reflecting a change in focus within the area of investigation and study. These changes can be seen as products of evolving concern regarding the role and practices of the business community, and its duties and responsibilities toward the wider society. Given this scenario, it is not the intention in this final chapter to formulate a grand theory of business ethics. Rather the objective is more modest: it is to explore how the current interest in business ethics can be located within an analysis of contemporary society which takes account of the prevalence of uncertainty along with the concomitant desire to (re-)establish some form of normative order and continuity within social life. Hence it will be argued that business ethics may be seen as a socially constructed 'field' of study which inevitably reflects broader changes and controversies within western society.

Postmodernist debates and business ethics

It has become axiomatic to associate contemporary times with change and uncertainty – be it social, cultural, environmental or technological. This is even reflected in the debates regarding how best to classify and analyse contemporary society and its institutions. For heuristic purposes it is initially helpful to follow the distinction, embedded in these debates, that has been made between the different but related foci of 'epistemology' and 'periodization' (e.g. Parker, 1992).

As we have demonstrated earlier in Chapter 1, epistemology is concerned with the criteria by which we determine what does and does not constitute warranted, or valid, knowledge. Currently there are strong epistemological disagreements concerning the way in which warranted knowledge about social and natural phenomena can, and should be acquired. For instance, the 'official' (Anthony, 1986) rationalist basis of a variety of management disciplines have increasingly been subject to various critiques e.g. accountancy (Tinker, 1985); corporate strategy (Knights and Morgan, 1991); human resources management (HRM) (Townley, 1994) and organization theory (Reed and McHugh, 1992). Although substantively varied, epistemologically these critiques share a postmodernist desire to:

1. Demistify those disciplines through a rebuttal of what is seen as the rationalist, or 'modernist', tendency to present those disciplines as objective, value-free and technical enterprises.
2. Point to how such a modernist perspective is grounded in an objectivism expressed in terms of a putative theory-neutral observational language.
3. Reject the objectivist view that the essentials of the world are to be discovered through the exercise of managers' privileged reason (i.e. rationality) and replace it with a social constructivist view of management knowledge which exposes and disrupts the taken-for-granted assumptions that underpin ostensibly neutral management practices – thereby casting them in a new light.

In contrast, the debate about periodization is concerned with how one might best categorize the contemporary period within which we are located. Hence, Smart (1992) suggests that three questions can be identified:

1. Is the present period best understood in terms of a continuity, or evolution, of the past – i.e. is it still appropriate to conceptualize the present as an extension, or development of industrial society?
2. How might the role of technology be best understood and evaluated – especially the potential effects of information technology?
3. What are the implications of such changes upon the social structure, lifestyles, and political processes?

For some, the current period marks a definite break with the modernist past, hence it is classified as being 'postmodern'. According to Ryan (1988) 'postmodernity' was originally developed as an architectural concept which, among other things, referred to randomness, anarchy, and fragmentation in contrast to the monolithic architectural structures of modernism. This would suggest that society and its institutions are moving from a modern to a postmodern epoch characterized by a search for new organizational methods of coping with an increasingly turbulent and thereby uncertain world. Thus, for example, Clegg (1990) labels the current levels of accelerated social, economic, political and technological change as 'the postmodern condition'. In this light it would be possible to view the field of business ethics as encapsulating a variety of searches for a new, and institutionalizable, moral order for 'business'. The epistemological debate in postmodernism adds a further dimension to this view.

Postmodernist epistemology leads to the outright rejection of prescriptive approaches to business ethics, and sanctions ethical relativism, because all knowledge is perceived as being an outcome of variable social construction. Moreover it seems to have devastating implications for both organizational research and management practice. It demands from the researcher reflexivity and acceptance of their role as partisan participant in interest-laden discourse and divesting themselves of allusions to the role of detached observer occupying a neutral position. For the manager, because any claim to privileged knowledge becomes open to question, their recipes of knowledge, their roles and their statuses become (more) ambiguous and open to critique.

These debates concerning periodization and epistemology, have important implications for both the study and practice of business ethics. Best and Kellner (1991) seem to indicate the potential impact of both postmodernist themes for business ethics when they observe that postmodern theory

> ... rejects modern assumptions of social coherence and notions of causality in favour of multiplicity, plurality, fragmentation, and indeterminacy. In addition, postmodern theory abandons the

rational and unified subject postulated by much modern theory in favour of a socially and linguistically decentred and fragmented subject. (1991, p. 4)

Thus Bauman (1993) in advocating a postmodernist approach to ethics contends that there is a need to reject the traditional reliance on a belief in universal moral absolutes and rationalism and instead to accept that today the individual '... moves, feels and acts in the context of ambivalence and is shot through with uncertainty' (1993, p. 11). The radical critique contained within a postmodernist approach to ethics lies in the contention that traditional, normative, ethics is essentially a mechanism of social control and domination in which the individual's analysis and evaluation of their own and others' behaviour is an output of the social construction of knowledge. Bauman, in rejecting both universalism and the possibility of a cognitively accessible rationality rooted in human objectivity, contends that the prescriptive emphasis inherent in much of traditional ethical thought is a product of the modernist era and its allusions to rationalism. As such it is now in need of being supplanted by an approach which enables the individual to challenge the *status quo* and to develop their own ethics.

However, the uncertainty and ambiguity inherent in much of contemporary social life can result in people becoming 'expert-dependent' (Bauman, 1995, p. 12) for ethical guidance and instruction in how to lead one's life (see also Illich, 1977). For Bauman, and other postmodernists, such reliance in misplaced, one cannot learn how to lead one's life from an 'ethical instruction manual', or by relying upon the words of 'ethical gurus', whether alive or dead. All that happens is that the individual introjects and objectifies the partiality of a particular significant other. For Bauman the responsibility for dealing with and resolving the problem is ultimately one's own. The individual must come to terms with the inherent uncertainty of social life. Ethical thought does not provide a panacea for the age-old question: how should one live one's life?

However, both postmodernist themes are problematic. While postmodernist epistemology poses an important challenge to modernist orthodoxy, it also has its own contradictions that are rarely addressed since it can be seen as sanctioning relativism. For instance, Townley's Foucauldian analysis (1994) portrays HRM as involving the social constitution of knowledge and order – a process of representation in which organizational worlds are rendered 'known, visible and potentially manageable' (p. 144). Power is made invisible by the presentation of information as an objective fact ostensibly 'independent of the interests of those who produce it' (p. 145). But if we accept this postmodernist claim that all knowledge is the outcome of such partial constructivist processes, what therefore is the epistemological status of Townley's, and other postmodernists, own accounts?

Is there a danger that they construct discourses about discourses that inadvertently assert an implicit claim to privilege for their own accounts through some epistemological backdoor? Alternatively, if that contradiction is avoided, postmodernism must lead to the adoption of a relativistic argument that concludes that since all knowledge is socially constructed, there are no good reasons for preferring one representation over another. In this they would undermine the epistemological basis of any possible critique of the *status quo*. In this manner postmodernism can ambiguously promote a disinterestedness that tacitly supports the *status quo* by engendering a silence about current practices rather than critique (Neimark, 1990, pp. 106–10).

While the epistemological theme in postmodernism is evidently problematic, the argument that the current period represents a fundamental break with the past is for some, also open to question (e.g. Harvey, 1989; Best and Kellner, 1991; Bertens, 1995). For instance, the current period is sometimes perceived as being continuous with modernism. Giddens (1991) for example, contends that the current period can be best understood as being one of 'late' or 'high' modernity (1991, p. 3), while Touraine (1995) contends that, to date, we have been living in a world of 'limited modernity' (1995, p. 366) and are only now on the brink of entering 'full' modernity.

In a similar vein writers such as O'Neill contend that postmodernism is 'the child of modernism' (1995, p. 16), while Mestrovic maintains that, postmodernism is neither new or original, 'it pretends to rebel at modernity, whereas it merely extends it' (1991, p. 28). Berger *et al.* while noting the social changes brought about by modernity with its emphasis upon progress, rational thought, and the application of science and technology, also observe that

> … it has not fundamentally changed the finitude, fragility and mortality of the human condition. What it has accomplished is to seriously weaken those definitions of reality that previously made that human condition easier to bear. (1973, p. 166)

Perhaps it is here that it is possible to locate the concerns raised by postmodernist writers within a more conventional analysis of business ethics and thereby provide an account that relates business ethics to its social context.

Giddens contends that modernity can be understood as being

Contextualizing business ethics

> … a post-traditional order, but not one in which the sureties of tradition and habit have been replaced by the certitude of rational knowledge. Doubt, a pervasive feature of modern critical reason, permeates into every life as well as philosophical consciousness, and forms a general existential dimension of the contemporary social world. (1991, p. 2)

By extolling the power of human reason and holding out the promise of progress, modernism had paradoxically institutionalized criticism and uncertainty concerning what the criteria of progress should be, the methods by which it might be obtained, and whether it is even desirable. Indeed the increasing secularization of western society, as a byproduct of the Enlightenment and industrialization, may have only replaced the belief in an immutable God-given order to life with a growing realization of the uncertainty and fallibility of human reason. Giddens (1991), Berger *et al.* (1973), and Beck (1992) all indicate how such uncertainty is pervasive within contemporary western society.

At the macro-level, there is the doubt concerning the idea, and promise, of 'progress' through the process of industrialization. Beck (1992) contends that 'risk' is inherent within the period of reflexive, or high, modernity. Risk may be defined as

> a systematic way of dealing with hazards and insecurities induced and introduced by modernization itself. – Along with the growing capacity of technical options (Zweckrationalitat) grows the incalculability of their consequences. (1992, p. 21)

At the organizational level, the perceived need to cope with uncertainty and insecurity has been institutionalized by the development of various corporate strategy-making processes (Whittington, 1993) and forms of organizational flexibility (Clegg, 1990). The latter has often entailed repeated exhortations to maintain high performance by stimulating innovation and various attempts at instilling in employees a common sense of purpose, or moral involvement, as traditional compliance-based forms of management control breakdown (Wood, 1989). More recently, there has been the introduction of 'risk management' and 'risk assessment' procedures by which decision makers may seek to prepare in advance for potential technological and environmental disasters. Similarly the individual is confronted with growing uncertainty and insecurity as a consequence of the increased pace of unpredictable social change arising from new organizational forms, technologies and modes of employment. Simultaneously, the individual is also the subject of intense and pervasive attempts to influence their consumption patterns and lifestyles arising from the need to stimulate and maintain the market economic system.

So it is hardly surprising that some commentators have pointed to the variety and intensity of means by which the individual is constrained and encouraged to construct a concept of self-identity which reflects the power of external mechanisms of classification and evaluation (e.g. Rose, 1989; Townley, 1994). The paradox here, as Berger *et al.* (1973) indicate, is that the variety and incommensurability of such pressures to conform generate further uncertainty. If this were not enough, Beck observes that traditional forms of coping with anxiety and insecurity in socio-moral milieus, families, marriage and male-female roles are failing. (1992, p. 153)

Here, Beck appears to echo writers such as Bellah *et al.* (1985, 1992), regarding the demise of 'community' in contemporary society. With community came psychological security – an awareness of one's role, position, and identity in a relatively stable, and comprehensible, social world. With the breakdown of community comes normlessness, uncertainty and anxiety. It is in just such a cultural context that one can discern the attraction of, and the raison d'être for, business ethics.

Contemporary society appears to manifest serious contradictions. For instance, along with the need for order, control and certainty there is the need to cope with change, disorder and uncertainty. Business ethics may be conceptualized as a 'field' of both discourse and practice which may be understood as a contemporary cultural reaction to the need for some form of guidance as a means of restoring a sense of order and control in an otherwise confusing and uncertain social world. But while attempting to satisfy this need business ethics itself expresses epistemological doubt and uncertainty. In these senses business ethics can be conceptualized as being both an expression of, and a reaction to, the prevalence of anomie (i.e. normlessness) within contemporary society.

The concept of anomie is most closely associated with the work of Durkheim (1933, for instance). However, Durkheim is usually represented as an apologist who provides a functionalist legitimation of the *status quo*. Mestrovic (1991) and Cladis (1992) however, give an altogether more complex and radical account of Durkheim. For Cladis, Durkheim was concerned with developing a theoretical reconciliation between the ostensibly opposing theories of liberalism and communitarianism. While liberalism conceptualizes the individual as autonomous, communitarianism presents an image of the individual as socially determined – a product of, and captive to, their cultural milieux. Cladis contends that Durkheim's primary aim was to provide a theoretical account of how the two might be reconciled, 'a communitarian defense of liberalism' (1992, p. 2) so as to correct what he saw as the over-emphasis upon individualism which had arisen with industrialization.

Far from being a supporter of the Enlightenment's concern with progress and the power and value of human reason, Durkheim countered by stressing the importance of feelings and emotion as essential facets of the human condition. At the individual level of analysis therefore, Durkheim presents a powerful critique of the view of the individual as a rational entity. But within this critique, there also lies an analysis which questions the very rationale of what has come to be known as the Enlightenment project – the pursuit and attainment of progress by the application of human reason to social and technological development.

It is Durkheim's suspicion of the promise of the Enlightenment, when combined with his concern to counter what he held to be the adverse influence of classical economic liberal thought upon both the individual and society, which gives Durkheim a contemporary relevance for business ethics.

One important expression of this is Durkheim's understanding of the relationship between 'moral individualism' and 'moral polymorphism' – the variety of social spheres and collectives which provide a mixture of social settings and experiences within which the individual is located and which contribute to the richness and diversity of the individual's social and moral beliefs. It is the richness and diversity of social experience which, ideally, would contribute to the complex and dynamic nature of Durkheim's image of 'organic solidarity' as an ideal-type presentation of modernity, as opposed to the form of social solidarity found in premodern (i.e. traditional societies), which he termed 'mechanical solidarity' (Durkheim, 1933).

Implicit in Durkheim's analysis is the recognition of the inevitability of conflict and uncertainty regarding appropriate modes of behaviour given the plurality of social settings and contexts within which the individual gains social experience. For Durkheim, it was the dominance of liberal economic thought within an industrializing French society which gave grounds for concern. Like Adam Smith, Durkheim argued that economic self-interest should be embedded within a plurality of other, contending, social and moral relationships. As Wolfe observes

> it is not simply that Adam Smith never thought to extend the principle of self-interest to all social relations; on the contrary, Smith recognized that to do so would destroy the very realm of morality that made economic self-interest possible in the first place. (1989, p. 30)

Thus for Durkheim, individual economic self-interest, inherent in free market economic philosophy, should not be the predominant ethos underpinning an individual's social behaviour. It is the balance between the competing moral, and social spheres of Durkheim's 'moral polymorphism' which has altered in the latter part of this century. The increasing penetration of free market ideology into other areas of social life which has increased what Mestrovic calls economic anomie.

> Economic anomie occurs when people's material desires override their real conditions, and economic anomie eventually produces a variety of other forms of anomie – political, domestic, religious, and so on. (1991, p. 75)

Thus, writers such as Wolfe (1989), Bellah *et al.* (1992) and Stivers (1994) all emphasize the impact of the free market system on social behaviour and attitudes. Stivers draws attention to the contemporary importance attached to 'efficiency' (1994, p. 8); Bellah *et al.* indicate the extent to which market pressures have come to overshadow and dominate social life (1992, p. 85); Wolfe demonstrates the influence of the Chicago school of economics on contemporary social life and thought (1989, p. 51). The end result, is what Bellah *et al.* suggest is the acceptance by many of the, 'market maximizer as the paradigm of the human person' (1989, p. 91).

But this is not to suggest that the power of free market philosophy has entirely overwhelmed other modes of social thought. Wolfe, for example, notes that the Chicago school – epitomized by Milton Friedman – is not representative of the academic discipline of economics as a whole. Nor indeed is it immune from criticism, even from conservative writers (e.g. Gray, 1993). Likewise, Giddens (1991, p. 195) in drawing attention to the persistence and resurgence of religious belief, indicates the plurality and continuity of social beliefs. In this respect, it is important to remember the historical and contemporary influence that religious thought has had upon business ethics (e.g. McHugh, 1988; Vogel, 1991).

Having noted the need for some caution, it is still possible to accept that *laissez-faire* economic thought and policies are pervasive. Wolfe emphasizes this when he illustrates the importance of the Chicago school, and how their perspective differs from that of Adam Smith. According to Wolfe, Adam Smith was a pluralist in the sense that he acknowledged that economic activity was only one of various areas of social activity which collectively provided a moral environment within which economic activity took place. But in the justification for capitalism offered by Milton Friedman and his disciples

> claims are not made for a capitalist *economy* within a society held together by non-capitalist values, but, for the first time in Western intellectual history, for a specifically capitalist *society*, in which market freedom will serve as the moral code defining every form of social interaction. (1989, p. 30)

Thus 'progress', achieved through the application of human reason, has become allied to the claimed benefits of economic liberalism and its encouragement of competitive individualism grounded in self-interest. For Mestrovic (1991) this alliance has exacerbated the level of social fragmentation. Meanwhile it is here that one can begin to comprehend the unease and anxiety surrounding the policy of privatization in the UK. The application of market principles to areas of activity such as healthcare and transport have given rise to much concern regarding whether or not there are areas where is it inappropriate to apply free market principles to their provision and management. The belief that certain goods and services should be provided on grounds of social need is at odds with an economic ideology which maintains that one's moral obligations to others can be addressed only by first giving priority to one's own desires and priorities (Wolfe, 1989, p. 30).

For Mestrovic, this situation of social fragmentation with its emphases upon the individual, the ephemeral, the new, and consumerism, when combined with a tacit relativism, constitute the preconditions of the postmodern epoch. He claims that

> ... postmodernity is an age in which only a sleepwalker could deny that contemporary portraits of life resonate with Baudelaire's and Durkheim's portraits that emphasize cynicism, disgust and decadence. Our age is drowning in ... anomie yet the positivists tell us that anomie does not exist and cannot be measured. (1991, p. 107)

As such, contemporary anomie is expressed as a perpetual dissatisfaction with life combined with a desire for improvement riddled with uncertainty regarding what constitutes 'improvement' and how it might be attained. Mestrovic's preconditions of postmodernity have ironically institutionalized anomie by the encouragement of competitive individualism and yet obscured it through the maintenance of allusions to Enlightenment's discourse progress through the exercise of rationality. Thus

> ... the most pressing and controversial modern social problems centre on the lack of business ethics, the selfishness of the so-called 'me generation', and the rise of hyper-individualism. (Mestrovic, 1991, p. 174)

Therefore it is within today's contradictions, tensions and uncertainties that the competing objectives and formulations of business ethics can be understood. The 'field' is both an expression of the concerns of the Enlightenment regarding material progress and human well-being through the application of the power of human reason – while simultaneously querying such a possibility. Thus it can be seen as both contributing to the on-going development of the free-market economic system, while providing a potent means for criticizing the application of a *laissez-faire* rationale which displays epistemological angst. By problematizing the conduct and objectives of 'business', business ethics facilitates a broad-ranging inquiry into the nature of contemporary society that may be understood as an attempt at resolving the growing incidence of anomie. As such it is a 'field' with many 'crops'. The heterogeneous nature of this field is indicative of the complexities of current society, their problematic impact on social life and the availability of different disciplinary perspectives. But with its own epistemological, disciplinary and theoretical diversity business ethics is itself an expression of anomie – perhaps more a 'Tower of Babel' than a 'field'.

Ultimately business ethics is an evolving social product of uncertain times in which doubt is developing with regard to the benefits and possibility of ostensible 'progress' through the power of 'human reason'. In many respects the debates and dilemmas of business ethics thus encapsulate the messiness of the human condition while attempting to provide the means of ameliorating that predicament.

Anthony, P.D. (1986) *The Foundation of Management*. Tavistock, London.   **References**

Bauman, Z. (1993) *Postmodern Ethics*. Basil Blackwell, Oxford.

Bauman, Z. (1995) *Life in Fragments: Essays in Postmodern Morality*. Basil Blackwell, Oxford.

Beck, U. (1992) *Risk Society: Towards a New Modernity*. Sage, London.

Bellah, R.N., Madsen, R., Sullivan, W.M., Swidler, A. and Tipton, S.M. (1985) *Habits of the Heart: Individualism and Commitment in American Life*. University of California Press, Los Angeles, CA.

Bellah, R.N., Madsen, R., Sullivan, W.M., Swidler, A. and Tipton, S.M. (1992) *The Good Society*. Vintage Books, Random House, New York.

Berger, P.L., Berger, B. and Kellner, H. (1973) *The Homeless Mind: Modernization and Consciousness*. Penguin, Harmondsworth.

Bertens, H. (1995) *The Idea of the Postmodern: A History*. Routledge, London.

Best, S. and Kellner, D. (1991) *Postmodern Theory: Critical Interrogations*. Macmillan Press, London.

Cladis, M.S. (1992) *A Communitarian Defense of Liberalism: Emile Durkheim and Contemporary Social Theory*. Stanford University Press, Stanford, CA.

Clegg, S.R. (1990) *Modern Organizations: Organization Studies in the Postmodern World*. Sage, London.

Derry, R. and Green, R.M. (1989) Ethical theory in business ethics: a critical assessment. *Journal of Business Ethics*, 8, 855–862.

De George, R.T. (1987) The status of business ethics: past and future. *Journal of Business Ethics*, 6, 201–211.

Durkheim, E. (1933) *The Division of Labour in Society*. The Free Press, Collier–Macmillan, London.

Giddens, A. (1991) *Modernity and Self-identity: Self and Society in the Late Modern Age*. Polity Press, Cambridge.

Gray, J. (1993) *Beyond the New Right: Markets, Government and the Common Environment*. Routledge, London.

Harvey, D. (1989) *The Condition of Postmodernity: An Enquiry into the Origins of Cultural Change*. Basil Blackwell.

Illich, I. (ed.) (1977) *Disabling Professions*. Martin Boyars, London.

Knights, D. and Morgan, G.(1991) Strategic discourse and subjectivity. *Organization Studies*, 12(2), 251–274.

Lewis, P.V. (1985) Defining business ethics: like nailing jello to a wall. *Journal of Business Ethics*, 4, 377–383.

McHugh, F.P. (1988) *Keyguide to Information Sources in Business Ethics*. Nichols, New York.

Mestrovic, S.G. (1991) *The Coming Fin De Siècle*. Routledge, London.

Neimark, M. (1990) The king is dead, long live the king. *Critical Perspectives on Accounting*, 1(1), 103–114.

O'Neill, J. (1995) *The Poverty of Postmodernism*. Routledge, London.

Parker, M. (1992) Post-modern organisations or postmodern organisation theory? *Organisation Studies*, 13(1), 1–17.

Reed, M. and McHugh, M. (eds) (1992) *Rethinking Organization*. Sage, London.

Robertson, D.C. (1993) Empiricism in business ethics: suggested research directions. *Journal of Business Ethics*, **12**, 585–599.

Rose, N. (1989) *Governing the Soul: The Shaping of the Private Self*. Routledge, London.

Ryan, M. (1988) Postmodern politics. *Theory, Culture and Society*, 5(2/3), 559–76.

Smart, B. (1992) *Modern Conditions, Postmodern Controversies*. Routledge, London.

Stivers, R. (1994) *The Culture of Cynicism: American Morality in Decline*. Basil Blackwell, Oxford.

Tinker, A.M. (1985) *Paper Prophers: A Social Critique of Accounting*. Reinhart & Winston, London.

Touraine, A. (1995) *Critique of Modernity*. Basil Blackwell, Oxford.

Townley, B. (1994) *Reframing Human Resource Management: Power, Ethics and the Subject at Work*. Sage, London.

Vogel, D. (1991) Business ethics: new perspectives on old problems. *California Management Review*, 34(4), 101–117.

Whittington, R. (1993) *What is Strategy – And Does It Matter?* Routledge, London.

Wolfe, A. (1989) *Whose Keeper?: Social Science and Moral Obligation*. University of California Press, Los Angeles, CA.

Wood, S. (1989) New wave management? *Work, Employment and Society*, **13**(3), 379–402.

Index

DATE DUE